English Vocabulary in Use

Advanced

Vocabulary reference
and practice

with answers

Second Edition

Michael McCarthy
Felicity O'Dell

CAMBRIDGE
UNIVERSITY PRESS

CAMBRIDGE
UNIVERSITY PRESS

University Printing House, Cambridge CB2 8BS, United Kingdom

Cambridge University Press is part of the University of Cambridge.

It furthers the University's mission by disseminating knowledge in the pursuit of education, learning and research at the highest international levels of excellence.

www.cambridge.org
Information on this title: www.cambridge.org/9781107637764

© Cambridge University Press 2013

First published 2002
Second Edition 2013

Printed in Italy by L.E.G.O. S.p.A.

A catalogue record for this publication is available from the British Library

ISBN 978-1-107-63776-4 Paperback

Contents

Thanks and acknowledgements

Many people have contributed to this book. Above all, we would like to thank our editors at Cambridge University Press, especially Colin McIntosh, Claire Cole, Sarah Almy, Brigit Viney and Sabina Sahni, whose expert guidance steered us and our manuscript through the whole process from start to finish. They set the deadlines that motivated us to get the book finished, provided feedback on drafts and chased us when we lagged behind. We are also grateful to the students and staff at various institutions who assisted in reviewing and piloting the material in different parts of the world: Wayne Rimmer, Garan Holcombe, Rachel Connabeer, Alex Latimer, Hayden Berry, Glennis Pye and Vânia Moraes. Equally, we thank the many other teachers and users of the previous edition of the book who have, over the last 15 years, given us invaluable feedback and constructive criticism which we have tried to take into account in this new edition. Alison Silver, as usual, proved to be the most expert and professional of editors when the typescript passed into her hands and made many useful comments and suggestions that have improved the book. We are also grateful to the corpus managers at CUP for providing us with the ever-growing Cambridge English Corpus, without which our vocabulary research would have been considerably impoverished. Andrew George and the Production Team at CUP led the book with utmost efficiency through its final stages, and we thank them too, as well as Darren Longley for the proofreading. What shortcomings that may remain must be laid entirely at our door.

Michael McCarthy
Felicity O'Dell

Cambridge, February 2013

Introduction

To the student

This book has been written to help you expand your vocabulary at the advanced level. You already know thousands of English words, but to express yourself fully and in a sophisticated way at the advanced level, you will ideally need between 6,000 and 8,000 words, so increasing your vocabulary is very important for your general progress in English, as well as for any academic, professional or vocational needs you may have where English plays an important role. At the advanced level, as well as learning new words, you will need to learn more about the subtle connotations of words, aspects of register and style and how words combine into collocations, compounds and fixed phrases. In this book, there are around 3,460 new words and expressions for you to learn. You will find them on the left-hand page of each unit. Every new word or phrase is used in a sentence, or in a conversation, or is in a table, or has a picture with it, or has some explanation of what it means. On the right-hand page there are exercises and other activities to help you practise using the words and to help you to remember them. Where our research shows that learners frequently make errors, we give you advice on how to avoid the most common ones, as well as other useful language tips. The book has been written so that you can use it yourself, without a teacher. You can do the units in any order you like, but we have grouped them into themes, so you might wish to work through several units on a particular area of vocabulary before moving to a new one.

The Answer key at the end of the book is for you to check your answers to the exercises after you do them. The key sometimes has more than one answer. This is because often there is not just one correct way of saying something. Where you are asked to talk about yourself, in the *Over to you* activities, we do not provide answers, since this is your opportunity to work completely independently and in a very personal way, so everyone's answer will be very different.

The Index at the end of the book has all the important words and phrases from the left-hand pages. The Index also tells you how to pronounce words. There is a table of phonemic symbols to help you understand the pronunciation on page 278.

You should also have a dictionary with you when you use the book. You can use a paper dictionary, an electronic one, or you can go to Cambridge Dictionaries Online at http://dictionary.cambridge.org/ Access to a dictionary is useful because sometimes you may want to check the meaning of something or find a word in your own language to help you remember the English word. Sometimes, you will also need a dictionary for the exercises; we tell you when this is so.

To learn a lot of vocabulary, you have to do two things:

1 Study each unit of the book carefully and do all the exercises. Check your answers in the key. Repeat the units after a month, and then again after three months, and see how much you have learnt and how much you have forgotten. Repeating work is very important.

2 Develop ways of your own to study and learn new words and phrases which are not in this book. For example, every time you see or hear an interesting phrase, write it in a notebook, and write who said it or wrote it, and in what situation, as well as what it means. Making notes of the situations words are used in will help you to remember them and to use them at the right moment.

We hope you like this book. When you have finished it, you can go to the other books in the series which have more specialised titles: *English Idioms in Use*, *English Phrasal Verbs in Use* and *English Collocations in Use*, which are available at advanced level, as well as *Academic Vocabulary in Use*. There are also separate books of tests available, where you can test yourself on what you have learnt from the books in the series. Find out more at the Vocabulary in Use website: http://www.cambridge.org/elt/inuse.

To the teacher

This book can be used in class or as a self-study book. It is intended to take learners from an upper-intermediate level of vocabulary to an advanced level. The vocabulary has been chosen for its usefulness in everyday situations, and we consulted the Cambridge English Corpus, a billion-word-plus written and spoken corpus of present-day English which includes a huge learner corpus, to help us decide on the words and phrases to be included and to help us understand the typical problems learners encounter at the advanced level. We also consulted the English Vocabulary Profile to make sure that the words in the book are a representative sample of vocabulary that is typical of the Common European Framework levels C1 and C2. Visit the English Vocabulary Profile at http://www.cambridge.org/elt/inuse.

At the advanced level, as well as learning a large number of new words and expressions, learners are often directing their efforts towards academic, professional or vocational needs, and so we have tried to offer a modern, sophisticated vocabulary that will underpin their work in other areas. The new vocabulary (on average 40 items per unit) is presented with explanations on the left-hand page, and there are exercises and activities on the right-hand page. There is an Answer key and an Index with pronunciation for all the target vocabulary. The key at the end of the book is for students to check their answers to the exercises after they do them. The key sometimes has more than one answer. This is because often there is not just one correct way of saying something. Where students are asked to talk about themselves, in the *Over to you* activities, we do not provide answers, since this gives learners the opportunity to work completely independently and in a very personal way, so everyone's answer will be very different.

The book focuses not just on single words, but on useful phrases and collocations, and the vocabulary is illustrated in natural contexts. The book is organised around everyday topics, but also has units devoted to basic concepts such as time, modality, manner and varieties and style. Typical errors are indicated where appropriate, based on information from the Cambridge Learner Corpus, and the most typical meanings and uses are focused on for each key item.

The right-hand pages offer a variety of different types of activities, some traditional ones such as gap-filling, but also more open-ended ones and personalised activities which enable learners to talk about their own lives. Although the activities and exercises are designed for self-study, they can be easily adapted for pairwork, groupwork or whole-class activities in the usual way.

When the learners have worked through a group of units, it is a good idea to repeat some of the work (for example, the exercises) and to expand on the meaning and use of key words and phrases by extra discussion in class, and find other examples of the key items in other texts and situations. This can be done at intervals of one to three months after first working on a unit. This is important, since it is usually the case that a learner needs five to seven exposures to a word or phrase before they can really begin to know it, and no single book can do enough to ensure that words are always learnt first time. It is especially important at the advanced level to discuss in detail the meanings and uses of words and phrases and how they combine and collocate with one another.

When your students have finished all the units in this book, they can move on to the more specialised higher level books in this series: the advanced levels of *English Idioms in Use*, *English Phrasal Verbs in Use* and *English Collocations in Use*, or they may wish to work on academic vocabulary by using *Academic Vocabulary in Use*, all by the same authors as this book. They can also test themselves on the knowledge they have gained from this and the other books in the series by using the separate books of tests that accompany the series. You can find out more at the Vocabulary in Use website: http://www.cambridge.org/elt/inuse

We hope you enjoy using the book.

1 Cramming for success: study and academic work

A Study and exams

Before an exam, some students cram[1] for it. Even if you're a genius[2], you'll have to do some revision. If the exam happens every year, you can revise by looking at past papers[3]. Some things can be memorised or learnt (off) by heart. But rote-learning[4] is not sufficient for most subjects. It is also possible to use mnemonics[5]. However, all things considered, the best idea is to bury yourself in your books[6] and to study intensively[7] until you know the subject inside out[8].

[1] study in a very concentrated way for a short time   [2] an exceptionally clever person   [3] exam papers from previous years   [4] learning purely by repetition   [5] /ni'mɒnɪks/ tricks that help you remember something, for example: 'i' after 'e' except after 'c' is a mnemonic for English spelling (e.g. friend, but receive)   [6] spend the maximum time studying   [7] in a very focused way   [8] know it completely

B Academic writing

composition could be just 50–100 words, often used for school work
essay longer than a composition, more serious, hundreds or thousands of words
assignment a long essay, often part of a course, usually thousands of words
project like an assignment, but emphasis on student's own material and topic
portfolio a collection of individual pieces of work, may include drawings and other examples of creative work as well as writing
dissertation a long, research-based work, perhaps 10–15,000 words, for a degree or diploma
thesis a very long, original, research-based work, perhaps 80–100,000 words, for a higher degree (e.g. PhD)

It's a good idea to start with a mind map[1] when preparing an essay. Always write a first draft[2] before writing up the final version. Your essay should be all your own work; plagiarism[3] is a very serious offence in colleges and universities. It is an increasing problem because it is so easy to cut and paste from materials available on the internet, and students have to sign a plagiarism form to say that the work they are handing in is all their own and that they acknowledge[4] any sources they have used. There is usually a deadline[5]. After the essay is submitted[6], it will be assessed[7] and usually you can get feedback[8].

[1] diagram that lays out ideas for a topic and how they are connected to one another   [2] first, rough version   [3] /'pleɪdʒərɪzəm/ using other people's work as if it was yours   [4] give details of   [5] date by which you must hand in the work   [6] handed in; *formal*   [7] evaluated and given a grade   [8] comments from the teacher/tutor

C Aspects of higher academic study

University academics carry out[1] research and are expected to read academic journals[2], which publish papers/articles on specialised subjects. If a library does not have a copy of a book or journal, you may be able to access it online[3] or you can usually get it through an inter-library loan[4]. Open educational resources[5] are particularly convenient for many students. Academic study can be very demanding, and some students drop out[6], but the majority survive till finals[7] and become well-qualified[8] members of their future professions.

[1] less formal is do research   [2] magazines with academic articles (we do not use the word *magazine* to talk about this kind of academic publication)   [3] get hold of (it) on the internet   [4] system where libraries exchange books/journals with one another   [5] online materials that can be freely used by teachers and students anywhere   [6] leave the course before the end because they cannot cope   [7] last exams before the end of a college or university course   [8] with the right formal qualifications

Exercises

1.1 Correct the wrong usage of words to do with written work in these sentences.

1 His PhD assignment was 90,000 words long and was on the history of US place names.
2 Little Martha did her first dissertation in school today. It was called 'My family'.
3 We have to hand in an essay at the end of the course. It can consist of up to five different pieces of work.
4 The teacher gave us the title of this week's project today. We have to write 1,000 words on the topic of 'If I ruled the world' and hand it in next Monday.
5 At the end of this course, you have to do a 5,000-word thesis which will be assessed, and the grade will contribute to your final degree.
6 I think I'll do a study of people's personal banking habits for my MSc composition. It has to be about 12,000 words.
7 I've chosen to do the portfolio instead of the two exams, because I like to do one single piece of work where I can research something that interests me personally.

1.2 Rewrite this text using words and phrases from the opposite page instead of the underlined words.

When I'm studying in a very focused way because I'm preparing hard for an exam, I don't see any point in looking up exam papers from previous years, nor is there any point in just learning things by memory. I know some people develop very clever memory tricks to help them remember the material, but there's no real substitute for rereading and going over the term's work. It's a good idea to have some sort of diagram to organise your ideas, and memory-learning is useful, but in a limited way. At the end of the day, you just have to read a huge amount until you feel you know the subject 100%.

1.3 Answer these questions.

1 What do we call the first attempt at writing something, e.g. an essay?
2 What word means 'the date by which you must do something'?
3 What word means 'using someone else's ideas as if they were yours'?
4 What are more formal words for 'to hand in' and for 'to mark'?
5 What phrasal verb do we use when someone doesn't complete their course?
6 What is another word for an academic article? Where can you read them?
7 What is the name of the system for getting books from other libraries?
8 What word means 'the comments you get back from the teacher about your work'?
9 What word can you use for a person who is extraordinarily intelligent?
10 What is a more formal way of saying 'do research'?

1.4 Choose the best word from the opposite page to complete these sentences.

1 If you quote an article in an essay, you must .... your source, giving details of author and title.
2 Open educational .... can be particularly useful for students who do not have easy access to a university library.
3 How much .... have you done for tomorrow's maths exam?
4 Don't forget to sign the .... form and hand it in with your dissertation.
5 Some people take a long time to find suitable work even though they are very ....
6 Orla has had a .... published in the *British Medical Journal*.
7 All students need a username and password to be able to ...access........... journals online.
8 Caspar is bound to do well in his mechanics exam – he knows the subject .... out.

2 Education: debates and issues

A Opportunity and equality

All education systems may ultimately be judged in terms of **equality of opportunity**[1]. This is often referred to in the debates over **selective**[2] versus **comprehensive**[3] **schooling**[4]. The main issue is whether everyone has the same opportunities for educational achievement or whether **elitism**[5] of one sort or another is **inherent in**[6] the system.

League tables[7] for schools and colleges may actually help unintentionally to **perpetuate**[8] inequalities, while claiming to promote the raising of standards. Inevitably, league tables divide educational institutions into good and bad, resulting in a **two-tier system**[9], or at least that is how the public **perceives**[10] it. The ability of **better-off**[11] parents and **well-endowed**[12] schools to push children towards the institutions at the top of the league may, in the long term, have the effect of **depressing**[13] opportunity for the **less well-off**[14] or for children from home environments that do not provide the motivation to **excel**[15].

Financial support can help to make educational opportunity more equal. There are, for example, **scholarships**[16] or **bursaries**[17] that make it possible for less privileged youngsters to afford **tertiary**[18] education. There are **student loans**[19] which allow **undergraduates**[20] to pay for their **tuition fees**[21] and living expenses while they are studying. But few would claim that real equality of opportunity has been achieved.

[1] when everyone has the same chances [2] pupils are chosen, usually for academic reasons, for entry, though, in the case of some private schools, parents' ability to pay school fees may be a factor in selection [3] everyone enters without exams and education is free, paid for by the government [4] education received at school [5] when you favour a small, privileged group [6] existing as a basic part of something [7] lists of schools or colleges, from the best down to the worst, based on exam results and, sometimes, other criteria [8] make something continue for ever [9] a system with two separate levels, one of which is better than the other [10] sees, considers [11] richer [12] receiving a lot of money in grants, gifts from rich people, etc. [= **endowments**] [13] reducing [14] poorer [15] achieve an excellent standard [16] money given to pay for studies, usually provided on the basis of academic merit [17] money given to pay for studies, usually provided on the basis of need [18] education at university or college level [19] money that students can borrow from a bank while studying and then pay back once they are in work [20] students doing a first degree [**postgraduates** = students doing a further degree] [21] money paid to receive teaching

B Other debates and issues

Some people think we should return to an emphasis on **the three Rs**, the traditional, basic skills. [reading, writing and arithmetic] **Literacy** and **numeracy** are skills no one can afford to be without. [the ability to read] [the ability to count / do basic maths]

Language help

Notice how compound adjectives like *well-off, well-endowed, high-achieving, badly-performing* can be used in comparative and superlative forms, e.g. *better-off, best-endowed, higher-achieving, worst-performing.*

Curriculum reform is often done for political reasons rather than for good educational ones. [changes to what is covered in the national **syllabus** = plan of what is to be studied]
Nowadays, **lifelong/continuing education** is an issue, and creating opportunities for **mature students** is important. [education for all ages] [adult students older than the average student]
Special needs education is expensive because class sizes need to be small or **one-to-one**. [education for children who cannot learn in the normal way, because they have some disability] [one teacher and one pupil, not a group]
Children are unhappy at school if there is a lot of **bullying**. [threatening behaviour]
Some headteachers complain that getting to grips with constant new government **guidelines** on what schools should be doing is a **distraction** from what they ought to be focusing on. [advice (often official) on how something should be done] [takes attention away]

Exercises

2.1 Complete the collocations by filling in the missing words according to the meaning given in brackets.

1 .... tables (lists of schools from best to worst)
2 .... education (entry to schools is decided by exam results)
3 equality of .... (when everyone has the same chances)
4 .... inequalities (make inequalities continue for ever)
5 .... education (at university or college level)

2.2 Rewrite these sentences so they are more formal by using words and phrases from the opposite page instead of the underlined words. Make any other changes that are necessary.

1 Inequality is <u>built into</u> the education system.
2 <u>Giving access only to privileged groups</u> is bad for the country in the long term.
3 <u>Education where everyone gets into the same type of school without exams</u> is a basic political ideal in many countries.
4 A <u>system where there are two levels</u> of schools <u>reduces</u> the opportunities for children from <u>poorer</u> families and favours those from <u>richer</u> families.
5 Some private schools <u>have lots of wealth and receive gifts of money</u>, and this means they can have better resources.
6 All parents want their children to <u>achieve the best possible results</u> at school.
7 Emphasis on the three Rs is <u>considered</u> by parents to be the key to success.
8 The government is increasing its provision for education <u>that young people can enter after finishing secondary school</u>.

2.3 Correct these statements about words or expressions from the opposite page. Correct each of them twice – once by changing the definition and once by changing the word being defined.

1 One-to-one education is another way of saying continuing education.
  One-to-one education means a situation where there is one teacher and one student.
  Lifelong education is another way of saying continuing education.
2 Numeracy refers to the ability to read.
3 A student who is doing a doctorate is an undergraduate.
4 Excelling is when a pupil uses frightening or threatening behaviour towards another child who is smaller or less powerful in some way.
5 Tertiary education is the stage that follows primary education.
6 Comprehensive schools choose the best students to study there.
7 Guidelines list schools from good to bad according to their exam results.

2.4 Complete each sentence with a word from the opposite page.

1 Matt won a .... because of his excellent academic record.
2 Zara's parents said that starting a rock band with her friends would be too much of a .... from her studies.
3 The report contains some interesting .... on how best to prepare for exams.
4 There were two .... students in my class at university but most of us were just 19.
5 Katia wouldn't have been able to go to university if her grandparents hadn't paid her tuition .... for her.
6 Most undergraduates need to take out a student .... to cover their costs while they study for a degree.
7 Primary schools usually spend a lot of time on the .... Rs.
8 At university I was lucky enough to have a lot of .... tutorials, just me and the tutor!

3 At work: colleagues and routines

A Colleagues

Philip is **my opposite number**[1] in the company's New York office. We have a good **working relationship**[2] and there's a lot of day-to-day **collaboration**[3]. Having a **counterpart**[4] like Philip in another branch is a great support. Last month we got a new boss, who quickly established a good **rapport**[5] with everyone. She likes us to **take the initiative**[6]. The company is very **hierarchical**[7]; there's a **pecking order**[8] for everything. I do a **job-share**[9] with a woman called Rose, which suits us as we each have childcare responsibilities. I socialise with my **workmates**[10] outside of work, but we try not to **talk shop**[11] on those occasions.

[1] has the same position / does the same job as me [2] way of communicating and working together [3] working together to achieve shared ... valent of *opposite* ... /ræˈpɔː/ ... ınication/relationship ... ɛing told what to do /ˌhaɪəˈrɑːkɪkəl/ ... ture with important [8] a system where some people have the right to get benefits/promotions before others [9] an agreement where two people each share the same job [10] colleagues you are friendly with (especially in non-professional occupations); *informal* [11] talk about work; *informal*

> **Common mistake**
> Be careful with the spelling of technician. Don't forget the 'h'.

B During the day (different work patterns)

I do fairly **mundane**[1] tasks. Occasionally I have to **meet a deadline**[2] or they need someone to **volunteer**[3] for something. Then the job is more **rewarding**[4] and **stimulating**[5]. Sometimes I have a heavy **workload**[6] but at other times it can be quite light.

[1] ordinary, not interesting [2] have something finished by a fixed day or time [3] offer to do something without being asked or told to do it [4] making you feel satisfied that you have done something important or useful, or done something well [5] encouraging new ideas or new thinking [6] amount of work I have to do

I start work at my machine at seven o'clock when I'm on the **day shift**. The job's **mechanical**[1] and **repetitive**[2]. All I ever think about is **knocking off**[3] at three o'clock. The shift I hate most is the **night shift**. I start at ten and work till six in the morning. It's a bit **monotonous**[4]. It's not a **satisfying**[5] job – I feel I need something a bit more **challenging**[6].

[1] you don't have to think about what you are doing [2] the same thing is repeated every day [3] finishing work; *informal* [4] boring because it never changes [5] (does not) make me feel pleased by providing what I need or want [6] that tests my ability or determination

I have a pretty **glamorous**[1] job. I'm a pilot. But the hours are **irregular** and **anti-social**[2]. I'm not **stuck behind a desk**[3], but long-haul flights can be a bit **mind-numbing**[4]; most of the time the plane just flies itself. We work to very **tight schedules**[5]. But I shouldn't complain. I feel sorry for people who are **stuck in a rut**[6] or who are in **dead-end**[7] jobs.

[1] very exciting, which everyone admires [2] do not enable one to have a normal social life [3] sitting at a desk all day; *informal* [4] extremely boring [5] very strict or severely limited timetables [6] stuck/trapped in a job they can't escape from [7] with no prospects of promotion

I started off as a **technician**[1]. After retraining, I worked for a software company, and later I **went in with**[2] a friend and we formed our own software company as a **start-up**[3] in 2009, so now I'm **self-employed**. My husband is **freelance**[4] – he works for several different companies as and when they need work done – he's a computer **programmer**[5].

[1] person whose job involves practical work with scientific or electrical equipment [2] formed a business partnership with [3] a small business that has just started [4] or works freelance [5] someone who writes computer programs

Exercises

3.1 Correct seven mistakes in this paragraph.

I'm a tecnician in a factory. I think I have a good work relationship with my colleagues. I tried to establish a good report with them from the very beginning. The person I like most is my opposite member in our office in Paris. My boss likes me to make the initiative. Generally, when I socialise with my jobmates outside of work, we try not to talk about shop, but it's not easy and sometimes we have a good gossip about colleagues and events at work.

3.2 Match the left and right-hand columns to make pairs of sentences.

1 We often work together.
2 The firm's rather hierarchical.
3 Peter's my counterpart.
4 We work to a tight schedule.
5 I don't think I'll be promoted before her.
6 Jess and I work half-and-half.

- a There are several levels of management.
- b Deadlines have to be met.
- c It's a job-share.
- d Collaboration is a good thing.
- e We do the same job but he's based in Rome.
- f There's a strict pecking order in the company.

3.3 Use words and phrases from the opposite page to complete these sentences.

1 A good friend suggested we set up a small company together, so I .... her and we formed a .... in 2012.
2 I'm really tired; I've had a very heavy .... recently.
3 I don't want an office job. I don't want to spend all day stuck ....
4 I'd hate to feel trapped in my job and to be stuck in ....
5 I work for different companies at different times as it suits me. I'm ....
6 I used to work for someone else, but now I'm my own boss; I'm ....
7 I stopped working in the hamburger restaurant. It was such a dead ....
8 When I was working in the factory, all I could think of all day was the moment when I could knock ....
9 Being a hospital nurse is a good job, but you can't go out much with friends. The hours are a bit .... (*two possible answers*)

3.4 Choose adjectives from the box to describe the jobs below. You can use more than one for each job. Add other adjectives of your own.

> glamorous   stimulating   repetitive   stressful   monotonous   varied
> mechanical   mundane   challenging   mind-numbing   rewarding

1 assembly-line worker in a car factory
2 supermarket shelf stacker
3 public relations officer in a multinational company
4 bodyguard to a celebrity
5 surgeon

6 lifeguard on a beach
7 receptionist at a dentist's
8 private detective
9 refuse collector in a city
10 night-security guard

3.5

Over to you

Answer these questions about yourself.

- Describe a mundane task which you have to do in your work or daily life.
- Are you good or bad at meeting deadlines? Explain why.

4 At work: recruitment and job satisfaction

A Getting a job

Look at this **job ad**[1] for a position in a software development company.

Are you looking for a stimulating and challenging position in a fast-moving and dynamic[2] industry?

Primeloc Software needs ambitious sales professionals with the talent and **drive**[3] to develop a **rewarding**[4] career in software sales. You will work in **close-knit**[5] teams, developing relationships with a wide range of clients nationally and internationally. If you have previous IT **sales experience**[6], a good, up-to-date knowledge of industry software needs, if you're a **team player**[7] with a strong desire to succeed, this may be the job for you. If you **fit this description**[8] and are seeking a **lucrative**[9] career in software sales, then contact us.

[1] ad; *informal* = advertisement   [2] energetic and forceful   [3] strong motivation   [4] giving you a lot back   [5] working in a close relationship   [6] experience of selling things   [7] someone good at working closely with other people   [8] have these qualities   [9] producing a lot of money

Language help

The text has some words with similar meanings connected to work. It is a good idea to learn them in pairs: stimulating and challenging (job), fast-moving and dynamic (industry/profession), seeking a career in ... and looking to work in ... . Note: we say look *to*, meaning consider or plan, not look *for*.

B Expressions connected with working life

In many countries, women are allowed **maternity leave** and men **paternity leave** if they're having a baby. If they adopt a child, they may have a right to **adoption leave**. [time away from work to prepare for and look after a new baby / adopted child]

What **perks** (*informal*) / **(extra) benefits** (*formal*) do you get in your job? [extra things apart from salary, e.g. a car, **health insurance**]

What does **job satisfaction** mean? [a feeling that your job is worth doing and fulfils you] Is it just having a pleasant **workplace** or is it more than that? [the place where you work] Can a **run-of-the-mill** job be satisfying? [ordinary, not special or exciting]

What's your **holiday entitlement**? I get four weeks a year. [number of days you have the right to take as holiday]

Do you get regular salary **increments** or do you have to ask for pay rises? [increases/rises; *formal*]

Most people think they are **overworked and underpaid**. (often said together as an informal, humorous fixed expression)

Because of the bad financial situation, the company announced that there would have to be **voluntary/compulsory redundancies**. [people losing their jobs, by offering to do so / having no choice]

During the strike, the airport managed to continue running with a **skeleton staff** of volunteers. [the minimum number of workers needed to keep operating]

The people on the **interview panel** at the last job I applied for were so unfriendly that I got very nervous. [the group of people interviewing someone for a job]

Exercises

4.1 Rewrite these sentences so they are more formal by using words and phrases from the opposite page instead of the underlined words.

1 Do you often look at the job <u>ads</u>?
2 I <u>haven't worked in Sales before</u>.
3 Developing good apps for phones and tablets is a <u>money-making</u> activity.
4 I thought I would apply for the job, since <u>it sounded just like me</u>.

4.2 Find expressions on the opposite page which mean the *opposite* of the underlined words or phrases.

1 a <u>loosely organised</u> team
2 a <u>very frustrating</u> job
3 a person with <u>low motivation</u>
4 a <u>rather static and slow-moving</u> profession
5 a <u>drop in salary</u>

6 <u>compulsory</u> redundancy
7 a <u>full</u> staff of workers
8 someone who <u>has a light workload and is paid a lot</u>

4.3 Use words from the box to fill the gaps in the text below.

> team player   rewarding   holiday entitlement
> run-of-the-mill   job satisfaction   drive   seeking

Careers for people who are going places

If you're an out-of-the-ordinary person who is ¹.......................... more than just a ².......................... job, ecotourism offers a stimulating and ³.......................... career with many opportunities for professional and personal development. If you are a ⁴.......................... with a strong, positive personality and plenty of ⁵.......................... and motivation, if you want a job with lots of travel opportunities, great ⁶.......................... and a generous ⁷.......................... , and if you think you can show leadership and deal with challenging and sometimes unpredictable situations, ecotourism may be the right career for you. If you really want to go places, contact us now and click here for our online application form.

The title and last sentence of the job ad above play with the double meaning of the expression to go places. What are the two meanings? Use a dictionary if you are not sure.

4.4 Each sentence in these pairs of sentences contains a mistake. Correct them.

1 She was on mother leave for three months after the birth of her baby. Then her husband took father leave for three months.
2 Sarah has been on adapted leave since she and Brian welcomed their new two-year old child into their family. Brian took volunteer redundancy from his job, which means he is at home too.
3 My holiday titlement is four weeks a year. The atmosphere in my place for work is very pleasant, so I'm happy.
4 When I applied for the job, I was looking for join a dynamic team. However, the interview jury gave an impression of complete boredom and lack of drive.
5 The factory had to operate with a skeletal staff during the economic crisis. There had been a large number of compulsive redundancies.
6 I get some good parks in my new job. I get a company car and free health security.

4.5 *Over to you*

Use a dictionary and write down adjectives that describe your personality in relation to qualities that might be sought in job ads, e.g. *talented, self-reliant*.

5 At work: careers

A Carl's career in sales

When Carl left school, he took the first job he was offered – in **telesales**[1]. He thought **telemarketing**[2] sounded quite glamorous but soon found that most of the people he phoned hated **cold calling**[3] and put the phone down when he tried the **hard sell**[4]. However, he persevered and found he became quite skilled at persuading customers to **part with their money**[5]. He then moved into a job on a **TV shopping channel**[6] where he specialised in selling **merchandise**[7] for the leisure market. He did so well at this that he set up his own sportswear company and **hasn't looked back**[8] since.

[1] + [2] selling or marketing goods and services by phone   [3] phoning people who have not requested a call in order to try to sell them something   [4] attempt to sell something by being very forceful or persuasive   [5] spend money   [6] a TV channel devoted to selling products   [7] products that are bought and sold   [8] has moved forward successfully

B Buying and selling

A person's **purchasing power** is the ability they have to buy goods, i.e. the amount of money they have available.

If you **shop around,** you try different companies or shops to see which offers best value.

If you want to buy something, you need to find a shop that **stocks** it. [keeps a supply of it = **keeps it in stock**]

If you **trade something up,** usually a car or a house, you buy one that is of higher value than the one you had before. (*opp.* = **trade down**)

People sometimes make a purchasing decision based on **brand loyalty.** [confidence in that particular make and a tendency always to choose it]

Supermarkets sometimes sell an item for less than it cost them just so that they attract a lot of people into the shop where they will also buy more profitable items – the item being sold at a low price is called a **loss leader.**

For a company to sell its products, it has to **price** them appropriately. [give them a price]

If a company finds a **niche market,** it finds a specialised group of customers with particular interests that that company can meet.

If an item is said to **come/go under the hammer,** it is sold at an **auction.** [sale of goods or property where people make gradually increasing **bids** and the item is then sold to the highest **bidder**]

C Tina's business career

A few years ago Tina started her own software development business which turned out to be very **lucrative**[1]. However, she got increasingly irritated by all the **red tape**[2] involved in the **administration**[3] of a business and when a larger company contacted her with a **proposition**[4] suggesting a **takeover**[5], she was interested. At first the two companies could not agree on all the details of the agreement but they managed to **reach a compromise**[6] and **hammer out a deal**[7] without too much delay. In many ways Tina was sad that her company had been **swallowed up**[8] but she has used the money raised by the sale of her **capital assets**[9] to **invest in**[10] a business **start-up**[11]: an online **holiday property letting agency**[12].

[1] producing a lot of money   [2] bureaucracy (negative)   [3] organisation and arrangement of operations   [4] formal offer   [5] agreement in which one company takes control of another one (compare with **merger** in which two companies join together to become one company)   [6] come to an agreement in which both sides reduce their demands a little   [7] talk in detail until a business agreement is made   [8] taken over by a larger company   [9] buildings and machines owned by a company   [10] put money into   [11] new company   [12] a business organising the rental of holiday houses and flats

Exercises

5.1 Match the two parts of these business collocations from the opposite page.

1 loss	☐	a agency
2 capital	☐	b channel
3 purchasing	☐	c leader
4 shopping	☐	d tape
5 hard	☐	e power
6 letting	☐	f loyalty
7 brand	☐	g assets
8 niche	☐	h sell
9 red	☐	i market

5.2 Look at A and B opposite. Fill the gaps in these sentences.

1 A world-famous painting will go .... the hammer in London tomorrow.
2 It's a sensible idea to shop .... a bit before buying a computer.
3 Sally made the right decision when she quit her old job and set up her own business – she hasn't looked .... since the day it opened.
4 I don't mind trying a hard sell on a person who has already expressed an interest in our products, but I hate .... calling.
5 It can be quite hard to persuade my dad to .... with his money.
6 I'm going to make a .... for the dining table that is up for auction tomorrow.
7 My current job is in .... I spend all the day on the phone.
8 They produce special clothes for people who practise yoga and have really cornered this .... market.
9 The shop I went to didn't .... the printer I wanted so I'm going to order it online.

5.3 Replace the underlined words with a word or phrase from C with a similar meaning.

1 As their business interests were quite different, it took them a long time to <u>come to an agreement</u>.
2 If you want to go into the import and export business, you had better be prepared for a lot of <u>bureaucracy</u>.
3 At the moment they are discussing the possibility of <u>buying up another company</u>.
4 Sportswear is a very <u>profitable</u> business to be in at the moment.
5 Banks will only lend a <u>new business</u> money if they have a realistic business plan.
6 A number of small companies have been <u>taken over</u> by that huge multinational in the last six months.
7 Hassan has made a rather interesting <u>suggestion</u> about setting up a business together.
8 Chloe is much better at the creative side of business than the <u>organisation</u> involved in running a company.

5.4 Choose the best word to complete each sentence.

1 I hope we'll be able to *keep / reach* a compromise when we meet tomorrow.
2 I think those new games consoles are *priced / purchased* too high at the moment.
3 The shops are hoping to sell a lot of *capital assets / merchandise* connected with the royal wedding.
4 My sports car was so expensive to run that I decided to trade it *down / up* for something much cheaper.
5 Helga has never looked *back / out* since she started her own business ten years ago.
6 There's a lot of *loss leader / red tape* involved in setting up a new business.

6 Managing a business

A Managing business agreements

to **put in / submit a tender**: to supply a written offer to do a job for an agreed price
to **win a tender**: to be given a job, after submitting a tender
to **meet/miss a deadline**: to supply / fail to supply something by the agreed time
a **penalty clause**: part of a contract specifying what will happen if an agreement is broken
an **outstanding** account: an account that has not yet been paid
to **default on a payment**: to fail to pay something that had been agreed
to **distribute**: to supply goods to shops and companies
to **ship an order**: to send out goods that have been ordered –
nothing to do with boats; what is sent is the **shipment**
to **expire**: to end – of something that was agreed for a fixed period;
the noun is **expiry**, used most commonly in the phrase **expiry date**
[date when something, e.g. a document **expires** or **runs out**]

STAFF MORALE...

B Problems in business management

These are some of the issues that business managers
sometimes have to deal with:
how to improve staff **morale**[1]
how to encourage effective **teamwork**[2]
how to avoid **bankruptcy**[3] or **liquidation**[4]
how to cope if the **stock market**[5] **crashes**[6]

whether to offer staff **bonuses**[7] or not
how to secure enough **funding**[8]
how to compete with other businesses in the
same **sector**[9]

[1] amount of confidence felt by a person or group   [2] working together for a common purpose
[3] a situation in which a person or business has no money to pay debts   [4] cause a business to close, so
that its assets can be sold to pay its debts   [5] market for buying and selling of **part shares** [investments]
in companies   [6] suddenly fails   [7] extra money, usually based on good performance or **productivity**
[rate at which goods are produced]   [8] money given by the government, an organisation, or bank, to
allow an activity to be carried out   [9] area of economic activity (collocates with **financial/retail/health/
public/private sector**)

C Success in management

Successful business people don't work hard. They work very, very hard. I think we all get that bit. But
the willingness to do this should come from the fact you are doing exactly what is right for you and the
kind of person you are, i.e. that you feel total **affinity**[1] with your role.

Working very hard but with little emotional affinity for that work can bring **short-term**[2] **financial
reward**[3], but also brings with it serious **'soul' damage**[4] if you do it for too long. But that truly **tuned-in**[5]
feeling that comes from affinity helps you to see opportunity where others don't; to give the extra 5%
where others can't and to bring that bit of **zip**[6] to the job where others won't.

Connected to affinity is the balance between head and heart that's important in your role as manager
or **entrepreneur**[7]. The head gives you clear, rational thinking in areas like the **risk assessment**[8]. Your
heart provides the emotional **propulsion**[9] to drive ideas from the imagination into action, to tune into
that most underrated of business skills – your **intuition**[10] – better and perhaps, most important of all,
to inspire others. That is the way that you will **deliver great results**[11].

'How to be lucky in business' by Douglas Miller

[1] feeling close to someone or something, because of something that is shared   [2] immediate (*opp.*
= **long-term**)   [3] money gained (notice the collocation)   [4] emotional and spiritual harm   [5] well-
adjusted (a radio or TV is tuned in to a particular station)   [6] energy; *informal*   [7] someone who
starts their own business, used especially of someone who sees a new opportunity   [8] working out how
much risk might be involved in something   [9] force that pushes something forward (verb = **propel**)
[10] ability to know or understand something immediately without needing to think about it   [11] produce
great results (notice the collocation)

Exercises

6.1 **Rewrite these sentences using the word in brackets.**

1 Do you have many accounts which have yet to be paid? (OUTSTANDING)
2 Until what date is your contract valid? (EXPIRE)
3 Is there anything in the contract saying what will happen if we don't deliver what we promise? (CLAUSE)
4 It is very important that you complete your work by the agreed time. (MEET)
5 We would like to invite companies to send us proposals as to how they would do the job and what they would charge for it. (SUBMIT)
6 It is company policy to take legal action against customers who fail to pay their accounts. (DEFAULT)
7 Our factories send their products to customers by rail. (DISTRIBUTE)
8 We received a large number of items we had ordered from the States this morning. (SHIPMENT)

6.2 **Complete the sentences using a word or phrase from B opposite.**

1 If you want to make money on the .... you have to follow what is happening on Wall Street.
2 Staff .... has improved a lot since we gave everyone free membership of the local sports centre.
3 Unfortunately, the company was forced into........................... .
4 The government provides a lot of .... for various arts projects.
5 Do more people work in the public or the private .... ?
6 Andy was really pleased to get a .... just before his holiday.

6.3 **Match each of these pieces of advice to a problem in B.**

1 Think carefully about who you ask to work together on the same project.
2 Prepare yourself well before you go to the bank.
3 Make sure you do not price your products too cheaply.
4 Remember to let your employees know much you value their work.
5 Work out what kind of effect this will have on productivity.

6.4 **Complete these sentences about the text in C.**

1 The writer wants people to feel .... with the work they do.
2 He suggests that it is not enough to receive financial .... for your work, you need to feel ....-in to what you are doing.
3 He wants managers and .... to find the right balance between head and heart.
4 Your head can help you when it comes to the .... of risk.
5 Your heart gives you the emotional .... to put your ideas into action.
6 Your heart also helps you trust your ....

6.5 **Match the two parts of the business collocations from the opposite page.**

1 win	☐	a	a payment
2 miss	☐	b	account
3 an outstanding	☐	c	a tender
4 default on	☐	d	results
5 penalty	☐	e	term
6 deliver	☐	f	date
7 long	☐	g	clause
8 expiry	☐	h	a deadline

7 Describing yourself

A Character and personality

Chinese astrology organises years into cycles of 12, and asserts that the year you are born in affects your character. Each year is named after an animal.

animal	year	characteristics
RAT	1972, 1984, 1996, 2008	imaginative, charming, generous, quick-tempered, **opportunistic**[1]
BUFFALO	1973, 1985, 1997, 2009	conservative, **methodical**[2], conscientious, **chauvinistic**[3], a born leader
TIGER	1974, 1986, 1998, 2010	sensitive, emotional, tends to **get carried away**[4], stubborn, rebellious, courageous
RABBIT	1975, 1987, 1999, 2011	affectionate, **obliging**[5], sentimental, **superficial**[6], often **insecure**[7]
DRAGON	1964, 1976, 1988, 2000	fun-loving, popular, a **perfectionist**[8], gifted, may sometimes be **tactless**[9]
SNAKE	1965, 1977, 1989, 2001	charming, **intuitive**[10], stingy
HORSE	1966, 1978, 1990, 2002	**diligent**[11], independent, **placid**[12], outgoing, can be selfish and cunning
GOAT	1967, 1979, 1991, 2003	elegant, artistic, always ready to complain, over-anxious
MONKEY	1968, 1980, 1992, 2004	witty, **magnetic personality**[13], good company, can be **distrustful**[14]
ROOSTER	1969, 1981, 1993, 2005	industrious, **shrewd**[15], **supportive**[16], decisive, **extravagant**[17]
DOG	1970, 1982, 1994, 2006	**down-to-earth**[18], **altruistic**[19], **morose**[20], **sharp-tongued**[21]
PIG	1971, 1983, 1995, 2007	intellectual, tolerant, **naive**[22], often materialistic

[1] using situations for own benefit
[2] systematic, careful
[3] too patriotic
[4] become too excited and lose control
[5] ready to help
[6] not caring about serious things
[7] not confident, uncertain about your own abilities
[8] someone who is not satisfied if things are not 100% perfect
[9] inclined to say things that upset or offend people
[10] understanding instinctively
[11] hard-working
[12] calm, does not easily become excited or angry
[13] personality that attracts people to you
[14] not trusting, suspicious of others
[15] having good judgement
[16] gives help or encouragement
[17] spends too much money or uses too much of something
[18] practical and sensible
[19] thinking of others rather than yourself
[20] gloomy
[21] inclined to speak in a severe and critical way
[22] without enough experience of life, trusting too easily

B Positive and negative associations

Charming, generous – is that how you think of yourself? Selfish, cunning – that can't be me! Some words in the chart above have positive associations, others negative ones. Here are some words from the chart together with other words that share some aspects of their meaning. The table shows which have positive and which have negative associations.

positive	negative	positive	negative
generous, unstinting	extravagant, immoderate	shrewd, astute	cunning, sly
resolute, dogged	stubborn, obstinate	sober, serious	morose, sullen
thrifty, frugal	stingy, parsimonious	witty, pithy	brusque, terse
diligent, industrious	work-obsessed, (a) workaholic (noun)	tolerant, open-minded	unprincipled, unscrupulous
idealistic, principled	dogmatic, inflexible	chatty, talkative	verbose, garrulous

Exercises

7.1 Read the comments and then answer the questions.

1 'I wish Tatyana would calm down and not get so over-excited about things.'
2 'Graham thinks his country is better than any other country and doesn't listen to reason.'
3 'Alice can always be relied upon to make the right decision.'
4 'Sophie is always so calm.'
5 'Rowan is such a practical and sensible person.'
6 'Andrey has a tendency to say things that upset people.'

	name		name
1 Who is placid?		4 Who is often tactless?	
2 Who is down-to-earth?		5 Who is shrewd?	
3 Who tends to get carried away?		6 Who is chauvinistic?	

7.2 Which colleagues does the speaker have a positive opinion of and which a negative one?

'Eliza, my boss, is very astute and she can be very witty, but I find her assistant, David, a bit sullen and obstinate. Julie, who I sit next to, is a bit stingy and extremely work-obsessed. I do a lot of work with Marco, who's very obliging, supportive and tolerant.'

7.3 Fill the gaps with words from the opposite page. You are given the first letter(s) and clues to the meaning in brackets.

1 He's rather o........................ . He always tries to use situations to his own advantage. (devious)
2 She has an i........................ approach to life rather than a rational one. (instinctive)
3 My father was a somewhat quick-tempered and m........................ sort of person. (gloomy)
4 He was a very altruistic person, almost to the point of being n........................ . (too trusting)
5 Aisha has a m........................ personality. Everyone is drawn to her. (attractive)
6 Jack is a very conscientious and m........................ worker. (careful, systematic)
7 I find Janine a bit b........................ and rude. (speaks in a quick and rude way)
8 She's fun-loving but she can be a bit s........................ at times. (doesn't care about serious things)
9 I think Max is i........................ . (doesn't have much confidence, not really sure of himself)
10 I'm always happy to go out for a meal with Kerstin. She's such g........................ c........................ . (pleasant and entertaining to spend time with)
11 She was very c........................ in speaking out against corruption. (brave, unafraid to speak or act)
12 Owen's a p........................ . He's never happy if he doesn't get an A-grade in every test.

7.4 Find adjectives on the opposite page related to these abstract nouns.

1 altruism	4 placidity	7 distrust	10 unscrupulousness
2 parsimony	5 industriousness	8 terseness	
3 diligence	6 rebellion	9 naivety	

7.5 The adjectives you found in the exercise above are more common in formal contexts. Give a synonym for each word that would be more likely to be used in informal situations (e.g. a friendly, informal conversation). Use a dictionary if necessary.

7.6 **Over to you**

Answer the questions about yourself and people you know. If possible, compare your answers with someone else.

- Which animal in the Chinese horoscope best represents you? To what extent do the characteristics apply to you?
- Arrange a selection of adjectives and descriptive phrases from A into three columns under the following headings: *describe me | might describe me | do not describe me*.

8 Describing others: appearance and mannerisms

A Adjectives connected with size, weight and general appearance

She introduced me to a tall, **slender** woman who looked very serious. [thin in an attractive way]
He was too **scrawny** to be a football player. [unattractively thin and bony-looking]
A **lanky** teenager walked in. [very tall and thin, and usually moving awkwardly]
A **gangling/gangly** youth approached him. [tall, with long, thin arms and legs and rather awkward movements; often used of men and boys]
A number of the children in the class were **obese**. [very fat, in an unhealthy way]
She's the rather **stout** woman wearing glasses over there. [with a quite fat, solid body; used of men and women]
My grandfather was a **stocky** man with big hands and broad shoulders. [short and with a body that is wide across the shoulders and chest]

B Aspects of appearance and complexion

Hi Jessica,

Guess who I bumped into the other day? Our old college mate, Rob Parsons! First thing I noticed was he's put on weight (he used to be so **lean**[1] and **wiry**[2], didn't he?) and he's got a **double chin**[3]. He looked so **unkempt**[4]. I wonder why he doesn't look after himself. His sister was always the opposite – **never a hair out of place**[5] and **immaculate**[6] clothes, remember? But they were different in appearance too, weren't they? He has a rather **swarthy**[7] complexion. His sister's was more **sallow**[8]. I must say he looked a bit **haggard**[9] and exhausted. He's probably working too hard. Anyway, how are things with you?

Beth

[1] thin and healthy   [2] thin but strong   [3] fat around the chin   [4] untidy, scruffy (the opposite would be *smart* or *neat*; 'kempt' does not exist)   [5] always well-dressed, neat and smart-looking   [6] in perfect condition, smart   [7] dark-coloured, used about skin   [8] yellowish   [9] his face looked thin and tired

C Facial expression

A: What are you **grinning** at?
B: You've got ice cream on your nose – it looks so funny! [giving a big smile]
Look at those models **pouting** for the photographers! [positioning their lips in a sexually attractive way]
She said if her daughter doesn't get what she wants, she **pouts** for the rest of the day. [positions her lips in a look of annoyance]
You don't have to **grimace** every time I eat raw garlic. I happen to think it's delicious. [make an expression of pain or strong dislike]
I arrived late and she just **scowled** at me. [gave a bad-tempered, angry look]
He was **leering** at us. I felt very uncomfortable and wanted to leave. [looking in an unpleasant, sexually interested way]

D Mannerisms and actions

I asked him for advice but he just **shrugged his shoulders**. [lifted his shoulders up and down to show he didn't know or couldn't answer]
He **folded his arms** and **crossed his legs** and waited for me to speak. [crossed one arm over the other close to his body] [crossed one leg over the other while sitting]
He sat there **twitching** nervously as he waited for his interview. [suddenly making small movements]
She **bites her nails** all the time. It drives me crazy!
She **clenched her fist** and told him to get out of the room at once. [closed her hand tightly because of anger]
He just kept **tapping/drumming his fingers** on the table, looking impatient. [made quick, light hitting movements]

Exercises

8.1 Rewrite these sentences using words from A opposite instead of the underlined words.

1 She looks as if she needs a good meal; her body is so <u>thin and bony</u>.
2 Marian and David are very suitable for each other; they're both rather <u>tall and thin</u> individuals.
3 Being <u>extremely fat</u> is very unhealthy.
4 A <u>very tall, thin, bony, awkward-looking</u> boy carried our bags for us.
5 They were taking photos of a beautiful, <u>thin</u> model.
6 A <u>short</u> man <u>with broad shoulders</u> offered to lift the stone so we could look underneath.
7 That <u>quite fat</u> woman on the left of the photo is Charlie's wife.

8.2 Use words from B opposite to write a sentence describing each of these pictures.

1 .... 2 .... 3 .... 4 ....

8.3 What are these people doing?

  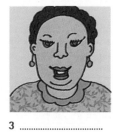 

1 *He's grimacing*..... 2 .... 3 .... 4 ....

5 .... 6 .... 7 .... 8 ....

8.4 Answer these questions. Use a dictionary if necessary.

1 The verb *to pout* has two meanings on the opposite page. What are they?
2 If someone scowls at you, how are they probably feeling?
3 What is the difference between a *swarthy* complexion and a *sallow* complexion?
4 When would you clench your fist?
5 When do people normally shrug their shoulders?
6 What might you do with your fingers on a table if you were nervous or impatient?
7 In what situations do people typically (a) fold their arms, (b) cross their legs?
8 If someone is 'lean and wiry', which of these adjectives are true of them: *thin, fat, healthy, weak, ill-looking, strong*?

9 Describing others: personality and character traits

A Adjectives to describe people's personality or behaviour

word	meaning	example
impetuous	acts on a sudden idea without thinking first; often negative	She's so **impetuous**; I wish she would consider things before acting.
impulsive	similar to *impetuous*, but can be used in a more positive way	His **impulsive** generosity led him to give money to anyone who asked for help.
effusive	gives exaggerated expression of pleasure, praise or gratitude	She always gives me such an **effusive** welcome when I visit her.
excitable	easily excited by things	He's a very **excitable** child; he needs to calm down.
pushy	always selfishly promoting one's own position or interests; *informal*	She's so **pushy**, it's typical of her to demand a pay rise for herself and not care about the rest of us.
self-conscious	nervous or uncomfortable because you know what people think about you or your actions	Freddie seemed **self-conscious** and uncomfortable when he had to make the announcement at the party.
well-balanced	calm and reasonable and showing good judgement	The teacher said Maddy was a **well-balanced** child who got on well at school.
taciturn /'tæsɪtɜːn/	reserved or says very little (generally negative)	He was a bit **taciturn** when I first met him. He hardly said a word.

B Sociability

Chloe's such an **introvert**. Her brother Mark is so **outgoing** and is such an **extrovert**. Strange, isn't it? [inward-looking and quiet] [energetic and friendly, finds it easy to be with others] [outward-looking, energetic and sociable]

Mr Rogers is such a **diffident** man. He seems to have quite low **self-esteem**. [lacks confidence] [has a low opinion of himself]

English people are traditionally thought of as rather **reserved**. [not immediately sociable]

Barbara tends to be rather **aloof**. I don't know if she's just shy. [unfriendly and not sociable]

My aunt Annie can be very **haughty** and **disdainful** at times, but she's lovely really. [unfriendly and thinks herself better than others] [does not believe others deserve respect]

I've always found Professor Mactoft very **unapproachable**, but his colleague Dr O'Daly is very **approachable**. [not easy to be sociable with or start a conversation with] [the opposite]

Natasha is very **conceited** and **self-important**, but Rachel is such a **modest** person. [thinks herself wonderful] [has an exaggerated sense of her importance] [prefers not to exaggerate her own qualities]

Joe is always so polite and **respectful**. I wish he would be more informal and just treat me as his equal. [treating someone well and politely, often with admiration]

C Character traits

Arjen is a somewhat **naive** person; he thinks love can solve all the world's problems. [/naɪˈiːv/ willing to believe simple things, perhaps because of inexperience]

Telephone salespeople often take advantage of **gullible** people. [easily deceived]

My father was a very **conscientious** man; he never took time off work unless he was really sick. [/ˌkɒntʃiˈentʃəs/ always took his work very seriously]

She's a **restless** individual. I don't think she'll ever settle down in a job. [not satisfied with what she is doing now and wanting something new]

You are so **obstinate** and **pig-headed**! Why don't you listen when people give you advice? [unwilling to change, despite persuasion] [similar to *obstinate* but stronger; *informal*]

Exercises

9.1 **Answer these questions.**

1 Why would most people rather have an approachable teacher or boss than an unapproachable one?
2 What is a stronger and less formal way of saying *obstinate*?
3 If someone is *diffident*, do they have little or lots of self-confidence?
4 How could you describe a greeting from someone that showed exaggerated pleasure?
5 Do you think it would be easy or difficult to have a friendly conversation with a taciturn person?
6 Which tends to be more negative, *impetuous* or *impulsive*?
7 Which would most people rather be described as, *conscientious* or *self-conscious*?
8 If you're *outgoing*, are you more likely to be seen as an introvert or an extrovert?

9.2 **Rewrite the underlined parts of the sentences using the words in the box, making any other changes necessary.**

> restless   well-balanced   aloof   conceited   haughty
> excitable   naive   self-esteem   pushy   outgoing

1 Don't be so <u>over-proud of your achievements</u>! You're not the only one to get an A-grade!
2 People who have <u>a poor opinion of themselves</u> can find it difficult to achieve their goals.
3 He's generally a <u>happy, sociable</u> sort of person.
4 She is a person <u>who is generally quite reasonable and who shows good judgement</u> overall.
5 You always seem <u>unable to settle down</u>. What's the problem?
6 He's so <u>easily excited</u>. He should try to calm down more.
7 She <u>believes rather simple things</u> when it comes to politics.
8 He's <u>just pursuing his own interests</u> and cares little what happens to others.
9 Frances was very <u>unfriendly and would not take part in things</u> at the party.
10 At times, Joel is quite <u>cold and unfriendly and acts as if he's better than the rest of us</u>.

9.3 **Complete the table. Some of the words are not on the opposite page.**

adjective	noun	adjective	noun
excitable		reserved	
gullible			diffidence
	disdain	pig-headed	
impetuous			respect
obstinate		self-important	
approachable		modest	

9.4 **These sentences contain words from the table in 9.3. Rewrite the sentences using the other form of the word. For example, use a noun instead of an adjective and vice versa.**

1 One of her main character traits is that she is impetuous.
2 It's difficult to get him to change his ways. He displays a high level of obstinacy.
3 Luke shows a lot of reserve, but his wife is known more for her approachability.
4 One of her nicest characteristics is that she is modest.
5 She shows a lot of respect for her elders. It's important in her culture.
6 Being pig-headed seems to be a family trait among my relatives.
7 She is so full of self-importance; it irritates everyone.
8 Online identity thieves prey on people being gullible.

9.5 **Over to you**

Choose five words from the opposite page that you feel describe you. Be honest!

10 Relationships: friends forever

A Love and romance

When Tom met Lily, it was **love at first sight**. [love began the first time they saw each other]
She **fell head over heels in love** with him. [fell deeply and madly in love]
Nick **only has eyes for** Sophie. He's not interested in other girls. [is only attracted to]
Lauren was more than **infatuated with** Dave; she was completely **besotted with** him.
[romantically obsessed with] [almost stupidly or blindly in love with]
I've often seen Matt and Ellie at the cinema together, but it's purely a **platonic relationship**.
[affectionate relationship between people of the opposite sex that is not sexual]

B Friendships and other positive relationships

Anona and I **hit it off** immediately; we're true **soulmates**. [liked each other the moment we met]
[people who feel close in spirit and understand each other deeply]
The moment I met Rob, I could see he was **a man after my own heart**. [someone you admire
because they do or think the same as you; also **woman after your own heart**]
Charlie and I **get on like a house on fire**. [have a very good, enjoyable relationship]
Jim and Tony have been **bosom friends/buddies/pals** for years. [very close, good friends]
Marta and Carmen are **inseparable**. [always want to be together, very close]
There's a close **bond** between Rushda and her aunt. [relationship or feeling of togetherness]

C General social relationships: collocations

The replies in these conversations are another way of saying what the first speaker says.

A: You seem to be very similar to Ben – the way you think and look at life.
B: Yes, we've always been **kindred spirits**.

A: What a nice wedding! Ian and Sally seem to be perfect for each other.
B: Yes, such a **well-matched** couple!

A: Our Spanish friends are always phoning their brothers and sisters.
B: Yes, well, I think **family ties** in Spain are much stronger than here.

A: I've never met Kay but I know several people she knows.
B: Yes, she said you have a number of **mutual acquaintances**.

A: Gareth has a lot of respect for Clare.
B: Yes, he **holds her in high regard**.

A: Sarah and Anna are very close these days. I'm sure they share all their secrets.
B: Yes, they're **as thick as thieves**.

D Nouns and adjectives

adjective	noun	example
adoring	adoration	The parents gazed at their new-born baby with a look of tender **adoration**.
affectionate	affection	He never shows much **affection** for his children.
amiable	amiability	She always treats us with great **amiability**.
considerate	consideration	'Have some **consideration** for the other students!' she said angrily.
faithful	faithfulness	**Faithfulness** is the key to a good marriage.
fond	fondness	Over the years she developed a **fondness** for Mario that went beyond a purely business relationship.
loyal	loyalty	He was a great team captain who inspired **loyalty** in the players.

Exercises

10.1 Match up the words on the left with words on the right to make expressions. Then use the expressions to complete the sentences below.

1 love ☐   a pals   4 hit ☐   d spirits
2 head ☐   b it off   5 kindred ☐   e at first sight
3 bosom ☐   c acquaintances   6 mutual ☐   f over heels in love

1 When Patrick met Andrea, it was ....
2 Phil and Colin look at life in the same way. They're ....
3 Ever since they worked together, Lucy and Sue have been ....
4 I was introduced to Zoe by some ....
5 They just looked at each other and fell ....
6 When Joss and I met, we immediately ....

10.2 Fill the gaps in these sentences.

1 Rachel only has .... for Mark these days. She's crazy over him.
2 They look such a .... couple. I wonder if they will get married?
3 Sheila and I have always got .... like a house ....
4 He's completely .... with her. I've never known him to be so much in love before. He's like a teenager. (*two possible answers*)
5 Greg would do anything for his boss – he holds her in very high ....
6 I think she was quite right to say what she did – she's a woman after my own ....
7 The children must be planning something – they look as .... as thieves.
8 They spend most of their holidays in the south of Italy because of their .... ties there.

10.3 Complete the table. Some of the words are not on the opposite page.

noun	adjective	noun	adjective
	loyal	respect	
consideration		affection	
passion			romantic
	devoted	support	
	fond		amiable
	faithful	trust	
adoration			infatuated

10.4 Now complete these sentences, which include words from the table above, using the correct preposition. Use a dictionary if necessary.

1 She's absolutely devoted .... her mother and visits her every day.
2 I've always had a lot of respect .... my boss, and I do enjoy my job a lot.
3 She's been so loyal .... me all these years, I can't let her down now.
4 He's very supportive .... his colleagues; they're very lucky.
5 I'm quite fond .... Jack, but that doesn't mean I want to marry him.
6 He puts a lot of trust .... me, and I feel I can trust him too.
7 I feel very affectionate .... him but I'm not in love with him.
8 Sophie and Dan are as passionate .... each other as they were ten years ago.

10.5 **Over to you**

Answer these questions, giving a reason why. Name someone in your life who ...

• you feel a close bond with   • is a real soulmate for you   • is a person after your own heart

11 Relationships: ups and downs

A Friendship

Friends are people who are much more than mere **casual acquaintances**[1]. **True friends** are always there when you need them, as you are for them. We expect **loyalty**[2] from our friends, despite our faults, and should give it in return, never speaking ill of them **behind their backs**[3]. As well as having friends and casual acquaintances, we have relationships with **colleagues, allies** and **partners.**

[1] person you know, but not very well
[2] support in good or bad times
[3] say bad things about us when we are not there

Here are some qualities of friendship and their opposites:

quality	opposite
loyal (adj.), **loyalty** (noun)	**disloyal** (adj.), **disloyalty** (noun)
supportive [always supports you]	**unsupportive, critical**
honest, truthful	**dishonest, untruthful**
respectful (adj.), **respect** (noun)	**disrespectful** (adj.), **disrespect** (noun)

B Problematic relationships

I used to think of Kate as a friend but I now realise she has been **two-faced towards** me. [insincere; pleasant with someone and then unpleasant about them behind their back]
Russia and America were **allies** in the war. [countries or people who join together to fight for a common cause]
We were **business partners** but now we're **bitter/ arch rivals.** [people who own a business together]
[people in competition with each other in a negative, aggressive way]
Indeed, I could say we are now **sworn enemies.** [people who will always hate each other]
Terry has been **disloyal to** me on a number of occasions.
OK, I was **dishonest with** you. I'm sorry, but I didn't want to hurt you.
Sam has been very **distant towards** me recently. [not friendly, cold]
Jamie has always been **scrupulously honest** in his dealings with us.
I would expect **complete and unswerving loyalty** from a true friend.
Monica has always been my **staunchest ally** at work. I can always rely on her to support me.
I was amazed that someone who called herself my friend could be so **deeply critical of** me.

C Breakdowns: expressions and collocations

Unfortunately, relationships sometimes **break down** because of **genuine misunderstandings.**
[collapse] [not understanding something correctly]
A **rift** can develop between two people or groups. [serious disagreement that divides people]
There's been a lot of **discord** in the office lately. [disagreement and discontent]
My father and I **don't see eye to eye** on most things. [have different opinions]
Jack and his sister have **been on bad terms** for a long time. [have a poor relationship]
His love affair with Anna has **turned sour.** I think they'll **split up.** [become bad] [separate]
Our marriage **has had its ups and downs,** but basically we're OK. [had good and bad times]
a **bumpy relationship** [up and down like a car on a road with bumps]
a **broken home** [family split up by divorce]
a **family feud** [/fjuːd/ quarrel in a family causing bad feeling for many years]

Exercises

11.1 Give the opposites of these adjectives.

1 loyal
2 truthful
3 honest
4 supportive
5 distant
6 respectful

11.2 Some words in these sentences have been used incorrectly. Rewrite the sentences using the correct word from A.

1 We both own the company: we're business rivals.
2 I've made several casual colleagues since moving to London, but no close friends yet.
3 Were Britain and the USA colleagues in the First World War?
4 The two companies hate each other: they're acquaintances.

11.3 Fill the gaps with suitable adjectives or adverbs from the opposite page.

1 You need .... allies at work who won't let you down.
2 His .... honesty is a quality I greatly admire.
3 I don't know why she was so .... critical of him; it seemed very unfair.
4 Her .... and .... loyalty to him was a mistake. He betrayed her in the end.
5 Ted and Hilary were .... rivals at work, but seemed to get on well outside the office.
6 When all my other so-called friends drifted away, Jack always remained a .... friend to me.

11.4 Fill the gaps with a suitable preposition.

1 I know I'm not perfect, but I've never been dishonest .... you.
2 She's very critical .... her colleagues.
3 Why are you always so disloyal .... me?
4 A true friend would never talk .... your back.
5 I hate being .... bad terms .... people.
6 I realise that people can often be two-faced .... their boss.

11.5 Rewrite the underlined phrases to give the *opposite* meaning.

1 Sandra and her sister <u>shared the same opinion</u> on a lot of things.
2 Carla's affection for Andrew has <u>grown stronger</u> lately. I expect they'll <u>get engaged</u>.
3 Our relationship <u>stayed firm</u> because we were <u>truthful</u> to each other.
4 Henry's brothers are <u>close friends</u>.

11.6 Use expressions from the opposite page to describe these situations.

1 Roger has phoned – he's still at the station. He thought I was picking him up and I thought he was getting a taxi. It was a ....
2 The kids have been unhappy since their parents divorced. They come from a
  ....
3 Her marriage has been both good and bad at different times. It has
  ....
4 The two union leaders have had a serious disagreement which has split them. A serious
  ....
5 Two of the brothers have not spoken to their other brother for 20 years because of something bad that happened. I think it's a ....

12 Emotions and reactions

Strong desires

Pregnant women **crave / have a craving for** strange things like tuna and banana pizza! [want very strongly]

Young children often seem to **thirst / have a thirst for** knowledge. [feel very strongly that you want]

Sometimes my cousin just **yearns to** be on her own with no family responsibilities. [if you **yearn to do / yearn for / have a yearning for** something, it means that you want something that you do not have and, often, can never have]

An Olympic gold medal is probably the most **coveted** sporting prize. [**to covet** something means to want to possess it very much]

Reacting to other people's emotions

Jane tried to **defuse** the tension by changing the subject. [make a dangerous or tense situation calmer]

Tim was very angry with his daughter and it took her a long time to **placate** him. [stop someone feeling angry]

An independent advisor has been brought in to **conciliate** between the unions and the employer. [end a disagreement between two people or groups by acting in a friendly way towards both sides; *formal*]

Although **appeasing** the enemy postponed the war for another year, it did not ultimately prevent it from happening. [end a disagreement by giving the other side an advantage that they are demanding (normally used in a disapproving way); *formal*]

> ### Language help
> A useful adjective from *placate* is **implacable**. It is used about someone's opinions and feelings and means that they cannot be changed, e.g. *I cannot understand the implacable hatred that he still feels for his old rival.* (Note: *placable* doesn't exist.)

Being extremely happy

exultant: feeling great pleasure and happiness, usually because of a success (more formal than **ecstatic**) Sarah was in an **exultant** mood / was **ecstatic** after her great exam results.

to rejoice: be extremely happy; *formal* Everyone **rejoiced** at the news of her recovery.

jubilant: expressing great happiness, especially at a victory; *formal* There were **jubilant** shouts as the results of the referendum were announced.

bliss: perfect happiness (often collocates with **utter** and **sheer**; adjective = **blissful**; the adverb **blissfully** often collocates with **happy**, **ignorant** and **unaware**) We had a fabulous holiday on a beautiful island – seven days of **utter/sheer bliss**. They are **blissfully happy** even though they're poor.

There are a number of colloquial expressions which mean to be very happy.

You look **full of the joys of spring** today. Why are you smiling all the time?

My daughter's just had a baby girl. We're **thrilled to bits** at the news.

I feel **on top of the world**. It's great to have a job again.

I've been **floating/walking on air** ever since I heard I got into drama school.

A: How did you feel when you scored the winning goal? B: I was **over the moon**!

Exercises

12.1 Choose one of the words below each sentence to fill the gaps.

1 I often find I .... sweet things when I'm studying, but I try to resist!
  A thirst   B crave   C hunger
2 Martha is very good at .... difficult situations.
  A placating   B appeasing   C defusing
3 Everyone is .... to bits that Karim was so successful in the competition.
  A blissful   B thrilled   C exultant
4 If he has a tantrum, you mustn't try to .... him. Don't give in!
  A conciliate   B appease   C defuse
5 When Lorna retires, there will probably be a lot of internal applicants for what must be the most .... job in the company.
  A yearned   B craved   C coveted
6 Fortunately, her parents were .... ignorant of what was going on.
  A jubilantly   B blissfully   C exultantly

12.2 Read the comments. Then answer the questions.

ROWAN: 'I just want to learn more and more about science, history, everything.'
LAURA: 'I can't believe I won first prize! Wow!! I never thought I'd do it! Yippee!!'
KATIE: 'I'm just longing to return to my homeland again. But I don't think I ever will.'
WILLIAM: 'I'd give anything to own that motorbike of Nick's. It's so fantastic!'
ASHLEY: 'Calm down, there's no need to be so cross.'

	name
1 Who is yearning to do something?	
2 Who is placating someone?	
3 Who has a thirst for something?	
4 Who covets something?	
5 Who is in an absolutely jubilant mood?	

12.3 Match the sentence beginnings on the left with the endings on the right.

1 Lucy has been walking   ☐   a on top of the world since he got his PhD.
2 Beth is full   ☐   b unaware of all the problems.
3 Amanda seems to be blissfully   ☐   c to bits when he won the medal.
4 Everyone rejoiced   ☐   d on air since she got her promotion.
5 Sam is feeling   ☐   e when they heard that the war had ended.
6 His parents were thrilled   ☐   f of the joys of spring.

12.4 Answer these questions.

1 If a politician talks about someone appeasing someone else, is he/she expressing approval?
2 Would fans be more likely to be called jubilant or blissful if their team won the World Cup?
3 If someone tried to conciliate between two neighbours who each claimed the other was too noisy, what would that person be trying to do?
4 If you are trying to placate someone, is it likely that they are (a) angry or (b) over-excited?
5 If, after a conflict, someone is thirsting for revenge, is it likely they are ready to forget the conflict or not?

12.5   **Over to you**

Think of an occasion (a) when you felt ecstatic about something, and (b) when you had to defuse a difficult situation. If possible, compare your experiences with someone else.

13 Negative feelings

A Antipathies and aversions

Antipathy is a feeling of strong, often active, dislike or opposition towards something or someone, e.g. **Antipathy** towards the government increased during the economic crisis. **Aversion** is a feeling of intense dislike or an unwillingness to do something. It is often used in the phrase **have/feel an aversion to**, e.g. I felt an instant aversion to the new manager. Arrogance has always been my **pet aversion**. [the thing I dislike most of all]
Averse to means opposed to, usually used with **not**, e.g. I'm **not averse to** a good night out. [I enjoy a good night out]

B Negative feelings

noun	meaning	adjective	verb	examples
loathing	intense hatred	loathsome	loathe	I just loathe people who tell lies.
abhorrence	intense disgust	abhorrent	abhor	We all find her behaviour abhorrent.
scorn	lack of respect for something	scornful	scorn	There was a scornful note in his voice.
irritation	a feeling of being annoyed	irritating irritated*	irritate	Her comments gave me an intense feeling of irritation.
distress	a feeling of being extremely upset or worried	distressing distressed*	distress	Being told that my best friend was seriously ill was very distressing.
alarm	a feeling of being very worried or frightened	alarming alarmed*	alarm	The advance of the enemy troops across the river was an alarming development.

C Adjectives with negative connotations

She was very **offhand** with everyone. [showed a rude lack of interest in others]
The Director's personal assistant can be very **officious**. [too eager to tell others what to do]
He makes very **ostentatious** displays of his wealth, with big, flashy cars, designer clothes, etc. [displaying wealth or possessions in a vulgar way]
She's become very **pompous** since she was elected to Parliament. [too formal and showing that you think that you are more important than other people]
She boasts about reading philosophy books – she's so **pretentious**. [tries to appear more serious or important than she is]
What **puerile** behaviour! Grow up! [silly and childish]
Because I rushed it, my essay was a bit **sloppy**. [not taking care in the way you work; *informal*]
Joanna can be very **fickle**. [changes her feelings suddenly without reason]
Oh, stop being so **nit-picking!** [too concerned about unimportant details; *informal*]
The customs officer was such an **obnoxious** man. [unpleasant and rude]

D Being extremely unhappy

I felt utterly **dejected** when I didn't get the job. [unhappy and disappointed]
She looked **forlorn** gazing into the distance. [sad, alone and not cared for]
I was **devastated** when I heard of the death of a good friend of mine. [very shocked and upset]
The missing child's parents were **distraught**. The neighbours tried to calm them. [extremely worried and upset]
You're looking a bit **down** today. Anything wrong? [unhappy; *informal*]
He always looks so **miserable** and never seems to smile! [very unhappy]

Exercises

13.1 Rewrite the sentences using the form of the word in bold indicated in brackets. Make any other necessary changes.

1 I am strongly **averse** to people who always want to be the centre of attention. (noun)
2 He's always **scornful** of our amateur theatrical productions. (verb)
3 She has an **abhorrence** of injustice, wherever it occurs. (verb)
4 I do not have an **aversion** to a vegetarian diet. I've just never tried it. (adjective)
5 His attitude **irritated** me very much. (adjective) (*two possible answers*)
6 The news was **alarming** to us all. (adjective ending in -*ed*)

13.2 Answer the questions.

1 If you are distressed by a piece of news, are you (a) angry, (b) upset, (c) depressed?
2 If you find something loathsome, what emotion do you feel towards it?
3 If someone feels antipathy towards another person, do they (a) just not like them, (b) feel annoyed by them, (c) actively and strongly dislike them?
4 If someone irritates you, do you feel (a) deep anger, (b) annoyance, (c) hatred towards them?

13.3 Match the sentence beginnings on the left with the endings on the right.

1 We were distraught		a so I offered to buy him a coffee.
2 She felt dejected		b by the death of so many good friends.
3 He was looking a bit down		c who rarely laughed or enjoyed herself.
4 They were utterly devastated		d when our cat went missing.
5 She was quite a miserable person		e because she failed the exam.

13.4 Add words to complete the sentences.

1 The dictator's palace was very .... , with gold ceilings and marble statues everywhere.
2 One of my friends is a bit .... ; he has a new girlfriend every week!
3 She thinks I'm .... because I like opera, but I think that's unfair. I like pop music too.
4 The lawyers were very .... - .... when they were dealing with old Mrs Carson's complicated will.
5 The decorators were very .... and didn't paint the kitchen properly.
6 He's an .... person; absolutely nobody thinks he's nice.
7 The receptionist was very .... with me, considering I had been kept waiting so long.
8 The Minister made a very .... speech, and seemed full of his own importance.
9 Their behaviour was silly and .... I wish they would act more maturely.
10 The man at the museum was very .... , telling us to be quiet and not to touch the exhibits.
11 She looked a bit .... because all her friends had gone to a party and she was not invited.
12 We were .... when our friends didn't arrive and we heard there'd been an accident on the motorway.

13.5

Over to you

Answer the questions. If possible, compare your answers with someone else.

- Name three things that you loathe doing.
- Are there any ideas that you find abhorrent? Why?
- Have you ever felt an instant antipathy to someone?
- Do you have a pet aversion? If so, what is it?

14 Birth and death: from cradle to grave

A In the beginning

Pregnancy[1] is the nine-month period when a woman is expecting a baby. It begins with **conception**[2], when the mother's egg is **fertilised**[3] and an **embryo**[4] **implants**[5] in the mother's **womb**[6] or **uterus**[6]. Most mothers **conceive**[7] naturally but some are helped by **fertility drugs**[8] or other procedures such as **IVF**[9]. As the **foetus**[10] grows, it is fed through the mother's **placenta**[11]. After 40 weeks, the mother usually **goes into labour**[12]. If this doesn't happen naturally, she may **be induced**[13]. Usually, a mother is helped to **give birth**[14] by a **midwife**[15]. Sometimes a surgeon is needed to **deliver**[16] the baby by **caesarean section**[17].

[1] (adj. = **pregnant**)   [2] time when sperm and egg meet and a baby starts to form   [3] made to start developing into new life   [4] developing baby   [5] fixes itself   [6] organ inside the mother where the fertilised egg develops into a baby; uterus is a more medical word than womb   [7] become pregnant   [8] drugs that help a woman to become pregnant   [9] **in vitro fertilisation**: process that fertilises a woman's egg in a laboratory; babies born this way are sometimes referred to as **test tube babies**   [10] what the embryo developing in the uterus is known as from eight weeks onward   [11] organ connecting the developing baby to the mother and giving it food   [12] goes into the last stage of pregnancy where the womb starts the process of pushing the baby out of the body   [13] be helped medically to start the process of labour (noun = **induction**)   [14] have her baby   [15] nurse who specialises in helping women when they are giving birth   [16] help the mother to give birth (noun = **delivery**)   [17] operation in which the mother's abdomen and womb are cut open to allow the baby to be removed

> **Language help**
> **Expect** when it means 'expect a baby' is only used in the continuous form. *Helena and her sister are both **expecting*** (NOT ~~expect~~).

B At the end

More and more people these days are living to a **ripe old age**[1]. My aunt, for example, that's my **late**[2] father's sister, is 93. She's been a **pensioner**[3] for more years than she worked. She lives in **sheltered accommodation**[4] but she's not at all **doddery**[5] or **gaga**[6]. At her age she's lucky, of course, still to **have all her wits about her**[7]. Funerals are changing a lot too. I went to one recently where there was a cardboard **coffin**[8] in the colours of the dead man's football team. And at the **wake**[9] his sister told me she'd put it in her **will**[10] that her own **ashes**[11] are to be sent up in a rocket! I think it's good that funerals are more about celebrating a person's life rather than just about **mourning**[12]. As for me, I think I'd prefer an ordinary family-only **cremation**[13]. But then I'd quite like to have my ashes **scattered**[14] at sea, as I love sailing.

[1] living well into old age; usually used in the phrase **to live to a ripe old age**   [2] now dead   [3] elderly person, receiving an old age pension from the state   [4] special housing, usually for old people, where care staff also live   [5] weak and unable to walk well, usually because of old age; *informal*   [6] unable to think clearly because of old age; *informal*   [7] is still able to think and react quickly   [8] box where the dead person is put   [9] gathering of family and friends after a funeral   [10] legal document saying what is to happen to your possessions after your death   [11] remains of a body after cremation (see 13)   [12] expressing sadness after someone's death (the mourners have been **bereaved**)   [13] service at a place called a **crematorium** where a dead body is burnt (as opposed to a **burial**, where the body is buried in the ground)   [14] spread around

C Death in different registers

expressions of sympathy: Please accept my **condolences**. (*formal*) I was so sorry to hear/learn of your **loss**. (*informal*)

euphemisms for 'to die': **to pass away, to pass on, to pass over**

colloquial expressions for being close to death: **to be at death's door, to be on your last legs** (often used about machines, e.g. My laptop's on its last legs)

newspaper words: **fatalities** [dead people], **perished** [died], **slaughtered** [violently killed]

legal words: **the deceased** [the dead person], **to bequeath** [to leave something in a will; noun = **a bequest**], **to inherit** [to receive something from someone who has died; noun = **an inheritance**], to die **intestate** [without having made a will]

Exercises

14.1 Complete these sentences with words from A opposite.

1 If Liz doesn't .... soon, she's going to ask her doctor for a fertility test.
2 Karen went into .... at midnight and gave .... only four hours later.
3 Did Amy have a natural .... or a .... section?
4 The .... provides the baby growing in the mother's .... with all the food it needs.
5 The first test .... baby was born in 1978.
6 As well as helping with the birth, a trained .... usually visits the mother before and after the birth to check that everything is going well.
7 Laila's .... a baby – it's due in the middle of October.
8 During the nine months of .... , the baby developing inside the mother is often referred to as a ....

14.2 Correct these sentences, which use the vocabulary in B and C.

1 The whole country is in morning after the President's death.
2 I'd like my dust scattered in my favourite forest.
3 My extinct grandfather was a shepherd all his life.
4 I'm afraid her elderly step-mother has just passed off.
5 My car is on its last leg.
6 My father inherited me his gold watch in his will.
7 Mrs Wilson seems to have been at death's window for years.
8 Over 2,000 people were perished in the earthquake.
9 It was amazing there were no fertilities when the bridge collapsed.
10 My aunt left me a request of £500 in her will.

14.3 Write sentences with the same meanings, using the word in brackets and making any appropriate changes.

1 Both my sisters are pregnant at the moment. (EXPECT)
2 Twins were born to Amanda Harrison last Monday. (BIRTH)
3 She has been taking medication to help her conceive. (FERTILITY)
4 All my grandparents lived to their 80s or 90s. (RIPE)
5 My neighbour is 90 but she is still very mentally alert. (WITS)
6 Unfortunately, the deceased died intestate. (WILL)
7 John bequeathed £1,000 to each of his three nephews. (INHERIT)
8 I was so sorry to hear of your loss. (CONDOLENCES)

14.4 Choose words or expressions from the box to complete these texts.

deceased	bequest	bequeathed
inherited	slaughtered	pensioner
perished	passed away	fatalities

Yesterday was indeed a black day for our country. Twenty-five people ¹........................... in an earthquake. Five more people were ²...........................in a terrorist bomb attack and there were ten road accident ³........................... . Among the ⁴........................... was one of our most popular young politicians.

I'm very sad to have to tell you that my grandfather ⁵...........................last month. He had been a ⁶........................... for some years. He had considerable savings and ⁷........................... each of his grandchildren quite a large sum of money. I'd love to spend some of the money I ⁸...........................on something really special. He also left a very large ⁹........................... to the university where he worked for most of his life.

15 Free time: relaxation and leisure

A Adjectives describing free-time activities

adjective	meaning	possible examples
rewarding	gives you a lot of positive experiences	doing voluntary work, helping charities
fruitful	produces good results	collaborating/cooperating with someone in an activity
lucrative	makes a lot of money	selling designer jewellery, writing video games
therapeutic /θerəˈpjuːtɪk/	makes you healthy in body and/or mind	gardening, yoga, jogging
relaxing/calming	reduces stress, gives a peaceful feeling	reading, listening to music, meditation
time-consuming	takes a long time to do	being president of a club, being a member of a committee

I enjoyed being secretary of the sports club but it was very **time-consuming**. I had to give up two evenings a week to do it.
The conservation work I do is very **rewarding**. I feel I'm doing something good and useful.
Photography has been a **lucrative** pursuit for her. She often sells her pictures to magazines.
Painting is such a **therapeutic** activity. It makes me feel good, and teaches me patience.

B Informal expressions: how people spend their leisure

Rob's a real **culture vulture**; he goes to the theatre regularly and to every art gallery he can find. [big fan of anything cultural]

I'm a bit of a **couch potato**; I spend hours every day just watching TV. [physically very inactive person]
Diana loves playing tennis but only as an **amateur** – she'd never want to be a professional. [someone who does something as a hobby, not a job]
Fatima's a bit of a **dabbler**; she does a hobby for a couple of weeks, then she gets bored and starts something different. [person who never keeps doing one activity for long]
Matt does a lot of **chores** at the weekend – things like shopping and mowing the **lawn**. [boring tasks that have to be done] [grass]
Laura's a **shopaholic**. She buys all sorts of things she doesn't need. [person addicted to shopping; compare alcoholic: addicted to alcohol]
Joe **is** heavily **into** downhill skiing these days. [is very involved in]
I **went off** football and I took up golf instead. [stopped liking, lost interest in]
She **locks herself away** for hours in front of the computer and goes online every night. [isolates herself from the world]
He's totally **hooked on** motor racing these days. [is addicted to]
What do you **get up to** at weekends, Mariana? [do]
Do you have a hectic social life? Yes, I have a pretty **full diary**. [a lot of activities]
Mark is a **keen participant** in all the community activities in his village. [takes part enthusiastically]

> **Language help**
> Words like **shopaholic**, **workaholic** and **chocaholic** are used in a light-hearted way and are different from **alcoholic** which is a serious and medically recognised condition.

Exercises

15.1 Fill the gaps with a suitable adjective from A opposite. There may be more than one possible answer.

1 I find writing poetry very............................ . It helps me to get a truer understanding of myself and gives me a good feeling inside.
2 I enjoy selling the pictures I paint, but it's not very .... I only made £300 last year.
3 Gardening is very .... It reduces stress levels and calms you down.
4 I've had a .... partnership with Jane for several years: she plays the piano and I play the violin. It's been very good for both of us.
5 Doing unpaid work at the hospital has been a .... experience for me.
6 I would like to be on the club committee, but I've heard it's very .... , and I don't have a lot of free time.

15.2 Solve these riddles, based on words in B opposite.

1 I am a vegetable that sits where humans sit. What am I?
2 I enjoy shopping a bit too much. What am I?
3 I am a bird that eats the flesh of art. What am I?
4 I do some of this and some of that, but never all of this or all of that. What am I?

15.3 Answer the questions.

1 Which of these is your least favourite chore – washing your clothes or tidying your room?
2 How often is it usually necessary to mow a lawn?
3 Does an amateur footballer get paid for playing a match?
4 If you say that someone 'dabbles in photography', are they a serious photographer?
5 When it comes to sport, do you prefer to be a spectator or a participant?

15.4 Give alternatives for the underlined words.

1 My daughter's <u>extremely interested in</u> folk music. She downloads a lot of traditional folk songs.
2 He <u>isolates</u> himself in the attic and plays with his model railway for hours on end.
3 She's <u>totally addicted to</u> football these days. She watches every match on TV.
4 I have a <u>long list of social appointments</u> for the rest of the month.
5 What do you <u>engage in</u> when you aren't working, Nigel?
6 Martine <u>performed with enthusiasm</u> in the end-of-term concert.

15.5 Complete the dialogues with a word or expression from the opposite page. B agrees with A by saying the same thing in a different way.

1 A: Going for a swim helps you forget your everyday worries, doesn't it?
   B: Yes, it's very ....
2 A: Dan spends every evening watching rubbish TV.
   B: That's true. He's a terrible ....
3 A: I'm not so keen on playing in the school orchestra as I used to be.
   B: Yes, I've .... it too.
4 A: I'd like to join a drama group but it would mean giving up lots of evenings and weekends.
   B: Yes, it can be a very .... activity.
5 A: I don't think I can fit in a tennis match with you for another couple of weeks.
   B: No problem. I've got a very .... too.
6 A: Someone said I could make some money out of those necklaces I make in my spare time.
   B: I agree. I think it could prove very .... for you.

16 All the rage: clothes and fashion

A Dressing for work

Many students, both male and female, would agree that they often look **scruffy**[1] in their T-shirts and jeans. However, those who go in to the world of business have to make a rapid transition and learn about **dress codes**[2] in the workplace. Business **attire**[3] needs to project a professional image, and clothing that **reveals**[4] too much **cleavage**[5] (for women), your back, your chest or your **midriff**[6] is not appropriate, even in a casual business setting. For women, see-through **fabrics**[7] should be avoided, and skirts should not be too tight or too short, though nobody wants to look **frumpy**[8]. For men, trousers should not be too tight, or shirts too open. Women often need a good choice of **outfits**[9] and men find a good range of **suits**[10], ties and casual trousers and jackets **invaluable**[11]. **Accessories**[12], e.g. jewellery, shoes and **cufflinks**[13], can also enhance the professional look. Some offices have **dress-down days**[14], often Fridays, when staff can wear more casual clothes. In other jobs, of course, people are required to wear **uniforms** or **protective clothing**, such as **overalls**[15] and **safety helmets**[16].

[1] untidy [noun: scruff = person who dresses in an untidy way] [2] accepted way of dressing in a particular social group [3] clothing; *formal* [4] show [adj.: revealing = (of clothes) that show a lot of flesh] [5] space between a woman's breasts [6] part of the body between the chest and the waist [7] materials [8] old-fashioned and boring [9] set of clothes for a particular occasion [10] jacket and trousers in the same material [11] extremely useful [12] extra items added to clothing for useful or decorative purposes [13] decorative objects used to fasten the cuffs on men's shirts [14] days when people wear less formal clothes [15] (plural noun) piece of clothing covering all the body, usually worn over other clothing to protect it when working [16] hat to protect the head

> **Language help**
> *Invaluable* means extremely valuable. The opposite of *valuable* is **valueless** or **without value**.

B Words and expressions about clothes

Clothes can be described as **scanty**[1], **skimpy**[2], **baggy**[3], **clingy**[4], or **chic**[5].
Sometimes an invitation to a more formal party will ask people to dress in **smart-casual**[6] clothes. **To be glammed (up) / dressed up / done up to the nines** means to be dressed in a very fashionable or very formal way. Some people choose to buy **designer (label) clothes** but most people prefer to buy clothes more cheaply **on the High Street**[7]. People who can afford to sometimes have clothes **made-to-measure**[8]. But more often people buy their clothes **off the peg/rack**[9].

[1] revealing a lot of flesh [2] short, using little material [3] loose, e.g. a sweater [4] close-fitting [5] /ʃiːk/ modern, stylish [6] clothes that are informal but clean, tidy and stylish [7] from ordinary, much less expensive shops [8] made especially for them [9] ready-made

C Being in fashion

A few years ago denim jackets were **all the rage**. [very fashionable]   The woman was dressed in **the height of / the very latest fashion**. [an extremely fashionable way]   The magazine has **up-to-the-minute** fashion articles. [dealing with the most recent trends]   The film has **set a new trend** for the silk top the star wore. [started a new fashion]   A **trend-setter** is a person whose style is followed by others. High heels are **on trend** this year. [fashionable]   Large handbags are this year's **must-have item**. [thing that everyone wants]   If a fashion/trend **catches on**, it becomes popular.   A **slave of/to fashion** is someone who is strongly influenced by fashion. [used in a disapproving way]   Your new outfit really **suits** you. [looks good on you]

D Clothes in metaphors

to speak **off the cuff** [without having prepared anything]   **to be hand in glove with someone** [to have a close working relationship with someone]   to do something **on a shoestring** [spending as little as possible]   **no frills** [simple and plain]   **to put someone in a straitjacket** [restrict someone's freedom]   **to draw a veil over** something [not to talk about something]   **to have something up your sleeve** [to have a secret plan or idea]

Exercises

16.1 **Answer these questions.**

1 What do you mean if you call someone 'scruffy'?
2 What is the dress code in a workplace you are familiar with?
3 What kinds of clothes are not appropriate for a job interview?
4 What might be appropriate clothes to wear for a job interview for a man and for a woman?
5 What is your favourite outfit?
6 And what accessories would be required for this outfit?
7 What would you put on if you had a dress-down day at work?
8 What sorts of work require staff to wear a uniform?
9 What kind of jobs need protective clothing to be worn?
10 If a woman says she finds a particular outfit 'invaluable', does she mean it's very expensive, extremely useful or absolutely useless?

16.2 **Fill the gaps with words or phrases from B or C opposite.**

1 Goodness me, you're done up to .... ! Where on earth are you going?
2 The sign outside the bar said: 'Dress .... – no jeans or trainers.'
3 I'm surprised to see girls wearing such .... dresses in this cold weather.
4 I can't afford .... clothes. I buy most of my outfits on the ....
5 Lucy is always dressed in the .... of fashion – she always looks very .... !
6 As soon as Amy gets home from work, she changes from her smart suit into tracksuit bottoms and a comfortable, ... , old jumper.
7 Very high heels remain .... trend this season.
8 These bracelets were last year's ....-have item.

16.3 **Rewrite the underlined parts of these sentences using phrases from D opposite.**

1 I'm no good at speaking <u>if I haven't had time to prepare what I want to say</u>.
2 Simon is bound to have <u>some plan in readiness</u> for tomorrow's meeting.
3 I think we should <u>keep quiet</u> about what happened on Monday, don't you?
4 Be careful what you say to Helen – <u>she works very closely</u> with the boss.
5 The new legislation <u>means we are not able to act as we wish</u>.
6 We'll still have a great party even if we have to do it <u>as cheaply as possible</u>.

16.4 **Here are more metaphorical uses of clothes words. Explain the literal and metaphorical meanings of the underlined words and expressions. Use a dictionary if necessary.**

1 We'll have to <u>tighten our belts</u> if you stop working full-time.
2 We wanted to leave but were <u>hemmed in</u> by the crowd and couldn't escape.
3 Phil's got so many books – his room is <u>bursting at the seams</u>.
4 The negotiations have been <u>cloaked in</u> secrecy ever since they began.
5 If she wins the prize again this year, it'll be a real <u>feather in her cap</u>.

16.5
> **Over to you**
> 1 What is all the rage in your country at the moment?
> 2 What are your favourite fabrics?
> 3 What do you think about people who are a slave to fashion?
> 4 How interested are you in being up-to-the-minute with fashion?
> 5 What sort of people start new fashion trends?
> 6 What item of clothing would you most like to have made-to-measure?

17 Home styles, lifestyles

A Home

A **squa** /skwɒt/ n empty building where people start living without the owner's
permis:
A **hove** /'hɒvəl/ very small, dirty house or flat in a bad (or **run down**) condition.
Rented :ion can be either **furnished** or **unfurnished**. [with or without furniture]
A **pent** ury flat at the top of a building.
Council or **social housing** is rented accommodation provided by the state for people who
cannot afford to buy their own homes. A **council estate** is a large group of such housing.
High-rise (flats) or **tower blocks** are flats in a tall, modern building with a lot of floors.
A **granny flat** is a set of rooms for an elderly person, connected to a relative's house.

B Idioms and expressions relating to *house* and *home*

expression	meaning	example
get on like a house on fire	get on very well with someone	Happily, my mother-in-law and I have always **got on like a house on fire.**
a household word/name	something/someone everyone knows	Nike has become a **household name.**
on the house	free of charge	The restaurant owner offered us coffees **on the house.**
home truths	information that is true but not pleasant or welcome	It's time he was told some **home truths** about the way he's been behaving!
nothing to write home about	nothing special	The town is OK but **nothing to write home about.**
hit home	become fully understood or fully felt	The difficulty of managing without a regular salary is **hitting home** now.
make yourself at home	make yourself feel comfortable in someone else's home	Please just **make yourself at home** while I get dinner ready.

C Idioms and metaphors relating to *life*

expression	meaning	example
life in the fast lane	a way of life that is full of activity and excitement	As a rock star, Joe lived **life in the fast lane.**
have the time of your life	have a wonderful time	Paula's **having the time of her life** in Canada.
get a new lease of life	become more energetic and active than before	When Sue moved jobs, she seemed to **get a new lease of life.**
a dog's life	a very unhappy and difficult life	Roger had **a dog's life** in the army.
lead a sheltered life	have a life that is protected from unpleasantness (also **lead a busy/quiet/normal**, etc. **life**)	Kyoko has **led a very sheltered life** and may find it hard to adapt to the big city.
(not) be a matter of life and death	(not) be very serious	If we miss the last train, **it's not a matter of life and death.**
take your life in your hands	do something very dangerous	**You're taking your life in your hands** if you cross the road here – go to the zebra crossing!
breathe new life into	bring new ideas and energy to something	When Orla joined the staff, she **breathed new life into** the school.

Exercises

17.1 Complete the following table about the types of accommodation in A opposite.

accommodation	What kind of person lives there?	Would you like to live there? Why/Why not?
squat	Example: a homeless person or someone who wants to make a political statement about property ownership	Example: I wouldn't like it because you never know when you might be evicted.
furnished accommodation		
social housing		
granny flat		
high-rise		
hovel		
penthouse		

17.2 Fill the gaps in these sentences with words and phrases from B and C opposite.

1 From the moment we met, we got on like a house ....
2 Mandy's so selfish, she deserves to be told a few ....
3 The new restaurant is OK but nothing really to ....
4 So what that you didn't get the promotion – it's not a matter of ....
5 I'm not sure I'd like to have a celebrity lifestyle, living life in the ....
6 As a child, the writer .... a sheltered life in a small village in the back of beyond.
7 We need someone to come and .... some new life into the project.
8 We soon managed to .... ourselves at home in our holiday cottage.

17.3 Choose expressions from B and C opposite to replace the underlined words in these sentences.

1 We had the most marvellous time on holiday this year.
2 As soon as spring comes, I feel as if I'm becoming energetic and active again.
3 The problems caused by the floods are only making themselves fully felt now.
4 I imagine that being a servant in the past must have been very hard and tedious.
5 All over the world, everybody knows about McDonald's.
6 He's taking a big risk if he gets in a car with Paul at the wheel!
7 Because we were such frequent customers, the restaurant gave us a meal free.
8 Our holiday apartment was quite adequate but not particularly special in any way.

17.4 Here are some more expressions with *home* and *life*. Use the context to work out what the underlined expressions mean.

1 The poet said that he had had a period of depression but that he had never considered taking his own life.
2 The comedy duo's superb performance brought the house down.
3 Our customers come from many different walks of life – we have doctors, shop assistants, computer programmers, you name it!
4 The system turned out to be a house of cards – it didn't take much to bring it down.
5 Whenever my nephews arrive for a visit, they eat us out of house and home.
6 I love having Tim around – you can rely on him to be the life and soul of the party.

18 Socialising and networking

Nouns for social events

Hi Rebecca,

How's life? Things have been really hectic on the social front here. It seems to be nothing but parties! Frankie and Joe had their **housewarming**[1] last week, now that they've decorated and got all their furniture in. A lot of our friends seem to be getting married lately – Josh went to his friend Mick's **stag party**[2] last weekend – they went to Spain for it! And next week, my old schoolmate Angela's having her **hen night**[3]. It's **fancy dress**[4] too. I think I'll go as Cleopatra. The wedding's at the end of the month. I think the **wedding party**[5] will include a lot of our year from school; that'll be nice. They're having the **reception**[6] at the Royal Hotel, very posh. The following week Josh has got his annual company ball. It's a **black tie**[7] affair.

Meanwhile, I've got the **launch party**[8] for my new book coming up next month and I have the usual **girls' night out**[9] with Amy and Izzie every few weeks. Oh, and there's a **leaving do**[10] at the office next week. We're going to be exhausted by the end of the year!

Hope to hear from you soon. Karen x

[1] a party to celebrate moving to a new house or flat   [2] a party before a wedding for the future husband and his male friends   [3] a party night out before a wedding for the future wife and her female friends
[4] everyone dresses up in costume   [5] usually refers to the main group of close family and friends at a wedding, rather than to the reception after the wedding   [6] a formal party, e.g. after a wedding or to meet an important visitor   [7] a formal event at which men have to wear dinner jackets and black bow ties
[8] a party to celebrate the publication of a new book or product   [9] an evening out just for female friends
[10] a party to celebrate somebody leaving a job or institution (**do** is an informal noun)

Networking

Advice on networking

We interviewed some successful business people about networking. Here are some of their comments.

'**Exchange**[1] business cards. **Do lunch**[2] with useful people. Don't be afraid to **hobnob with**[3] the boss. Go for it!'

'Make sure you **rub shoulders with**[4] the people who really matter. Every moment counts in networking.'

'**Socialising** is meeting people purely for pleasure but **networking** is making contacts that are going to be useful to your business or career, so, don't just leave it to chance – plan your networking.'

'Try to **be proactive**[5] in the workplace.'

[1] give each other   [2] have lunch; *informal*   [3] be friendly with someone who is important or famous, sometimes with negative associations   [4] mix socially with people; *informal*   [5] taking action yourself rather than waiting for something to happen

Expressions for social activity

I don't like the people Chris **hangs out with / knocks around with**. [spends social time with; *informal*]
(*Said to your host*) I hope I'm not **outstaying my welcome**. [staying too long]
Sandy's a real **party animal**. [someone who loves going to parties]
I hate it at my new job – everyone's so **cliquey**. [a **clique** is a disapproving word for a small group of people who spend time together and do not allow others to join them]
It was good at the club last night. Pete Esterhaus was there with his **crowd**. [his group of friends / the people he socialises with; *informal*]
Lizzy and Rob are always together. Are they **an item**? [having a romantic relationship; *informal*]
Joel isn't very happy because Fran **stood him up** last night. [didn't arrive for a date they had made]

Exercises

18.1 Look at A opposite and decide what kind of party you might be invited to if ...

1 a friend of yours is about to get married and is having a party before the wedding (depending on whether you are male or female).
2 you are going to help a friend celebrate on the day of their wedding.
3 some friends have just moved into a new flat.
4 a friend has just had a book published.
5 your local council is arranging for important people in the area to meet a visiting dignitary.
6 you have friends who love dressing up as characters from famous films.

18.2 Rewrite these sentences by replacing the underlined words with an expression from the opposite page that means the same thing. There may be more than one possible answer.

1 It's always good to see Hugh, but somehow he always manages to <u>stay too long</u>.
2 I'm going to a dinner at the Royal Plaza Hotel tonight. It's an event <u>where you have to wear a dinner jacket and bow tie</u>.
3 Don't forget your old friends when your film becomes a hit and you're <u>socialising</u> with the rich and famous.
4 We're going to have <u>a night out just for us girls</u> on Friday.
5 We must invite Jasmine to our do. She's a real <u>lover of parties</u>!
6 Don't always wait for people to do things for you. You should be more <u>prepared to take action yourself</u>.
7 It's good to see you! We must <u>have lunch together</u> sometime and discuss business.
8 It irritates me the way he's always <u>being so friendly</u> with the managers.

18.3 There is one mistake in each of these sentences. Correct the mistakes.

1 He usually hangs over with his college friends at the weekend and they go to football matches and things.
2 Nella and her friends are very clique. They don't mix with anyone else.
3 I'd better go home now. You've been very kind, but I don't want to stay out my welcome.
4 She said she wanted to go out with me, then she stood me down!
5 Rita and Nick are an article. They've been together for months. Didn't you know?
6 Laurie's crowds are really fun people. I often meet up with them in town.

18.4

> ### Over to you
> Answer the questions. If possible, compare your answers with someone else.
>
> - Which of the types of party listed in A have you had personal experience of? How did you enjoy them?
> - Who do you mostly knock around with? Are any of your friends party animals?
> - Have you ever rubbed shoulders with anyone famous? If not, who would you most like to rub shoulders with?

19 The performance arts: reviews and critiques

A Useful adjectives for describing works and performances

That TV series is **overrated**. [not as good as people say]

The plot was so **hackneyed**! [done so often it is boring]

The play was **disjointed** and difficult to follow. [unconnected and not in a clear order]

The film *Green Aliens from Mars* was a bit **far-fetched**. [impossible to believe]

The play was a bit **risqué**, and some religious leaders criticised it. [/rɪˈskeɪ/ against accepted social standards and likely to shock some people]

It was a **gripping** film from start to finish. [exciting and keeping your attention the whole time]

It was a **harrowing** documentary about war and refugee camps. [extremely upsetting]

It's a **moving** story about a child whose mother dies. [making you feel strong emotion, especially pity or sadness]

What a truly **memorable/unforgettable** performance. [you remember it long after]

The ballerina's performance was **understated**. [done or expressed in a simple but attractive style]

The play was long and **tedious**. [boring]

That new stand-up comedian is **hilarious**. [extremely funny]

> **Language help**
> The adjectives above can be used equally well about writing.
> *The plot of the novel is* **far-fetched/hilarious/unconvincing**, etc.

B Success and failure

The audience clearly loved the play – the **applause** was deafening. [clapping to show enjoyment] So it's not surprising that it got **glowing reviews**. [excellent reviews]

The audience called for several **encores** after his concert. [/ˈɒŋkɔːz/ calls from the audience to perform some more]

She got a **standing ovation** as Juliet in *Romeo and Juliet*. [the audience stood up and applauded at the end of the performance]

Her latest album has already won three **awards**. [prizes/honours, e.g. 'Best album of the Year']

Sam Dell won the award for 'Best **up-and-coming** actor'. [likely to become very successful]

The critics generally agree that her new symphony is a **masterpiece**. [very great work of art]

She has become **typecast** as a middle-aged mother in TV drama series. [always associated with that type of role]

His latest opera was **panned/slated** by the critics, which is strange, since all his previous works have been universally **lauded**. [very negatively criticised] [highly praised]

The play **bombed** in London's West End, although it had been really successful in New York. [was a failure]

The show was **booed** on the first night. [got disapproving noises from the audience]

The new TV soap has turned out to be a **total flop**. [complete failure]

Novak was definitely **miscast** as the father in that film; he was very **unconvincing**. [was the wrong person for the role] [not seeming real or true]

C Nouns relating to performing

Megan did well in the **audition** and is now busy going to **rehearsals** for the play. [short performance where actors show what they can do, hoping to get a role] [practice performances]

I liked her **interpretation** of the song 'Yesterday'. [way of understanding and performing it]

I prefer the original **version** by the Beatles. [one of several performances that exist] None of the **covers** are as good in my opinion. [versions that are not the original]

The actor's **portrayal** of the mother in the film was very tender. [the picture she created]

Exercises

19.1 Give an adjective from A which is *opposite* in meaning to the following words.

1 credible, believable ....   4 exaggerated ....
2 original, innovative ....   5 coherent, smooth-flowing ....
3 underrated ....   6 fascinating ....

19.2 Now use other adjectives from A instead of the underlined words in these sentences. Make any other changes that are necessary.

1 The musical <u>shocked some people because they thought it was immoral</u> and was attacked by several politicians and religious figures.
2 Her dance performance was <u>one of those you will never forget</u>, simply marvellous.
3 I can't remember the last time I saw such a <u>film that keeps you in suspense and totally absorbed all the time</u>.
4 It was a play <u>that aroused very deep emotions in me</u>.
5 It's a film <u>that is difficult to watch without getting very upset</u>.
6 His first stand-up routine <u>had the audience falling off their seats with laughter</u>.

19.3 Fill the gaps in this paragraph with words from the opposite page. The first letter is given to help you.

Two new musicals opened last week. The first, *Dogs*, turned out to be a total
¹f.......................... . It was loudly ²b.......................... by the audience and ³p.......................... by critics, who had praise only for the male lead's ⁴i.......................... of his role. The other show, *Danger*, has, however, received ⁵g.......................... reviews and has been given a standing
⁶o.......................... at every performance so far.

19.4 Read the text below and underline the words or phrases that match the eight definitions. Use a dictionary if necessary.

1 the way an actor creates a picture of a person
2 he/she is the wrong actor for that part
3 a film/book/play that keeps you in suspense
4 keep you in suspense / constantly excited
5 up-and-coming
6 a film which huge numbers of people will go and see
7 a police or crime theme
8 a very great work of art

Cliffhanger not to be missed

In this latest blockbuster cops-and-robbers movie from the Holdart Studios, budding Hollywood star Fletch Packline plays country-boy Ricky Smart, who gets involved with a gang of criminals intent upon stealing ten million dollars from a Chicago bank. Packline's portrayal of the confused small-town boy caught up in big city crime is convincing, but Julia Fischer as his long-lost sister is somewhat miscast. Not a masterpiece, but it will certainly keep you on the edge of your seat.

19.5 **Over to you**

Answer the questions. Explain your answers.

1 Do most actors like to become typecast?
2 Is it true that a standing ovation shows that the audience disliked the performance?
3 How do you think an actor might feel before an audition for a big part?
4 How much are you influenced by reviews that either universally laud or pan a show?

20 The visual arts

Changing tastes

Throughout the centuries, people have tended to be suspicious of the new art movements of their period. At the end of the 19th century, for example, people were shocked by **Impressionism**[1], criticising its practitioners as careless **daubers**[2]. Later, when faced with **Cubist**[3] paintings, the public were puzzled by those too. The **Surrealists**[4] were initially **deemed**[5] crazy. **Op-art**[6] was criticised because its **subject matter**[7] was said to consist of nothing of significance. However, nowadays, liking **Surrealism**[8] or Op-art is considered perfectly acceptable, and images from these **schools of art**[9] appear everywhere, from posters to advertising campaigns. Perhaps because of the ubiquity of advertising, people tend to be more **visually literate**[10] than they used to be, and so are perhaps **inured to**[11] surprises. Perhaps new movements in art will meet with less hostility in future.

Mmmm... Intriguing...

[1, 3, 4, 6, 8] types of artist and schools of art of the last 150 years [2] someone who paints quickly and carelessly (disapproving) [5] considered; *formal* [7] content [9] art movement [10] educated with regard to art [11] not affected by

B Words for commenting on art

original: new in a special and interesting way (*opp.* = **predictable**)
highbrow: intended for educated, intelligent people (often disapproving) (*opp.* = **lowbrow**)
impenetrable: extremely difficult to understand (*opp.* = **transparent**)
sophisticated: showing advanced skills and understanding (*opp.* = **primitive**)
challenging: demanding considerable effort to be understood (*opp.* = **undemanding**)
dazzling: inspiring great admiration because it is brilliant in some way (*opp.* = **pedestrian**)
evocative: calling up images and memories (*opp.* = **uninspiring**)
thought-provoking: making people think (*opp.* = **unstimulating**)
exquisite: having rare beauty or delicacy (*opp.* = **clumsy**)
intriguing: interesting because it is strange or mysterious (*opp.* = **dreary**)
peerless: better than any other (*opp.* = **run-of-the-mill**)
tongue-in-cheek: not intended to be taken seriously despite appearing serious (*opp.* = **earnest**)
priceless: extremely valuable (*opp.* = **worthless**)
skilful: clever, masterly, done well (*opp.* = **poorly done**)

C Art and metaphor

Notice how words connected with art can be used when talking about literature.

The writer **paints** his hero in a fascinating **light**. Minor characters are more **shadowy** or **sketchy** but they are also **depicted** quite powerfully even though the **focus** is, inevitably, on the two central characters. These are **portrayed** with great sensitivity. The heroine is particularly **colourful** and we see how her character is **shaped** and **moulded** by events. Some say the author **illustrates** his **motifs** in a **black-and-white** fashion, but the **image** he creates to **illuminate** the evils of slavery will remain with me for ever.

Exercises

20.1 Choose a word from the text in A opposite to answer the questions.

1 What is the early 20th century school of art which shows unusual or impossible things happening?
2 What is the mid 20th century school of art which has its origins in optical illusions?
3 What is the early 20th century school of art which depicts people or objects as a set of geometric shapes?
4 What is the late 19th century school of art whose aim was to represent the effects of light on people or scenes?
5 What phrase can be used to mean the content of a painting or other work of art?
6 What phrase can be used to describe someone with an educated understanding of art?

20.2 Read the sentences and answer the questions.

1 Rod enjoys painting but he's a dauber not an artist.
Does the speaker have a high or low opinion of Rod's work?
2 Curious as it now seems, the artist's work was deemed morally dangerous.
Is this sentence more likely to come from a formal or informal source?
3 The sculptor is now inured to criticism.
How is the sculptor affected by criticism?
4 While at art school, Matilda was particularly interested in the Cubist school of art.
What is the difference between art school and school of art?

20.3 Look at the adjectives in B opposite. Divide them into these categories:

usually positive associations   usually negative associations   negative or positive associations

20.4 Choose one of the words from each pair of opposites in B and think of a work of art (of any kind) that you could apply it to. Write a sentence explaining why it applies.

EXAMPLE *I think that the paintings by Salvador Dali could be called intriguing, because he uses such curious and surprising images.*

20.5 Choose the correct word to complete these sentences.

1 I think that the artist's cartoons are usually rather *highbrow / dreary / lowbrow* as they are intended to appeal to a mass audience.
2 When an artist sent in an ordinary red brick to an exhibition, no one was sure whether it was *impenetrable / run-of-the-mill / tongue-in-cheek* or intended as a serious statement.
3 Although the artist's early work is very sophisticated, some of his later pieces are surprisingly *primitive / thought-provoking / original* in style.
4 I find pictures of dull grey street scenes rather *dreary / peerless / dazzling*.
5 The design on that china plate is *earnest / exquisite / transparent* – however did they manage to paint such fine detail?
6 Although his photographs are quite *challenging / evocative / intriguing*, it is worth making the effort to understand them.

20.6 Make a verb–noun–adjective word formation table with these words from C opposite.

> paint   sketch   depict   portray   colour   shape   illustrate   illuminate

20.7 **Over to you**

This website gives you a wealth of links to art galleries and museums worldwide:
http://www.museumland.com/ Visit this site and follow up any links that interest you.
Note any useful vocabulary you come across.

21 Talking about books

A Blurbs

A **blurb** is a short text, usually printed on the back cover of a book, describing what the book is about and sometimes including quotes from critics. Here are some examples.

Woman of Snow is a **poignant**[1] **chronicle**[2] of childhood in a small American town. Nora Delaye is the youngest child in a …

The third novel by this **acclaimed**[3] writer, this is a **compelling**[4] tale of mystery, love and betrayal in a **lugubrious**[5] setting reminiscent of the …

A **macabre**[6] and **chilling**[7] account of an unsolved murder that tears a village apart …

A **page-turner**[8] full of brilliant moments of **insight**[9] and an unparalleled depth of feeling, this is a **gripping**[10] and **enigmatic**[11] tale that unfolds in …

A **breathtaking**[12] achievement, a journey of self-discovery that enchants and saddens, with a combination of **wry**[13] humour and **evocative**[14] scenes of life in …

Jim Lawless, the **eponymous**[15] **protagonist**[16] of Arkrow's latest novel, is a confused young man seeking a meaning in life. It is an **engaging**[17] tale, which …

[1] /ˈpɔɪnjənt/ moving and sad   [2] description of a sequence of events   [3] praised by the public   [4] very interesting and engaging   [5] rather dark, mournful and gloomy (**lugubrious** is often used of people too) [6] /məˈkɑːbrə/ often cruel or disgusting, concerned with death   [7] causing great fear   [8] powerful story that keeps you interested   [9] the ability to understand what something is really like   [10] so interesting or exciting that it holds your attention totally   [11] mysterious   [12] amazing   [13] in the face of a bad situation   [14] which arouse memories or images   [15] who has the same name as the title of the book [16] main character   [17] pleasant and interesting

B Some other types of books

A **journal** is a written record of what you have done each day, e.g. a learning journal; it is also a publication containing academic articles, published at regular intervals, e.g. every three months. **Memoirs** /ˈmemwɑːz/ are a written record of a person's own life, typically by a politician or military figure.

An **encyclopedia** is a book or set of books containing articles arranged in alphabetical order, dealing with the whole of human knowledge or part of it.

An **anthology** is a collection of, for example, poems or short stories by different authors.

A **manual** is usually a technical book with instructions, for example, a car manual.

A **logbook** is a book that records events and times, etc., for example, all the journeys made by a lorry or ship.

C Other expressions for talking about books

I'm reading a book about the history of Ireland. It's **compulsive reading**. [difficult to stop once you've started; *formal*] *Or* It's one of those books you just **can't put down**. [*informal*] It's very **informative**. [gives a lot of useful information]

Nancy Dreifus's novel about mental breakdown, published in 1950, was **ahead of its time**. [contained ideas that no one else had yet thought of or discussed at that time] Her 1955 book *Exciting Careers for Women* was **a product of its time**, though the ideas seem tame and old-fashioned, even sexist now. [was a reflection of that time]

Bertram's latest novel is not a difficult book; in fact it's rather **lightweight**. [not complex; slightly negative connotation] It's good **bedtime reading**. [nice to read in bed] His last one was **heavy going** and I just couldn't **get into** it. [difficult to read] [become involved/engage with] Nonetheless, his books always attract a wide **readership**. [number of people who read them]

Common mistake

An academic publication containing articles by different authors that is issued periodically (e.g. three times a year) is normally called a *journal* (NOT ~~magazine~~).

Exercises

21.1 **Which names for types of books or other reading material from B opposite would best fit these statements?**

1 It's by General Rogers, who led the allied forces during the recent war.
2 It's so badly written I don't know how anyone could learn how to use the camcorder by reading it.
3 I recommend it. If you want to read a typical selection of modern poets, it's excellent.
4 The latest issue contains a paper by Professor Susan Frith, in which she presents a new theory of the human mind.

21.2 **Rewrite these sentences using words or phrases from the opposite page to describe the experience of reading particular books.**

1 I just could not seem to become involved in the story, so I stopped reading it.
2 It's not very serious, and it's easy to read.
3 It's dense and very difficult to read.
4 Take it to bed with you; it's just right when you're settling down at night. All the time I was reading it, I just couldn't wait to get to the next page.
5 You find yourself wanting to read more, it's so fascinating.
6 The book is full of useful information.
7 Her second novel did not attract a large number of readers.
8 This book contains some great moments of true understanding of how things are.
9 It is a pleasantly interesting tale about a boy who nurses an injured bird.
10 Mena Harrap's self-help book was a reflection of the time it was written, but what was true in the 1980s doesn't necessarily apply nowadays.

21.3 **Fill the gaps in these sentences with appropriate adjectives from the opposite page, based on the meaning in brackets.**

1 The story takes place against a rather .... background in 18th century London. (mournful and gloomy)
2 It's full of .... comedy and satire. (humour despite a bad situation)
3 The book is a .... documentation of abuse in a prison. (frightening)
4 The novel is full of .... passages depicting life in Australia at the turn of the 19th century. (arousing memories or images)
5 It's a very .... novel; you never really know what is happening until right at the end. (mysterious, puzzling)
6 The novel is a .... portrayal of life in a coal-mining community during the last economic recession. (moving and very sad)
7 John Farr's latest novel is a .... masterpiece. (very impressive, great)
8 *House of the Dead* is a .... story of torture and death in a medieval castle. (cruel and dark)
9 The novel's .... heroine, Maria Selune, leaves home at the age of 18 and travels through Asia. (who has the same name as the book's title)
10 Laisha and Asoka are the .... in this unusual tale of rural family life. (main characters)

21.4 **Match the things you might find in particular kinds of books with an appropriate type of book.**

1 a section on 'troubleshooting' / problem-solving ☐   a encyclopedia
2 an article about waterfalls, with pictures ☐   b journal
3 a record of a recent examination or test of a lorry ☐   c manual
4 a day-to-day record of life during a war in 1776 ☐   d logbook

21.5

Over to you

Think of a book you read and enjoyed recently. Which words from this unit describe it best?

22 Food: a recipe for disaster

A Describing food products

Food production has become increasingly industrialised and globalised, and so knowing what our food contains has become more and more important. Labels do not always help. Adjectives such as 'wholesome[1]', 'farm fresh' and 'homemade' can be rather vague and meaningless, while the international numbering system for additives[2] is often incomprehensible to people. Some familiar descriptions, however, do have a clear official meaning, for example 'wholefoods[3]', 'free-range[4] eggs', 'gluten-free[5] bread' or 'contains no artificial colours or preservatives[6]'. Clear and scientifically accurate descriptions can be vital for people who suffer from food allergies[7], for vegetarians or vegans[8] who want to know exactly what is in a product, as well as being important for consumers looking for natural or unprocessed[9] foods or those concerned about animal welfare[10] who may wish to avoid food produced by battery-farming[11] methods and so on. With the growth in popularity of convenience foods[12], alongside public health concerns over bad diet and obesity, simple and unambiguous nutrition labels[13] are more important than ever. An example of a simple system is traffic-light labelling[14], which indicates high (red), medium (amber) or low (green) levels of such things as fat, sugar and salt. Finally, good labelling tells us where the food was produced and under what conditions, for example fair trade[15] products.

[1] good for you   [2] substance added to food to improve its taste or appearance or to preserve it
[3] foods that have not had any of their natural features taken away or any artificial substances added
[4] produced by farm animals that are allowed to move around outside and are not kept in cages or stalls
[5] not containing a protein which is contained in wheat and some other grains   [6] chemicals used to stop food from decaying   [7] condition that makes a person become ill or develop skin or breathing problems because they have eaten certain foods or been near certain substances   [8] person who does not eat or use any animal products, such as meat, fish, eggs or cheese   [9] which have not been treated with chemicals that preserve them or give them extra taste or colour   [10] taking care of animals
[11] system of producing a large quantity of eggs or meat cheaply by keeping a lot of birds in rows of small cages   [12] foods that are almost ready to eat or are quick to prepare   [13] labels that indicate how the food influences your health   [14] labels with colours like traffic lights that give information on nutrition   [15] a way of buying and selling products that makes certain that the original producer receives a fair price

B Food metaphors

Inviting Jackie and her ex-husband to the same party was a **recipe for** disaster. [situation sure to lead to]
When asked why he didn't turn up to the exam, he **cooked up a story** about his kitchen being flooded. [made up, invented]
The film has **all the ingredients of** a box office hit. [all the necessary characteristics]
I'm not going to call him. I'm going to let him **stew** for another few days at least. [worry or suffer, especially about something you think is that person's fault; you can also say **stew in your own juice**]
It's kind of you to invite me, but ballet isn't really **my cup of tea.** [not the type of thing that I like]
The police **grilled** the suspect for hours, but eventually let him go. [asked a lot of questions]
I'm sure this is going to be another of his **half-baked** schemes that never comes to anything. [unrealistic or not thought through properly]
Let's hire a karaoke machine – that'll **spice up** the office party. [make more lively]
Rick has started hanging around with some **unsavoury** characters. [unpleasant, morally offensive]
They started their business with high hopes but things soon **turned sour.** [went wrong]
Let's go for a coffee and you can tell me all the **juicy** gossip. [exciting and interesting]

Exercises

22.1 **Read the comments and then answer the questions.**

1 Carlos: 'I never buy eggs that come from battery farms. They have no flavour.'
2 Beth: 'I can't be bothered cooking. I just buy ready-made meals and tins of stuff.'
3 Rowan: 'It worries me that farm animals are sometimes treated so badly.'
4 Hannah: 'I can't eat curry. It makes me come out in red spots.'
5 Thomas: 'I want my food to be 100% natural.'
6 Atsuko: 'I always buy coffee that gives growers in developing countries a decent price.'

	name
1 Who seems most concerned about animal welfare?	
2 Who wants food without additives or preservatives?	
3 Who uses a fair trade product?	
4 Who has a food allergy?	
5 Who uses convenience foods?	
6 Who prefers a free-range product?	

22.2 **Complete the sentences. The first letter of the missing word is given.**

1 The label gave no n............................ information whatsoever, so I didn't know if it was good or bad for me.
2 The t........................ - .... system of labelling is easy to understand with just three familiar colours.
3 I try to make my diet as w............................ as possible and not eat things which I know are bad for me.
4 It's sometimes difficult to find u............................ foods – everything seems to contain chemicals or preservatives of some kind.
5 My sister has to have a g............................ - .... diet as wheat makes her ill.
6 The laws governing b............................ f............................ were changed recently and birds must have larger cages now.
7 I'm a vegetarian but I don't think I could ever become a v............................ . I would find the diet too restrictive.
8 My diet is mostly natural foods, with nothing taken away or added, because I buy a lot of w............................ .

22.3 **Rewrite these sentences using the metaphors from B opposite. You are given a clue in brackets.**

1 My mother asked me a lot of very searching questions about where I had been last night. (grill)
2 I feel I need a complete change of career, something more exciting to make my life more interesting. (spice)
3 What's been happening while I was on holiday? You must fill me in on all the interesting gossip. (juice)
4 Don't tell her that her phone has been found. Let her suffer for a bit longer – perhaps she'll be more careful with it in future. (stew)
5 He wanted me to go to the match with him, but rugby just isn't something I like. (tea)
6 They lived together happily for many years, but things changed for the worse when his mother came to live with them. (sour)
7 Patience combined with interest in your pupils is bound to lead to success for a teacher. (recipe)
8 Lance's ideas are never thought through properly. (bake)
9 There were some very unpleasant and offensive characters at that party. (savoury)
10 He has invented a crazy scheme for making money on the internet. It has all the necessary characteristics of a complete disaster. (cook, ingredient)

23 Dinner's on me: entertaining and eating out

A Paying the bill

We'll **split the bill**, shall we? [each person will pay for him/herself]
Lunch **is on me** today. [I am paying for you; *informal*]
Would you like to **join us** for dinner at the City Plaza hotel? [come with us]
We'd like you to **be our guest**. [we will pay; *formal*]
Let me **get this**. [pay the bill; *informal*]
I was **wined and dined** every night by the New York office. [invited out to restaurants]

B Describing service

A new Italian restaurant called Bella Roma has just opened in the High Street, and we went there the other night to try it. I couldn't help comparing it to the Casa Italia, where we ate last week. In the Bella Roma, the service was **impeccable**[1] and quick; at the Casa Italia it's always a bit **sluggish**[2]. In the new place the waiters are **courteous**[3] and friendly without being **overbearing**[4]. In the other place they tend to be **sullen**[5] and the service is rather **brusque**[6], which I find very **off-putting**[7]. But at Bella Roma they'll **go out of their way**[8] to give you what you want.

[1] perfect, cannot be faulted   [2] rather slow   [3] polite   [4] too confident, too inclined to tell people what to do   [5] bad-tempered, unwilling to smile   [6] quick and rude   [7] makes you feel you do not want to go there again   [8] do everything possible

C Food preferences

I **have a sweet tooth** and can never say no to cakes or biscuits. [love sweet things]
I won't have dessert, thanks. You're lucky being so slim, but I'm afraid I have to **count the calories** / I have to be a bit **calorie-conscious** these days. [be careful how many calories I eat]
I'll just have a small **portion** of dessert, please. I'm on a diet. [amount of a particular food that is served to one person]
I like to end the meal with something **savoury** like cheese. [salty in flavour, or with herbs]
Ben's a bit of a **fussy eater**. [person who has very particular demands when eating]
No, thanks, I won't have wine. I'm **teetotal**. [never drink alcohol]
Before I book the restaurant, do you have any particular **dietary requirements**? [special needs or things someone cannot eat; *formal*]
I won't have any more wine, thanks. I don't want to **overdo it**. [eat or drink too much]

D Entertaining at home

A: Why not come home and eat with us? You'll have to **take pot luck**, though. [eat what we're eating, nothing special]
B: Thank you. Shall I **bring a bottle**? [usually means a bottle of wine]
A: Should I wear a suit on Friday?
B: No, no, it isn't a **dinner party**, it's just an **informal get-together**. [rather formal dinner with guests] [informal group of people meeting for a meal/drinks, etc.]
B: Does anyone want **seconds**? [a second helping/serving of a dish]
B: Oh, yes please. It was delicious.
A: Can I pour you some juice? **Say when**. [tell me when I have served enough]
B: **When!** ['That's enough, thanks']
A: **Help yourself** to some **nibbles**. [things like nuts, crisps, etc., before a meal]
A: We have to leave at six. We can **grab a bite to eat** on the way. [have a quick meal]
B: Or we could get a **takeaway** when we get there. [ready-cooked meal bought to take home]

Common mistake

Note the spelling of the past tense of *pay. My friend **paid** the bill* (NOT ~~payed~~).

Exercises

23.1 Rewrite the underlined parts of these sentences using expressions from A opposite.

1 When we eat out as a group, <u>each person usually pays for their own food and drink</u>. (*Use a shorter expression meaning the same.*)
2 Let me <u>pay for this one</u>. You can pay next time. (*Use an informal expression.*)
3 Visitors to the company's head office in London are always <u>taken out to</u> the best restaurants. (*Use a phrase with two words which rhyme with each other.*)
4 <u>Fancy coming with us</u> for lunch tomorrow? (*Use a more formal expression.*)
5 No, please. Put your credit card away. <u>I'm inviting you for dinner.</u> (*Use an informal expression.*)
6 <u>I'd like to pay for you</u> at the theatre tomorrow night. (*Use a formal expression.*)

23.2 Rewrite the underlined parts of these sentences using expressions from the opposite page to describe food and drink preferences.

1 I <u>never drink alcohol</u>. (*Use an adjective.*)
2 I <u>don't really like sweet things</u>. (*Use an idiom.*)
3 <u>Are there things you can't or mustn't eat?</u> (*Use a formal/polite expression.*)
4 Just a small <u>amount of food</u> (use one word) for me, please. I don't want to <u>eat too much</u>. (*Use an expression that means the same.*)
5 She's become <u>very careful about how many calories she's eating</u>. (*Give two different ways of saying the same thing.*)
6 Sasha is such a <u>choosy person when it comes to food</u>. It's difficult to find things she likes. (*Use an expression that means the same.*)

23.3 Give words from the opposite page which contrast with or are the opposite of these phrases.

1 a sweet dish
2 a friendly waiter
3 a formal gathering
4 rude staff
5 quick service
6 dreadful service

23.4 Which expressions on the opposite page mean ...

1 eat whatever your hosts are eating at home, not a special dish for you?
2 tell me when I've poured enough in your glass?
3 get a quick meal or some other food that does not take a long time?
4 small items you eat before a meal, or perhaps at a reception?
5 another portion of what you have just eaten?
6 a semi-formal party in someone's house, probably not a meal?

24 On the road: traffic and driving

A Driving and traffic regulations

In the UK, you must **give way**[1] at a **give-way sign** and at a roundabout, where traffic coming from the right **has the right of way**[2]. You must give way to pedestrians at a **pedestrian crossing**[3].

In some countries, **sounding/beeping**[4] **your horn** is prohibited, except in emergencies.

GIVE WAY

In most countries, **jumping**[5] **a red light** is a serious offence, as is **reckless**[6] **driving**.

In many parts of the world, **drink-driving**[7] can result in a heavy fine or imprisonment. Drivers may be asked by a police officer to take a **breathalyser**[8] test. **Hit-and-run**[9] accidents are almost always considered to be grave offences and may result in a **ban**[10] for several years and/or imprisonment. In the UK, less serious breaches of traffic regulations may lead to **penalty points**[11] on the driver's licence. In many countries, **on-the-spot**[12] fines may be issued for careless driving and other offences.

In the European Union, **exhaust emissions**[13] must meet certain standards, and the car must be **roadworthy**[14], which includes a minimum depth of **tyre tread**[15], and driving with a **bald**[16] tyre is against the law.

[1] stop at a junction if there is traffic passing before entering a bigger road   [2] is allowed to go before other traffic   [3] often called a *zebra crossing* when it has black and white stripes   [4] *beeping* is less formal than *sounding*   [5] not stopping at   [6] very dangerous, without any care for others   [7] driving after consuming alcohol above the official limit   [8] instrument you breathe into to measure alcohol level   [9] running over or into someone and not stopping   [10] removal of one's driving licence   [11] negative points which are added up over time and which can result in the loss of your licence   [12] given at the scene of the offence   [13] waste gases produced by the vehicle   [14] in a condition that it can be driven safely   [15] the depth of the grooves in the tyre rubber   [16] one which has lost its tread

B Traffic problems

It was the rush hour, and there was a long **tailback**. [line of slow or stopped traffic]

You have to pay a **toll** on the new motorway. [a charge you have to pay to use the road]

There was a **pile-up** involving ten cars, because of the fog, so the road was closed and we were **diverted** onto a narrow country lane. [crash between several or many cars] [directed away from our road]

Overnight snow caused **disruption** this morning on many roads, but it has cleared now. [when a system, process or event is prevented from continuing as usual or as expected]

I had stupidly parked in a **tow-away zone** and came back to find my car had gone! [area where your car may be taken away if you park illegally]

I only parked for a few minutes outside the station, but when I came out my car had been **clamped**. [fitted with a metal device on the wheel to prevent it from moving]

I saw two men fighting next to their cars. I think it was a case of **road rage**. [anger or violence between drivers because of difficult driving conditions]

The road was wet and I **skidded** on a bend and almost crashed. [lost control of the steering so that the car slid across the road]

There was a **head-on collision** on the main road between here and the next village last night. [two vehicles hitting each other directly in the front]

Language help

Many of the items in this unit are phrases or collocations. Always learn and record the words together.

There was an accident at the junction between the A476 and the A53 this morning involving a lorry carrying a load of glue. Traffic has been stuck there for the last three hours. (*Radio announcement*)

Exercises

24.1 Fill the gaps in these sentences using words and phrases from the opposite page.

1 We can't park here; it's a .... zone.
2 There was a five-mile .... on the motorway because of road works.
3 Fog caused a number of .... , one of which involved 15 cars.
4 If it's a .... sign, you don't have to stop if the road is clear, but if it's a stop sign, then you must always stop.
5 Who has the .... at a pedestrian crossing in your country? Cars or pedestrians?
6 It was a .... accident, but the police have a description of the car.
7 The permitted level of .... is to be lowered in an attempt to reduce air pollution in big cities.
8 He was given a .... test and it was discovered he had consumed a huge amount of alcohol. He was charged with .... , fined and given three .... on his licence.
9 In some countries, drivers .... their .... just because they get frustrated. As a result, the city streets are incredibly noisy.
10 The accident caused a lot of .... in the city centre and traffic did not return to normal till several hours later.

24.2 Respond to these comments as in the example, so that your response explains the meaning of the underlined words. Use words from the opposite page.

1 A: I came out and saw a big metal thing on my wheels.
   B: *Oh, so your car had been clamped!*
   A: Yes. I had to pay a lot of money to get it released.
2 A: As I drove round the corner, there was some ice on the road and I lost control of the steering.
   B: Oh, so you ....
3 A: The two women were obviously having an argument about the way one of them had driven. Then suddenly they started hitting each other!
   B: Oh, I guess it was a case of ....
4 A: The police officer looked at two of my tyres and said they were illegal.
   B: Oh, so your tyres were .... , were they?
5 A: The road was closed. Two lorries had come straight at each other and crashed.
   B: Oh, so it was a ....
6 A: The police officer fined me there and then. I have to pay up within seven days.
   B: Oh, really? I didn't know they could give ....
   A: Yes. You have no choice. They just give it to you and you can't dispute it at the time.
7 A: The man at the garage said my car wasn't in a fit condition to be driven legally.
   B: Oh, so it's not ....
8 A: They charge a lot to drive across the new bridge!
   B: Oh, really? Do you have to pay a .... ? I didn't know that.

24.3 What do you think the underlined expressions mean? Write their meaning in your own words. Use a dictionary if you can't work out the meaning from the context.

1 There were three separate accidents in the city centre during the rush hour and soon there was total gridlock. It took about two hours to clear.
2 The police car made me pull over and they checked my lights.
3 I had a minor bump yesterday. It wasn't serious, but one of my lights got smashed.
4 My car conked out on the motorway and I had to ring for assistance. It cost me £100.
5 He's a bit of a back-seat driver, so don't be surprised if he criticises your driving.

25 Travel and accommodation

A Booking travel and holidays

Here are some choices you may make when booking travel or holidays.

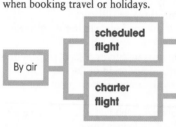

By air

scheduled flight — first, business or economy class / route (e.g. via /vaɪə/ Amsterdam) / airline (e.g. low-cost such as EasyJet or national carrier such as Emirates)

charter flight — inclusive / all-in package / flight only / extras (e.g. airport taxes, insurance)

A **scheduled flight** is a normal, regular flight; a **charter flight** is a special flight taking a group of people, usually to the same holiday destination. Some airline tickets may have **restrictions** (e.g. you can only travel on certain days). Such tickets can offer good **value for money** but, if you cancel, they are **non-refundable**[1] or you may have to pay a **cancellation fee**. Some tickets allow a **stopover**[2]. **Inclusive / All-in packages** normally include accommodation and **transfers**, e.g. a coach or a **shuttle bus** to and from your hotel, in other words the price is **inclusive of** transfers.

[1] you can't get your money back   [2] you may stay somewhere overnight before continuing to your destination

Sea travel is normally on a **ferry**, and the journey is called a **crossing**, but you can have a holiday on the sea if you **go on a cruise**. For some people, a luxury cruise is the **holiday of a lifetime**[1]. You may decide to book a **berth** in a **shared cabin**[2], or to have a single or double cabin. For more money, you can often get a **deluxe** cabin, perhaps on the **upper deck**[3]. Cruises often go to **exotic**[4] islands where you can **get away from it all**[5].

[1] one you will always remember   [2] a bed in a cabin with other people   [3] the higher part of the ship, which is often bigger and more comfortable   [4] unusual or exciting   [5] escape your daily life and routines

Train travel allows you to relax as you travel and look at the countryside through the windows of your **carriage**. Train **tracks** link major towns but you may have to **change trains**[1] if you are not able to get a **through train**[2].

[1] get off one train and on to another   [2] or **direct train** which takes you directly to your destination

Car hire is another way of **getting around**[1]. When you book it, you may have to choose whether you want **unlimited mileage**[2]. There may also be **extras** to pay such as accident insurance. If you hire a car, it gives you the freedom to **come and go as you please**[3].

[1] travelling to different places; *informal*   [2] /ˈmaɪlɪdʒ/ you can travel as many miles as you like for the same price   [3] go where you want when you want

B Accommodation when travelling

Some people like **camping**[1] while others prefer hotels. Or you can have a **self-catering**[2] holiday, such as staying in an apartment or **chalet**[3]. You can also choose to stay in a **guest house**[4] or an **inn**[5]. Some types of accommodation offer **half board**[6] or **full board**[7].

[1] sleeping in a tent or a caravan   [2] where you do your own cooking   [3] /ˈʃæleɪ/ small cottage or cabin specially built for holiday-makers   [4] small, relatively cheap hotel   [5] similar to a pub, but also offering accommodation; sometimes in an attractive old building   [6] usually breakfast and one other meal   [7] all meals

Exercises

25.1 Use vocabulary from A opposite to express these sentences more briefly.

1 It was a regular flight which the airline runs every day.
It was a scheduled flight.
2 I hate those special flights where everyone is booked to the same holiday destination.
3 The ticket allowed us to spend up to three nights in Singapore on the journey from London to Sydney.
4 You can get a bed on the ferry in a little room with three other beds.
5 Our seats were in the part of the train that was nearest to the engine.
6 The bus or taxi to your hotel is included in the cost of the holiday.
7 It was a cheap fare, but there were some things you were not allowed to do.
8 The ticket is relatively cheap, but you can't get your money back if you have to cancel.

25.2 Match the words on the left with their collocations on the right.

1 holiday	☐	a catering
2 full	☐	b for money
3 self-	☐	c mileage
4 unlimited	☐	d bus
5 exotic	☐	e of a lifetime
6 value	☐	f board
7 shuttle	☐	g train
8 through	☐	h airline
9 low-cost	☐	i class
10 economy	☐	j island

25.3 Which expressions in the box do you associate with each of the holidays below? Use a dictionary if necessary. Each expression may go with more than one type of holiday.

to rough it	to keep on the move	to just drift along
an exhilarating experience	to sleep under the stars	a cosy atmosphere
to be out in the wilds	a real learning experience	to come and go as you please
to lounge around	to be your own boss	to spend a fortune on entrance fees

1 self-catering holiday
2 camping at a beach resort
3 staying in an inn or a guest house
4 skiing holiday, staying in a chalet
5 trekking holiday, camping in the mountains
6 cruise
7 sightseeing holiday staying in a hotel in a historic city
8 touring holiday, in a hire car

25.4 Complete these sentences with expressions from 25.3.

1 It was a lovely cruise; we just .... all day.
2 I prefer self-catering because I like to ....
3 Camping is OK if you don't mind ....
4 Skiing is always such ....
5 Sightseeing's great but it's easy ....
6 The guided tour of the ancient ruins was ....
7 Inns and guest houses usually have quite ....
8 I'd hate to stay in just one place on my holiday – I much prefer ....

26 Attracting tourists

Describing tourist destinations

If you're the type of traveller who wants to **escape the crowds**[1], **get off the beaten track**[2] and **get back to nature**[3], take a closer look at Suriname. Suriname's **tourist sector**[4] is relatively modest and the emphasis is on what makes the country different for the **discerning**[5] traveller. Other Caribbean nations may **boast**[6] better sand, sea and sun, but because of that, you won't find **hordes**[7] of people in Suriname. What you will find is a **wealth of**[8] wildlife with a huge range of **flora and fauna**[9]. More than 12% of the country is given over to **national parks**[10] and **nature reserves**[11] and large **tracts**[12] of the country are covered by **virgin**[13] rainforest. So, if you are **seeking something out of the ordinary**[14], click here for more information.

[1] go where there are not many people [2] go to places tourists don't normally go, somewhere different/ unusual [3] live a natural, rural style of life [4] tourist industry; *formal* [5] showing good judgement, especially about style and quality [6] this use of *boast* is for listing the good qualities of a place; *formal* [7] crowds, in a negative sense [8] large amount of; *formal* [9] plants and animals; a fixed phrase (Latin) [10] areas of a country that are protected by the government because of their natural beauty or because they have a special history [11] areas of land protected in order to keep safe the animals and plants that live there, often because they are rare [12] areas of land; collocates with *large, vast, huge* [13] original and natural [14] looking for something different (*seek* is rather formal)

B Travel advertisements

Unwind[1] in **Ubeda**, **recharge**[2] in **Positano**, all from under **£800**.

Taste of the bush[3] – all travel in air-conditioned **4x4**[4] vehicles.

Enjoy the **scenic**[11] wonders of a tropical **paradise**[12]. **Ecotourism**[13] at its best.

Waterfront[5] villas, self-catering, sleep up to six. **Stunning**[6] locations. **Unbeatable**[7] prices. Phone now.

Savour[14] the renowned landscapes in our **heartland**[15].

Awe-inspiring[8] national parks

Rambles, hikes and **treks**[9]

Unrivalled[10] programme.

Send for our brochure.

[1] /ʌnˈwaɪnd/ relax, reduce your general level of stress [2] get back your energy (like recharging a battery) [3] wild, areas covered in grass, bushes or trees (especially in Africa and Australia) [4] pronounced *four by four*; vehicles with driving power on all four wheels [5] on the edge of the sea or of a river [6] extremely beautiful [7] no other company can offer cheaper ones for the same service [8] it fills you with a sense of the power and beauty of what you are looking at [9] these words represent a scale of length and difficulty: a **ramble** is a long, pleasant walk, not too demanding; a **hike** is more demanding, suggesting more difficult terrain; a **trek** is usually of several days over wild country [10] no other holiday programme can match this [11] having views of the attractive, natural things in the countryside [12] a perfect place or situation (often collocated with *tropical* when describing somewhere hot and sunny) [13] the business of organising holidays in a way which helps local people and does not damage the environment [14] enjoy or taste (often used in advertisements) [15] the inland areas furthest away from the sea or from borders with other countries

Exercises

26.1 **Complete the expressions and collocations in these sentences, using words from A.**

1 Malaysia .... some of the loveliest beaches in Asia.
2 The tourism .... is very important to the economies of many developing countries.
3 It is vital that tourism should not damage the flora and .... of beautiful areas of this spectacular landscape.
4 Most tourists like to feel free to .... off the .... track.
5 Most people don't like to travel to places where there will be .... of other tourists.
6 People who spend all their time in big cities often like to .... back to .... when they go away for a holiday.
7 If you're .... something out of the .... , why not try a snowboarding holiday? It's certainly different!
8 When I travel, I always try to .... the crowds and find somewhere quiet.
9 There are vast .... of unspoilt land in the north of the country, with .... rainforests and a .... of wildlife.
10 The country has fabulous national .... and nature .... where you can camp or stay in basic accommodation.

26.2 **Use words from B opposite to fill the gaps, based on the words given in brackets.**

1 This company is excellent and their prices are .... (RIVAL)
2 The .... beauty of the coastline is unforgettable. (SCENE)
3 There are some absolutely .... beaches in the north. (STUN)
4 I think SunTravel Vacations is .... when it comes to value-for-money holidays. (BEAT)
5 The mountains were so .... Some were over 5,000 metres high. (AWE)
6 We rented a .... villa. It was nice to be so near the beach. (WATER)
7 I just want somewhere quiet and relaxing to .... for a week. (WIND)
8 Everyone needs to .... their batteries now and again. (CHARGE)

26.3 **Answer the questions.**

1 Order these words from the most physically demanding to the least physically demanding: ramble, trek, hike.
2 What verb might you find in travel advertisements meaning enjoy?
3 What adjective can be used with *traveller* to mean one who knows exactly what he or she wants in terms of quality and style?
4 Where would you find the bush?
5 How do you say this and what does it mean: 4x4?
6 If somewhere was described as a 'paradise', would that be positive or negative?

26.4

Over to you

Write a short paragraph describing what for you would be the perfect holiday. If possible, compare your ideas with someone else.

27 Describing the world

A Climate

Travelling from north to south in Nigeria, one passes through a fascinating series of landscapes. **Rainfall**[1] in the south-east can be extremely high in the wet season, whereas the northern part of the country is **arid**[2] and **prone to**[3] **drought**[4] during the dry season. (*Nigeria*)

[1] the amount of rain that falls, for example in a month or in a year   [2] dry   [3] tending to have a particular negative characteristic   [4] long period without rain

B Vegetation

More than 30 percent of the landscape of Canada lies inside the Arctic Circle, where the land can stay frozen for up to nine months of the year. In these regions, known as the **tundra**[1], **vegetation**[2] is limited. Further south, dense, **coniferous**[3] forests known as *taiga* cover large areas of land. Towards the border with the United States are the grasslands of the **prairies**[4] and the mixed, temperate forests. (*Canada*)

[1] area in north with no trees and permanently frozen ground   [2] plant life   [3] trees that are **evergreen** [in leaf all year round] and produce cones, unlike **deciduous** trees, which lose their leaves in winter   [4] flat grasslands in Canada and northern USA (similar to steppes in Asia or pampas in South America)

C Agriculture

Rice is the main crop grown in the south, along with tea, cotton, fruit and vegetables. The rice is planted in flooded **paddy fields**[1]. A good year can see two crops of rice and one of vegetables harvested. In the drier, hillier north and west, farmers generally harvest a single crop of **cereals**[2] and, in addition, **tend**[3] sheep and cattle. (*China*)

[1] fields planted with rice growing in water   [2] type of grass cultivated to produce a grain, i.e. a food plant like rice, wheat or maize   [3] take care of

D Industry

France is one of the world's leading industrial nations. It is home to large **manufacturing**[1], steel and chemical industries. The country is an important and major producer of aircraft and cars and is **at the forefront**[2] of technology and engineering. Its sizeable nuclear industry **generates**[3] a significant proportion of the nation's electrical power. (*France*)

[1] producing goods in large numbers   [2] in an important position   [3] produces/creates

E Population

Brazil is a vibrant mixture of peoples. Some **are descended from**[1] **indigenous**[2] tribes, others from the Portuguese who were the colonial power in Brazil for 300 years. Many Brazilians have African **ancestors**[3] brought over in the 17th century as slaves to work on sugar plantations. During the 20th century, large numbers of European **migrants**[4] **settled**[5] in the south. Brazil is also home to the largest Japanese community outside Japan, as large numbers of Japanese settled there in the 20th century. (*Brazil*)

[1] are related to someone who lived in the past   [2] existing naturally in that place   [3] relatives from earlier times: we are our ancestors' **descendants**   [4] people who move to live in another country or another part of their own country (often for reasons of economic need; an **emigrant** is someone who leaves a country, an **immigrant** is someone who moves to live in a country)   [5] made their homes

Exercises

27.1 Match the two parts of the collocations from the opposite page. Note the words are not all in bold.

1 coniferous ☐   a plantation
2 industrial ☐   b industry
3 paddy ☐   c forest
4 chemical ☐   d field
5 sugar ☐   e nation

27.2 Here are some other words which collocate with the words in the right-hand column in the exercise above. There are three for each of the five words. Can you match them?

> coffee   deciduous   dense   civilised   manufacturing   oil   pharmaceutical
> rain   magnetic   rubber   tea   textile   wheat   independent   sovereign

27.3 Complete the sentences using a word from the box. There may be more than one possible answer.

> descendants   ancestors   migrants   emigrants   immigrants

1 I believe my .... came to Britain from France in the 17th century.
2 Many .... left Russia for France after the Revolution in 1917.
3 The USA has traditionally welcomed .... from all over the world.
4 Our largest cities are full of .... looking for work and a better life.
5 Some Scots are said to be the .... of 16th century Spanish sailors shipwrecked off the Scottish coast.

27.4 Rewrite the underlined words using words and expressions from the opposite page.

1 Recently, the country's economy has suffered a decline in industry <u>concerned with making things</u>.
2 The university has long been <u>in a very important position in</u> agricultural science.
3 The river delta <u>tends to suffer</u> catastrophic flooding on a regular basis.
4 One can often see local shepherds <u>looking after</u> large flocks of sheep on the hillsides.
5 In the late 18th century, migrants <u>made their home</u> in the uncultivated lands towards the north of the country.
6 In the <u>extremely dry</u> southern provinces, <u>plant life</u> is sparse.
7 In the cold northern regions, the landscape consists mostly of <u>permanently frozen ground with no trees</u>.
8 The tribes <u>that have always existed naturally</u> in the eastern jungles are now facing threats to their way of life.
9 The farmlands are dotted with woods <u>that lose their leaves in winter</u>, while the large forests <u>of trees that are always in leaf</u> provide the country with much-needed timber.
10 The <u>flat grasslands</u> of the northern USA experienced a severe <u>long period with no rain</u> last year.

27.5 **Over to you**

If your country is not one of the ones on the opposite page, write a short paragraph about it in the same style, or else choose another country and do the same.

28 Weather and climate

Weather conversations

Here are some less common but nonetheless useful words about weather so that you can have typical weather conversations where you agree with someone by using a near-synonym. In these examples, B replies using more informal language.

A: Bit **cold** today, isn't it?
B: Yes, it's **chilly/freezing/nippy**, isn't it?

A: It's **hot**, isn't it?
B: Yes, it's **boiling/sweltering/roasting**!

A: It's a bit **windy** today!
B: Yes, really **blowy/breezy**, isn't it?

A: What **oppressive/sultry** weather!
B: Yes, isn't it **stifling/heavy/close**?

A: What a **downpour/deluge**!
B: Yes, it's **chucking it down / it's pouring**!

A: Isn't it **humid** today?
B: Yes, horrible **muggy/clammy/sticky** weather!

B Climate and metaphors

Climate metaphors are often used, particularly in written English. The word **climate** can refer to the general atmosphere or situation in society.

His secrecy and dishonesty created a **climate of distrust**.
The government reforms have contributed to a **climate of change**.
The words **cultural, current, economic, financial, moral, political, social** and **prevailing** all collocate strongly with **climate** in this social sense.

She has a very **sunny disposition** – she's hardly ever miserable.
Though they won the championship last year, the outlook for the team is less **sunny** this year.
Unfortunately, our plans met with a **frosty** reception.
I'm **snowed under** with work – I'll never get through it all in time.

After the company accounts were examined, the manager left **under a cloud**.
Don't let your love for him **cloud your judgement**.
The soldiers were hit with a **hail of bullets**.
The Prime Minister was greeted with a **hail/storm of abuse**.
I've only a **hazy memory** of my first day at school.
The truth is hidden **in the mists of history**.
The article sparked off a **whirlwind** of speculation.
They had a **whirlwind romance** and got married just a month after they met.

The horses **thundered** down the racetrack.
Thunderous applause followed his speech. (Note that **thundery** is used to describe stormy weather while **thunderous** describes a loud, deep noise.)
The **winds of change/discontent/democracy** are blowing across the country.

Exercises

28.1 Respond to these statements about the weather. Agree using slightly more formal language like that of speaker A in the conversations on the opposite page.

1 It's a bit nippy outside, isn't it?
2 What a sweltering day!
3 Isn't it muggy here?
4 It's blowy, isn't it?

5 Close today, isn't it?
6 It's chucking it down!
7 It's clammy today, isn't it?
8 What a sticky day!

28.2 What are the metaphorical meanings of these words from B opposite?

1 sunny – *pleasant and positive*
2 frosty
3 to cloud

4 snowed under
5 whirlwind
6 hail

7 climate
8 hazy
9 to thunder

28.3 Find collocations for these words. You will find some on the opposite page, but use a dictionary to find more if necessary.

1 .... climate ....

2 prevailing ....

3 to cloud ....

4 the winds of ....

5 a frosty ....

6 a hail of ....

28.4 Read the text below and find words in it which mean the following.

1 average
2 dry
3 height above sea level
4 distance from the equator
5 rain and snow

6 rays from the sun
7 make less extreme
8 situated very far from the sea
9 differing weather conditions at different times of the year

Schemes for dividing the Earth into climatic regions are based on a combination of indices of mean annual temperature, mean monthly temperature, annual precipitation totals and seasonality. The climate of a place is affected by several factors. Latitude affects the amount of solar radiation received, with the greatest in equatorial regions and the least in polar regions. Elevation affects both temperature and precipitation; mountainous areas are generally cooler and wetter. Location close to the sea or to large bodies of water moderates temperature; continental areas are generally more arid and more affected by extremes of temperature.

28.5 **Over to you**

Answer these questions for yourself.

- Would you prefer to live in a hotter climate or a cooler one? Why?
- How would you describe the cultural climate in your country at the present time?

29 Brick walls and glass ceilings

A Buildings

To **build something/someone up** can be used metaphorically to mean to praise someone or something in a way that will increase expectations of them: The press has **built up** the young footballer so much that it must be extra pressure on him.

Note how **cement** is used to fix bricks firmly in place and to make relationships more solid. It can be used in this way both as a noun and a verb: Let's have a drink together **to cement** our partnership.

To come up against a brick wall is used metaphorically, meaning to meet a barrier: When I tried to find out who had opened my letters, I **came up against a brick wall**.

Ceiling can be used to suggest a limit to something: They put a **ceiling** on the number of planned redundancies.

The **glass ceiling** is a phrase used to refer to an invisible barrier that stops people, especially women, from rising to top positions at work.

Roof is used in a number of common metaphors: The **roof fell in** on my world on the day he died. [My world collapsed ...]

Conversely, the **floor** can **give way** metaphorically when you faint.

The colloquial phrase **go through the roof** is used about prices, meaning to increase in a rapid, uncontrolled fashion.

Hit the roof means get very angry: My mother will **hit the roof** when she sees what we've done.

Window, both literally and metaphorically, means an opening.

A **window of opportunity** is a chance to do something special: If you see a **window of opportunity**, then take advantage of it.

If a quality or idea **goes out (of) the window**, it means it departs: Once the boys started going around together, common sense **went out of the window**.

As a very tall building, **tower** conveys an idea of distance from ordinary people. If someone lives in an **ivory tower**, he/she does not know about the unpleasant and ordinary things that happen in life: Academics are often criticised for living in their **ivory towers**.

If a person is a **tower of strength**, they are extremely strong (in an emotional rather than a physical sense): Our friends were a **tower of strength** when our house burnt down.

If a person or thing **towers above** something or someone, they are either outstandingly tall or outstanding in some other positive way: Lauren **towers above** all her classmates although she is actually one of the youngest students.

B Entrances

Gateway is used metaphorically in the phrase **be a gateway to**, meaning give an opportunity to get somewhere: A degree in law is a **gateway to** a well-paid job.

Door can also be used in a similar way to gateway above, but it is also used in many other metaphorical phrases as well: Failing his final exams **closed/shut** a lot of **doors** for him. Knowing several languages **opens doors** when it comes to finding work. The new year gives us the opportunity to **close the door on** the past and make a fresh start.

Doing something **through/by the back door** suggests doing it unofficially: Joe came into the business **by the back door** – the manager knew him from university.

Unfortunately, the decision was taken **behind closed doors** and no one knows exactly why it was made.

Key can be used as a noun to suggest the importance of something: This research may **provide/hold the key to** developing a cure for cancer.

Knowing the right people is **the key to success** in that country.

Exercises

29.1 Match up the words to make metaphors. Explain what each metaphor means.

1 glass ☐   a strength
2 ivory ☐   b opportunity
3 brick ☐   c ceiling
4 back ☐   d tower
5 window of ☐   e wall
6 tower of ☐   f door

29.2 Complete these sentences with the appropriate verb.

1 The price of fuel has .... through the roof.
2 We hope that this scientist's work may .... the key to solving the problem.
3 A degree in economics .... the door to a number of interesting job opportunities.
4 Whenever you try to initiate something in this company you find that, sooner or later, you .... up against a brick wall.
5 Lucy's father .... the roof when he saw that she'd dyed her hair purple.
6 Bill .... over all the other lawyers in his firm. He is by far the most able.
7 Her argument with the board last year has, unfortunately, ... a lot of doors for her in this company.
8 The roof .... in on their world the day that war was declared.

29.3 Rewrite the underlined parts of these sentences using one of the expressions on the opposite page.

1 My brother is always <u>enormously supportive</u> whenever I have a problem.
2 We'll never know what the US and Russian Presidents said to each other <u>when they met in private</u>.
3 The fee for this work will depend on the time it takes, but <u>cannot be more than</u> $20,000.
4 The cost of petrol <u>has risen dramatically</u> in the last six months.
5 Having children often <u>makes a marriage stronger</u>.
6 Winning an Olympic medal can <u>provide an opportunity to develop</u> a career in the media.
7 The <u>most important</u> decision we have to take now is where to locate our business.
8 The professor has spent all his life <u>in one university or another</u> and really finds it very difficult to cope in the real world.
9 Lena has <u>always said what an incredible person Max is</u> – I hope I won't be disappointed when I meet him.

29.4 Here are some more metaphors based on aspects of buildings. Can you guess what the underlined expressions mean and rewrite them?

1 He earns very little, barely enough to <u>keep the wolf from the door</u>.
2 The speaker's request for questions was met with <u>a wall of silence</u>.
3 Working on this project together should help to <u>lay the foundations</u> for a good relationship in the future.
4 Jack's prolonged illness left his business <u>in ruins</u>.
5 This government should <u>clean up its own backyard</u> before criticising other countries.

29.5 **Over to you**

Which of the metaphors in this unit also work as metaphors when translated literally into your own language? Look at exercise 29.4 as well as the opposite page.

30 Taking root and reaping rewards

Parts of a plant

Here are some metaphors based on parts of trees and plants.

Seed(s) is often used to talk about the start of an idea or feeling: **the seeds of success, the seeds of discontent, the seeds of revolution.**

Root(s) is used to suggest the origins of something. You can talk about **going back to your roots**, for example, meaning going back to the place where your family came from. You can also talk about **the root of a problem** or **the roots of a tradition**. **Putting down roots** means settling down and making your home in one place: After travelling the world for a couple of years, I was ready to go home and **put down some roots.**

When an idea becomes known or accepted, it can be said to **take root**. The **grassroots supporters** of an organisation or society are the ordinary people in it, not the leaders.

Deeply and **firmly** collocate with **rooted**: Its origins are **firmly/deeply rooted** in the 19th century.

Stem is used as a verb to signify that something originates in something else: Her discontent **stems** from a traumatic experience she had last year.

Bud is used in the expression **nipped in the bud** [flower before it opens] [stopped before it develops into something]: He's showing signs of neglecting his work – we'd better **nip that in the bud.**

The adjective **budding** can also mean showing promise of future development: She's a **budding** young actor.

A **branch** is something that grows off or **branches out** from a main organisation. We talk about **branches of a shop** or a **business branching out into new directions**: We don't have the blue sweater in your size here, but you could try our Oxford Street **branch.**

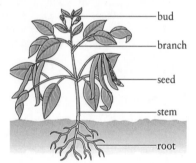

- bud
- branch
- seed
- stem
- root

Metaphorical verbs connected with plant growth and gardening

The new boss is planning to **weed out** older or less experienced staff. [get rid of]

The government will probably have to **prune back** its proposals. [cut/limit]

At last she **is reaping the rewards of** all her years of study. [is getting results from]

Because we didn't protest about the change, we are now **reaping what we sowed**. [experiencing the logical results of our actions – usually used in negative contexts]

The journalists **have dug up** some interesting facts. [have discovered]

The idea **was germinating** while we were on holiday. [was beginning to develop]

Out-of-town shopping centres **have been sprouting up** all over the country. [have been appearing quickly in large numbers]

Our business **is flourishing**. [is doing very well]

A deciduous tree **sheds** its leaves. [loses] Companies can **shed employees/jobs**. People can **shed worries/inhibitions/weight.**

Plants can **thrive**; so can people and things [grow/develop well and successfully]: The language school is **thriving** – student numbers are up from last year.

She loves her high-powered job and seems to **thrive on** stress and crises!

Plants **fade, wither, shrivel** and **wilt** when they die. These verbs can be used metaphorically: Hopes of finding survivors are **fading**. [becoming smaller]

Revenues/donations/profits have **shrivelled** in recent years. [become less]

It was so hot in the classroom that the students were starting to **wilt**. [lose energy]

A **glance/look/remark** can **wither** or **be withering** [make the recipient feel scorned]: She gave him a **withering look.**

Exercises

30.1 Match up the pairs to make collocations.

1 nipped ☐   5 to reap ☐   a of the problem   e roots
2 a budding ☐   6 to take ☐   b root   f in the bud
3 grass ☐   7 the seeds ☐   c Olympic athlete   g rewards
4 the root ☐   d of discontent

30.2 Fill the gaps in these sentences.

1 Alec has spent most of his life in London, but he is keen to get back to his .... when he retires. His family came from Scotland, so he'll move there.
2 The business is firmly .... in Western Australia.
3 The idea took some time to .... root, but it's very fashionable now.
4 His grandfather sowed the .... of the business's success.
5 The US bookshop chain is opening a number of .... in the UK.
6 It's about time she .... down some roots.
7 The idea for her novel .... from her interest in mountain climbing.
8 The West Side Drama College turns out a hundred .... actors every year.

30.3 Divide the verbs in the box into two groups: verbs associated with growth and health and verbs associated with decline and death.

> fade   flourish   germinate   shrivel   sprout   wilt   thrive   wither

30.4 Suggest three nouns that each of these adjectives could describe.

1 budding   ....
2 flourishing   ....
3 withering   ....
4 fading   ....
5 deeply rooted   ....
6 thriving   ....

30.5 Rewrite the sentences using plant metaphors instead of the underlined words.

1 My hopes of getting a job are <u>disappearing</u>. Unemployment is at an all-time record.
2 The firm is <u>cutting</u> the labour force in order to reduce costs.
3 She <u>got rid of</u> her inhibitions at the party and danced with everyone!
4 He and his wife are now <u>receiving</u> the rewards of many years of hard work building up their business.
5 The party is trying hard to <u>get rid of</u> the extremists and create for itself a more moderate political image. They want to reflect the views of their <u>ordinary</u> supporters.
6 Some people seem to <u>grow and develop</u> on difficult challenges.
7 A blogger <u>found out</u> some alarming facts about government spending.
8 Well, if you won't study for your exams, don't be surprised if you <u>suffer the negative consequences of your actions</u>.

30.6 Over to you

- Do you have any responsibilities that you would prefer to shed at the moment?
- Can you think of a situation where you reaped the rewards of something you did?
- What in your life is flourishing at the moment?
- Where are your family's roots?

31 The animal kingdom

A Describing animals and birds

mammal: animal that gives birth to live babies, not eggs,
and feeds them on its own milk (e.g. cat, cow, kangaroo);
a kangaroo is a special kind of mammal called a **marsupial**
[its young grow in a **pouch** in front of the mother]
rodent: e.g. mouse, rat   **reptile**: e.g. snake, lizard
carnivore: animal that eats a diet that is mainly or
exclusively meat (e.g. lion, tiger, hyena)
herbivore: animal that eats a diet that is mainly or exclusively grass/vegetation (e.g. deer, cow)
predator: animal that hunts/eats other animals (e.g. eagle, lion, shark)
scavenger: animal that feeds on dead animals which it has not killed itself
warm/cold-blooded: warm-blooded animals (e.g. mammals) have temperatures that stay the
same; cold-blooded animals (e.g. reptiles) have to control their temperature by taking in heat
from outside or by being very active

B Describing typical animal behaviour

Our old cat is a very **docile** creature. [behaves very gently]
These birds are so **tame,** they will sit on your hand. [not afraid of humans, usually because of
training or long involvement with humans]
Dogs and horses became **domesticated** thousands of years ago. [live with or are used by humans]
There are **wild** cats in the mountains. [opposite of domesticated]
A **savage** wolf killed three of the farmer's sheep. [extremely violent or wild]
A **fierce** dog guarded the gates. [behaves aggressively]

C Life of animals and birds

As more buildings and roads are constructed, the **natural habitat** for many species is
shrinking. [preferred natural place for living and breeding]
The arctic tern is a bird which **migrates** from the Arctic to the Antarctic, a round trip of over
70,000 km. **Migration** is when animals travel long distances to get to a different habitat.
The **dodo** is a large flightless bird which was once found on an island in the Indian Ocean
but **became extinct** in the seventeenth century. [died out]
You can see lots of animals in the big **game reserves / game parks** in Africa. [areas of land where
animals are protected from hunting, etc.; **game** can be used to mean animals or birds that are hunted]
There is a **bird sanctuary** near here. [protected natural area where birds can live and breed]
We went to the local **animal (rescue) shelter** to see if we could get a dog there. [place where
stray cats, dogs, etc., i.e. pets that have lost their home are given food and a place to live]

> **Language help**
> A *dodo* is now used to mean someone or something out of touch or obsolete.

D Human exploitation of animals and birds

Many people are opposed to **blood sports** such as foxhunting and bullfighting. [sports whose
purpose is to kill or injure animals]
Some people refuse to wear clothing made of natural animal fur since they are opposed to **the
fur trade.** [the selling of animal furs for coats, jackets, etc.]
Poachers kill hundreds of elephants every year to supply **the ivory trade.** [people who hunt
animals illegally] [the buying and selling of ivory from elephants' tusks]
Animal rights activists often demonstrate outside research laboratories where animals are
used in experiments. [people who actively campaign for the protection and rights of animals]
Rhinos are hunted for their **horn** which is said to have healing powers. [hard pointed, often
curved, part growing from the head of an animal]

Exercises

31.1 Rewrite the underlined phrases in these sentences using words from the opposite page.

1 There are a lot of different types of <u>squirrels, rats, mice and things like that</u> living in the woods.
2 A whale isn't a fish, as it doesn't lay eggs. It's actually <u>an animal that gives birth directly</u>.
3 There are some interesting <u>turtles and crocodiles and that sort of thing</u> near the river.
4 Everyone thinks these animals <u>eat meat</u>, but in fact they <u>only feed on certain kinds of leaves</u>.
5 The mother bird protects her eggs from <u>animals that attack them</u>.
6 Many different species have <u>died out</u> because their habitat has been destroyed.

31.2 Fill the gaps in these sentences using adjectives from B on the opposite page to describe gentle or aggressive behaviour, or the relationship between animals and humans.

1 Sheep are generally rather .... animals, but the other day a ram attacked our dog.
2 Lions can look very .... with their huge teeth and large heads.
3 Horses were probably first .... many thousands of years ago.
4 Some dolphins are very .... and will swim along with human beings.
5 I don't think .... birds should ever be hunted. They should be left in peace in their natural surroundings.

31.3 Here are the beginnings of some words related to animals and birds. Can you fill in the missing letters? You are given a clue as to the meaning.

1 h........................... (natural home)
2 s........................... (protected place)
3 r........................... (protected area, often for big game)
4 s........................... (creature that eats flesh of, e.g. birds killed by other animals)
5 s........................... (pet that has wandered away from home)
6 m........................... (animal that carries its young in a pouch until the young are fully developed)
7 m........................... (travelling a long way to live somewhere else for a while)
8 d........................... (an extinct bird or an out-of-touch person or idea)

31.4 Answer these questions.

1 What do we call sports that deliberately injure or kill animals for pleasure?
2 What name is given to the activity of buying and selling elephants' tusks?
3 What do we call people who illegally hunt or catch animals or fish?
4 What arguments would animal rights activists have against the fur trade?
5 What is the most valuable part of the rhino and the reason why it is hunted?
6 Where might you go to get a pet if you want to give a home to one that no longer has one?
7 Where might you go in Africa to see wild animals?
8 What do you call creatures like mammals that always have approximately the same temperature?
9 What is used to describe creatures like reptiles and is the opposite of the answer to 8?

31.5 Complete the following table. Do not fill the shaded boxes. Use a dictionary if necessary. In the noun and adjective columns, mark which part of the word is stressed.

noun	verb	adjective
carnivore		
herbivore		
predator		
poacher		
migration		
domestication		

32 Our endangered world

You probably already know a lot of words for talking about the environment, pollution, and so on. In this unit we focus particularly on collocations (words that are often used together). Try to learn these and use them in your writing.

A Threats and potential threats to the environment

Shrinking habitats[1] are a threat to biodiversity[2], in terms of both plants and animals, and endangered species[3] need legal protection if they are to survive. Although some climate change sceptics[4] disagree, many scientists believe that global warming[5] will increase. This will encourage polar ice to melt resulting in rising sea levels and climatic changes. Carbon (dioxide) emissions[6] from the burning of fossil fuels[7] are contributing to the greenhouse effect[8]. In addition, population growth exerts severe pressure on[9] finite resources[10], and the ecological balance[11] may be upset by uncontrolled deforestation[12]. Demographic projections[13] suggest the world population will continue to grow exponentially[14], putting extra pressure on depleting resources[15]. Waste disposal[16] is an increasing problem and toxic waste[17] is contaminating[18] many rivers and seas. Safe water may become an increasingly precious commodity[19], leading to issues of water security[20]. One of the worst-case scenarios[21] is that there will be no tropical rainforests left by the year 2050. Our only hope is that pristine environments[22] such as Antarctica can be protected from development and damage so that at least these habitats are preserved.

[1] places where animals live and breed which are decreasing in size   [2] variety of different types of biological species   [3] types of animals/plants which are in danger of no longer existing   [4] people who do not believe that climate change is a serious issue   [5] steady rise in average world temperatures   [6] carbon dioxide gas from factories, cars, etc.   [7] coal, oil, etc.   [8] warming of the Earth's surface caused by pollution, where gases trap and redirect heat back down to the Earth's surface   [9] puts great pressure on; *formal*   [10] limited resources that will eventually run out / be exhausted   [11] balance of natural relationships in the environment   [12] unrestricted destruction/clearing of forests   [13] forecasts about the population   [14] grow extremely rapidly   [15] resources that are reducing   [16] getting rid of waste   [17] poisonous waste materials   [18] poisoning (something)   [19] very valuable substance   [20] ability to ensure that a population has safe drinking water   [21] the worst possibilities for the future   [22] perfectly clean/untouched/unspoilt areas

B Responses to environmental issues and problems

Look at these newspaper headlines and note the useful phrases.

GOVERNING PARTY IN BID TO IMPROVE GREEN CREDENTIALS[1]

[1] reputation for positive support of the environment and for making policies that reflect this

PROPHETS OF DOOM AND GLOOM[2] SHOULD LISTEN TO SCIENTIFIC EVIDENCE, SAYS PRIME MINISTER

[2] people who always make the most depressing or pessimistic predictions about the future

SUSTAINABLE DEVELOPMENT[3] THE ONLY ANSWER FOR EMERGING COUNTRIES, SAYS UN COMMISSION

[3] development of industry, etc. which does not damage the environment or social and economic stability, and which can continue over a period of time

RENEWABLE ENERGY[4] – GOVERNMENT DEVELOPS NEW STRATEGY

[4] energy produced using sun, wind or crops rather than coal or other fuels which cannot be replaced once used

> **Common mistake**
> People cause damage to the environment (NOT ~~damages~~).

Exercises

32.1 Make these sentences formal by using words and phrases from A opposite instead of the underlined words, making any other necessary changes.

1 All that carbon-what's-it-called gas put out by cars and factories is a major problem.
2 These flowers here are a type there's not many left of, so it's illegal to pick them.
3 A lot of wild animals have to survive in smaller and smaller areas where they can live.
4 A lot of Patagonia is a completely spotless area that's never been touched.
5 We have to look after the things we use on this planet because they won't last for ever.
6 If the cutting down of trees continues, there will be no forest left ten years from now.
7 Burning coal and oil and stuff like that causes a lot of pollution.
8 The sea will get higher if this heating up of the world continues.
9 Increasing population puts really big pressure on economic resources.
10 The way things all balance one another in nature is very delicate.

32.2 Complete the following table, using a dictionary if necessary. Do not fill the shaded boxes.

noun	verb	adjective	adverb
climate			
demography			
	project		
	sustain		
	contaminate		
		toxic	
	deplete		

32.3 Correct the mistakes in this paragraph.

Profits of boom and gloom are always saying that we are heading for an environmental catastrophe, and that unless we adopt a policy of attainable development we will cause irreparable damages to the planet. The worst place scenery is of a world choked by overpopulation, the greenhouse affect and traffic gridlock. Much of what is claimed is exaggerated, but politicians are influenced by such voices and are always trying to improve their green potentials in the eyes of the voters.

32.4 Match words on the left with words on the right to make collocations about the environment.

1 renewable ☐
2 demographic ☐
3 precious ☐
4 polar ☐
5 waste ☐
6 greenhouse ☐
7 worst case ☐
8 climate change ☐

a scenario
b sceptic
c effect
d energy
e projections
f disposal
g commodity
h ice

32.5 *Over to you*

To find more vocabulary connected with environment and conservation issues, visit the websites of major conservation organisations such as the World Wildlife Fund (WWF) (www.worldwildlife.org) or Friends of the Earth (www.foei.org).

33 Here to help: customer service

A Good service

Read these comments by someone about a company they recently used.

They're a good company. They always make sure you get a **prompt**[1] reply to any **query**[2] and they're very **responsive to**[3] complaints. When I rang to ask if I could change the delivery date, they were very **accommodating**[4] and **got back to**[5] me within ten minutes with a new date. Whenever I ring, I get **impeccable**[6] service; they're always very helpful and **obliging**[7], whatever the problem is.

[1] quick, without delay   [2] ˈkwɪəri :stion or enquiry   [3] they listen, take things seriously and act
[4] willing to understand and help   [5] called (or wrote) with an answer   [6] 100% perfect   [7] willing and happy to do things for someone

B Adjectives connected with bad service

adjective	meaning	example
incompetent	failing through insufficient skill, knowledge or training	It wasn't just bad service; they were completely **incompetent**.
impersonal	lacking a personal element or feeling of human warmth	I find supermarkets so **impersonal**.
shoddy	poor quality (of service or of goods)	They repaired my car but the work was very **shoddy**.
substandard	below the standard expected (often used about actions)	It was a **substandard** performance altogether for such a big company.
uncooperative	not supportive, unwilling to work together	The secretary was very **uncooperative**, so I ended up doing it myself.

There's a huge **backlog** of orders and they can't deliver for three weeks. [number which are waiting to be dealt with]
They never seem to have any **sense of urgency** when you ring them. It's exasperating. [feeling that your request is important or urgent]
They have a **helpline**, but it's useless; they always **put you on hold** every time you ring. [telephone number where you can get help if you have problems] [make you wait]
The home button on my tablet stopped working but it was still **under guarantee/warranty** so I didn't have to pay to get it repaired. [having a written promise by a company to repair or replace a faulty product]

C Service encounters on the internet

Most big companies offer a **secure site** where you can **set up an account,** and they have a **privacy policy** guaranteeing **secure transactions**. [web address where no outside person can read your details] [enter all the details necessary to open an account] [set of rules to make sure your account is private] [business exchanges which protect, e.g., your credit card from use by someone else]
The hotel website lets you check **availability** and has all the information you need on its **home page.** [whether they can supply something, e.g. a room for when you want it] [main or first page of a website]
This site has a very good **FAQ** link where you can find answers to the most important questions. [frequently asked questions (pronounced as initials)]
This online bookshop is excellent: you can **browse** and it has a very good **site index.** [look at the list of goods/services offered before buying] [alphabetical list of contents of website]
Most large online stores offer **immediate dispatch** and a **nationwide** service. [goods will be sent at once] [covering the whole country] You can also **track** your order so you know when it will be delivered. [follow]
Do you buy clothes online or do you prefer to buy them **in-store**? [in a real shop]

Exercises

33.1 Fill the gaps with appropriate words or phrases from the opposite page. There may be more than one possible answer.

1 I rang to complain and they put me .... for about 15 minutes. Then I spoke to someone who promised to ring me again, but they never got .... me. I'll have to call them again.
2 They promised immediate .... of the goods I ordered, but I've been waiting over a week now, and nothing has arrived.
3 I've always found the company very .... to complaints and enquiries.
4 I was expecting a .... reply to my email, but I've been waiting two weeks now, and still haven't had an answer.
5 I asked why they hadn't dealt with my order yet and they said there was a .... of orders which had built up over the New Year's holiday.
6 In my opinion, the goods and the service were both pretty .... I would have expected better quality from such a famous firm.
7 Staff in that shop are so .... ; they are genuinely helpful.
8 I rang the .... , but they couldn't solve my problem.
9 I think you need to try a musical instrument before you buy it, so I would recommend you buy your guitar .... rather than online.
10 Most online stores ask you to .... account before you can buy things.

33.2 Here are some links from internet sites. Match them with the list of functions.

1 `Track your order`   4 **Check availability**   7 `At a glance site map`

2 **Returns policy**   5 ○ Browse our categories   8 `Your basket ⇨`

3 **FAQ**   6 Gallery   9 **Privacy and cookies**

a look through the range before buying
b the most commonly asked questions
c rules for protecting your personal details and whether the site may leave tracking and other software on your computer
d with one look you can see what the website contains
e goods you have chosen but not yet paid for
f see if the goods you want can be supplied
g look at pictures of something or someone
h rules for sending back goods you are not satisfied with
i follow the progress of your order

33.3 Replace the underlined words with words from the opposite page.

1 The plumber we got lacked the necessary skills and he caused a flood in our kitchen.
2 If you have any questions about the service, there's a helpline you can ring.
3 The new TV came with a two-year promise to repair or replace a faulty item.
4 The service has no feeling of human warmth about it; they just treat you as a number.
5 Do they offer a service that covers the whole country?
6 The service they gave me couldn't have been better.
7 It's a website which safely protects all your personal details.
8 It didn't feel like a business exchange that was safe, so I cancelled it and logged off.

33.4

Over to you

If possible, compare your answers with someone else.

- Do you have a backlog of anything at the moment?
- Have you had any recent experience of someone being very accommodating towards you?
- Have you ever rung a helpline? If so, what for, and was it a successful call?
- Has anyone who has served you been uncooperative recently? What was the situation?
- Was your last major purchase online or in-store? Which way of shopping do you prefer and why?

34 Authorities: customs and police

Entering a country

On arrival in most countries, you have to show your passport or national identity card, possibly a **landing card**[1] and often a **customs declaration form**[2]. You may need a visa and a **vaccination certificate**[3], depending on **entry regulations**[4]. Alternatively, some passengers can use e-passport gates which make use of **facial recognition technology**[5]. Customs officers carry out **spot checks**[6] on people's baggage to find **banned or restricted goods**[7] and to check that you haven't gone over your **allowance**[8]. They may use **sniffer/detector dogs**[9] to **detect**[10] drugs, tobacco, cash and explosives. In most cases, you have to **clear customs**[11] at the **port of entry**[12]. Some passengers may wish to be recognised as **refugees**[13] and claim **asylum**[14].

[1] form with your personal details and date of arrival   [2] form showing how much money and what goods you are carrying   [3] paper proving you have had the necessary health injections   [4] rules about who can enter a country and for how long   [5] computer application that can automatically identify a person from a visual image   [6] checks done as a sample, rather than checking everyone or everything
[7] items that are forbidden or only permitted in specified quantities   [8] amount permitted by law
[9] specially trained dogs who locate specific items using their sense of smell   [10] find something hidden
[11] successfully get through baggage checking   [12] the port or airport where you first enter a country
[13] people who have escaped from their own country for political reasons   [14] /əˈsaɪləm/ to request permission to stay in another country to avoid **persecution** back home [cruel treatment because of race, religion or political beliefs]

Policing the streets

The police **enforce** the law. [make people obey]
A police officer can **stop and search** you if there is a **suspicion** you are carrying drugs, weapons or stolen property. [belief that something may be the case]
The police cannot normally enter your home against your wishes without a **search warrant**. [official permission from a judge or magistrate to search a home]
Many roads have **safety/speed cameras** to ensure people aren't **exceeding the speed limit**. [going faster than the permitted speed]
Traffic wardens issue **parking tickets**, with fines for illegal parking. [people whose job it is to make   ive their cars where it is not allowed]
The police also use **surveilla**   /səˈveɪləns/   niques, including CCTV (**closed-circuit television**) to monitor public   centres and airports. [television system sending signals to a limited number of screens]

Other types of policing

security forces: often a name for the army and police working together
plain-clothes police: police who do not wear uniform
undercover police: police who do not wear uniform
drug squad: police specially trained to fight the illegal drug trade
anti-corruption squad: police specially trained to discover and fight **bribery/corruption** [dishonest behaviour usually involving using money illegally to gain favours]
cyber crime: computer crime (there are many types, including **cyber terrorism, cyber warfare, phishing** = tricking people on the internet to give up personal information, particularly bank account details)

Common mistake

Police is a plural word. *The police are trying to combat crime.*

Exercises

34.1 Rewrite these sentences using phrases and collocations from A opposite instead of the underlined words.

1 You'll have to show a <u>paper proving that you have had injections</u> for infectious diseases when you enter the country.
2 People entering from war-torn countries often <u>ask for permission to stay to avoid political oppression in their own country.</u>
3 You have to <u>take your baggage through customs</u> if you arrive on an international flight at San Francisco airport, even if you are flying on within the USA.
4 You may have to fill in a <u>paper saying how much money you're bringing into the country</u> before going through customs control.
5 At the airport now, they use <u>a system that checks that the photo in the passport is actually of the person using the passport.</u>
6 *Passenger to airline cabin attendant:* Could you give me <u>one of those papers for filling in my passport number and personal details</u> before we arrive, please?
7 At the airport, the security guards had <u>those special dogs that can smell drugs.</u>
8 You'll need a visa; the <u>rules about who can enter the country</u> are very strict.
9 You have to fill in the <u>city where you first entered the country</u> in this box here.

34.2 Match the words to form collocations.

1 detector	☐	6 spot	☐	a squad		f ticket	
2 landing	☐	7 closed-circuit	☐	b television		g dogs	
3 cyber	☐	8 drug	☐	c goods		h crime	
4 speed	☐	9 parking	☐	d check		i warrant	
5 search	☐	10 restricted	☐	e camera		j card	

34.3 What do we call ...

1 a police officer who does not wear uniform?
2 a person whose job it is to check that no one is parked illegally?
3 police officers engaged in combating dishonest use of public funds?
4 the official paper you sometimes find stuck on your windscreen when you park illegally?
5 the type of police officer who might try to infiltrate a group suspected of terrorism?
6 the police and army considered as a single body?

34.4 Choose a word from the box to complete each sentence. Put it in the correct form.

> detect   suspicion   exceed   search   enforce   refugee   persecution   allowance

1 An official stopped the man because a sniffer dog had .... something in his suitcase.
2 During the Civil War many .... crossed the border into neighbouring countries.
3 Throughout the centuries many people have suffered .... for their religious beliefs.
4 Ella was fined for .... the speed limit.
5 It is a police officer's duty to do all he or she can to .... the law.
6 When you come into this country, the tobacco .... is 200 cigarettes per person.
7 There are restrictions on the powers the police have to stop and .... people.
8 The police have had .... about the activities at that address for some time now.

34.5 **Over to you**

If you have internet access, look up information concerning entry and immigration formalities for different countries, which are often available in English, and note any new vocabulary. For example, for regulations about the UK, see http://www.ukba.homeoffice.gov.uk/ or for Australia, see http://www.immi.gov.au

35 Belief systems

A People and their beliefs

person	definition	related words
adherent (of)	a person who supports a particular idea or party	adherence, to adhere to
convert (to)	someone who has taken on a new set of beliefs	conversion, to convert
fanatic	(disapproving) someone with a very strong belief that something is great	fanaticism, fanatical
radical	someone who believes there should be extreme change, often political	radicalism, to radicalise
reactionary	(disapproving) someone opposed to change or new ideas	reaction, to react

B A definition of one belief

FEMINISM   The modern feminist movement **seeks** equal political, economic and social rights for women. The main theoretical **assumption**[1] shared by all branches of the movement **derives from**[2] the belief that there has been a historical tradition of male **exploitation** of women. Feminists are **anxious** to **eradicate**[3] this exploitation, giving both genders equal opportunities, for example, in terms of education and employment. In some workplaces, for example, feminists have complained about employers being **biased in favour of**[4] male staff or **prejudiced against**[5] female employees and they have **campaigned** for **maternity/paternity leave**[6] and childcare facilities to allow women to combine family and work **commitments**[7] more easily.

[1] unquestioning acceptance that something is true   [2] has its origins in   [3] abolish or get rid of
[4] showing an unreasonable liking for, based on opinions rather than facts   [5] showing an unreasonable dislike for, based on opinions rather than facts   [6] time off for a mother/father around the time of a baby's birth   [7] responsibilities, things that you must do

C Other words and expressions relating to believing

Jan's **viewpoint / point of view** is that we should just wait and see what happens next. [way of thinking about a situation]

The boy produced a barely **credible** excuse for arriving late. [believable; *opp.* = **incredible**]

I was **incredulous** when she told me she was quitting her job to go to New Zealand. [not wanting or able to believe something]

He's very **gullible** – he believes anything you tell him. [easily tricked into believing things that may not be true]

You should try to be less **subjective** about the situation. [influenced by beliefs or feelings rather than facts; *opp.* = **objective**]

Can't you find a more **plausible** excuse than that? [convincing; *opp.* = **implausible**]

Many scholars **attribute** this anonymous poem **to** Dante. [consider something to be caused or created by]

I **presume** that Meena told you what happened. [believe something to be true although you are not totally certain]

We should **give her the benefit of the doubt.** [accept that someone is telling the truth even though it is not certain]

You should **take** what he says **with a pinch of salt** – he's inclined to exaggerate. [do not totally believe what you are told]

Exercises

35.1 Complete the word table. Do not fill the shaded boxes.

noun – person	noun – abstract	verb	adjective
adherent			
convert			
radical			
			reactionary
fanatic			

35.2 Find words and expressions in the text in B with the following meanings.

1 wants to achieve ....
2 has its roots in ....
3 very much want to ....
4 completely get rid of ....
5 unfair treatment ....
6 organised activities to try to achieve something ....
7 time off work ....
8 duties ....

35.3 Choose the correct word in the sentences below.

1 A gullible person believes everything even if it is *plausible / implausible*.
2 I don't find his story at all *credible / incredulous*.
3 When marking exams, try to give candidates the *advantage / benefit* of the doubt.
4 A fanatic is someone with a very *objective / prejudiced* point of view.
5 The law says that you must be *derived / presumed* innocent until proven otherwise.
6 It is better to take her promises with a pinch of *salt / pepper*.
7 In the essay you must summarise the economic problems of this area and conclude by giving your own *point of view / assumption* about what the government should do to solve them.
8 The play has been *presumed / attributed* to Shakespeare.

35.4 Choose words from the box to complete the sentences below.

> adherents   attribute   commitments   converts   eradicate
> objective   pinch   prejudiced   subjective

1 The charity aims to .... poverty in this region within five years.
2 It has been said that .... to a religion can often be much more active supporters of the religion than people who were born into it.
3 The Town Council has been accused of being.......................... against cyclists.
4 The criteria for judging the Poem of the Year competition are, inevitably, to some extent ....
5 Many of the self-professed .... of this philosophy have never even read its basic texts.
6 Historians .... the origins of this philosophy to Ancient Greece.
7 A judge must try to remain .... and not let personal values influence his or her decisions.
8 Family .... undoubtedly have an impact on people's attitudes to their work.
9 I take anything said by an election candidate with a .... of salt.

35.5 **Over to you**

If you have internet access, look up a world view that interests you, e.g. feminism, Marxism, humanism, Buddhism or any -ism that you want to research. Make notes about (a) the origins of the -ism, (b) what its basic beliefs are, and (c) what differences there are between its different branches (if it has them).

36 Festivals in their cultural context

A Describing festivals

Read this short text about a Kenyan cultural festival.

The Mombasa Carnival **falls** in November each year in this Kenyan city. People from all over the country and the world travel to Mombasa to participate in the **festivities**. The carnival **features** people dressed in **spectacular** costumes **parading** through the city's streets performing traditional songs and dances to **celebrate** their cultures. Promoting integration within this multicultural region remains the **focus** of the carnival.

noun	verb	adjective
There are big **celebrations** on New Year's Day.	New Year's Day **is celebrated** in many ways. The festival **celebrates** the New Year.	
The **festival** is held in March. [special day(s)/event] The **festivities** go on for days. [enjoyable activities]	–	There was a **festive** mood in the village during the spring holiday.
The **parade** in the town square was a very colourful **spectacle**.	On the anniversary of the battle, soldiers **paraded** through the streets. *	The parade is always very **spectacular**. *
Everyone in the village attends a big **feast** in the evening [big meal to celebrate something].	During the national holiday, there is a whole week of **feasting** and celebrations.	–
Many of the customs have their origin in ancient **ceremonies**.	–	A **ceremonial** procession goes through the streets of the city.
The festival is a time of **renewal**.	Each year, the festival **renews** the national spirit of the people.	The celebrations at the end of the war brought **renewed** hope to the people.

* There is no verb for *spectacle* and no adjective for *parade*.

B Other words and phrases connected with festivals

A lot of people are very **superstitious**, especially about numbers and colours. [have illogical beliefs about hidden forces in nature]

The festival celebrated the **centenary/bi-centenary** of the country's independence. [100th anniversary / 200th anniversary]

The Rio de Janeiro Carnival is always a very **flamboyant** and **raucous** event. [extremely colourful and exaggerated] [very noisy]

The Festival of the Dead is very **sombre** and **atmospheric**. [serious, heavy and sad] [had a special feeling or atmosphere] It can be **traced back to pagan times**. [its origin may be found in] [the times when people believed that nature had special powers]

The annual holiday **commemorates** all those who died in the country's civil war. [respects and remembers officially; *formal*]

Exercises

36.1 Use words and phrases from A opposite to rewrite the underlined words. Use the word class indicated and make any other necessary changes.

1 For Christians, Christmas is a celebration of the birth of Jesus Christ. (verb)
2 The festival events included parades, sports and musical gatherings. (noun, plural)
3 There was a feeling of celebration about the whole weekend. (adjective)
4 For people who live in the country, the spring festival renews the fertility of the land. (noun)
5 There was an atmosphere of ceremony as the military bands took part in a parade around the main square. (adjective, verb)
6 People were in a mood for a festival when the harvest was successfully completed and a huge meal was held in the village. (adjective, noun)
7 You should go and see the lantern festival. It's always spectacular. (noun)
8 The festival is always on the first Monday in July. It is in memory of a famous battle. (verb, verb)
9 It was the 100th anniversary of the founding of the university and the 200th anniversary of the city itself. (noun, noun)
10 The gymnastic display involving 300 children was a real spectacle. (adjective)

36.2 Here is an extract of someone talking about a festival using rather informal language. Write it as a more formal description, using words and expressions from the box instead of the underlined words. Make any other necessary changes.

| parade | atmospheric | focus | associate | trace back to | raucous |
| pagan | symbolise | sombre | superstitious | flamboyant | renewal |

Well, it was called the Festival of Flowers, and it was to do with the coming of spring, after the dark, serious winter months. It was a time of everything being new again. Its origin can be seen in the religious tradition of taking flowers to offer them to the gods. Spring flowers were the main thing in the festival, and there was always a big group of people marching through the streets. It was all very lively and extremely colourful and probably rather noisy, and there was a great atmosphere. The flowers meant new life, and people thought they would be guaranteed a good harvest later in the year if they were offered to the gods. Nowadays, most people don't have such funny beliefs about nature, but there are still some festivals that are all about nature's special powers celebrated every year.

36.3 **Over to you**

Answer the questions for yourself. If possible, compare your answers with someone else.

- Which of these important days are celebrated in your country? What happens on them?
  Mother's Day   Independence Day   May Day   Valentine's Day
- What is the most important day of the year in your country? What does it symbolise or commemorate? What does it feature? What are its origins? What sort of atmosphere does it have?

37 Talking about languages

A Some major world language families

English belongs to the **Indo-European** family of languages. [major group of languages in Europe and parts of Asia] English is part of the **Germanic** group of languages within the Indo-European family, along with, for example, Swedish and Dutch.
Other Indo-European language groups include Indo-Iranian, Romance and Slavic, and Semitic languages are a branch of the Afro-Asiatic family.

in writing 以书面形式

в письменной форме

γραμμένο

서면으로

yazılı olarak

مَكتوبا

family name	examples
Sino-Tibetan	Chinese, Burmese
Indo-Iranian	Hindi, Farsi, Bengali
Romance	Spanish, Romanian, French
Altaic	Japanese, Korean, Turkish
Austronesian	Malay, Filipino, Maori
Slavic	Polish, Russian, Bulgarian
Semitic	Arabic, Hebrew
Dravidian	Malayalam, Tamil
Austro-Asiatic	Vietnamese, Khmer

B Specialist terms for talking about language

Syntax: the grammar and word order
Different languages express **modality** in different ways. [meanings such as possibility and necessity] English does it with **modal verbs** like *must*, *could* and *should*.
Phonology: the sound system, i.e. pronunciation and intonation
All languages have **phonemes**, such as /b/ and /v/. [different sounds that distinguish meanings]
English has ten **diphthongs**. [sounds made by combining vowels, such as /eɪ/ and /aʊ/]
Lexicon: specialised term for vocabulary
English **derives** much of its vocabulary from **Graeco-Latin** words as well as **Anglo-Saxon** words. [originally from Greek and Latin] [language of England from 500–1000 AD]
Orthography: specialised term for writing systems and spelling
The English alphabet has 26 **characters**. [letters or symbols] Some writing systems, such as Chinese, are not alphabetic but have **pictograms** or **ideograms**. [characters representing pictures] [characters representing ideas/concepts]
Morphology: how words are formed
In English, there are three **morphemes** in *unthinkable*: *un*, *think* and *able*. [units of meaning]

C Other useful words for talking about language

Many words in English are **polysemous**. [they have a number of different meanings] The meaning will usually be clear from its **context**. [the language or situation around it]
Words are often used in a **metaphorical** way – a way that is not **literal**, e.g. *to see the light* meaning 'to understand something' rather than literally to see a light.
Language **usage** inevitably changes with time. [the way words are used] Some words become **obsolete** while new words are **coined**. [fall out of use] [of words, created]
Any language has a number of different **registers**. [style of language used in a particular situation, e.g. formal, informal] **Jargon** is used to describe a specific type of language that is used by a particular group of people sharing a job or interest, e.g. **military jargon**, **computer jargon**.

Exercises

37.1 Which language family do these languages belong to?

1 Russian   5 Malay
2 Chinese   6 Spanish
3 Hebrew   7 Hindi
4 Dutch   8 Japanese

37.2 Rewrite these sentences using more appropriate technical terms from B opposite instead of the underlined words.

1 The <u>writing system</u> of Burmese is quite difficult for a foreign learner.
2 Japanese uses several different writing systems with hundreds of <u>letters and symbols</u>.
3 The <u>vocabulary</u> of a language like English is constantly changing. A lot of new technical words are <u>based on</u> roots <u>from Latin and Greek</u>, rather than <u>words from the period pre-1000 AD</u>.
4 Unlike English, some world languages have very few vowel <u>sounds</u> and no <u>combinations of vowels</u>.
5 This ancient and beautiful alphabet uses <u>characters that symbolise pictures</u> to express meaning.
6 <u>Meanings connected with probability and obligation are</u> expressed in different forms in different languages.

37.3 Complete the word formation table below. Use a dictionary if necessary. If your dictionary gives pronunciations, mark any differences in stress between the noun form and the adjective form.

noun	adjective	change in stress?
orthography		
lexicon		
modality		
metaphor		
polysemy		

37.4 The sentences below are examples of the different types of language in the box. What is each an example of?

> obsolete language   computer jargon   metaphor   polysemy

1 Life is a journey and sometimes your path will be rocky.
2 Marry, thou are roinish, forsooth.
3 It's not fair that boy with the fair hair won all the prizes at the fair.
4 What kind of external storage device do you have access to?

37.5 **Over to you**

Answer these questions, and if possible, compare your answers with someone else.

- Which language family is your language included in?
- How many vowel phonemes does your language have?
- Does your language have diphthongs?
- How is your language written?
- Which languages do words in your language tend to derive from?
- How are words formed in your language?
- How does your language express modality?

38 History: since the dawn of civilisation

A History – the great and the ordinary

Archaeologists[1] patiently work among the remains of past civilisations, trying to understand once-powerful vast empires[2], kingdoms[3] and dynasties[4]. Since the dawn[5] of civilisation, societies have recorded the reigns[6] of kings and emperors, the fate of their heirs[7] and successors[8] and major events such as coronations[9], wars and conquests[10]. All this can be recorded in manuscripts[11] or on stone tablets. When an heir succeeds to the throne and is crowned, we usually learn how long he/she reigns. Meanwhile, the lives of the ordinary people, the peasants[12] and labourers[13], the pattern of their days, the migrations[14] of social groups, often go unrecorded, and archaeologists and historians have a tougher task in interpreting whatever shreds[15] of evidence remain. But for many, this is the real history and archaeology, the true key to our past.

[1] person who studies the material evidence of past societies [2] group of countries ruled by a single person [3] individual countries ruled by a king or queen [4] different rulers who are all from the same family, or a period of time that a country is controlled by them [5] beginning [6] period that a king, queen or emperor rules [7] person who is legally entitled to continue the work of someone important who has died or who has the same position as they had [8] person who takes over from another person [9] event when a king or queen receives his/her crown [10] when someone or an army defeats and takes over another country [11] texts written by hand [12] person who works on the land and earns little, usually having a low social status [13] person who does unskilled manual work [14] moving from one place to another in large numbers [15] very small amounts

B Historical eras

In ancient Egypt, the Bronze Age began about 4,000 years ago. [period when the metals copper and tin began to be used to make weapons, tools, etc.; we also talk of the Stone Age, the Iron Age]
Life in medieval times was hard. [of or from the European Middle Ages, i.e. 1000–1500 AD]
I love the great Renaissance art of Italy. [period of new growth of interest and activity in the arts especially in Europe in the 14th to 16th centuries]
Magnificent architecture and works of art were created in Central America in the pre-colonial era. [period before Europeans arrived in large numbers and took power; opp. = post-colonial]

C Military history

infantry: soldiers on foot (uncountable)
cavalry: soldiers on horseback (uncountable)
(suit of) armour: metal protective clothing worn by soldiers
chariot: two-wheeled vehicle pulled by a horse and used in ancient times for racing and war
galleon: large sailing ship with three or four masts used in the 15th to 18th centuries

D People

warlord: a military leader who controls a country or, more often, an area within a country
slave: person legally owned by someone else and who has to work for them (noun = slavery)
ruler: leader of a country
explorer: someone who travels to places that no one is thought ever to have visited in order to find out what is there
merchant: someone who buys and sells things in large amounts, especially by trading with other countries
monarch: neutral term for a king or queen (a country with a king or queen at its head can also be called a monarchy)
the nobility: collective term for people of the highest social rank in a society

Exercises

38.1 Which words on the opposite page are these definitions of?

1 The period during which someone is king or queen ....
2 A family that rules during different generations ....
3 Someone who is legally entitled to take power or control when someone dies ....
4 A text written by hand ....
5 The event when a king or queen receives a crown ....
6 Several different countries ruled by one person ....
7 A metaphorical expression meaning 'the beginning' of something ....
8 A small amount ....
9 A historical era when the use of copper and tin to make weapons and implements began ....
10 The period in the history of many countries before European conquerors arrived ....

38.2 Complete the table, using a dictionary if necessary. Do not fill the shaded boxes.

person	noun	verb
	kingdom	
emperor		
successor		
		crown
	conquest	
archaeologist		
	reign	
	labour	
	migration	
ruler		
monarch		

38.3 Match the beginnings and endings of the sentences.

1 The sailors ☐   a marched for three days.
2 The emperor drove ☐   b led his army into battle.
3 The infantry ☐   c drew a map of the island.
4 The nobility ☐   d boarded the galleon.
5 The cavalry ☐   e traded with the local tribespeople.
6 The warlord ☐   f lived in large, expensive houses.
7 The merchant ☐   g a chariot with two black horses.
8 The explorer ☐   h galloped across the field.

38.4 Here are some of the words from the opposite page used in a metaphorical way. Read the sentences and answer the questions about the underlined phrases.

1 The princess swept into the room like a galleon in full sail. Was the princess (a) small and awkward or (b) large and stately?
2 He doesn't mind criticism and it's often hard to penetrate his armour. Is the person described likely to be (a) thick-skinned or (b) physically strong?
3 There has been a renaissance of interest in the harp. Has interest (a) increased or (b) decreased?
4 No one should be a slave to tradition. Does the writer think people should (a) always follow tradition or (b) not always follow tradition?
5 Nigel has a positively medieval attitude towards the role of women in society. Does Nigel have (a) a liberal, open-minded attitude or (b) a very old-fashioned, conservative attitude?

39 The haves and the have nots

A Definitions of poverty

United Nations definition: 'Fundamentally[1], poverty is a denial[2] of choices and opportunities, a violation[3] of human dignity[4]'...

[1] in a basic and important way   [2] not allowing people to have   [3] act that spoils or destroys something   [4] worth

type and aspect of poverty	definition	comments
absolute poverty	being poor according to a fixed minimum standard; sometimes called the poverty line	In 2011, people with less than $1.50 to live on a day were defined as being below the poverty line/threshold. This sum does, of course, regularly change.
relative poverty	being poor in relation to others around you	This kind of poverty depends on a person's social context[1]. It takes into account that there is no income equality between countries.
extreme poverty	living below the poverty line	People living in extreme poverty will be lacking in material possessions and money. Another word for extreme poverty is penury.
human poverty	being poor in a range of ways, not only financial	This kind of poverty takes into account such social factors as shelter[2], nutrition[3] (people living in poverty are more likely to be malnourished[4]), literacy[5] levels (people living in poverty are more likely to be illiterate), sanitation[6], access to education and healthcare. People lacking these basic aspects of life are said to be deprived[7].

[1] situation   [2] having a place to live that is protected from the weather   [3] food that people take into their body   [4] suffering from ill health because of poor food (noun = malnourishment/malnutrition)
[5] ability to read and write   [6] systems for taking dirty water and waste from homes to ensure good hygiene   [7] noun = deprivation [lacking in things considered necessary for a pleasant life]

B Other expressions relating to wealth and poverty

Most of the world's population can be classed as poor. [categorised]
Only a small minority of people in the world enjoy affluence / are affluent. [wealth; wealthy]
It's a very poor country – over 60% of the population live on or below the breadline. [having the level of income of an extremely poor person]
When your income is low, it is hard to make ends meet. [have enough money to buy all you need]
At this time, many people left the poverty-stricken countryside to go to the city. [affected by poverty]
The charity's main aim is to improve healthcare in impoverished areas of the world. [poor, without much money to live on]
Everywhere in the city you see destitute people living in shop doorways or under bridges. [without money, food, home or possessions; noun = destitution]
When we were first married, we were living from hand to mouth, so it's nice to be able to spend a bit more now. [having just enough money to live without suffering]
Ever since I lost my job, money has been tight. [there has not been much money]
We'll have to tighten our belts now that Mum has lost her job. [spend less than before]
Many of the people in this area are in the lowest income bracket. [the group earning the least money]

Common mistake

We say *the rich* and *the poor,* meaning rich people and poor people (NOT ~~the riches~~ and ~~the poors~~).

English Vocabulary in Use Advanced

Exercises

39.1 Complete the second sentence so that it means the same as the first one.

1 The number of deprived children is increasing.
The number of children facing .... is increasing.
2 There is much less illiteracy in the world than there used to be.
There are far fewer .... people in the world than there used to be.
3 Our family enjoyed relative affluence at that time.
Our family enjoyed a relatively .... lifestyle at that time.
4 It is wrong to deny people their basic human freedoms.
.... of people's basic human freedoms is wrong.
5 There are more destitute people in the city than before.
The problem of .... in the city is increasing.
6 Poverty could be said to violate human dignity.
Poverty could be said to be a .... of human dignity.

39.2 Choose one of the words in the box to complete each of the sentences below.

> absolute   threshold   impoverished   relative   fundamental   shelter

1 Some people in a middle income bracket claim that they are living in .... poverty simply because they have fewer material possessions than their neighbours.
2 Anyone who has experienced living below the poverty .... will always be anxious never to return to that state.
3 Food and .... are two of the most important human needs.
4 There is a .... difference between not having a lot of money and being destitute.
5 It is not very meaningful to talk in terms of .... poverty when you compare people who live in very different contexts.
6 His family were once quite affluent, but in the last few years they have become increasingly
....

39.3 Complete the sentences.

1 An increasingly large number of families are living on the bread ....
2 Most of the people who live in this street are in a higher income ....
3 It all depends on your social .... whether you feel poor or not because you don't own a car.
4 It can be hard for students to make .... meet.
5 If we all tighten our .... , we should be able to manage all right.
6 I was surprised how poverty-............................ the villages looked given the richness of the surrounding farmland.

39.4 Choose the best word to complete each of these sentences.

1 A person who sleeps in a cardboard box on the street and begs for money can best be described as *impoverished / destitute*.
2 Without my husband's income, we were very much living from hand to *mouth / foot*.
3 When we were children, money was always *small / tight*.
4 Even children with rich parents can be *deprived / destitute* in terms of love and affection.
5 An increasing number of people live below the *penury / poverty line*.
6 The table shows the proportion of people in each income *section / bracket*.
7 Many of the children here are *classed / grouped* as living in poverty.
8 The country has great extremes of poverty and *influence / affluence*.
9 Children who don't get enough food will suffer ill health as a result of *nutrition / malnourishment*.
10 Inadequate *sanitation / deprivation* can have serious health consequences.

40 British politics

Influencing political decisions

www.parliament.uk

Ordinary citizens in the UK can have their say in political life in a number of ways. They can:

- **Lobby**[1] MPs and Members of the House of Lords about a particular issue.
- **Petition**[2] the House of Commons to tell MPs about views on an issue and request action.
- Comment on **legislation**[3] going through Parliament during the **committee stage**[4] of a Public **Bill**[5] in the House of Commons.
- Submit evidence to a **Select Committee**[6] inquiry **scrutinising**[7] the work and policies of the government.

[1] try to influence the opinions of MPs and Lords [2] formal process involving sending a written appeal to an MP, following a set format, which is then presented to the Commons by the MP [3] possible future laws [4] period after a proposed law has been discussed by Parliament when it is looked at in detail by a group of people [5] proposal for a law currently under discussion [6] committee that checks and reports on some aspect of government work · [7] looking very closely at

Lobbying and petitioning

Methods of lobbying vary and can range from sending letters, making presentations, providing **briefing**[1] material to Members and organised **rallies**[2]. Often the result lobbyists are seeking for the MP or Lord to vote a certain way on a specific issue. However, this decision will **ultimately**[3] be **down to**[4] the MP or Lord's own judgement and the influence (if any) that existing party policy will have on them.

[1] informational [2] large political meetings or demonstrations [3] in the end [4] the responsibility of

The public can petition the House of Commons to make MPs aware of their opinion on an issue and to request action. All that's needed is that the petition is properly **set out**[1] and has the signature and address of at least one person. The text of the petition is published in **Hansard**[2]. There is a procedure for petitions in the Lords but it is very rarely used. Generally, MPs will **present**[3] all petitions they receive from their **constituents**[4]. MPs present petitions by either giving a short statement in the debating chamber of the House of Commons or by simply placing the petition in the Petition Bag (which hangs on the back of the **Speaker's**[5] Chair). A copy of the petition is sent to the appropriate government department. Government departments are expected to offer **observations**[6] on all **substantive**[7] petitions.

[1] in the correct format [2] the official record of parliamentary business [3] make something known [4] people who voted for them, people in their constituency [political region] [5] MP with responsibility for controlling the way parliamentary business is done [6] comments [7] of significance

Select Committees

There is a Commons Select Committee for each government department, examining three aspects: spending, **policies**[1] and administration. Some Select Committees have a role that **crosses departmental boundaries**[2], such as the **Environmental Audit**[3] Committee. Other Commons Committees are involved in a range of ongoing investigations, like **allegations**[4] about the **conduct**[5] of individual MPs. Lords Select Committees do not **shadow**[6] the work of government departments. Their investigations look into specialist subjects, taking advantage of the **wide-ranging**[7] **expertise**[8] of the Lords and the greater amount of time (compared to MPs) available to them to examine issues. Committees in the House of Lords concentrate on five main areas: Europe, science, economics, communications and the UK **constitution**[9].

[1] official plans of action [2] deals with different departments [3] closely examines environmental consequences of government decisions [4] complaints that have not been proven [5] behaviour [6] follow closely to see how a job is done [7] covering many subjects, diverse [8] high level of knowledge or skill [9] full set of laws of a country

Exercises

40.1 Are these statements about the texts true or false? Explain why.

1 A lobbied MP has to do what his or her constituents request.
2 MPs make a statement in the Commons about all the petitions they receive.
3 You can read Hansard to find out what has been happening in Parliament.
4 Government departments should comment on all the petitions they receive.
5 The Public Accounts Select Committee shadows a specific department.
6 Select Committees do not look at how individual MPs behave – that is up to the law courts.
7 Lords are felt to have more time to give to committees than MPs.
8 Lords Select Committees focus on the same key areas as those of the Commons.

40.2 Match up the words to make collocations. Note that not all the nouns are in bold on the opposite page.

1 debating	☐	5 wide-ranging	☐	a chair	e stage
2 select	☐	6 Speaker's	☐	b department	f policy
3 committee	☐	7 party	☐	c material	g expertise
4 government	☐	8 briefing	☐	d chamber	h committee

40.3 Now choose one of the expressions from 40.2 to complete each sentence.

1 MPs discuss proposed legislation in the .... of the House of Commons.
2 Before Question Time in Parliament, Ministers have to read a lot of .... provided by their advisors.
3 She was elected to the House of Lords because of her ....
4 Many journalists gave evidence to a .... investigating the behaviour of the press.
5 I am not quite sure what .... is on renewable energy.
6 The bill has had two readings in the House of Commons and is now going through the .... of procedures.
7 The .... is situated between the two sets of benches in the Commons so that its occupant can more easily control the debates.
8 The Treasury in the UK is the .... which deals with the country's finances.

40.4 Complete these sentences with words from the opposite page.

1 The .... of individual MPs may be investigated if it is thought they have not behaved honestly.
2 There have been a number of .... claiming that the Speaker is not doing his or her job properly.
3 On this particular issues, it is .... to the individual MP how he or she votes.
4 It is the role of the Health Select Committee to .... the work done in the Department of Health and to deal with any relevant issues arising from that.
5 A petition to Parliament has to be .... out in accordance with strict rules.
6 The work of this committee is complex because it .... departmental boundaries.
7 There is a lot of .... in the House of Lords because of the very different professional backgrounds among its members.
8 This committee .... the decisions made by the Department of Transport.

40.5

Over to you

Answer these questions about politics in your own country.

- How easy is it for ordinary citizens to lobby MPs?
- How easy is it for ordinary citizens to petition MPs?
- Does the legislative process have a committee stage?
- Do ordinary citizens play any part in committee decisions in relation to government?

41 International politics

A United Nations

The UN is an international organisation **constituted**[1] in 1945 to make the world a better place for **humanity**[2]. From its **foundation**[3], it has **pursued**[4] these key aims:
To keep peace throughout the world.
To **establish**[5] friendly relations between countries.
To work together to improve people's lives by **conquering**[6] poverty, disease, **illiteracy**[7] and environmental destruction, and to encourage respect for each other's rights and freedoms.
To be a centre for supporting nations in achieving these goals.
In other words, the UN stresses the importance of **negotiation**[8] when there are disagreements between countries. It is opposed to **injustice**[9] and **upholds**[10] the rights of **minorities**[11] but it will only support military **intervention**[12] if its Security Council agrees that this is **justified**[13].

[1] formed (used about an official organisation)   [2] all people   [3] time when it was **established** [founded]   [4] try to achieve (*pursue* with this meaning collocates with words like *aim, goal, career, strategy*)   [5] set up, put in place   [6] beating, getting rid of   [7] inability to read or write   [8] discussions in an attempt to reach an agreement   [9] unfairness   [10] supports   [11] groups of people who differ racially or in some other way from most of the people in the place where they live (*minority* collocates with adjectives like *ethnic, religious, oppressed*)   [12] involvement in a difficult situation in order to improve it   [13] caused by a good reason

B Political movements

A political **movement** is a group of people with the same beliefs who work together in the attempt to achieve something. They often make use of a **slogan,** a short phrase that catches people's attention and is easy to remember. The aim of a political movement might be the **liberation** of a minority perhaps or the **integration** of one particular social group into the society from which it is, or feels itself to be excluded. Members of a political movement sometimes go on a **march,** a walk where they can demonstrate their **solidarity** with others sharing the same attitudes and aims.

C International conferences

A major international conference is currently meeting in Rio. **Delegates**[1] from 60 different countries are attending. Their aim is to determine ways in which each country can minimise the energy requirements of its **infrastructure**[2] with a view to slowing the rate of global warming. The governments of each country **recognise**[3] the importance of these discussions and have **undertaken**[4] to support any programme of measures agreed on by the conference. Although some of the issues under discussion are **undeniably**[5] **delicate**[6], the conference has so far shown more **unity**[7] than is **customary**[8] in such gatherings.

[1] representatives   [2] basic systems and services such as transport   [3] accept   [4] promise   [5] certainly   [6] needing to be handled with great skill   [7] being together as one   [8] usual

Exercises

41.1 Choose a word from the box to complete each sentence.

> pursue humanity justify conquer
> negotiations injustice establish minorities

1 The organisation's aim is to .... illiteracy throughout the continent.
2 There is still too much .... in the world today.
3 The rights of ethnic .... are sometimes neglected by national governments.
4 The government wants to .... a committee to work on reducing poverty.
5 It is hoped that the current .... will lead to a positive outcome.
6 The best hope for all of .... is that nations should get better at respecting each other.
7 It is impossible to .... the use of force in such a situation.
8 Lesley is determined to .... her goal of becoming a barrister.

41.2 Complete the word formation table. There are two nouns for five of the verbs.

verb	noun
constitute	
	foundation
undertake	
	negotiation
justify	
	conquest
	liberation
	unity
	delegate
recognise	

41.3 Choose the correct word to complete each sentence.

1 Are you planning to go on the protest .... tomorrow?
  A slogan   B march   C unity   D movement
2 It's quite a .... subject, so take care how you bring it up.
  A customary   B deniable   C delicate   D justified
3 The country's economy can only develop once it has a good ....
  A humanity   B liberation   C solidarity   D infrastructure
4 The party .... not to reduce spending on international aid.
  A integrated   B undertook   C conquered   D recognised
5 It is now nearly 100 years since the .... of the organisation.
  A foundation   B negotiation   C infrastructure D movement
6 Chris is going to the conference as our ....
  A humanity   B solidarity   C slogan   D delegate

41.4 Complete each sentence with a word from the same root as the word in brackets.

1 It is .... true that the project is likely to meet with some opposition. (DENY)
2 Is it .... in your country to take a gift if you visit someone's house? (CUSTOM)
3 It is wrong that there is still so much .... in the world. (JUST)
4 The workers expressed their .... by organising a huge demonstration. (SOLID)
5 Left-wing political .... were particularly powerful in the early 20th century. (MOVE)
6 On the whole this society is very well .... (INTEGRATE)

42 The letter of the law

Legal verbs

to bend the law/rules: to break the law/rules in a way that is considered not to be very harmful
to contravene a law: to break a law (noun = **contravention**)
to infringe a law/rule: to break a law/rule (noun = **infringement**)
to impeach a president/governor: to make a formal statement saying that a person in public office has committed a serious offence (noun = **impeachment**)
to lodge an appeal: to make an official request that a previous judgement should be changed
to uphold/overturn a verdict: to say that a previous decision in court was correct/incorrect
to pervert the course of justice: to make it difficult for justice to be done (noun = **perversion**)
to quash a conviction: to change a previous official decision that someone was guilty
to set a precedent: to establish a decision which must usually, in English law, be taken into account in future decisions
to award/grant custody to: to give one parent or adult the main responsibility for a child, especially after separation or divorce
to annul a(n) agreement/marriage/law: to declare that it no longer exists and never existed (noun = **annulment**)
to sue someone: to take legal action against someone
to allege: /əˈledʒ/ to say that someone has done something illegal without giving proof (noun = **allegation**)
to amend a law: to make changes to a law (noun = **amendment**)

The verdict is...

Crimes

crime	meaning	verb	criminal
discrimination	unfair treatment on grounds of sex, race or nationality	discriminate (against)	
embezzlement	stealing money that is in your care or belongs to an organisation that you work for	embezzle	embezzler
harassment	making a person feel anxious and unhappy (sometimes for sexual reasons, sometimes to get, e.g., a debt repaid)	harass	
insider trading/ dealing	illegal buying and selling of shares by someone who has specialist knowledge of a company	do/practise insider dealing/ trading	insider trader/ dealer
money laundering	moving money obtained illegally so that its origin cannot be traced	launder money	money launderer
perjury	lying when under oath	commit perjury	perjurer
trespass/ trespassing	go onto someone else's land without permission	trespass	trespasser

Words and expressions with law

A **law-abiding** person is someone who always obeys the law.
A **law-breaker** is someone who – often and deliberately – does not obey the law.
If you **take the law into your own hands,** you do something illegal to punish someone because you feel the legal system will not punish that person.
If you **lay down the law,** you say with great force what you think should happen.
If someone is **a law unto himself/herself,** he or she behaves in a way which is independent and not the way in which most other people behave.

Exercises

42.1 Choose the correct verbs from A to fill the gaps. Put the verb in the correct form.

1 The governor on the province was .... for wrongful use of state money.
2 The prisoner decided to .... an appeal against the court's decision.
3 The appeal court .... the verdict of the lower court and the prisoner was released.
4 In English law, a previous legal decision usually .... a precedent for future decisions.
5 Judges almost always .... custody to the mother rather than the father.
6 I'm not asking you to break the rules, just to .... them a little.
7 You .... my legal rights by not allowing me to vote.
8 Witnesses charged with perjury are accused of .... the course of justice.
9 The marriage was .... because the man had never properly divorced his first wife.
10 The Supreme Court .... the murder conviction and the man was freed.

42.2 Which of the crimes in B might each of these people be charged with?

1 A camper who spent a night on a farmer's land without asking permission.
2 A businessman who diverted funds from the account of the company he worked for into his own personal account.
3 An employer who gave a job to a man although he was less suitable for the post than a woman applicant.
4 A witness who gave false evidence in court.
5 A person who kept making inappropriate comments about a colleague's personal appearance.
6 A board member who took advantage of what they knew about the business's plans to make a profit on the stock market.

42.3 Choose a noun from each of these verbs to complete each sentence.

impeach   allege   contravene   annul   harass   infringe   pervert   amend

1 Parliament is currently discussing a number of .... to the current laws on citizenship.
2 Amy took her employer to court for .... in the workplace.
3 Some people consider .... of others' rights as being as serious a crime as theft.
4 By taking on work for a competitor Nathan was in .... of the terms of his contract.
5 The trial was criticised by many as a .... of justice.
6 To suggest that Sue took the money is a very serious ....
7 The circumstances are such that I think the judge may agree to a(n) .... of their marriage.
8 The .... of a president has only taken place a couple of times in US history.

42.4 Choose an expression from C to complete each sentence.

1 You should let the police deal with the situation – it's far too risky to ....
2 Sam started getting into trouble when he got in with a gang of habitual ....
3 You shouldn't start .... on your first day in a new job.
4 Masha will never be able to get Vadim to conform – he's ....
5 Jack is far too .... to agree to bring extra cigarettes into the country.

42.5 **Over to you**

- Write a paragraph describing the main aspects of the law in your country. For example, which of the crimes in B do you hear most about?
- Find out more about the law in the UK. Note down at least ten more useful legal words and expressions. If you have access to the internet, look on this website: http://www.britishlaw.org.uk/

43 War and peace

A War and violence

War is often seen as **a last resort**[1] when relations between states break down totally and **diplomacy**[2] and such measures as economic **sanctions**[3] have failed. The decision to take military action is rarely made lightly, since even the best-planned military operations carried out with the benefit of the latest hi-tech **weaponry**[4] inevitably result in **civilian casualties**[5]. Military **intervention**[6] may be carried out with the goal of **regime change**[7], but it is often the leaders of **tyrannical**[8] regimes who are the most difficult to **overthrow**[9]. Even more tragic than wars between states is **civil war**[10], which often begins with civil **unrest**[11] and **clashes**[12] between **rival**[13] **ethnic**[14] religious or political groups, and may **escalate**[15] into **all-out**[16] war and end in the **brutal suppression**[17] of one group by another or, in extreme cases, **ethnic cleansing**[18] and **massacres**[19]. **Conflict resolution**[20] may take years to bring into effect, and **mistrust**[21] and **hatred**[22] between groups within the same country may continue for many years.

[1] something you do when everything else has failed   [2] activities concerning the relationships between governments   [3] official orders, such as the stopping of trade, taken against a country to make it obey international law   [4] weapons in general / of different types   [5] people injured or killed who are not members of the military or the police   [6] intentionally becoming involved in a difficult situation to improve it or stop it from getting worse   [7] changing the government or leader of a country, especially by force   [8] using power in a cruel way over people in a country or group   [9] remove somebody from power using force   [10] war between groups who live in the same country   [11] disagreement or fighting between groups   [12] fights or arguments   [13] who compete against one another   [14] national or racial   [15] become greater or more serious   [16] complete and total   [17] violent and cruel ending of the right or freedom to do something   [18] organised attempt by one racial or political group to completely remove from a country or area anyone who belongs to another particular racial group, using violence to achieve this   [19] the killing of large numbers of people   [20] finding a way to end conflict and the negative feelings between groups   [21] lack or absence of trust   [22] feeling of intense dislike

B Other words and expressions relating to war and peace

Powerful West African rulers **waged war on** their neighbours in the 19th century. [fought a war against]

Hostilities finally ceased after five years of bloodshed. [acts of war]

The invading army **besieged** the city. [attacked by surrounding it for a period of time (noun = **siege**)]

The patrol was **ambushed** on a remote highway. [attacked unexpectedly from secret positions (noun = **ambush**)]

The two armies signed a **truce** in 2011. [agreement during a war to stop fighting for a time]

A **ceasefire** was declared in 2009. [agreement between two armies or groups to stop fighting]

A **peacekeeping force** entered the country in 2009. [neutral soldiers who keep the peace in a divided society]

International observers monitored the ceasefire. [outside, neutral people or body]

The rebels fought a long **campaign** against the dictatorship. The **rebellion** lasted ten years before the dictator was defeated. [planned group of military activities] [people fighting against their government]

A **suicide bomber** killed 25 people at a military base yesterday. [person who lets off explosives, deliberately killing themselves in the process]

C Metaphors of warfare

The government is **waging war on** drink-driving.

Paparazzi are **besieging** the star's Hollywood home.

A major advertising **campaign** was planned to launch the new cosmetics range.

Several companies are **battling** to win market supremacy in sales of smartphones.

We have a major **fight on our hands** if we are to save the company from bankruptcy.

A **fleet** of bullet-proof cars followed the President's limousine. [a fleet normally consists of a large number of ships]

Exercises

43.1 **Fill the gaps with words from A opposite.**

1 When .... and economic .... had failed, the Cabinet voted to take military action.
2 Occasional violence between the two groups eventually .... into all-............................ civil war.
3 The government forces were accused of carrying out ethnic .... by executing members of the rival tribe.
4 During the war, a .... occurred in a village near the border. Some 150 women and children were shot by enemy troops.
5 The war brought about .... change. The former dictator was .... and forced to flee from the country.
6 The process of conflict .... was successful and the country has now been at peace for ten years.
7 War should always be a last .... when all other avenues have been explored.
8 There were many civilian .... as a result of the bombing raid.
9 There were violent .... between police and demonstrators in the capital city.
10 The armed forces moved a large amount of .... to the battlefront, including tanks, artillery and missile launchers.

43.2 **Replace the underlined words using an appropriate form of the word in brackets.**

1 The irrational dislike of people of other ethnic groups is one of the root causes of conflict. (HATE)
2 The involvement of the United Nations in the situation helped to restore peace. (INTERVENE)
3 The political groups that opposed one another finally negotiated a peace agreement. (RIVAL)
4 The general was a cruel and violent dictator who ruled for 18 years. (BRUTE)
5 There had been a longstanding feeling of not trusting each other between the two tribes. (TRUST)
6 The fight against the government began in 2010. (REBEL)

43.3 **Choose a word from the box to complete the sentences below, using an appropriate form.**

> ambush   observers   truce   suicide   wage
> siege   ceasefire   campaign   peacekeeping

1 A .... bomber disguised as a police officer killed 15 people in an attack today.
2 The UN sent in a .... force to keep the two sides in the civil war apart.
3 A convoy of lorries was .... by enemy soldiers in a remote valley yesterday.
4 International .... monitored the election and concluded that it had been fair.
5 The government has .... war on the drug cartels for the last ten years.
6 The .... of the city lasted six months before the enemy troops were pushed back.
7 After a year of fighting, the two sides agreed to a .... to enable peace negotiations to start. (*two possible answers*)
8 The army fought a long .... to free the country from the enemy forces.

43.4 **Match the sentence beginnings on the left with the endings on the right.**

1 The President was besieged   ☐   a advertising campaign to launch the new phone.
2 Our team is battling   ☐   b war on child poverty.
3 He had a fight on   ☐   c fleet of white limousines.
4 The company planned a major   ☐   d by reporters as she stepped out of her car.
5 The government set out to wage   ☐   e to reach the semi-finals.
6 The band arrived in a   ☐   f his hands to convince everyone he was right.

44 Economy and finance

In this unit we focus particularly on collocations (words that are often used together).

A International aid and development

European countries have, in recent years, turned their attention to supporting real and **sustainable development**[1] in Africa. There are many **encouraging signs** that such projects have **taken root**[2]. In the five years up to 2011, a score of African countries **achieved economic growth** of more than 4% per year. Foreign direct investment also rose. Africa's share in world trade now shows real signs of **recovering from a long decline**. From Ghana in the west to Ethiopia in the east and Mozambique in the south, Africa's economies have consistently grown more rapidly than those of almost any other region of the world. A dozen countries' economies have expanded by more than 6% a year over a period of six or more years. But many millions of people in Africa still live in **deep poverty**[3] and more **determined efforts** are needed to tackle the problem. The European Union is committed to supporting and **allocating**[4] **funds** and **development grants**[5] to those African governments which are **pursuing**[6] **policies** to reduce and **eradicate**[7] **poverty** and **improve access to** healthcare, education and clean water supplies.

[1] development which can continue over a long time   [2] started to be accepted   [3] *abject poverty* is also a collocation   [4] giving to be used for a particular purpose   [5] money to help development   [6] *following policies* is also a collocation   [7] completely get rid of something bad

B Collocations related to the noun *debt*

Countries often find it impossible to **repay debt**. The **debt burden** is too great. **Easing the debt burden** or **cancelling debt** helps **debtor countries/nations** free themselves from the problem of **incurring** more and more **debt**. **Alleviating debt / Debt relief** for poor countries should be a priority.

repay — *burden* **DEBT** *alleviate* — *incur*
ease — *cancel* *relief* *debtor countries/ nations*

C Trade and cooperation

Free trade agreements often cause disputes between countries, especially when one country thinks the other is engaged in **restrictive practices**[1]. Occasionally, **trade wars** erupt, and **sanctions**[2] or **embargoes**[3] are **imposed** on countries that may not be **lifted** for long periods. On the other hand, countries closely related economically and enjoying good relations have the possibility of entering into **monetary union** and having a **single currency**.

[1] the placing of unfair restrictions, e.g. limiting imports   [2] restrictions on what a country may import/export   [3] total prohibitions on importing/exporting certain goods

D Economic difficulties

If an economy is badly affected by war, we may refer to it as a **war-torn** economy. Economies in a bad state are often referred to as **ailing** economies. **Devaluation/Revaluation** of the currency may be necessary. [reduction/increase in value against other currencies]

Common mistake

The verb meaning to reduce the value of a currency is to devalue (NOT ~~devaluate~~).

Economies may **go into recession** and not **come out of / emerge from recession** for several years. Indeed, countries may even suffer a **double-dip**[1] recession. A country may suffer from a **slump in prices**[2] for its goods. **Lower taxes** may be introduced to **boost the economy**[3] when it is in recession.

[1] recession which ends and then begins again after a short time   [2] serious fall/collapse in prices   [3] give the economy a lift

Exercises

44.1 Try to remember the collocations in A opposite. Fill the gaps in these sentences.

1 Development is important, but it should be .... development, not the kind that only lasts a short time.
2 The government is .... a policy of giving aid only where it is used to .... poverty. (*Give two answers for the first one.*)
3 There have been some .... signs that development projects are .... root in many countries.
4 Millions of people still live in .... poverty. (*Give two answers.*)
5 The economy has .... from its decline and is now doing well.
6 The struggle to .... economic growth in developing countries is a constant one.
7 Governments often .... funds for specific overseas development projects.
8 The goal should be to improve .... to better healthcare and education for the poor.

44.2 Rewrite these sentences about debt using more appropriate language from the opposite page to replace the underlined words.

1 Over a period of five years, the country <u>got</u> huge debts which it could not <u>pay back</u>.
2 <u>Countries in debt</u> are completely at the mercy of wealthier nations.
3 <u>The weight of debt</u> is so great in some countries that their economies are collapsing.
4 Wealthier countries could do a lot to <u>make</u> the debt of poor countries <u>less heavy</u>, and indeed, in some cases, could <u>forget</u> the debt altogether. (*Give two answers for the first one.*)
5 Over a period of three years, the country suffered a <u>two-stage</u> recession.
6 The following year, there was a <u>severe collapse</u> in the price of crude oil.
7 While some countries <u>lowered the value of</u> their currencies, one country alone <u>increased the value of</u> its currency due to its strong economy.
8 Urgent measures were needed to <u>improve</u> the economy.

44.3 Answer the questions using vocabulary from the opposite page.

1 What kind of war can break out between countries concerning imports and exports?
2 Which two verbs are used with *sanctions* and *embargoes* to mean (a) 'placing' and (b) 'removing'?
3 What is the name for activities which make free trade difficult or impossible between countries?
4 What kind of agreement is it when two or more countries decide to share a single currency?
5 What do we call sums of money given to poor regions to assist their economic growth?
6 What can we call an economy that is devastated by armed conflict?
7 What adjective beginning with the letter 'a' can be used to describe an economy in a bad state?
8 What noun can follow 'debt' to create a phrase meaning 'removing debt'?

44.4 Now use the answers from 44.3 to rewrite the words in bold.

1 **Sharing the same currency** was agreed between the five countries in 2003.
2 The government introduced a package of measures to rescue the economy, **which was in a bad state**.
3 The two Trade Ministers got together to try to abolish **activities that made trade difficult**.
4 A **major dispute concerning exports and imports** broke out between the two countries in 1999.
5 The economy, **which has been seriously affected by the war**, is slowly recovering now that peace has come.
6 The United Nations **placed** sanctions on the country in 1995 and did not **remove** them until 2008.
7 The region received a **large amount of money to help it grow economically** from the World Bank.
8 **Removing debt** has been crucial for some developing nations.

45 Personal finance: making ends meet

A Cash, cheques and cards

I was **broke/skint** at the end of last month. [had no money left] (broke = informal; skint = very informal)

I'm **rolling in** it this month; I got a payment of £3,000 for some work I did. [have a lot of money; *informal*]

It's sometimes difficult **to make ends meet** with three children and only one parent working. [to survive financially]

Things are a bit tight at the moment. [my finances are not good; *informal*]

I was **strapped for cash** and had to borrow money from my parents. [needed cash and had very little; *informal*]

She gave me a cheque for what she owed me but it **bounced**. [the bank refused to pay it]

Who shall I **make** this cheque **out to / payable to**? [What name shall I put on it?] (payable to = slightly more formal)

The easiest way to pay your household bills is by **direct debit** or by **electronic transfer**. [a regular automatic payment, e.g. every month] [movement of money online between two bank accounts]

Shall we **put/stick** this meal **on** my credit card? Then we can forget it. (*informal*)

Could you **charge** it **to** my credit card, please? (*formal*)

The **APR** for this credit card is 23%, which is 2% lower than my other card. [annual percentage rate of interest]

My card **expires in/on** 05/15. The **expiry date** is 05/15. [is not valid after]

Credit card fraud has increased in recent years. [illegal use of someone's card or account]

A: Is this a credit card or a **debit card**? [card where the money is taken directly from your bank account]

B: Actually, it's a **store card**. [credit card issued by a store/shop for that store]

I went to **withdraw** some money / **get** some money **out** but I forgot my **PIN** and the **ATM** swallowed my card after three wrong attempts. [take money from my account; get money out = informal] [personal identification number] [automated teller machine, often just called a 'cash machine' or 'cashpoint']

B Savings, pensions, etc.

Victims of last year's rail crash will receive **lump sum**[1] compensation payments following a High Court decision today.

A **golden handshake**[2] of ten million pounds was paid to the boss of one of Britain's biggest companies today. This was in addition to an annual **bonus** of two million pounds.

People with well-managed **share portfolios**[3] have done better on the **stock market**[4] than individuals who buy **stocks and shares**[5] privately.

The thieves stole Mr and Mrs Bateson's **life savings**[6], which they kept under their bed in a metal box.

Johan Carslow left only a very small sum to his family in his **will**[7]. It was hardly enough to **cover**[8] the cost of his funeral.

Ms Rafstedt had **borrowed**[9] heavily to finance the building of a new house and found herself deeply in debt, which led her to commit the robbery.

[1] single, large payment [2] large payment to someone on leaving a job [3] combination of investments of different kinds [4] organisation which controls the buying or selling of parts of the ownership of companies [5] parts of the ownership of companies which people buy as investments in the hope of making a profit [6] money saved over many years [7] official statement of what a person has decided should be done with their money and property after their death [8] be enough money to pay for it [9] borrow money, e.g. from a bank (used without an object)

Exercises

45.1 Complete these sentences using words from the opposite page.

1 This is a credit card. If you want one that takes the money directly from your bank account, then you need a ....

2 She never used her card on 4th September. But someone did and bought hundreds of pounds of goods. It was a case of ....

3 I haven't got enough cash to pay for this meal; shall I just .... on my card? (*Give two answers.*)

4 I pay my rent by .... every month, so I don't have to do anything.

5 When I ran out of money in Thailand, my parents made an .... from their bank account to mine.

6 I'm sorry, I can't lend you anything at all. I'm absolutely .... (*Give two answers.*)

7 I couldn't pay for it last month as I was a bit .... for cash.

8 I have to be very careful how I spend my money because things are a bit .... right now.

45.2 Correct the mistakes in these sentences using vocabulary from the opposite page.

1 She got a huge golden hand when she left the company.

2 My old aunt Jessie is rich in it. Every time I go to see her she gives me £100.

3 My father got a bump sum when he retired, so he bought a weekend cottage.

4 She put her living savings into an online company and lost everything when it collapsed.

5 The bank tried to persuade me to put my money into a share folio, with stocks and shares in different companies.

6 If you need a very large sum of money, it's not a good idea to lend from friends or neighbours.

45.3 Match the beginnings and endings of the sentences.

1 Students often find it difficult to make	☐	a in her will.
2 She invested a lot of money on the	☐	b PIN as that's when I was born.
3 If you need cash, there's a	☐	c to cover the cost of the holiday.
4 I use 1-9-8-7 as my	☐	d ends meet.
5 She left a million euros	☐	e cashpoint in the supermarket.
6 The money was not enough	☐	f stock market and lost it all.

45.4

Over to you

Answer these questions for yourself.

- Look in your wallet or purse. What different types of card do you have?
- Give the date on which one of your cards expires.
- Approximately what is the current APR on your credit card?
- What can you do to prevent credit card fraud?

46 The media: in print

Typical sections found in newspapers and magazines

'One thing I always read in the paper is the **obituaries**[1]; it's so interesting to read about other people's lives. I also read the **editorial**[2] (or **leader**); it helps me form my opinion on things. Although national papers **cover**[3] all the important news, I find that if you just want to sell your car or something, the **classified ads**[4] (or **classifieds**) in a local paper is one possibility. I love the Sunday papers, especially the **supplements**[5] with articles on travel, food and fashion and so on. Last week there was a fascinating **feature**[6] on new technology in one of them. My daughter prefers magazines, especially the **agony columns**[7]. I just can't imagine writing to an **agony aunt**[8]. It amazes me how people are prepared to discuss their intimate problems publicly, but I know this sort of article really increases a publication's **circulation**[9].'

[1] descriptions of the lives of people who have just died [2] an article giving the newspaper editor's opinion [3] deal with (noun = **coverage**) [4] pages of advertisements in different categories [5] separate magazines included with the newspaper [6] an article or set of articles devoted to a particular topic [7] sections in a paper or magazine that deal with readers' private emotional problems [8] person, typically a woman, who answers letters in the agony column [9] number of copies sold by a newspaper or magazine

Some types of printed material

name	description/definition	example sentence
journal	a magazine containing articles about a particular academic subject	Part of John's doctoral research was published in an international chemistry **journal**.
	a book where you write about what happened to you each day	I kept a **journal** while I was working in Zambia.
newsletter	a regular report with information for people belonging to a particular group	Laura is in charge of producing a monthly **newsletter** for her tennis club.
pamphlet	small book with a soft cover, dealing with a specific topic, often political	The Conservative Party published a **pamphlet** on the future of private education.
press release	official written statement with information for the public	The company is going to issue a **press release** about its takeover plans later today.
leaflet	single sheet or folded sheets of paper giving information about something	I picked up a **leaflet** about the museum when I was in town.
brochure	small, thin book like a magazine, which gives information, often about travel, or a company, etc.	Do you have any **brochures** about Caribbean holidays?
prospectus	small, thin book like a magazine, which gives information about a school, college or university, or a company	Before you choose a university, you should send away for some **prospectuses**.
flyer	single sheet giving information about some event, special offer, etc., often given out in the street	I was given a **flyer** about a new nightclub which is opening next month.
booklet	small thin book with a soft cover, often giving information about something	The tourist office has a free **booklet** of local walks.
manual	book of detailed instructions about how to use something	This computer **manual** is impossible to understand!

Exercises

46.1 Without looking at A opposite, test your memory for words that mean …

1 the small advertisements in different categories found in newspapers ....
2 a person you write to at a magazine to discuss intimate emotional problems ....
3 the section of a newspaper which pays respect to people who have just died ....
4 an article in a newspaper which gives the editor's opinion ....
5 a separate magazine that comes free with a newspaper ....
6 an article or set of articles devoted to a special theme ....
7 the number of people buying a magazine ....
8 the way a newspaper deals with a particular subject ....

46.2 Fill the gaps in these sentences with appropriate words from B opposite.

1 I've decided to do my own car maintenance, so I've bought the .... for my particular model.
2 Someone was giving out .... in the town centre today about a festival that's going to take place on Saturday.
3 I love looking through holiday .... and dreaming about flying off to exotic places.
4 I never read political .... ; they're so boring.
5 I wish I'd kept a .... when I first started teaching.
6 The Central Bank has issued a .... announcing some changes in personnel.
7 I've read the .... and I like that university; I think I'll apply.
8 My son's school publishes a termly .... for parents, which reports on the previous term and tells us about upcoming events.

46.3 Sort this group of vocabulary items into those connected with *books* and those with *magazines*. Use a dictionary if necessary.

> spine   blurb   subscription   foreword   issue   index   edition   quarterly

46.4 From the context, guess the most likely meaning of the expressions in bold.

1 There's a new autobiography of the footballer Troy Sutton, but it was written by a **ghost writer**.
A someone who didn't have Sutton's permission
B someone who wrote it on his behalf
C Sutton wrote it but he used a different name

2 It makes sense to use **desktop publishing** for any sports club's newsletter.
A published by a school or college
B published only on the internet
C published using a home computer to design it

3 This book is a **facsimile** of an original edition published in 1693.
A an exact reproduction in every detail
B a modernised edition
C a copy made on a fax/ photocopying machine

46.5 Here are some expressions in bold not on the opposite page, which refer to how different types of printed material present their information. Match the sentences with the type of printed material. Use a dictionary if necessary.

1 It **lists** entry requirements. ☐ a a political pamphlet on poverty
2 It **exposes** serious problems in the industry. ☐ b a guarantee leaflet with a new camera
3 It **draws attention to** the fundamental issues. ☐ c a university prospectus
4 It **tells you all you need to know about** main sights. ☐ d a newspaper article
5 It's **packed with** useful tips. ☐ e a tourist brochure
6 It contains a lot of **small print**. ☐ f a booklet about buying a house

47 The media: internet and email

A The pros and cons of internet use

Here are some possible advantages (pros) and disadvantages (cons) of the internet.

pros	cons
email, **instant messaging**[1], **chat rooms**[2], **newsgroups**[3] **social networking sites**[4], **webinars**[5]	ISP[12] charges can be high for heavy users, people you've never met may get your **contact details**, your account may be **hacked**[13]
e-commerce[6] (e.g. internet banking, travel booking), **e-books**, **e-learning**	**download**[14] and **upload**[15] times can be slow, e-books don't feel the same as real books, e-learners may miss a 'live' teacher
accessing vast amounts of useful information, fun of just **browsing**[7] and **surfing the web**[8]	**spam**[16] and **junk mail**[17] can be annoying
ability to transfer **graphic images**[9] and sound files	can become **addictive**[18]
ability to send files as **attachments**[10], usefulness of **file-sharing**[11]	**cookies**[19] track your activities on the web
gaming – you can play video games with anyone in the world	many sites contain **offensive material**[20], **parental control**[21] may be necessary for children

[1] a kind of email where both people are online at the same time   [2] an online conversation between a group of people on topics chosen by them, where you can enter or leave the 'room' at any time   [3] a website where people with shared interests can get news and information   [4] websites that enable you to connect with other people, make new friends, exchange photographs, keep up with people's personal news, etc.   [5] online seminars   [6] all kinds of business done on the internet   [7] looking at different websites, with no particular goal   [8] moving from one website or web page to another, usually looking for something   [9] technical term for pictures, icons, diagrams, etc.   [10] files you send with email messages   [11] the practice of sharing computer data or space on a network   [12] (pronounced I-S-P) Internet Service Provider: a company that offers users access to the internet and services such as news, email, shopping sites, etc., usually for a monthly fee   [13] someone may access it illegally   [14] bringing files to your computer from the internet   [15] sending files from your computer to the internet or to another internet user   [16] unwanted advertisements and other material sent to you by email from companies   [17] another term for spam   [18] something you cannot stop doing, which has become out of your control   [19] pieces of software that are sent from the internet to your computer, which can follow and record what you do, which websites you visit, etc.   [20] material such as pornography, or extreme political views, or material that encourages hate and violence against people   [21] ability of parents to control which websites their children can visit

B Email and internet communications

I've **bookmarked** the CNN home page as I use it regularly to get the latest news. [put it in a list of websites I can access immediately]

If you **subscribe to** newsgroups, you often get hundreds of messages. [become a member of]

Some ISPs allow you to **screen out / filter out** unwanted mail. [prevent from reaching you]

Our **server** at work was **down** yesterday so I didn't get your message till today. [central computer that distributes email and other services to a group of users] [not working]

Do you have good **anti-virus software**? It's worth updating it frequently. [protection against computer viruses]

She must have changed her email address – the email I sent her **bounced**. [came back to me]

She often **posts** ridiculous details about her life on social networking sites. [adds them to her (home)page]

See also Unit 55.

Exercises

47.1 Match the words in the box with the explanations.

> attachment   cookie   spam   chat room   ISP   webinar

1 website where people with common interests can email each other online
2 a sort of class held live on the web
3 company that gives you access to the internet and offers news pages, shopping, etc.
4 program sent to your computer from the internet, used to follow your activities
5 file sent at the same time as an email message
6 unwanted material (e.g. advertisements) sent to you via the internet

47.2 Some of these pairs of opposites exist in the language of internet/computer communications, others do not. Tick the box for 'exists' or 'doesn't exist'. Use a search engine to find the answer on the web if you're not sure.

I DON'T HAVE A COMPUTER ANY MORE. I CAN DO EVERYTHING I WANT ON MY MOBILE!

word	opposite	exists	doesn't exist
delete	undelete		
download	upload		
update	downdate		
inbox	outbox		
online	offline		
install	uninstall		

47.3 Use the correct words from the table above to fill the gaps in these sentences. You are given a paraphrase of the meaning in brackets.

1 I sent a photo of my house by email to a friend in Canada, but it took ages to .... (transfer from here to there) and I spent 20 minutes .... (connected to the internet) just waiting for it to go.
2 I've had your message in my .... (a place where unread emails are stored) for two days, but haven't had time to read it yet.
3 I had a lot of trouble trying to .... (add to the programs already on my computer) that new software I bought.
4 How do I .... (restore something accidentally rubbed out) on this computer?
5 I edit my pictures .... (while disconnected from the internet) and then connect to send them.
6 This is an old version of the software. You can .... (get a new version) it online for free.

47.4 In your own words, say what the words in bold mean in these sentences.

1 A new law has given **e-signatures** the same legal status as handwritten ones.
2 **E-learning** will become more and more common as an alternative to traditional learning.
3 We have **e-enabled** everything you need to study on the internet.
4 **E-books** are selling faster than traditional books.
5 The **dotcom** economy has attracted hundreds of new businesses hoping to make a fortune.
6 With this smartphone, you'll never need a **tablet** or a laptop!
7 **Parental controls** provided by ISPs are vital these days.
8 I send about 40 texts per day. It's very **addictive**.

48 Advertising

A Promoting quality

Advertisers like language that suggests their product is of *especially high quality*.
Check out our latest smartphone – you'll love its **innovative** features. [original and interesting]
The design of our beds is **unsurpassed**. [the best there is]
Our dishwashers **leave other** dishwashers **standing**. [are much better than other dishwashers]
Sign up for exam courses that **put/leave** other courses **in the shade**. [make other courses seem insignificant]

B Promoting value for money

Advertisers like language that suggests things give you *good value for money*.
Rock-bottom prices in our sale! [extremely low]
Prices **slashed!** [dramatically reduced]
Bargains galore! [a huge number of products on sale at ridiculously low prices]
Order now and get a 10% **discount**. [reduction in the price]

C Promoting luxury and comfort

Advertisers like language that suggests *luxury and comfort*.
Pamper yourself with a full-body massage. [treat yourself to something luxurious]
Indulge yourself with our smooth, rich, perfectly blended coffee. [let yourself do or have something that you enjoy but which may be bad for you]
Enjoy a **sumptuous** meal in **opulent** surroundings. [both adjectives mean rich and special: sumptuous collocates most strongly with words relating to food and furnishings, and opulent with words relating to lifestyle]
Live **in the lap of luxury** for two weeks. [in a very luxurious way]

D Promoting scientific backing

Advertisers like language that suggests *scientific backing* for their product.
This **ergonomically designed** reading lamp provides the perfect light. [designed by studying people and their working or living conditions, especially in order to improve effectiveness]
Our health drink is medically **proven** to boost energy levels. [shown by research]
All our computers are **state-of-the-art**. [use the very latest technology]

E Promoting attractiveness

Advertisers like language that suggests their products *make us more attractive*.
Ties that will make you **stand out in the crowd**. [be noticed]
In our new styles, you're **guaranteed to turn heads**. [be noticed]
Our new lipsticks are **tantalisingly** appealing. [temptingly]
Have **fetching** feet and **alluring** ankles in our summer sandals. [both adjectives mean attractive]

F Common ways of advertising

Magazine and newspaper advertisements/adverts; classified ads; TV and radio commercials; posters; **billboards**[1]; **flyers**[2]; **trailers**[3]; sports sponsorship; banners; **sky-writing**[4]; **sandwich boards**[5]; brochures; carrier bags; **logos** on clothing and other products; **pop-ups**[6] on websites.
In addition, personalities often use TV interviews to **plug**[7] a new book or film.

[1] very large boards
[2] sheets of printed information
[3] brief excerpts from a film, TV or radio programme
[4] words written in the sky using smoke from a plane
[5] advertising posters hung at the back and front of a person who then walks around a busy area
[6] advertisements that appear on your screen suddenly
[7] advertise

Exercises

48.1 Complete each of these sentences with one missing word from the opposite page.

1 Enjoy a weekend in the .... of luxury.
2 Don't just follow the herd – take the chance to stand out in the ....
3 Don't miss the ....-bottom prices in our special May Day sale.
4 For the best in state-of-............................ camcorders, visit our website.
5 Why not .... yourself this Christmas with our new foam bath?
6 Take a look at our .... new fabric designs.
7 Our cosmetics .... all others in the shade.
8 You'll find bargains .... in our new discount superstore.
9 Why not .... yourself with our delectable chocolate desserts?
10 We're .... our prices this week for one week only! Huge reductions!

48.2 Match the beginnings and endings of the sentences.

1 The armchair is ergonomically ☐   a to boost the immune system.
2 She was distributing ☐   b for the new James Bond film?
3 He carried a sandwich ☐   c pop-up ads.
4 There was a huge billboard ☐   d designed to ease back pain and provide comfort.
5 It contains a herb proven ☐   e her new book.
6 Did you see that trailer ☐   f advertising a new soft drink.
7 My software is good at blocking ☐   g board advertising a clothing store.
8 She went on TV to plug ☐   h flyers for a charity concert.

48.3 Here are some phrases typical of advertising language. Which of the categories A to E opposite do they fit into? Some of them may fit into more than one category.

1 colossal discounts   5 developed by a team of international experts
2 fit for a king   6 we outshine the best of the rest
3 tantalisingly elegant   7 alluring, fetching and flatteringly fashionable
4 go on – spoil yourself   8 outstanding value

48.4 Look at F opposite. What are these examples of?

48.5

Over to you

Answer the questions for yourself. If possible, compare your answers with someone else.

- Are you influenced by advertisements? If so, what kinds of adverts and why? If not, say why.
- Have you bought anything in the last year because of an advertisement? What was it and why did the advertisement attract you?
- Can you ignore TV commercials or do you always watch them?
- Do you look at pop-ups when they appear on websites or do you immediately close them?

49 The news: gathering and delivering

A Gathering the news

There are a number of different types of journalism: print journalism[1], broadcast journalism[2], online journalism[3] and, increasingly citizen journalism. This is where ordinary citizens use social media to report, photograph and share news with others.

Professional journalists gather news in a number of different ways. They may get stories from pressure groups[4] which want to air their views[5] in public. Journalists also attend press conferences[6] where politicians or others may issue a statement or press release[7]. A person seeking publicity[8] will try to include a soundbite[9] in what they say.

Journalists also hunt for[10] stories by tapping useful sources[11] and by monitoring[12] international news agencies like Reuters. The more important a story is, the more airtime[13] it will achieve and the more column inches[14] it will be given in the newspaper or on the webpage, in other words, the more coverage[15] it will receive.

[1] newspapers and magazines [2] radio and TV [3] news websites [4] people trying to influence what other people think about a particular issue [5] express their opinions [6] meetings to give information to and answer questions from the press [7] give a formal announcement to the press [8] wanting to reach a wider audience [9] short memorable sentence or phrase that will be repeated in news bulletins and articles [10] look for [11] making use of people or organisations which regularly provide news [12] regularly checking [13] minutes given to it on radio or TV [14] space [15] media attention

B Delivering the news

A rag is an informal word for a newspaper and it suggests that it is not of very high quality. The gutter press is a disapproving term used about the kind of newspapers and magazines that are more interested in crime and sex than serious news.

Journalists produce copy, which has to be ready for a deadline. When everything is ready, the newspaper goes to press.

Previous issues of a paper are known as back copies. These are usually accessible in an online archive.

A story that is only to be found in one newspaper is an exclusive or scoop. All newspapers or TV news channels hope to run a story that no one else has discovered. A major story can be said to hit the headlines on the day it is published. At that time, the story breaks or becomes public knowledge.

A newspaper may be taken to court for libel or defamation of character if it publishes an untrue story that, for example, wrongly accuses someone of something.

Journalists of different political persuasions will put their own gloss/spin on a story. [present it in their own way]

Some journalists gather stories by muck-raking. [collecting scandal]

Generally, newspapers like to make stories sound more dramatic by using words like heroic and triumph even for some occurrence that is quite ordinary. [happening, event]

Language help

Media is a plural noun and should be used with a plural verb: *The media are blamed for a number of social problems.* However, some people treat it as if it were a singular word: *Social media has/have had a huge impact on our lives.* Media is often used as an adjective in phrases like media reports/coverage/attention/interest/hype.

Exercises

49.1 Match the two parts of the collocations from the opposite page.

1 air	☐	a groups
2 issue	☐	b conference
3 muck	☐	c bite
4 press	☐	d journalism
5 pressure	☐	e raking
6 citizen	☐	f sources
7 sound	☐	g a statement
8 tap	☐	h your views

49.2 Fill the gaps with words from the opposite page.

I started my career as a journalist working as a reporter on the local [1]........................ in my home town. The first thing I had to do was to take over the role of agony aunt. This was quite difficult for an 18-year-old boy straight out of school! Still, I managed to produce enough [2]........................ – ten column [3]........................, in fact – and in time for my first [4]........................ . When that first column of mine [5]........................ to press, I felt extremely relieved and was so proud that I sent the link to the online [6]........................ to everyone I knew!

49.3 Answer these questions about the words and expressions in B opposite.

1 Would you write to a chief editor asking for a job on his or her 'rag'? Why / Why not?
2 What do you think about newspapers if you refer to them as the gutter press?
3 What is it very important for journalists not to miss?
4 What two words might describe the kind of story that a journalist dreams of getting?
5 What two expressions refer to the moment of publication of a big story?
6 Which two crimes are mentioned in B and what do they consist of?

49.4 Rewrite these sentences so that they mean the same thing, using the word in brackets.

1 Every news report inevitably gives its own particular view of events. (SPIN)
2 I have to find some articles from some previous editions of *The Times*. (BACK)
3 The TV news yesterday broadcast something about my favourite singer. (RAN)
4 The floods took up more space in the papers than any other story this week. (COLUMN)
5 Politicians are always ready and willing to give their opinions to the press. (AIR)
6 The story about the scandal surrounding her uncle broke on her wedding day. (HIT)
7 Any newspaper does all it can to prevent being sued for libel. (CHARACTER)
8 Muck-raking is a characteristic activity of an inferior kind of newspaper. (PRESS)

49.5 Choose the best word to complete each sentence.

1 The President will be holding a press *release / conference* this afternoon.
2 The story *broke / hit* last night when it was the first item on the TV news.
3 Politicians are usually not slow to seek *coverage / publicity*.
4 The story has had a lot of *print / media* attention.
5 The story received a lot of *airtime / soundbite* on the radio.
6 *Social / Print* media have encouraged the development of citizen journalism.
7 Ricky deserves to be called a *hero / rag* – he acted with great courage.
8 Unfortunately, muggings are an everyday *occurrence / triumph* in this part of town.

50 Healthcare

Healthcare professionals

Many professionals are trained to help people stay healthy and to treat health problems. **Primary care** is provided by the doctors (also known as **physicians**) or nurses who the patient goes to first when they have a problem. This may happen at the doctor's surgery or sometimes during a **home visit**. A **locum** is a doctor who does the job of another doctor who is ill or on holiday.

Most medical care, whether it is for an **acute condition**[1] or a **chronic** condition, is provided through the primary care system. **Secondary care** is provided by specialists in special clinics or hospitals. Patients are **referred to** a specialist by their doctor. These may specialise, for example, in a particular **organ**[2] or a specific age group. Specialists (what they specialise in is in brackets) include, among many others: **ophthalmologists** (eyes), **cardiologists** (heart), **psychiatrists** (the mind), **dermatologists** (skin), **gynaecologists** (women), **paediatricians** (children), and **anaesthetists** (**anaesthesia** or stopping people from feeling pain during surgery).

There are also healthcare workers who focus on what is sometimes referred to as **alternative medicine** or **complementary medicine**[3], including: **acupuncturists**[4], **chiropractors**[5], **homeopathic doctors**[6] and **aromatherapists**[7].

[1] one that can be cured through treatment
[2] part of the body
[3] approaches that differ from conventional western approaches
[4] /ˈækjʊpʌŋktʃərɪsts/ people who treat patients by using needles at special points around the skin
[5] /ˈkaɪrəʊpræktəz/ people who treat patients by pressing joints in places where two joints are connected, e.g. the **spine**, or backbone
[6] /ˌhəʊmiəʊˈpæθɪk/ doctors who use tiny amounts of natural substances to treat an illness
[7] /əˌrəʊməˈθerəpɪsts/ therapists who use aromatic oils and massage

Health systems

In Britain, **healthcare**[1] is paid for through taxes and **national insurance**[2] payments taken directly from wages and salaries. The government decides how much will be spent on the **National Health Service**[3], but a lot of people feel they do not spend enough. Hospital treatment and visits to a **family doctor** (or **GP**[4]) at a **surgery**[5] or **clinic**[6] are free, but there is often a **prescription charge**[7]. Private healthcare is available and a large number of **insurance schemes** exist to enable people to **'go private'**[8].

[1] general expression for all of the services offered by hospitals, clinics, dentists, opticians, etc.
[2] tax paid by most working adults which covers the costs of healthcare for everyone
[3] British name for the service that covers hospitals, clinics, dentists, etc.
[4] doctor who looks after people's general heath (GP = **general practitioner**)
[5] small centre offering primary care, run by a single GP or a group of GPs (*surgery* can of course also mean the branch of medicine that involves carrying out operations)
[6] centre which specialises in treating a particular condition or group of conditions
[7] charge for the medication the doctor prescribes, which you pay at a pharmacy
[8] choose private healthcare

Exercises

50.1 What kind of medical specialist is each of these people?

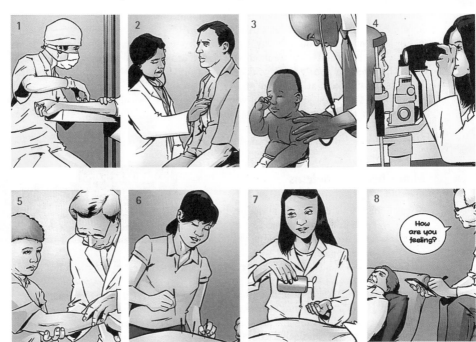

50.2 Choose a word from the box to complete each sentence.

> acute   chronic   condition   locum   organ   prescription   refer   surgery

1 I need to phone the .... to make an appointment for a blood test.
2 He suffers from .... bronchitis – it comes back year after year.
3 The doctor wrote me a .... for some painkillers.
4 The GP decided to .... Alex to a specialist.
5 Chris has a skin .... which is taking a long time to clear up.
6 I saw a very nice .... today because our normal GP was on leave.
7 The heart is the .... which pumps blood around our bodies.
8 Lydia had her appendix removed after an .... attack of appendicitis.

50.3 Correct the mistakes in the collocations in these questions about healthcare.

1 What is the name of your familiar doctor?
2 Is there a prescription price in your country?
3 In your country is there a similar structure of primary care and second care?
4 Do doctors often do home visitors in your country?
5 Are there insurance societies for private healthcare in your country?
6 When it comes to healthcare, do many people in your country make private?
7 How popular is complimentary medicine in your country?
8 Have you ever been to a specialist who practises some kind of alternating medicine?

50.4 **Over to you**

Now answer the questions in 50.3 for yourself. If possible, compare your answers with someone else.

51 Illness: feeling under the weather

A Feeling unwell

Some informal expressions that mean 'not well, but not seriously ill'.
A: You look a bit **off-colour** today. Are you all right?
B: I'm just feeling a bit **out of sorts**, it's nothing to worry about.
I was feeling a bit **under the weather**, so I stayed at home yesterday.
Katy's been **feeling poorly** for a while.
I'm **fighting off** a cold at the moment. [trying to get rid of]
Rani isn't in today; she's **gone down with** flu. [has caught, usually a non-serious illness]
I'm not going to work today. I've **come down with** a dreadful cold. (we say *come down* not *go down* with I)
Harry **suffers from** hay fever and sneezes a lot if he's near grass or flowers. [used for more long-term problems]

B Minor health problems

Note that **hurt** is different from **ache**.
My arm **hurts** where I banged it against the car door. [gives pain caused by an injury]
My back **aches** after all that digging yesterday. [persistent low-level pain]

> **Language help**
> You can call a physical pain a dull/nagging/throbbing ache but the noun hurt refers to emotional pain: *The break-up of their relationship caused them both deep hurt.*

The fixed expression **(the usual) aches and pains** is often used to refer in a non-serious way to minor problems.
Mum's feeling fine apart from the usual **aches and pains** (NOT ~~pains and aches~~).
The fixed expression **cuts and bruises** can refer to minor injuries. Jason had a few **cuts and bruises** when he fell off his bike, nothing serious (NOT ~~bruises and cuts~~).
Some other kinds of physical discomfort:
My hand's been **stinging** ever since I touched that plant. [sudden, burning pain]
My head is **throbbing**. [beating with pain]
I have a **stiff neck** from sitting in a draught yesterday. [pain and difficulty in moving your neck round]
She tripped on the uneven pavement and **twisted her ankle**. [injured by turning it suddenly]
I feel a bit **dizzy**. I think I should sit down. [a feeling that you are spinning round and can't balance]
She was a bit **feverish** this morning, so I told her to stay in bed. [with a high temperature/fever]
I feel quite **shivery / hot and cold**. I think I must have a temperature. [shaking slightly, usually because of a fever]
I've had a lot of **sleepless** nights recently. [without sleeping much]
I had a terrible **nauseous** feeling after taking the medicine, but it passed. [/ˈnɔːsiəs/ feeling that you want to vomit]
He was **trembling** all over; I knew it must be something serious. [shaking]
My nose is all **bunged up** today with this horrible cold. [blocked; *informal*]

C Getting better

I had a virus last week, but **I got over it** quite quickly. [got better, recovered]
Jo's **recovering from** a major operation. [getting better: used for more serious illnesses]
Dan felt terrible last week, but he's **on the mend** now. [getting better]
It's taking Hania some time to recover from her accident, but she's **over the worst** now. [past the most difficult period]
She'll **be back on her feet** again soon. [fully healthy again]

Exercises

51.1 Correct the mistakes in these sentences.

1 She was feeling out of the weather and a bit fevering so she took the day off.
2 I felt really off my colour yesterday and my head was throwing, so I took a painkiller.
3 I felt a bit off the sorts and seemed to have more pains and aches than usual.
4 Mo has back hurt after carrying that heavy suitcase of yours.
5 Gary has been fighting out cold for the last few days.
6 I'm sorry I won't make it to your party because I've gone down with flu.
7 Do you suffer of any allergies?
8 How did you get all those bruises and cuts?

51.2 Rewrite the underlined parts of these sentences using words and phrases from B opposite.

1 I was feeling quite as if I had a high temperature.
2 The smell of paint always made her feel that she wanted to vomit.
3 I felt as if my head was spinning, so I went and lay down for an hour.
4 My nose was blocked, so I got a spray from the chemist.
5 I got a pain in my neck from driving for a long time in an awkward position.
6 Joanna was feeling hot and cold and looked unwell, so I told her to go to bed.
7 My knee hurts today because I moved it awkwardly getting out of Andrei's sports car yesterday.
8 I didn't sleep at all last night.

51.3 Sort these everyday phrasal verbs and expressions connected with health and illness into two groups, depending on whether they have *positive* or *negative* meanings with regard to health.

suffer from   be over the worst   fight off   be on the mend
be back on one's feet again   get over   come down with   under the weather

positive	negative

51.4 Now fill the gaps using expressions from 51.3.

1 (*Someone speaking to a colleague just returned to work after an illness*) Hello, Dan, good to see you ....
2 (*Person ringing their place of work*) Nadja, I won't be in today, I've .... a cold.
3 (*Person in hospital, just beginning to get better, talking to a visitor*) Oh, I'm OK. I'm .... now. I still feel bad, but I should be out within a week or so.
4 (*Parent to a child with a cold*) Don't worry, darling. Everyone has a cold now and then. You'll .... it.
5 (*Someone ringing a workmate*) I'm trying to .... the flu, but nothing seems to help. I don't think I'll be at work tomorrow.
6 Hilary was quite ill last week, but she's .... now and should be back at work on Monday.
7 I feel a bit .... today, but I'm sure I'll be fine tomorrow.
8 I used to .... a dust allergy, but I don't think I do any more.

52 Medical language

A Medical information leaflets

Read these extracts from a leaflet included in a packet of painkillers.

Before taking this medicine, talk to your doctor or pharmacist if you:
- are taking **low-dose**[1] aspirin (up to 75 mg daily)
- suffer from **asthma**[2], or have a **past history**[3] of asthma
- have a connective tissue **disorder**[4]
- have a history of **gastrointestinal disease**[5] or suffer from **bowel**[6] problems
- are elderly as it increases the risk of **adverse reactions**[7]
- have heart problems, have had a previous **stroke**[8] or think you might be at risk of these **conditions**[9]

*DO NOT **EXCEED**[10] THE STATED DOSE OR **DURATION**[11] OF TREATMENT*

Like all medicines, these tablets may sometimes cause **side effects**[12] though not everybody gets them. Stop taking this medicine and seek medical help if you suffer from any of the following:
allergic reactions[13]
are sick and it contains blood or dark **particles**[14] that look like coffee grounds
pass blood in your **stools**[15]
stiff neck, headache, feeling sick (**nausea**), being sick (**vomiting**), fever and **disorientation** (not knowing where you are).

[1] measured amount of medicine that is relatively small [2] medical condition in which breathing becomes difficult because air passages have narrowed [3] record of medical conditions a person has experienced [4] illness of the body or mind [5] illness of the stomach or digestive passages [6] tube that carries solid waste out of the body [7] unwanted results [8] sudden change in blood supply to the brain causing loss of function of part of the body [9] illnesses or physical problems [10] take more than [11] length [12] unwanted effects in addition to the intended one [13] conditions affecting skin or breathing because of eating or coming into contact with certain substances [14] small pieces [15] medical term for **excrement** (formal) or **poo** (informal, childish)

B Medical metaphors

Social and other problems are often talked about as if they were illnesses.
symptom [medical meaning = problem indicating an illness]
The current spate of car thefts is a **symptom** of a deeper underlying problem.
This behaviour is **symptomatic** of his general lack of self-confidence.
The causes of a problem can be **diagnosed** and the outlook for a situation can also be referred to as the **prognosis**. [medical meaning = identify what illness a patient has] [medical meaning = how experts expect an illness to develop]
The medical meaning of the key word is given in brackets before the examples below.
[ailing = unwell, sickly] an **ailing** organisation [one that has a lot of problems]
The economy has been **ailing** for some time, but there are hopes of a recovery soon.
[rash = a lot of small red spots on the skin] a **rash of** burglaries [a number of similar things happening at the same time]
[fever = high temperature] World Cup **fever**, election **fever** [great excitement]
at **fever pitch**, to reach **fever pitch** [a point of very high intensity]
With a week to go before Anne's wedding, preparations had reached **fever pitch**.
[jaundiced = yellow-looking skin because of a liver problem] Experts in the history of the area take a rather **jaundiced** view of the likely success of the peace talks. [unenthusiastic or sceptical because of previous bad experiences]
[scar = mark left on skin after an injury such as a cut] **carry the scars of / be scarred by** [be permanently affected by a negative experience]
I'm afraid that children will always **be scarred by** experiencing war at a young age.
[infect = pass on an illness] I hope Helen's enthusiasm will **infect** everyone else. [pass on to]
[pulse = regular beating of heart, e.g. as felt on wrist] That journalist really **has his finger on the pulse** of public opinion. [understands how things are changing]

Exercises

52.1 **Choose the best word to complete each sentence.**

1 Anorexia is a serious eating *effect / disorder* in which a person tries to eat as little as possible.
2 The doctor asked me a lot of questions about my medical *history / story*.
3 Far more children these days are *asthmatic / allergic* to nuts than ever before.
4 It is important not to *overtake / exceed* the number of pills the doctor tells you to take.
5 Talk to your pharmacist if you suffer any *side / adverse* reactions to the tablets.
6 My grandfather had a *bowel / stroke* last year.
7 Doctors use the word stools but children talk about *poo / excrement*.
8 If you vomit, you *feel / are* sick.
9 *Disorientation / Disease* can be the result of a bang on the head.
10 Maria is not allowed to drive for the *duration / dose* of her treatment.

52.2 **Replace the underlined expressions with one of the metaphors from B. Make any other necessary changes.**

1 Excitement grew extremely strong as the day of the final match dawned.
2 Although industry is doing well in the north of the country, in the south it is weak.
3 The manager said that there had been a sudden large number of complaints about the hotel.
4 Unfortunately, she is still affected in a negative way by her divorce.
5 The problems we have experienced in our neighbourhood are evidence of wider problems in society.
6 What do you think the prospects are for the peace talks?
7 I voted for the Green Party because they seem to be in touch with what's happening.
8 The business has been having problems for some time now.
9 I'm afraid I have rather a sceptical view of the banking industry.

52.3 **The medical words in the box below are used metaphorically in the following text. Fill the gaps using these words. Use a dictionary if necessary.**

> ailing   fatal   disease   rash   paralysed   prognosis   fever   contagious

The country has been ¹............................ by the latest rail strike, with no rail services at all running today. The railway service has been ²............................ for some time, but if today's action is prolonged it may prove ³............................ to the rail industry. The Minister for Transport commented: 'The country has been suffering from a ⁴............................ of local strikes since the first one in Nortown last month. It was ⁵............................ and one strike led to another. Things reached ⁶............................ pitch last week and we can only hope that this ⁷............................ will come to an end soon.' The minister's ⁸............................ is that things will only start to improve once people appreciate the seriousness of the situation.

52.4 **Over to you**

Learn more medical vocabulary by going to the following website which provides information for people who want to learn more about a medical condition: www.nhsdirect.nhs.uk

53 Diet, sport and fitness

A Cholesterol and health

Our arteries circulate blood around the body and are essential to good health, but the blood flow can be **impeded**[1] by fatty **plaque**[2] that can **clog**[3] them. The production of plaque is associated with high levels of **cholesterol**[4] and clogged blood vessels can lead to a heart attack or a **stroke**[5]. Some foods, such as eggs and shellfish, while **nutritious**[6], are also **cholesterol-rich**, but, if eaten in moderation, do not significantly raise cholesterol levels or **pose a danger**[7]. 'Bad cholesterol' is counteracted by **fibre**[8] in our diet, and a **high-fibre** diet is often recommended by health experts. Fibre causes less fat to be absorbed by the blood vessels. Fibre-rich foods include fruit, vegetables, **lentils**[9], **oatmeal**[10], potatoes and wholemeal bread.

[1] slowed down or made difficult   [2] unwanted substance that forms on the surface of the arteries
[3] cause something to become blocked   [4] fatty substance found in the body tissue and blood of all animals   [5] sudden change in the blood supply to the brain causing loss of function of part of the body
[6] containing substances that your body needs to stay healthy (noun = **nutrition**)   [7] cause a problem
[8] substance in foods such as fruit, vegetables and brown bread, which travels through the body as waste
[9] very small dried beans that are cooked and eaten   [10] type of flour made from oats or a grain used to make **porridge** [a cooked breakfast cereal]

B Exercise and calories

One of the most efficient forms of **cardiovascular**[1] exercise is running or fast walking, which have been proved to have a positive effect in reducing cholesterol levels. This type of exercise lowers your blood pressure and can help **diabetics**[2] too by helping their **insulin**[3] work more effectively. Running or jogging is also a great way to **burn calories**, and you don't have to be excessively **sporty**[4]. Based on a calculation of your body weight in relation to the time you devote to an activity, a person who weighs 140 pounds (about 63 kilos) can burn 148 calories by jogging for 20 minutes. The same person doing half an hour of cycling at 15 mph (about 24 kph) could burn more than 330 calories. If you're **intent on**[5] losing weight, running, **brisk**[6] walking and fast cycling are excellent ways of doing so!

[1] relating to the heart and blood
[2,3] people suffering from **diabetes**, an illness in which the body cannot cope with **glucose** [sugar] because it does not produce enough **insulin** [hormone that controls the level of sugar in the body]
[4] good at or keen on sports
[5] determined to
[6] quick and energetic

C Sport and fitness metaphors

I **scored an own goal** when I told my boss it had only taken me a day to write the report. Now she wants me to write several a week. [made things worse rather than better]
My boss always seems to be **moving the goalposts,** which makes it very difficult to know what he wants. [changing the rules]
The new EU laws aim to provide a **level playing field** for all member states. [fair situation]
He's too young to be **in the running** for such a job. [seriously considered]
The two main parties in the election are still **neck and neck** in the opinion polls. [level with each other and equally likely to win]
Politicians often **skate around** a subject. [don't talk directly about]
The students all **sailed through** their exams. [passed very easily]

Exercises

53.1 Rewrite the underlined parts of the sentences using words and expressions from A and B opposite.

1 Eggs and shellfish are <u>full of substances that keep our bodies healthy</u>.
2 <u>Foods with a lot of cholesterol</u> are fine if eaten in moderation.
3 These foods do not necessarily <u>cause</u> a danger to health.
4 The most important thing is not to <u>slow down or prevent</u> the flow of blood.
5 Fatty plaque can <u>block</u> the arteries.
6 Scientists recommend a <u>diet with lots of fibre</u>.
7 Running is a good form of <u>exercise that affects the heart and blood circulation</u>.
8 <u>Fast</u> walking is also good for you.
9 Jogging is a great way to <u>use</u> calories.
10 To do enough of this kind of exercise, you don't have to be <u>a lover of sport or good at it</u>.

53.2 Answer the questions.

1 What two serious illnesses can result from clogged blood vessels?
2 What word could you connect to these words before the hyphen to mean 'with a lot of'?
............................-fibre ....-energy ....-calorie
3 What word could you connect to these words after the hyphen to mean 'with a lot of'?
protein- .... vitamin- ....
4 Why are lentils and oatmeal good for our diet?
5 What is another way of saying 'He is determined to do more exercise'?
6 Which people might be interested in helping their insulin to work more effectively?

53.3 What sports do each of the metaphors in C come from?

53.4 Rewrite these sentences using metaphors from C.

1 Elsa passed her exams without any difficulty at all.
2 I wish he'd get directly to the point.
3 I've been told that they are seriously considering me for the job of supervisor.
4 Although he meant it as a compliment, Rick didn't improve his chances with Helen when he told her she looked as if she had put on some weight.
5 The situation is hardly fair when 18-year-olds take the same exam as 15-year-olds.
6 It's hard to know what to do when the regulations seem to be constantly changing.
7 The two candidates are in exactly the same position in the race to become President.

53.5

Over to you

Answer the questions for yourself. If possible, compare your answers with someone else.

- How much exercise do you do every week?
- What type(s) of exercise do you do?
- Do you know how many calories you burn? (there are websites that tell you how to calculate this for the activities you do)
- What about diet? Do you think you could improve your diet? How?

54 Industries: from manufacturing to service

A Industries and industrial practices

expression	explanation	opposite expression	explanation
heavy industry	e.g. steel works, shipbuilding	light industry	e.g. manufacturing car parts, TV sets
manufacturing industry	making things, e.g. consumer goods	service industry	serving people, e.g. tourism, banking
high-technology (high-tech; *informal*) industry	involving computers, e.g. software industry	low-technology (low-tech; *informal*)	involving little or no computer technology
cutting-edge technology	involving new and innovative technology	conventional technology	using standard, proven technology
privatisation	e.g. selling off state railways to private companies	nationalisation / state ownership	when industry is owned by the government

Many big industries are run as **public-private partnerships.** [partly state-owned, partly owned by private industries or businesses]

The nuclear industry receives a huge **subsidy** from the government. [money/grants which enable it to stay in profit]

The government tries to encourage **inward investment.** [investment from foreign companies]

B Industrial practices

example	explanation
Most of the factory workers are on **piecework.**	they are only paid for the amount they produce
Child labour is a serious problem in some countries.	the employment of children to do adult jobs
In many countries, the right to **trade union representation** has only come after long struggles.	a union that negotiates wages and conditions for the people it represents
Many cheap electrical goods are produced in **sweatshops** in poorer countries.	factories where people work very long hours for low wages
Retraining and **reskilling** are necessary when an economy is modernised.	training people for new jobs and teaching them new skills

The big **multinationals**[1] often close factories as a **cost-cutting exercise**[2] and **relocate**[3] and **switch production**[4] to countries where labour and costs are cheaper.

In many cases, **components**[5] for cars are imported and then **assembled**[6] rather than manufactured in the country.

[1] big companies with operations in many different countries
[2] effort to reduce their costs
[3] move the company's offices (or, less commonly, production) to a different place
[4] move the centre of manufacturing to a different place
[5] parts
[6] put together

Exercises

54.1 Use expressions from the table in A opposite to rewrite the underlined parts of these sentences with more appropriate vocabulary.

1 The economy cannot depend only on <u>things like restaurants and hotels</u>. We need to encourage <u>industries that make things we can sell</u>.
2 In this area, there are a lot of <u>industries that use computers and things</u>, while in the north, they depend more on <u>industries that don't use such up-to-date technology</u>.
3 <u>The latest, innovative</u> technology is very expensive, so the company has to rely on <u>existing, standard</u> technology.
4 <u>The idea that industries should be owned by the government</u> is less popular than it was, but the trend towards <u>selling off these industries</u> has slowed down.
5 <u>Industry with big factories producing things like steel and so on</u> has declined, and now we're more dependent on <u>industry that makes things like radios and furniture</u>.

54.2 Give words or expressions which mean:

1 a combination of state ownership and private ownership
2 payment or grant from the government which enables a loss-making industry to continue
3 investment in a country by foreign companies
4 system of paying employees only for the amount they produce
5 an economy that depends on factories producing large quantities of cheap goods based on long hours and low wages
6 to change the location where goods are produced (*Give two answers.*)
7 to train people for new jobs and teach them new skills (*Give two answers.*)
8 a big company with operations in many different countries
9 an effort to reduce costs
10 using children to do adult jobs

54.3 Here are some more expressions relating to problems in industry. Make sure you know what they mean, then use them to fill the gaps in the sentences below. Use a dictionary if necessary.

> black market   copyright infringement   industrial piracy
> industrial espionage   money laundering

1 .... is a serious problem in many parts of the world, with factories producing illegal copies of top brand names.
2 It was a serious case of .... The designs for the new aircraft were photographed illegally and sold to a rival company.
3 .... is a problem for people who make a living writing books. Illegal editions mean that the author receives no payment.
4 .... is a huge international problem, as police and banks try to trace money from the illegal drugs trade and terrorism.
5 There is a big .... in the importation of untaxed luxury cars in some countries.

54.4

Over to you

Answer the questions for yourself. If possible, compare your answers with someone else.

- Have you worked, or do you see yourself working, in (a) a high-tech industry, (b) a service industry, (c) heavy industry? Describe your experience or say why you would like or not like to work in those environments.
- Would you buy an item if you believed child labour was involved in its manufacture? Why / Why not?
- What do you think of illegal imitations of famous designer brands? Would you buy such items? Why / Why not?

55 Technology and its impact

Technological advances affecting daily life

technology	examples of uses/ applications	example sentences with associated key words
digital technology	digital photography, digital video and audio recording; digital broadcasting	The sound quality of a **digital** tape recorder is superior to that of an **analogue** one. [non-digital]
wi-fi	a system for connecting electronic devices to the internet without using wires	The hotel has **wi-fi** in every room.
satellite communications	satellite navigation [SATNAV] systems; mobile phones	She doesn't use a road map now because her new car has **GPS** (global positioning system) built in, so she gave me her old plug-in **SATNAV**.
biotechnology	genetic modification of plants	**Biotechnology** companies are experimenting with new, **disease-resistant** crops for farmers. [with a high level of protection against diseases]
artificial intelligence (AI)	automatic translation; identification systems	Scientists working in **AI** are hoping to create computers that will be more and more like the human brain.
ergonomics	design of environments so people can work efficiently and comfortably	This car has **ergonomically designed** seats; they're very comfortable on long drives. [designed to give maximum comfort and efficiency]

B

How much of a techie* are you?

[* person who loves acquiring all the new technology]
Today we are all to some degree dependent on technology. How many of these things do you own or use?

a **smartphone** [a mobile phone that can be used as a small computer]
a **hands-free** earpiece and microphone for your mobile
a **smart ID card** for entering your workplace or college and using the facilities there

a **laptop (computer)** or **notebook**
a **desktop** computer for the home or office
an **MP3 player**
a **games console**
a **tablet** using a **touch screen** such as an iPad
an **e-reader** such as a Kindle
an **interactive flat-screen TV**
a **router** to let you connect to the internet from different devices

Language help

Technical (adverb = **technically**) means relating to the knowledge, machines and materials used in science and industry: *Removing the salt from sea water is a **technically** complex process.*
Technological (adverb = **technologically**) means relating to or involving technology: *Technologically, their company is a long way behind ours.* Note that technically – NOT technologically – can also be used to mean according to an exact understanding of the facts: *The recession is **technically** over but things are still difficult for many people.*

See also Unit 47.

Exercises

55.1 **Based on A opposite, what types of technology would you associate with the following?**

1 a round-the-world yachtsman/woman trying to establish his/her exact position
2 a designer creating a new type of computer keyboard which would be more efficient and comfortable to use
3 a scientist producing a new type of wheat which does not need to be sprayed against insects
4 a camera that does not use film
5 a computer that can make decisions for itself

55.2 **Which type of device in B opposite is the speaker talking about?**

1 I prefer it to my mobile because it's much bigger, but it's still not too heavy to carry around. I can Skype on it and take photos with it. I can access my emails wherever I am. I just can't make ordinary phone calls. ....
2 The picture is really good quality and it's fun being able to send in comments at the same time as you're watching a programme. ....
3 It's pretty small and light, but the screen and keyboard are not very big and I find the trackpad more awkward to use than a mouse. ....
4 I always use this rather than my laptop when I'm at home; I have it on a special table in my room next to my printer. ....
5 I used to have to take so many books when I went on holiday but now I don't need to. I just have to remember my charger! ....
6 I changed its position and now I can get online from any room in the house. ....

55.3 **Here are some other words and phrases connected with computers. Not all of them are on the opposite page. Fill the gaps in the sentences. Use a dictionary if necessary.**

> computer nerd   app   thumbnail   icon   screensaver   trackpad   techie   footprint

1 There are some good pictures of the Olympic Games on that sports website. You can look at .... pictures and then click on them to see the full-size version.
2 My younger brother's a real .... He never goes out, and all he ever thinks about is computers, computers, computers.
3 I'm a bit of a .... really; I love getting the latest mobile phone or digital camera.
4 I've downloaded a great new gaming .... onto my phone.
5 He has a really cool .... , which is a picture of planets, comets, stars and things all rushing towards you.
6 This new printer's got a smaller .... than the one I had before, which is good, since my desk is not very big.
7 Just click on that .... there to open the program.
8 I don't really like this .... on my laptop; I'd prefer a proper mouse.

55.4 **Complete the word beginning with 'techn...' in each sentence. Not all the words you need are on the opposite page.**

1 Karl got a good job as a lab techn........................... in the university.
2 In this country, young people techn........................... become adults at the age of 18.
3 Computer techn........................... makes huge advances every year.
4 Andrea has a very interesting techn........................... for remembering vocabulary.
5 Publicity photos of celebrities have usually been techn........................... enhanced.

55.5 **Over to you**

The language and terminology connected with computers changes very quickly. If you want to keep up with it, read computer advertisements in newspapers and magazines, or else visit the websites of well-known hardware and software manufacturers, and note any new vocabulary and how it is used.

56 Technology of the future

A Technology

Here are some things we are likely to see more of in the future.

smart buildings/ homes	computer-controlled buildings and homes where things like lighting, heating, security, etc. are completely automatic; the adjective **smart** can be used for anything that uses computers or information stored in electronic form (e.g. a smartphone, smart TV, smart car)
interplanetary travel and space tourism	travel to planets in outer space, either for exploration or for tourism
nanotechnology	science of developing and producing extremely small tools and machines by controlling the arrangement of atoms and molecules
keyhole surgery	medical operation in which a very small hole is made in a person's body to reach the organ or tissue inside

B The environment and nature

A **doomsday scenario** for the environment sees our **destiny** as a world choked with pollution where many plants and animals have become extinct. [the worst possible prediction, what will happen in the future] [the things that will happen to us in the future]

Many experts **foresee** a situation where traffic in **mega-cities** becomes completely **gridlocked**. [think that something will occur in the future] [cities of more than 10 million people] [unable to move at all]

The **population explosion** may lead to widespread food and water shortages. [rapid increase in population]

Genetic modification/engineering is already used to change fruit and vegetables so that they grow better. However, many people object to the idea of **genetically modified** (or **GM**) **food/ crops**. [changing genes] [food/crops created by changing the genes of the ingredients]

Gene therapy will be used to eradicate some diseases, thanks to our knowledge of **the human genome**. [changing genes in order to prevent disease or disability] [the 'map' or index of all the genes in a human being]

Some people **envisage** a world in which **designer babies** will be popular. [see a possible or probable situation in the future] [babies whose genetic characteristics are artificially created]

Cloning of animals, and even human beings, may become common. [making a genetically identical copy]

C Society and people

The breakdown of the traditional family structure has already occurred in some countries. In future, the **nuclear family**[1] may no longer be the main type of family unit, and more loosely defined relationships will develop. **Globalisation**[2] will increase, affecting how things are produced and sold, what we buy and how we communicate. The world has become a **global village**[3] and we will have more and more contact with other people in it. We may even make contact with **extraterrestrial beings**[4]. The **gulf**[5] between rich and poor nations will widen if we do not take **drastic measures**[6] now to improve the situation.

[1] family with father, mother and one or two children
[2] increase of trade around the world, with companies producing and trading goods in many different countries or the spread of similar social and cultural behaviour around the world
[3] a single community covering the whole world
[4] creatures from other planets
[5] gap/difference
[6] severe actions that have noticeable effects

Exercises

56.1 Match the words to make collocations.

1 gridlocked ☐   a explosion
2 genetic ☐   b village
3 human ☐   c traffic
4 population ☐   d genome
5 global ☐   e modification

56.2 Use the collocations in 56.1 to rewrite the underlined parts of the sentences.

1 Asia underwent <u>a dramatic increase in the population</u> in the latter part of the 20th century.
2 The crop had been subject to <u>having its genes altered</u>.
3 Since the advent of the internet, the world has become <u>one single community</u>.
4 <u>Times when the traffic cannot move</u> can cost the economy millions of pounds.
5 Scientists now understand <u>how the human genes are composed</u>.

56.3 What do we call …

1 a huge city with more than 10 million people? ....
2 medical operations where a very small hole is made in someone's body? ....
3 the science of making very small tools and machines by controlling atoms and molecules? ....
4 making an exact genetic copy of something? ....
5 creatures from other planets? ....
6 the process of altering human and animal genes? ....
7 the things that will happen to us in the future? ....
8 a baby whose genetic features have been chosen by its parents? ....

56.4 Rewrite the underlined words in these sentences using expressions from the opposite page.

1 The <u>worst possible prediction</u> is that we will destroy the world with nuclear weapons.
2 <u>Travelling to other planets</u> for scientific exploration will become normal in the coming centuries.
3 He belongs to a team of scientists who are trying to improve our understanding of the <u>index of all the genes in a human being</u>.
4 Governments need to <u>do things that will have a great impact</u> to save the planet.
5 Many people <u>see in their imagination</u> a world in which the poor simply get poorer. (*Give two answers.*)

56.5 Which words or phrases from the opposite page are associated with these sentences?

1 These tomatoes will stay fresh for several months. ....
2 A typical family is often said to consist of a husband, wife and 2.4 children. ....
3 This sheep is identical in absolutely every respect to the sheep standing next to it. ....
4 Thanks to this, doctors may be able to cure some genetic diseases. ....
5 The world is becoming a very small place in terms of economics and communication. ....
6 The company is planning to market two-week holidays on the Moon. ....

56.6

> **Over to you**
>
> Write five sentences under the heading *How I envisage the future*.
> Consider the future in terms of technology, the environment and society.
> If possible, compare your writing with someone else.

57 Energy: from fossil fuels to windmills

A Fossil fuels

Fossil fuels are sources of energy which were formed underground from plant and animal remains millions of years ago.
Several new **oil wells**[1] were constructed in the desert last year.
Offshore[2] drilling platforms explore the ocean bed for oil and gas.
Older **coal-fired**[3] power stations generally cause high levels of pollution.
The **coal mines**[4] in the north of the country are no longer profitable.
A new gas **pipeline**[5] was built to bring cheaper energy to the capital city.

[1] hole made in the ground for the removal of oil   [2] away from or at a distance from the coast
[3] using coal as a fuel   [4] deep hole or system of holes under the ground from which coal is removed
[5] very large tube through which liquid or gas can flow for long distances

B Renewable energy

Renewable energy is energy that can be produced again as quickly as it is used.

Onshore[1] **wind farms**[2] to get new government subsidies

Solar panels[3] to be installed on all government buildings

Hydroelectric[4] power station to be closed down

Biomass[5] not the answer, claims Energy Minister

Tidal power[6] and **wave power**[7] may meet future energy needs

Government to focus on **renewables**[8], Minister announces

Three new **nuclear**[9] power stations to be built

Geothermal[10] energy will last 1,000 years, says scientist

[1] on the land (*opp.* = **offshore**)   [2] group of wind turbines that are used for producing electricity   [3] devices that change energy from the sun into electricity   [4] producing electricity by the force of fast-moving water such as rivers or waterfalls   [5] dead plant and animal material suitable for using as fuel   [6] using the force of the sea tide to produce energy   [7] using the force of waves in the sea to produce energy   [8] note that **renewable** can also be used as a countable noun   [9] using the power produced when the nucleus of an atom is divided or joined to another nucleus   [10] using the heat inside the earth

Common mistake

Take care with the spelling of energy (NOT energie or energi).

C Using energy

What can ordinary citizens do to reduce energy **consumption**[1]? Some simple things include using fewer **power-hungry**[2] **appliances**[3] around the home, **monitoring**[4] your use of electricity and **consuming**[5] less energy by switching off unnecessary lights and entertainment systems that use power while on standby. Is your car a **gas-guzzler**[6]? Think about changing to a more **energy-efficient**[7] model. Think more about **food miles**[8] and buy local products so that fuel consumption in the transporting of goods is reduced. We can also reduce our **carbon footprint**[9] by planning travel more carefully and cutting out unnecessary journeys. Remember, the world's coal, oil and gas **deposits**[10] are **finite**[11]; one day they will run out, so think now about what you can do to consume less.

[1] how much is used of something   [2] that use a great amount of energy   [3] equipment, especially electrical equipment, used in the home, e.g. washing machines, fridges   [4] regularly watching and checking something over a period of time   [5] using (e.g. energy, time) especially in large amounts   [6] one that uses a lot of fuel; *informal*   [7] using only a little electricity, gas, etc.   [8] distance food is transported from where it is produced to when it reaches the consumer   [9] measurement of the amount of carbon dioxide that one's activities create   [10] layer formed under the ground, especially over a very long period   [11] having an end or lasting a limited time

Exercises

57.1 Choose words from the box to write labels for these pictures.

solar panels   wind farm   pipeline   offshore drilling platform   coal mine

1 ....   2 ....   3 ....

4 ....   5 ....

57.2 Rewrite the underlined parts of the sentences using words from A and B opposite. Make any other changes necessary.

1 A new 100-kilometre <u>metal tube</u> has been built to bring oil from <u>the holes in the ground for extracting oil</u> in the north of the country to a refinery on the coast.

2 The power station is <u>one that uses coal</u>, but it will soon be replaced by a <u>plant that uses atomic science</u>.

3 Fire has broken out on a drilling platform <u>in the sea</u>.

4 <u>Power from the tide or from waves</u> could solve the energy problems of countries with extensive coastlines. Other parts of the world may be able to use energy <u>from the heat inside the earth</u>.

5 '<u>Energy sources that can be renewed</u> are important,' the Prime Minister said. 'We intend to give grants for people to install <u>devices that turn the heat of the sun into electricity</u>, as well as developing <u>groups of turbines based on the land that use wind</u>.'

6 The country is developing two main energy sources: <u>the use of dead plant material</u> and power stations <u>that use the force of rivers</u>. At the same time, inefficient <u>deep holes for extracting coal</u> will gradually be closed.

57.3 Complete the sentences with words from C opposite.

1 We should consider the issue of .... when shopping for fruit and vegetables and try to buy local produce.

2 Most recent models of washing machines and other domestic .... use less power than older comparable models and are quite ....-................................ .

3 The company is trying to reduce its .... by allowing fewer foreign trips and encouraging the use of video-conferencing.

4 This car is a real ....-................................ . It has a very high fuel ....

5 We're .... our energy use at home and trying to .... less power.

6 The planet only contains a .... amount of oil and coal. One day the .... will run out.

57.4 **Over to you**

Write a short composition of about 75–100 words on the present and future energy sources your country uses now and is likely to develop in the future. Use words and expressions from this unit. If possible, compare your writing with someone else.

58 Space: no room to swing a cat

A Things occupying a lot of space

word	typical contexts of use	
extensive	Edinburgh has **extensive** traffic-free routes. The building contains **extensive** educational facilities.	
spacious	a **spacious** garden	The city of Washington is **spacious** and green.
roomy	a **roomy** car	The house was **roomy**.
rambling	a large, **rambling** building	a **rambling** mansion

I like Canada because I love **wide open spaces**. [large areas without buildings or trees]
Little white cottages were **scattered** across the landscape. [randomly across a wide area]
The problem with this university is that the buildings are rather **spread out** and it takes a long time to get from one place to another. [not close to one another]
Jack's bedroom is large with **ample room** for all his things. [more than enough space]

> **Language help**
>
> *Room can be used as an uncountable noun to mean space: Can you make room/space for me? There's plenty of room/space here. The sofa takes up a lot of room/space.*

B Insufficient space or things occupying too small a space

word	typical contexts of use	
cramped	**cramped** hotel rooms	living in small, **cramped** apartments
poky; *informal*	two **poky** little rooms	a **poky** little flat
congested	tanker traffic on the **congested** waterway the **congested** streets [full of traffic, people, etc.]	
compact*	a tiny, **compact** refrigerator	a **compact**, low, white villa

*Compact has positive connotations, whereas the other words in the table suggest negative connotations.

C Other words and expressions

I saw her at the carnival, but I couldn't get to her because I was **hemmed in** by the crowds. [surrounded by people and not able to move]
The city centre is always **bustling** with tourists at this time of year. [lots of people busily moving around]
There **isn't enough room to swing a cat** in his flat. [the flat is very small; *informal*]
We were **packed in like sardines** on the bus. [too many people in a small space; *informal*]
The government offices are an absolute **labyrinth**. [/ˈlæbərɪnθ/ vast and complex]
The river marks the **boundary** of the estate. [the edge of a large space]
We created more space by building an extension at the **rear** of our property. [back]
In these conversations, speaker B paraphrases what speaker A says. Note the verbs in bold.
A: There were 16 of us in a minibus that seated 10, and it was a long journey.
B: Yes, we were all **crammed into** that tiny space for over five hours!
A: There's not much room, is there? Can I sit between you and Mark?
B: Yes, you can **squeeze in** between us.
A: You've invited a lot of people to your party and it's only a small room.
B: Yes, it might be a bit of a **squash**!
A: Shall I put all those old papers into this rubbish bag?
B: Yes, just **stuff** them all **in** and we'll take it away later. (it suggests doing something quickly and without much care)

Exercises

58.1 Choose the most likely word from the box to fill the gaps, based on the typical contexts given in A and B opposite.

> compact   cramped   spacious   poky   extensive   roomy

1 You'd never get me to live in that .... little flat!
2 I'd prefer a .... car on a long journey.
3 This camera is nice and .... You can hide it in your pocket and not look like a tourist.
4 Her mother lived in a rather .... one-room apartment near the park.
5 The city centre is beautifully .... with many wide open squares.
6 The capital city has a(n) .... underground railway network.

58.2 How (not) to sell a house. Imagine you are an estate agent writing a description of a house for sale. Decide which of the words in italics is most suitable to persuade someone to buy the house. Use a dictionary for any words you are not sure of.

10 Kingsmead Road, Letchwood

The property is *rambling / spacious / a labyrinth*, with a *cramped / compact / poky* garden, and is situated only ten minutes away from the *bustling / congested / crowded* town centre. There are *excessive / extensive / expensive* leisure facilities nearby. Shops, banks, restaurants and other services are located in the pleasantly designed neighbourhood. Viewing by appointment.

Offers in the region of £620,000.

58.3 Rewrite the sentences using the words in brackets.

1 The kitchen is so small you can hardly move in it. (CAT)
2 There's plenty of space for your clothes in this wardrobe. (AMPLE)
3 I couldn't get out of my space in the office car park the other day. (HEMMED)
4 Holidays in Australia are great if you love vast landscapes without any towns. (OPEN)
5 I hate the London underground during rush hour. Everyone is pressing against one another in the trains. (SARDINES)
6 I dropped a glass and tiny pieces went all over the floor. (SCATTER)
7 The buildings in the holiday complex cover a wide area. (SPREAD)
8 The train was very full but I just managed to get on before the doors closed. (SQUEEZE)

58.4 Using words from B and C opposite, rewrite the underlined parts of these sentences.

1 There might be a lot of people on the bus at this time of day – I hope you don't mind.
2 I quickly put a few clothes and a couple of books in a rucksack and set off at once.
3 The Urals Mountains are what separates Europe from Asia.
4 We'll all have to try and fit into my little car; Larry hasn't got his with him today.
5 Your room is at the back of the hotel, so you won't hear any traffic.
6 I don't think we should try and fit everything into one suitcase. Let's take two.

59 Time: once in a blue moon

A Colloquial expressions relating to time

We only meet **once in a blue moon.** [very infrequently]
He's spent **all his born days** in the village. [all his life]
I'll be with you **in a mo / in a sec / in a tick / in less than no time / in a jiffy.** [very soon] (**mo** and **sec** are short for 'moment' and 'second')
Clive's been working here **for donkey's years / since the year dot.** [for a long time]
We can talk about this **till the cows come home,** but I'm not going to change my mind. [for ever]
Are you sure she gave you the book **for keeps / for good**? [to keep for ever]
She turned up just **in the nick of time** – she very nearly missed the train. [only just in time]
He was a famous athlete but now he's **over the hill / past it.** [too old]
She was a child film star but was already a **has-been** by the age of 20. [person who is no longer famous]
Sue did her homework **in a flash / at a rate of knots.** [very quickly]

Once in a blue moon

B Adjectives relating to the passing of time

adjective	meaning	common collocations
fleeting	brief or quick	glimpse, visit, smile, moment, appearance
lengthy	continuing for a long time	process, investigation, discussions, negotiations, delays
transient	lasting for only a short time; *formal*	effect, population, feeling, pleasure
persistent	lasting for a long time or hard to stop or get rid of	cough, problems, rumour, smell, accusations, critic, offender, failure, gossip
inexorable	continuing without hope of being stopped; *formal*	rise, slide, decline, pressure, advance of time
incipient	just beginning; *formal*	panic, rage, rebellion, stages, wrinkles, dementia
protracted	lasting for a long time or made to last longer; *formal*	negotiations, discussions, argument
lingering	taking a long time to leave or disappear	perfume, kiss, smile

C Other useful time words

Terrorists carried out **simultaneous** attacks on three places in the capital city. [happening at the same time]
Schools were closed for the **duration** of the President's visit. [amount of time that it lasted]
We should not **prolong** the meeting; we've already discussed the matter for an hour. [make it last longer]
I'm sorry, I can't change the date **at such short notice.** [just a short time before it is due to happen]
The teacher **repeatedly** warned the student that she would fail her exam. [many times]

Exercises

59.1 Put the words in the correct order to make sentences.

1 since / they've / same / living / the / house / year / the / been / in / dot
2 you / sec / I'll / with / a / in / be
3 to / keeps / Magda / it / John / for / gave
4 no / we / time / in / together / get / less / can / done / it / than
5 never / all / he's / his / been / than / nearest / born / town / further / days / in / the
6 nick / we / hospital / got / in / to / time / the / of / the

59.2 Which of the adjectives in B would you be most likely to use to describe the following?

1 a scent that remains in the room after its wearer has left
2 a feeling of joy that is short-lived
3 criticism that seems to go on and on
4 a headache that is beginning
5 a process that takes a long time
6 the never-ending ageing process – you can't stop its progress
7 a grin that lasts only for a moment
8 an investigation that takes a long time to complete

59.3 Match the adjectives on the left with the words on the right to make collocations.

1 lingering	☐	a events
2 fleeting	☐	b population
3 incipient	☐	c glimpse
4 inexorable	☐	d smile
5 persistent	☐	e peace negotiations
6 simultaneous	☐	f refusal
7 protracted	☐	g stages
8 transient	☐	h advance of time

59.4 Rewrite these sentences so that they keep the same meaning, using a form of the word in brackets.

1 We'll be ready to leave in a mo. (less)
2 Most of the members of the band may be in their sixties, but they're certainly not past it. (hill)
3 You can argue with him for ever, but he'll never see sense. (cow)
4 Kit promised he'd get here at a rate of knots and he kept his word. (flash)
5 I've told her many times not to phone me at work. (repeat)
6 The two events happened at the same moment. (simultaneous)
7 The hotel staff were very good; they let me cancel the reservation just a short time before. (notice)
8 I didn't want to make the meeting last longer. (long)
9 He had his moment of fame. Now he's no longer famous. (be)
10 The press were excluded during the delicate negotiations. (duration)

59.5

Over to you

Answer the questions for yourself.

- Would you like to work for the same company for donkey's years?
- What could you personally do happily till the cows come home?
- Do you think it's a good thing to spend all your born days in one place?
- Can you think of one thing that you do once in a blue moon?

60 Motion: taking steps

A Verbs of movement

verb	type of movement	reasons for type of movement
limp	uneven	one leg hurts
hop	on one foot, quickly	not using one foot
stagger	unsteady	drunk, ill
stumble	nearly falling	uneven surface
lurch	sudden or irregular	drunk, ill, walking on moving ship, etc.
tiptoe	quiet and on toes	not to be heard
amble	easy, gentle	pleasure or relaxation, no special aim
stride	long steps	purposeful
strut	proud, chest held out	to look important
tramp	firm, heavy steps	walking for a long time
trample	pressing repeatedly with feet	often wishing to destroy
stamp	pushing foot down heavily	anger, or just heavy-footed
trudge	heavy, slow, with difficulty	tired
chase	quickly	wanting to catch something or someone

B Metaphorical examples of motion

The maths lesson **limped** to a conclusion and everyone thankfully left the room.
Let's **hop** off the bus at the next stop. [quickly get off]
Miguel's business **staggered** on for a few years and then finally collapsed.
Lisa did **staggeringly** well in her exams. [amazingly]
The government has **lurched** from one economic crisis to the next.
Maria **takes** everything that life throws at her **in her stride**. [takes ... calmly]
Parents and teachers should try not to **trample** on children's dreams.
If the Campbells don't pay their bill this week, you'll have to **chase** them.
After several **stumbling** attempts at writing, Tom finally had a poem published.

C People and water move in similar ways

Crowds of tourists **flowed** across the square all day long.
As soon as the school doors opened, children **spilled** out into the playground.
People **streamed** into the lecture hall and soon there was standing room only.
People have been **pouring** into the exhibition all day.
A **trickle** of people appeared outside and by midday a crowd had gathered.
We **meandered** round the town, window shopping to our hearts' content.
Refugees have been **flooding** across the border since the start of the war.

D Taking steps

When you walk you **take (foot)steps**. Here are some adjectives often used with **taking (a) step(s)** in a metaphorical context.

backward   big   critical   decisive   first   giant
major   significant   **unprecedented** [never having happened before]

Common mistake

When talking metaphorically, people take **backward/decisive**, etc. steps (NOT ~~footsteps~~).

Exercises

60.1 The walking verb in each of these sentences is incorrect. Which verb would be a better choice for each sentence? Look at A to help you.

1 The old man strutted wearily homeward, his shoulders hunched in the rain.
2 The mother trudged across the bedroom doing her best not to wake the baby.
3 Look at all those baby rabbits stamping across the field!
4 Ever since he had an accident last year, he has stamped a bit.
5 The drunken men strode unsteadily out of the pub at closing time.
6 Please try not to stumble on the daisies – they look so pretty in the grass.
7 The small dog tramped after the postman and caught his trouser leg in his teeth.
8 The sea was so rough that even the sailors were tiptoeing around the decks.

60.2 Answer these questions about the sentences in B opposite.

1 How successful and enjoyable was the maths lesson?
2 Did Miguel's business come to a sudden end?
3 Did people expect Lisa to do so well in her exams?
4 Does the government seem to take each crisis smoothly and purposefully?
5 What kind of person do you think Maria is?
6 What do parents and teachers do to children's dreams if they trample on them?
7 How exactly might this person chase the Campbells?
8 How confident were Tom's first attempts at writing?

60.3 Look at the water words in each of the example sentences in C. What does the word suggest about the way the people in those sentences are moving?

60.4 Complete these sentences with a word from C, using the appropriate form.

1 The new traffic system allows vehicles to .... across the city without major disruptions.
2 There were such a lot of people at the talk that some were .... out into the corridor.
3 When I have a day off, I like to .... around town without a care in the world.
4 We expected to be very busy during the sale, but there was just a .... of people throughout the day.
5 As soon as the gates opened, people started .... into the football stadium. (*Give two answers.*)

60.5 Here are some more verbs of movement. Complete a table for them like the one in A opposite. Use a dictionary if necessary.

verb	type of movement	reason for type of movement
file		
saunter		
sidle		
glide		
mill around		

60.6 Which of the verbs in exercise 60.5 would these people probably do?

1 graceful dancers ....
2 guests at a cocktail party ....
3 schoolchildren going into a classroom ....
4 someone who is irritatingly anxious to make you like them ....
5 tourists exploring a city in a relaxed way ....

61 Manner: behaviour and body language

A Manners

Courtesy is still important nowadays. [politeness and respect]

The teacher said her Asian students were always very **courteous**. [polite and respectful]

She addressed the customer in a very **discourteous** manner. [impolite and lacking respect]

I hope I didn't appear **offhand** with her – it's just that I was in such a hurry. [showing a rude lack of interest in others]

The boy had an **insolent** expression on his face which irritated me. [rude and not showing respect (much stronger than discourteous)]

What's the **etiquette** at a traditional Chinese wedding? Do you know? I've had an invitation to one. [set of rules or customs for accepted behaviour in particular social groups or social situations]

Here, have a seat. Relax. There's no need to **stand on ceremony**. [behave in a formal way]

My elderly uncle and aunt are both rather **straitlaced**. [having old-fashioned and fixed morals]

Asking for more food at a formal dinner party is just not **the done thing**. [what you are expected to do in a social situation]

For the older generation, **netiquette** often includes using normal sentence punctuation in electronic communication. [code of behaviour when using the internet]

> **Language help**
>
> *Manners*, meaning the way we behave with one another socially, is plural: *We need to employ staff with good manners* (NOT good manner). *Manner* (singular) is a more formal alternative to 'way (of doing something)': *He greeted everyone in a friendly manner.*

B Body language and non-verbal language

Research shows that we communicate more through body language and non-verbal noises than we are aware. Here are some examples of how we indicate emotion through our non-verbal behaviour.

verb/expression	what it indicates	comment
raise your eyebrows	surprise or shock (either showing or causing)	either a person or behaviour can raise eyebrows
twitch	nervousness	repeated small movements with part of the body
flinch	pain or fear	sudden small movement
squirm	embarrassment or nervousness	move from side to side in an awkward way
smirk	self-satisfaction	smile (negative associations)
beam	happiness	broad smile (positive associations)
sniff at something	disapproval	breathe air in through your nose in a way that makes a noise
snort	disgust or great amusement	make an explosive sound by forcing air quickly up or down the nose
titter	nervousness or embarrassment	small laugh

Exercises

61.1 Complete the sentences with words from A opposite.

1 A light kiss on each cheek is the .... thing in some cultures when you meet someone you know.
2 Some people don't seem to follow any kind of .... when posting messages on social network sites and often post offensive or bullying material.
3 She was very .... and hardly looked at me when she replied.
4 Joanna and David always taught their children to have good ....
5 We don't stand on .... in this house – just help yourself to anything you want from the fridge.
6 I'm sick of your .... comments. It's time you learnt to speak politely to people. You're so rude!
7 For a young person, she's very .... and old-fashioned in her ideas and behaviour.
8 The school considers it important that students should always address their teachers in a .... manner. Anyone who behaves in a .... way will be reported to the Director.

61.2 Answer these questions.

1 *Bill was twitching all evening.* Do you think he was relaxed?
2 *Kate sniffed at every comment I made at the meeting.* How did Kate feel about my comments?
3 *Jack flinched when I touched his arm.* Why do you think he flinched?
4 *The teenagers' behaviour on the bus raised a few of the other passengers' eyebrows.* What must the teenagers' behaviour have been like?
5 *Look at the photo; Meg's smirking and Tanya's beaming.* Who does the speaker think looks nicer – Meg or Tanya?
6 *There was an occasional titter at the comedian's jokes.* Do you think the comedian was pleased at how his jokes were received?
7 *Ritva squirmed in her chair when Karl said her photo was in the paper.* How do you think Ritva felt?
8 *Their children had dreadful table manners.* How do you think the children behaved during meals? What sorts of things did they probably do?

61.3 Choose the best word to complete each of these sentences.

1 Brendan *sniffed / snorted* with laughter all through the play.
2 Whenever I'm tired or nervous, my eyelid starts to *twitch / flinch*.
3 Don't keep *squirming / smirking* in your chair like that – sit still and behave yourself.
4 The students *twitched / tittered* when the teacher tripped over the wastepaper basket.
5 The dentist stopped drilling as soon as he felt me *flinch / snort*.
6 She *twitched / beamed* with happiness all through the wedding ceremony.

61.4 Draw lines connecting the words and expressions on the right with the parts of the body mostly involved in the behaviour.

eyes   mouth   nose
no specific part of the body

snort   titter   smirk   twitch
raise your eyebrows   beam
squirm   flinch   sniff

61.5 *Over to you*

Imagine that someone who is going to live and work in your country asks you about what is considered to be good/bad manners and about codes of etiquette in your culture. What things would you consider important to tell them?

62 Sounds: listen up!

A Adjectives indicating lack of sound and their collocations

word	definition/explanation	example
silent	without noise or not talking; used for people and things that are perhaps unexpectedly or surprisingly quiet	They asked him several questions but he remained **silent**. The house was completely **silent**. **silent films/movies** [films made before sound was introduced]
quiet	without much noise or activity, or not talking much	It's very **quiet** here at night. [no noise] I had a **quiet** day at work. [not much activity] My dad was a **quiet** man. [didn't speak a lot]
noiseless	without noise (usually used as an adverb in formal or literary style)	He closed the door **noiselessly** behind him. [with no sound at all]
soundless	without sound (usually used as an adverb in formal or literary style to indicate an unexpected lack of sound)	The object vanished **soundlessly** into the night sky. Was it an alien spacecraft?

B Verbs for describing specific noises

The door **slammed** in the strong wind. [closed with a loud bang]
My bike wheel is **squeaking**. I need to get some oil. [high, irritating noise]
We could hear our neighbours' favourite rock music **pounding** through the walls. [dull, beating sound]
The old wooden door **creaked** as I opened it. [noise of friction of wood and/or metal]
The sausages **sizzled** in the frying pan and smelt delicious. [sound made by frying]
A shot **rang out** and the bird fell from the sky. [typically used for the sound of a gunshot]
From our cottage, we could hear the waves **crashing** on the beach below. [loud, heavy noise, typically used for waves]
He always **hoots/toots** his horn to let us know he's arrived. [sound made by a car horn]
I could hear police car sirens **wailing** all last night. [making a rising and falling sound]
She **hammered** at the door but nobody answered. [knocked very loudly and repeatedly]

C Some adjectives for noise and silence

There was an **eerie** silence in the old church. [rather scary]
The noise of the aircraft engines was **deafening**. [extremely and painfully loud]
He has one of those **grating** voices that gets on my nerves. [unpleasant, irritating]
She let out a **piercing** scream and fled as fast as she could. [high noise that hurts the ears]
Zara has a very **high-pitched** voice; it can be a bit irritating at times. [higher than most voices, like a whistle]
The recording was very faint, almost **inaudible**. [impossible to hear]

D Some fixed expressions connected with noise and silence

Everyone was so shocked and silent, **you could have heard a pin drop**. [there was total silence]
Hey you kids! Be quiet! **I can't hear myself think!** [said when people are making too much noise]
I need **peace and quiet** after a busy day at work. [calm and quiet period, after a noisy time]
You're **as quiet as a mouse**! I didn't hear you arrive at all. [very quiet indeed]

Exercises

62.1 Fill the gaps with appropriate forms, adjectives or adverbs, of the words *silent, quiet, noiseless* or *soundless*. Only *silent* may be used more than once.

1 This luxury car prides itself on its almost .... engine.
2 It's very difficult to find a .... place to live nowadays, even in the countryside.
3 Charlie Chaplin's .... films are as funny today as they were in the 1920s.
4 The great bird flapped its wings and rose .... into the evening sky.
5 The women kept up a .... protest in front of the laboratories.

62.2 Write a sentence which could come immediately before the following sentences, using verbs from the box and the word(s) in brackets, as shown.

slam   pound   creak   crash   sizzle   ring out   toot   squeak   wail

1 (door) ...... *The door slammed loudly.* ....
The wind must have blown it shut.
2 (shot) ....
Somebody was firing at the birds on the lake.
3 (door) ....
It was very old, made of oak and difficult to open.
4 (music, walls) ....
It was as if the musicians were playing in our bedroom.
5 (chicken, frying pan) ....
The sound and the smell made me even more hungry.
6 (rusty door hinges) ....
I think they need some oil.
7 (horn) ....
I looked out of the window and saw her car parked outside.
8 (waves) ....
It was wonderful to be so near the sea.
9 (police sirens) ....
There must have been an accident, or perhaps a robbery.

62.3 Which adjective can describe the following? The first letter is given.

1 An extremely loud noise, e.g. very loud music   d............................
2 A strange, almost scary silence   e............................
3 A high noise that hurts your ears   p............................
4 A harsh, irritating kind of voice   g............................
5 A voice that has a similar tone to a whistle   h........................-p............................
6 A whisper that is almost impossible to hear   i............................

62.4 Complete these expressions.

1 It was so quiet you could have ....
2 I've had some noisy, hectic days with all those kids, now I'm looking forward to some
....
3 Turn that music down! I can't .... !
4 I don't even notice that Jack is in the flat sometimes. He's ....

63 Weight and density

A Synonyms for *heavy*

There are a number of adjectives similar in meaning to *heavy*. Note their typical contexts.

adjective	typical contexts	example
weighty	abstract and physical things; usually includes the idea of 'seriousness'	a **weighty** tome [large book] discuss **weighty** issues
unwieldy	abstract and physical things; usually includes the idea of 'difficult to handle'	**unwieldy** system/bureaucracy an **unwieldy** object, e.g. a big box
cumbersome	often used for machines and equipment that are difficult to handle; also used for systems, structures, etc.	a **cumbersome** weapon a **cumbersome** process
burdensome	usually used of abstract things	a **burdensome** duty
ponderous	slow and clumsy because of weight but usually used for dull and excessively serious abstract things	a **ponderous** style, e.g. way of writing or speaking a **ponderous** thesis
lumbering	usually used of physical things; often suggesting 'heavy movement'	a **lumbering** truck a **lumbering** bear

B Phrasal verbs with *weigh*

I hate being **weighed down** with heavy suitcases when I travel. [carrying very heavy things] She looked tired and **weighed down** with problems.
We'll have to **weigh up** the alternatives before deciding. [consider and compare]
She **weighed out** a kilo of nuts and put them in a bag. [weighed a quantity of loose goods]
I have to confess something to you. It's been **weighing on me** for ages. [troubling my mind]
The discussion was getting heated, and then Kate **weighed in** with some uncomfortable financial arguments. [added more points to the argument]

C Making things more/less dense

You can put some flour in to **thicken** the soup, but you should **sift** it first, or it will go **lumpy**. [make thicker] [shake it in a sieve to separate the grains] [have solid pieces in it]
The soup has been in the fridge so long it's all **congealed**. [become thick and solid]
This curry powder is years old. It has completely **solidified** in the packet. [become solid]
Do you have some white spirit? I need to **thin** this paint. [make thinner]
As the rush hour ended, the traffic began to **thin out**. [become less dense]
The hairdresser **thinned** my hair **out** and it feels much lighter now. [made it less thick]
This fruit juice is very strong. Let's **dilute it / water it down** a bit. [add water]

D Adjectives connected with density

Many of the words above can be used both literally and metaphorically. More examples:

word	meaning	literal use	metaphorical use
impenetrable	impossible to move through	an **impenetrable** jungle/forest	**impenetrable** jargon
impervious (to)	liquid cannot pass through	an **impervious** material, e.g. glass	a person who is **impervious** to criticism

Exercises

63.1 Based on the typical contexts in A opposite, use the words in the box below to fill the gaps in the sentences. There may be more than one possible answer.

> lumbering   cumbersome   weighty   unwieldy   burdensome   ponderous

1 Applying for a visa is often a rather .... process and can mean filling in long, difficult forms.
2 He gave a very .... lecture on economic history that just bored everyone.
3 It is a really .... historical novel of over 1,000 pages, but it manages to instruct and entertain.
4 Seeing a great .... herd of elephants was the highlight for the tourists on safari.
5 She had so many .... obligations; her life was not her own.
6 The exam system was being increasingly criticised for becoming .... and overly bureaucratic.

63.2 Fill the gaps with a word from A that could collocate with all three nouns.

1 .... dinosaur / vehicle / goods train

3 .... encyclopedia / topic / issue

2 .... equipment / procedure / suitcase

4 .... tone of voice / sermon / narrative

63.3 Correct the wrong uses of phrasal verbs with *weigh* in these sentences.

1 I weighed on a kilo of flour and then added water to it.
2 He's very irritating. When you're trying to have a rational discussion, he always has to weigh through with his own selfish point of view.
3 I owe Gina £250; it's been weighing over my mind for weeks. I must pay her back.
4 We were weighed up with huge suitcases and bags, and the airport was terribly crowded; it was a nightmare.
5 I have to weigh in the various options before I decide which job to accept.

63.4 Answer these questions.

1 What does a hairdresser use thinning-out scissors for?
2 If there is dense fog, then it gets even denser, what verb could you use to describe the change?
3 What happens if you leave some coffee in the bottom of your cup for about a week?
4 What does 'Do not drink undiluted' mean on the instructions on a bottle of juice? What must you do before drinking it?
5 What might you sift when you are cooking?
6 If someone is impervious to insults, is it easy to upset them by calling them stupid?
7 If something is 'unwieldy', is it likely to be large or small?
8 If someone says a book is 'impenetrable', what do they mean?
9 What do you think it means to say that someone's philosophy is 'rather lightweight'?
10 Which verb can be used to describe a situation where heavy traffic is becoming less heavy?

64 All the colours of the rainbow

A Words and expressions for specific colours

pitch black: intensely black, used about darkness, night, etc. (**pitch** is an old word for tar)
jet black: intensely black, used about hair, eyes, etc. (**jet** is a black semi-precious gemstone)
scarlet: very bright red
crimson: strong deep red
shocking pink: an extremely bright pink
ginger: orangey red, used about hair and cats
navy: dark blue, used about clothes, not eyes
turquoise: greenish blue, used about fabrics, paint, sea, etc. but not usually eyes
lime: a bright yellowish green
beige: a light creamy brown
mousy: a light not very interesting brown, used only about hair
chestnut: a deep reddish brown, used about hair and horses
auburn: a red-brown colour, usually used about hair
A number of words for gemstones are also used as colour adjectives, e.g. **ruby** [deep red], **emerald** [bright green], **amber** [yellowy orange], **coral** [orangey pink], **sapphire** [deep blue], **jade** [dark green].

B Words for talking about colour

Red, blue and yellow are **primary colours**; by mixing them together you can make other colours. **Pastel colours** are pale shades of colour – pink, **mauve** [pale purple] and pale yellow, for example. **Strong colours** are the opposite of pastels. **Harsh colours** are colours that are unpleasantly strong. **Vivid colours** are strong, bright colours like scarlet or turquoise. **Fluorescent** colours are very bright colours which seem to glow in the dark. **Electric** blues or greens are extremely bright blues or greens. If white has a **tinge** of green, there is a very slight shade of green in it. If something is **monochrome**, it uses only one (or shades of one) colour, e.g. black, white and grey. The suffixes -y and -ish show that a colour is partly present, e.g. **bluey green, reddish brown**.

C Colour metaphors

blue = depression (to **feel blue**); physical or unskilled (**blue-collar workers**)
red = anger (to **see red** = to be very angry); danger (**red alert**, a **red flag**); special importance (All the competitors were given the **red-carpet** treatment. The day we met will always be **a red-letter day** for me.); communist or very left-wing in politics (People's views sometimes become less **red** as they get older.)
green = nausea (to **look green**) (People who are seasick often **turn/go green** and sometimes vomit.); envy (She turned **green with envy** when she saw her friend's new car.); care for the environment (**green tourism; the Green Party**)
black = depressing or without hope (a **black future**); anger (to look **as black as thunder**); illegality or incorrectness (**black market, black sheep of the family, black mark**) (During the war people bought many goods illegally on the **black market**. If I don't finish this report in time, that'll be another **black mark** against my name. My brother was the **black sheep** of the family, leaving school and home at the earliest opportunity.)
grey = lack of clarity (a **grey area**); brains (**grey matter, grey cells**)
white = purity (**white as snow, whiter than white**); being pale (She was so shocked that she went **white as a sheet**.); a **white-knuckle** [terrifying] ride at an amusement park such as Disneyland; office workers (**white-collar workers**)

Exercises

64.1 Match the colour to the picture it is most likely to be used about.

> navy   scarlet   ginger   pitch black   turquoise   chestnut

1   2   3   4   5   6

64.2 Put the words in the box under the best heading.

> ruby   emerald   coral   sapphire   lime   scarlet   navy
> jade   crimson   turquoise

red	blue	green

64.3 Answer these questions about the words in B.

1 Which of the following is not a pastel colour?
   A mauve   B pink   C scarlet
2 Which of the following colours can't be described as electric?
   A black   B green   C blue
3 Which of the following colours is a primary colour?
   A green   B orange   C yellow
4 If a speaker comments that a lipstick is rather a harsh red, what does the speaker think of the lipstick?
   A She likes it.   B She doesn't like it.
   C We don't know – she's stating a fact not giving an opinion.
5 Which is the closest synonym of a bright pink material?
   A a material with a tinge of pink   B a vivid pink material   C a pinkish material

64.4 Look at C opposite. Match the situations on the left with the responses on the right.

1 That child looks a bit green. ☐
2 He seems to have the blues most days. ☐

3 That TV programme always makes him see red. ☐
4 It's a bit of a grey area, isn't it? ☐
5 They seem to be trying to blacken his name. ☐

6 Do you like white-knuckle rides? ☐
7 White-collar workers earn more. ☐
8 They're going to vote for the Green Party. ☐

a No, they make me feel sick.
b Yes, it's not at all clear what we should do.
c Yes, but they need qualifications.
d I think he's going to be sick.
e Yes, they want to do their bit for the environment.
f Yes, he can't stand the presenter.
g Yes, ever since his wife left him.
h I wonder what they've got against him?

64.5 *Over to you*

Look up the colours below in a dictionary. Write down any new and useful expressions in example sentences of your own, e.g. *That sharp corner is a terrible black spot for road accidents.*

> black   white   red   blue   yellow   green

135

65 Speed: fast and slow

A Going fast

These verbs suggest going somewhere very quickly on foot or by a means of transport: **race, dash, tear**. I **dashed/raced/tore** to the station, just making it in time for the last train.

These verbs also suggest fast movement but are used mainly for going short distances: **nip, pop, zip, dart, whizz**. I **nipped/popped** into a nearby shop to buy a bottle of water only to see my bus **zip/dart/whizz** past.

The verb **bolt** also suggests fast movement over a short distance but it also has the added association of running away from something. The thieves **bolted** when the alarm went off.

The verb **career** suggests that something is moving rapidly and is out of control. The car skidded and **careered** down a bank. The company seems to be **careering** into financial ruin.

The verbs **scamper, scurry, scuttle** suggest small rapid steps, often of lots of small animals together. As we went into the dark shed, we saw mice **scampering** away and spiders **scurrying** into corners. Cockroaches **scuttled** into a crack in the floor.

These verbs emphasise the fact that speed is increasing: **speed up, accelerate. Accelerate** is used only about transport, whereas **speed up** can also refer to movement on foot. Both verbs can be used figuratively. We'd better **speed up** if we're going to get there on time. The growth of the company has **accelerated** since it started exporting.

B Going up or down fast

These verbs suggest a downward movement as well as speed: **plunge, plummet**. He put on a lifejacket and **plunged** into the icy water.

Notice that they are mainly used metaphorically. When export sales began to decline, our hopes of business success **plummeted**. After the death of his father, he was **plunged** into despair.

These verbs suggest a fast upward movement: **soar, rocket**. Notice that they are mainly used metaphorically and have strong associations with financial matters such as prices and share values. When our export sales **rocketed** our hopes **soared**.

The primary association of **soar** is with birds, and when it is used about people's feelings it provides associations of happiness and being carefree. My heart **soared** when I heard that he was coming home.

The opposite of **soar** and **rocket** in a financial context would be **slump** or **tumble**. Both suggest a rapid downward movement. Share prices **slumped** (or **plummeted**) on the stock market yesterday with telecommunications companies **tumbling** most dramatically of all.

C Going slowly

These intransitive verbs emphasise that the movement is slow: **crawl, creep**. They are often used metaphorically. Prices have been **creeping** up since May. It was rush hour and the traffic was **crawling**.

Totter also suggests a fairly slow movement, but it is one that is particularly unsteady as well. Mary **tottered** down the road laden with parcels and bags.

Sidle means to walk anxiously and nervously. Sam **sidled up** to the boss's desk and coughed to attract his attention.

Dawdle means to move more slowly than is necessary or to waste time. Don't **dawdle** on the way home.

Exercises

65.1 **Answer these questions.**

1 Would you be more likely to dash to the shops if you had plenty of time or if you were in a hurry?
2 If a car accelerates, does it speed up or slow down?
3 If you stop to look in shop windows, are you scampering or dawdling?
4 If traffic is said to be crawling, is it moving freely or is there a traffic jam?
5 If you plan to sell some shares, would you prefer their price to rocket or to tumble?
6 If a woman is wearing particularly high heels, is she more likely to scurry or to totter?
7 If a car slips on ice, is it more likely to be said to career or to dart across the road?
8 Who do you think is feeling more confident – a person who races up to greet you or someone who sidles up to greet you?
9 If you are thinking of buying your first flat, would you prefer the price of accommodation to be creeping up or to be soaring?
10 We sometimes say that people bolt their food. Does this mean that they eat fast or slowly?

65.2 **Would you be pleased or not to read the following headlines in your newspaper?**

1 **Taxes rocket in new budget**

2 **Shares plunge in uncertainty over US presidency**

3 **Economic growth tumbles to new low**

4 **Hopes soar for more Olympic medals**

5 **Profits plummet**

6 **Jobless figures creep up**

65.3 **Which do you think is the best verb to fill each of these gaps?**

1 When the car suddenly swerved to avoid hitting the dog, it .... out of control and crashed into a tree.
   A popped   B bolted   C careered   D dashed
2 When she switched the bathroom light on, she was horrified to catch a glimpse of cockroaches .... away into cracks in the tiles.
   A plummeting   B scuttling   C creeping   D nipping
3 I'm going to .... into town in my lunch hour. Can I get you anything?
   A bolt   B plunge   C totter   D nip
4 If you don't .... , you'll miss the bus and be late for school.
   A accelerate   B rocket   C speed up   D crawl
5 Meena's spirits .... when she learnt that she had won first prize.
   A plunged   B soared   C zipped   D tore
6 When the boy saw the fierce dog, he .... into the house.
   A dawdled   B careered   C tottered   D bolted
7 I'm just going to .... to the letter box to post these letters.
   A scurry   B totter   C plunge   D pop
8 Richard .... into the house, trying hard not to wake his parents.
   A soared   B crept   C scampered   D accelerated

66 Cause and effect

'Cause' verbs and their collocations

The differences between these verbs are best learnt by observing their typical collocations.

Cause usually collocates with negative results and situations.

The new computer system has **caused** us a lot of problems.

His stomach cancer was **caused** by exposure to radiation.

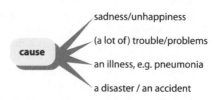

cause — sadness/unhappiness / (a lot of) trouble/problems / an illness, e.g. pneumonia / a disaster / an accident

Produce is more neutral, and deals with more concrete results. It is used in formal contexts.

Scientists can **produce** statistics and figures that can prove almost anything.

Cooking the dish for a long time at a very low heat **produces** the best results.

produce — a report / statistics/figures / good results / evidence

While *cause* usually collocates with negative situations, *give* can be used for positive or negative ones. *Give* is less formal than *cause*.

Our dog has **given** us a lot of pleasure over the years.

This car is **giving** me so much trouble, I'm going to get rid of it.

give — (a lot of) pleasure/happiness / a reason/motivation for something / (a lot of) trouble / good results

Generate is often used in contexts where people are forced to do more than usual, and in computer contexts. It sometimes has a rather negative feel. It is used in formal contexts.

It's going to be difficult to **generate** sufficient interest in the project.

The government will have to **generate** the extra funds somehow or other.

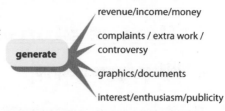

generate — revenue/income/money / complaints / extra work / controversy / graphics/documents / interest/enthusiasm/publicity

Language help

Cause and *give* are often used for things happening without people doing anything:
The hurricane caused terrible damage.
Produce and *generate* usually suggest some sort of intervention by people:
His presentation generated a lot of interest in the project.

Other 'cause' words

The news **provoked** a feeling of despair in everyone.
The events **precipitated** / **sparked off** a political crisis. [quickly, suddenly caused]
The invention of the car **brought about** great changes in society. [gradually produced]
Your action has **resulted in** a formal complaint from a member of the public. [produced]
His problems **stem from** his difficult childhood. [be a result of]
Have you any **grounds for** suspecting him? (cause, reason)
The proposal **has implications for** traffic in the area. [is likely to cause certain results]
My argument **is based on** the available data. [has been developed as a result of = the available data provide the basis for my argument]

Exercises

66.1 Decide which verb from the opposite page best fits each gap. There may be more than one possible answer.

1 The decision by the government to relax the regulations has .... a lot of investment in the poorer regions.
2 We need to .... a list of names and addresses by six o'clock tonight.
3 Her death was .... by a sign falling from a shop front in the heavy winds.
4 The Governor's remarks almost .... a full-scale war between the two regions.
5 His stupidity .... in none of us being able to get home that night.
6 Your letters have .... me so much pleasure. Please don't stop writing them.
7 The book .... a lot of anger amongst female readers.
8 I don't necessarily want to .... a crisis, but I have some bad news to tell you all.

66.2 A preposition is missing from each of these sentences. Add it in the correct place.

1 I have good grounds believing that he is lying.
2 My suspicions are based what I saw with my own eyes.
3 The government's decision has serious implications the economy.
4 His fear of flying stems a film he once saw.
5 I'm glad to say that all her hard work has resulted success.
6 The riots will probably bring a change of government.
7 A considerable amount of damage was caused the tornado.
8 The President's visit to the university sparked a number of demonstrations.

66.3 Rewrite these sentences using the word in brackets.

1 Because of the crash on the motorway, all traffic is being severely delayed. (CAUSED)
2 Thanks to your advice, we got there on time. (RESULTED)
3 There is a lot of interest in the minister's comments about tax law. (GENERATED)
4 She has many problems now as a consequence of her previous poor decisions. (STEM)
5 There were many flight cancellations because of bad weather. (BROUGHT)

66.4 Use any of the words and expressions from the opposite page to connect the events in the left-hand column with those in the right-hand column, as shown.

EXAMPLE *Scientists have produced statistics showing a direct link between smoking and cancer.*

1 scientists — stunning images and graphics
2 the higher taxes — statistics showing a direct link between smoking and cancer
3 icy roads — the break-up of his marriage
4 my old car — endless problems and involved me in a lot of expense
5 this software — riots in three cities
6 jealousy — a number of serious accidents this week

66.5 *Over to you*

Write sentences about something in your life which has:

- caused you a lot of problems
- given you a lot of happiness
- provoked a feeling of anger in you
- resulted in embarrassment for you
- brought about a change in your life.

67 Spot the difference: making comparisons

A Talking about similarity

collocation	meaning
I often feel there is a cultural **affinity between** London and New York. I **felt an affinity with** the writer as I read this novel.	closeness, similarity; feeling that different things/people have much in common
Her singing is more **akin to** that of Beyoncé than Adele.	similar in spirit/feel
To **use** a sporting **analogy**, middle age is like half-time at a football match.	see similarities that help us understand something
The picture this news article paints **does not correspond to** the truth.	is not equal to / does not match
It's a mistake to **equate** the price of something with its true value.	consider as the same
She knew that to apologise would be **tantamount to** admitting she had failed.	the equivalent of (normally used in negative contexts)
The goals of the two sides in the war have become almost **interchangeable**.	so similar that they could be exchanged one for the other
Mrs Burton's house was **indistinguishable from** all the others in the street.	so similar you cannot see the difference

B Talking about difference: adjectives beginning with *di*

example	contexts/comments
The **diverse** ethnic groups living in Malaysia give the country its cultural richness.	used to show a group is made up of different types of something
The **disparate** regions of Spain all have unique customs and cultures.	used for different types within a group, but emphasises separation and difference
This house is not **dissimilar** to the one I was born in.	very often used with *not*
They have widely **divergent** opinions.	often used to show contrasting opinions or ideas within a group
The Swedish and Norwegian languages are quite **distinct** from one another, even though they look similar when written.	used to describe differences where one might be deceived by similarities
It's easy to find our car in a car park because of its **distinctive** colour.	used to describe something that is easy to recognise because it is different
There are several **discrete** categories of verbs in English.	different and separate, not overlapping

Note the verbs associated with some of the adjectives above: to **differentiate** [to find a difference between], to **diversify** [to become or make more varied], to **diverge** [to move away, become more different from something], to **distinguish** [to notice the difference between two things].

Language help

Comparable (to) means similar in some way to something else:
The two girls are a comparable size. [about the same size]

Comparative means when comparing different things. These collocations are common:
comparative silence/freedom/comfort.

Exercises

67.1 One of these words is followed by a different preposition from the rest. Which word is it and which preposition does it need?

> akin   correspond   dissimilar   distinct   tantamount

Now use the words above and their prepositions in these sentences.
1 The state of Maine in the USA is not .... parts of Scandinavia. They both have lakes and forests.
2 To pretend I didn't want to be with her would be .... telling a lie.
3 What you say .... what I've heard too. I'm sure it's correct.
4 His life story is more .... a novel by Charles Dickens than a James Bond film.
5 The culture of the north of the country is quite .... that of the south, and it's a mistake to think they are the same.

67.2 Fill in the missing words.

1 There is a close affinity ....
Singapore .... Hong Kong; both are crowded, vibrant cities existing in a confined space.
2 I just cannot feel any affinity ....
his poetry; it's too dark and cruel.
3 This version of her essay is indistinguishable .... the first version. I can't see any changes.
4 It would be a great mistake to equate his shyness .... coldness or unfriendliness.
5 His ideas are not that dissimilar .... mine.
6 The temperatures in Moscow are currently comparable .... those in New York.

67.3 Choose the appropriate word in these sentences.

1 Spanish and Portuguese cultures are quite *diverse / distinct*, even though, to the outsider, they may sometimes appear similar.
2 The way they weave carpets in this region is not *dissimilar / divergent* to the way they are made in neighbouring countries.
3 English verbs do not always fit very easily into *distinctive / discrete* categories. For instance, is the verb *used to* an ordinary verb or a modal verb like *would*?
4 Seen from the widely *disparate / divergent* viewpoints of left and right, the problem either originates in too much freedom or in too much state control.
5 It would be very difficult to unite the *disparate / discrete* tribes and ethnic groups to form one coherent political force.
6 Her CD collection contains quite a *divergent / diverse* selection of music, with everything from classical to heavy metal.
7 The two suits I liked are a *comparable / comparative* price.
8 We walked part of the way home together and then our paths *differentiated / diverged*.
9 As he'd been to a boarding school, John loved the *comparable / comparative* freedom he had at university.
10 The business used only to make bicycles, but they've now *diversified / distinguished* into a range of other cycling products.

68 Difficulties and dilemmas

A Nouns relating to difficulties

Fairly small difficulties: **a snag, a hitch, a glitch. Glitch** usually refers to a technical problem of some kind. The other two words are more general.

More important difficulties:

A **setback** means that progress has been stopped by something.

A **stumbling block** is something that prevents action or agreement.

A **pitfall** is an unexpected difficulty (often used in the plural).

An **obstacle** is anything that stops progress, either literally or metaphorically.

An **impediment** is something that prevents free action, progress or movement.

A **dilemma** is a situation where a difficult choice has to be made between two, sometimes unpleasant, alternatives.

An **ordeal** is a severe experience, which is very difficult, painful or tiring.

B Adjectives relating to difficulty

adjective	meaning	collocations
problematic	full of problems or difficulties	relationship, situation, concept
abstruse	difficult to understand	theory, argument, philosopher
arduous	difficult, tiring, needing much effort	climb, task, journey
complex	difficult to understand as it has many parts	issue, problem, theory, process
convoluted	unreasonably long and hard to follow	explanation, sentences, theory
gruelling	extremely tiring and difficult	journey, work, match, expedition
insufferable	difficult to bear as it is annoying or uncomfortable	behaviour, heat, boredom, pain, person
obstructive	causing deliberate difficulties	person, measure, behaviour
tough	difficult to deal with or do	time, job, climate, decision
traumatic	shocking and upsetting	experience, past, childhood
wayward	changeable, selfish and/or hard to control	behaviour, child, person

Common mistake

Difficulty is used in the singular in the expression to have difficulty in doing something: I had great **difficulty in finding** a job at first (NOT great difficulties).

C Colloquial expressions relating to difficulties

Oh dear, more homework! **What a pain! / What a drag!** [What a nuisance!]

The software is good for editing still images, but editing video is a real **chore**. [boring job that has to be done]

What's eating him? / What's got into him? / What's bugging him? / What's (up) with him? [What's the matter with him?]

I can't face the **hassle** of moving house again. [situation causing trouble or difficulty]

My daughter keeps **hassling** me for a new bike. [asking again and again]

Having to listen to him singing is sheer **torture**! [used figuratively to refer to an unpleasant experience]

to slog (your guts out) / to grind / to graft / to flog yourself to death [to work hard]

in a fix / in a spot / in a hole / up against it / up to your neck [in a difficult situation]

The company's in a **sticky/tricky** situation now the workers are going to strike. [difficult]

I think I'm **off the hook / in the clear / out of the wood(s)** now. [freed from a difficult situation]

The **downside** of living here is the traffic thundering by. [the disadvantage of a situation]

Exercises

68.1 Choose the best word from the box to complete the sentences. Put the word in the plural if necessary.

> glitch   chore   impediment   dilemma   ordeal   pitfall   snag   stumbling block

1 Jane is caught in a terrible .... – should she move abroad with the man she loves or take the promotion she has been offered at work?
2 At first there were some .... with the software, but it's OK now.
3 Removing old files from my hard drive was a real .... – I spent four boring hours doing it!
4 The hostage is writing a book about his six-month ....
5 The proposal is very good. The only .... is that it is a little expensive.
6 Ian used to have a speech .... , but he's overcome it and is now an actor.
7 The leaflet gives new businesses information about typical .... to avoid.
8 Negotiations were going well until the issue of sick pay became a major ....

68.2 Which of the adjectives in B opposite might you use to describe:

1 a pupil who deliberately makes it hard for his teacher to continue with the lesson

....
2 an accident which affects the victim psychologically ....
3 a book that deals with very difficult ideas without simplifying them ....
4 a child who is very disobedient and self-willed ....
5 pain that is almost impossible to put up with ....
6 a speech that is very difficult to follow because the line of argument is very complex

....
7 an exhausting Arctic expedition ....
8 a decision that is not easy to make ....

68.3 Fill the gaps in this conversation using words from the opposite page.

A: What's got [1]............................. you, Paul? You look really fed up!
B: Oh, I don't know. I've been slogging my [2]............................. out at work and it's all getting too much. My wife says I should leave rather than go on flogging myself to [3]............................. . But I really can't face the [4]............................. of looking for something else at the moment.
A: What a [5]............................. ! I'm also in a bit of a [6]............................. .
B: Why? What's up [7]............................. you then?
A: I'm in a [8]............................. situation with my flat. The landlord's threatening to put the rent up. We've had quite a [9]............................. relationship for some time now, and I'm having great [10]............................. in finding somewhere else to live. That's the [11]............................. of living in Cambridge – it's beautiful but accommodation is so expensive. Still, at least my economics exam is over.
B: Great! How did that go?
A: Well, studying for it was sheer [12]............................. , but the exam itself wasn't too bad. It's a great relief it's over. Anyway, I hope you soon get through all your work and begin to feel off the [13]............................. soon.
B: Thanks. I think I'll feel out of the [14]............................. when this project is over.

68.4

Over to you

Answer these questions about difficulties you may have experienced in your life.

- When have you been in a dilemma? What were the choices that were facing you?
- Give an example of a project you were involved in that suffered a setback.
- Are there any downsides to living where you do at the moment?
- What obstacles have you had to overcome in your life so far?

69 Modality: expressing facts, opinions, desires

A Expressions based on modal verbs

I **must admit/confess/say** that I didn't enjoy the film.
You want me to lend you £1,000! **You must be joking!**
You **must have been frightened/worried/nervous/delighted/overjoyed** when you heard the news!
Don't look so miserable – **it may/might (well) never happen!**
What, may/might I ask, was the point of throwing your pen on the floor like that? (rather formal)
I was just strolling through the park when **who should I see/meet/bump into but** my boss.
Don't worry about spilling the wine. **Accidents will happen!** [accidents are inevitable]
The car **won't start.** What can I do?
That'll be Sean making that noise. He always plays his music very loudly.
A: Why are you so gloomy? The interview didn't go badly. **You might well** be offered the job, you never know.
B: **I should be so lucky!** [That is not likely!] All the other candidates were better qualified.

B Ways of expressing probability

The odds are he'll get the job. [it is likely that]
The odds are against her passing the exam. [it is unlikely that]
They **are bound to** get married in the end. [almost certain to]
She's **unquestionably** the best student in the class. [there is no doubt at all]
It was **apparent** that the negotiations were going badly [obvious].
She'll be here by five o'clock, **for sure.** [I am sure] (usually comes at the end)
In all probability we'll get the job finished on time. [it is very likely]
If you are not highly disciplined when you go on a diet, **the chances are** you won't succeed. [it is probable that]
There's every likelihood that the price of petrol will rise soon. [it is very probable]

C Ways of expressing obligation and lack of obligation

It is **essential** that you (should) take strong footwear with you.
Wearing a safety helmet is **obligatory** in this area.
The road was blocked. We **had no option** but to turn back.
We **have an obligation to** preserve the school's good name.
Some courses are **optional** but Maths and English are **compulsory.**

D Ways of expressing a desire to do something

I am **determined/anxious/eager/keen/resolved** to do whatever I can to help.
He **wishes/desires/yearns/longs** to return home. (all rather formal except *long*)
She has **ambitions/aspirations** to become Prime Minister.

Exercises

69.1 Look at A opposite. Match the situations on the left with the responses on the right.

1 Are you going clubbing tonight? ☐   a Shall I have a look at it?
2 I painted my house bright green last week. ☐   b They must be overjoyed.
3 The car won't start. ☐   c You must have been terrified.
4 You might win the lottery. ☐   d It'll be the Patels.
5 I'm afraid I've broken a cup. ☐   e What, may I ask, was the point of that?
6 Erica and Colin have just had twins. ☐   f I should be so lucky! Do you know what the odds are?
7 Someone's at the door. ☐   g You must be joking! I'm much too old.
8 I only just managed to escape. ☐   h Don't worry. Accidents will happen.

69.2 Rewrite these sentences using the words in brackets.

1 Sandra'll probably get the job. (LIKELIHOOD) *In all likelihood Sandra'll get the job.*
2 You must put on a life jacket. (OBLIGATORY)
3 I expect that Karl will take over his father's job. (ODDS)
4 You must do what the police officer says. (OPTION)
5 I'm sure they'll settle down eventually. (BOUND)
6 It's likely we'll meet someone we know at the party. (CHANCES)
7 We could see that there was going to be trouble. (APPARENT)
8 It's possible you'll end up with no job at all if you don't try. (WELL)
9 There's no doubt that this is the most serious problem we've encountered. (UNQUESTIONABLY)
10 With all this snow, the train will be late, definitely. (SURE)
11 I was in the park today, and I saw Marilyn. (SHOULD)
12 She really wants to get into university next year. (EAGER)

69.3 Write down three rules for a school using the words in brackets.

1 (ESSENTIAL) ....
2 (COMPULSORY) ....
3 (OPTIONAL) ....

69.4 Complete these sentences using the appropriate form of the words in brackets. Use a dictionary if necessary.

1 The town council expressed their .... to do what they could to help ease the traffic problems in the city. (DETERMINE)
2 The poem is about the poet's .... for his lost innocence. (YEARN)
3 Did you make any New Year's .... this year? (RESOLVE)
4 The President is .... that you attend her in her office immediately. (DESIRE)
5 Her .... to please is very touching. (EAGER)
6 She would have enjoyed her year abroad more had it not been for her .... for her boyfriend at home. (LONG)
7 Caroline is a very .... person. (AMBITION)
8 Steven has .... to be a great athlete. (ASPIRE)

69.5 Answer the questions.

1 Which verb from the opposite page could you use to make this sentence a little less formal?
It was a hard day. I was just yearning to get home and go to bed early.
2 *With his qualifications, he's bound to get a good job in the oil industry.* Does this sentence mean (a) he may work in the oil industry, (b) he has no choice but to work in the oil industry, or (c) he's almost certain to work in the oil industry?
3 Find four pairs of synonyms in the list of words. Which word is the odd one out?
resolved   eager   desire   likelihood   determined   obligation   keen   wish   probability

70 Number: statistics and quantity

A Changes in numbers and quantities

During the five years 2006–2011, internet use across the world was estimated to have increased **twofold**[1], while in China, it **quadrupled**[2]. In the developing world, internet use grew **by a factor of**[3] three.

The **drastic**[4] changes in interest rates resulted in a **threefold**[5] increase in the number of people unable to keep up their mortgage repayments.

The estimated number of stars in the Milky Way has been **revised upwards**[6] in light of recent discoveries.

The weather patterns have **deviated from the norm**[7] in recent years.

Sales **fluctuate**[8] from month to month.

Interest rates have **seesawed**[9] all year.

Share prices have been **erratic**[10] this last month.

[1] the suffix -fold means 'multiplied by that number' [2] increased by four times [3] multiplied by three [4] severe and sudden [5] twofold, threefold, etc. can be used as an adverb or adjective [6] changed to a higher number (you can revise something downwards to a lower number) [7] moved away from the standard or accepted pattern [8] keep going up and down [9] gone up and down at regular intervals [10] not regular and often changing suddenly

B More expressions for describing statistics and numbers

When the different amounts were added up, the **aggregate** was £600,000. [total]

I've **aggregated** all the figures. [added up all the different amounts]

The Finance Minister said the July rise in inflation was only a **blip**. [temporary change]

There seems to be a **correlation between** mathematical and musical ability. [connection between facts or things which cause or affect each other]

The percentage of **GDP expenditure** which goes on education varies considerably from country to country. [Gross Domestic Product: the total amount that a country produces] [the amount of money spent on something]

There's a **discrepancy between** our figures and yours. [difference between two things that should be the same]

The **ratio** of men to women in the Engineering Faculty was 3 to 1. [the relationship between two amounts, which expresses how much bigger one is than the other]

The company's figures were found to be **flawed** and the accountant was fired. [inaccurate]

She suffered **multiple** injuries in the accident. [very many of the same type, or of different types]

Our data are **inconsistent with** yours. [not in agreement with]

C Assessing quantity

Let me give you a **ballpark figure**[1] of how much money we expect to make this year. If I **tot everything up**[2], we begin to **run into six figures**[3]. There are a lot of **variables**[4] and our **projected figures**[5] may not be all that accurate. So I've **erred on the side of caution**[6] and I've **rounded things down**[7] rather than up in order to give you a **conservative**[8] estimate.

[1] guess believed to be accurate [2] add everything up (less formal) [3] get a figure over 100,000 [4] different factors that may change [5] planned figures [6] been cautious [7] make, say, 2.5 into 2 rather than 3 [8] cautious

Exercises

70.1 Use words from the opposite page to fill the gaps.

1 The chain has increased its number of restaurants .... in the last ten years. There were 20; now there are 80.
2 Many teachers were worried after the government announced it was going to cut its .... on schools.
3 The number of students enrolling for the course has increased by a .... of three, from 50 to 150 in just two years.
4 There was a sudden and .... rise in the number of serious road accidents during the extreme bad weather last winter.
5 We need to .... the estimate downwards from 3,000 to about 2,500.
6 There seems to be a .... between the two sets of data which suggests that the experiment was successful.
7 International trade is important to the country and makes up one third of its ....
8 The company .... its number of overseas branches from three to 12 in the space of five years.

70.2 Rewrite these sentences using the words in brackets so that they keep the same meaning.

1 The two reports of the accident appear to be inconsistent. (DISCREPANCY)
2 Oil prices were up one moment and down the next last year. (SEESAW)
3 Monthly average temperatures have been different from what we usually see this year. (DEVIATE, NORM)
4 The water levels didn't go up and down as much as we'd expected last year. (FLUCTUATE)
5 I don't need to know all the individual figures – just give me the total. (AGGREGATE)
6 His moods change – one minute he's happy, the next he's depressed. (ERRATIC)

70.3 Answer these questions.

1 If you give someone a ballpark figure, is it (a) precise or (b) rough?
2 If you round up 68.7, does it become (a) 69 or (b) 68?
3 If you want to give a conservative estimate when forecasting profits, would you prefer to (a) underestimate or (b) overestimate your figures?
4 If your weekly wage (in dollars) has just run into four figures, how much do you earn?
5 If you tot up all the numbers between 1 and 10, what do you get?
6 Name two variables that might affect a soft drinks company's projected profits.
7 If the ratio of girls to boys in a school is 1.5 to 1, are there more girls or boys?
8 If you err on the side of caution, do you (a) take care not to make any mistakes, (b) adopt a cautious attitude, (c) make errors through lack of caution?

70.4 Complete the word formation table below. Use a dictionary if necessary. Do not fill the shaded boxes.

verb	noun	adjective
deviate		
	discrepancy	
		flawed
		inconsistent
err		
		multiple

71 Permission: getting the go-ahead

A Permitting and agreeing that something may happen: verbs

All these verbs are formal and many are typically found in newspapers.

verb	meaning	example
accede	accept, but often associated with initial unwillingness	The factory owner **acceded to** the workers' demands.
acquiesce /ˌækwi'es/	permit something to happen, but often associated with a degree of secrecy or conspiracy	The Foreign Minister **acquiesced in** the plan to restrict imports from certain countries.
assent	agree to something, often associated with plans, proposals, ideas, etc.	The shareholders **assented to** the takeover.
authorise	give official permission	Only **authorised** people are allowed entry.
condone	approve or allow something which most people consider to be wrong	The judge **condoned** the use of reasonable force by police officers.
countenance	consider giving assent or permission, often used in negative contexts	No government would ever **countenance** abolishing taxes altogether.
endorse	give official approval to something	The cabinet has **endorsed** a proposal to change the way universities are funded.

B Permitting: phrasal expressions

The committee have been **given carte blanche** to investigate the problem and come up with a solution. [/ˌkɑːt'blɒnʃ/ complete freedom to do whatever they think necessary; *formal*]
The city has **given the go-ahead for** / **given the green light to** the new car park. [given permission for the building to start; *informal*]

C Prohibiting and disapproving: verbs

verb	meaning	example
bar	officially exclude, forbid someone access to something	Three students were **barred from** using the library because they had damaged books.
clamp down	use one's full power to prevent or limit something	The government has decided to **clamp down** on illegal immigration.
outlaw	make something illegal	Parliament has passed a bill **outlawing** smoking while driving.
veto /'viːtəʊ/	use one's official power to forbid	The President has **vetoed** the plan to open membership of the club to the public.

Common mistake

Regardless is not an adjective but an adverb. It means *not paying attention*.
It can be used on its own:
Her parents said she couldn't go to the party but she went to it regardless.

Or it can be followed by a phrase with *of*:
They built the extension to their house regardless of the fact that they had not received formal planning permission.

Exercises

71.1 Fill the gaps with a suitable verb which expresses the meaning in brackets. There may be more than one possible answer.

1 The committee were in favour of the proposal, but the President .... it. (used his/her official power to forbid it)
2 I would never .... the use of capital punishment, no matter how serious the crime. (approve or refuse to condemn)
3 The newspaper revealed that the Prime Minister had .... in the secret decision to sell arms to the dictator. (agreed to it, without openly admitting it)
4 The new bill going through Parliament will .... the use of unlicensed drugs by doctors. (make illegal)
5 The manager has .... the wearing of casual clothes to work on Friday. (used their official power to permit)
6 She has been .... from lectures because she disrupted one last term. (forbidden to enter/attend)
7 The President finally had to .... to demands for his resignation. (agree after being initially unwilling)
8 The police have announced that they are to begin to .... on motorists who exceed the speed limit. (take serious action to reduce the number of)

71.2 Find and correct the preposition errors in these sentences.

1 Alex parked his car outside the shop regardless to the No Parking sign.
2 The Minister said he would never accede for the union's demands.
3 It's time the police clamped down to cyclists going through red lights.
4 The President has assented at the latest world environment plan.
5 The Minister is likely to acquiesce with the proposal.
6 The college principal has given the green light on the students' proposal for an end-of-term festival.
7 The company been given the go-ahead at a new factory in the city.
8 The inspector had carte blanche for investigate every aspect of the business.

71.3 Look at these headlines containing further words and expressions connected with permission and prohibition. Match them with the news clips. Use a dictionary if necessary.

1 **GOVERNMENT TO LIFT EMBARGO ON COMPUTER IMPORTS**

2 **Railway franchise extended for five years**

3 **POLICE TO ADOPT ZERO-TOLERANCE OF HOOLIGANISM**

4 **NEW TRADE SANCTIONS ANNOUNCED**

a The company will be allowed to run services for the additional period, provided all conditions ...

b The hope is that firms will benefit from less severe competition in domestic markets if imports are subject to ...

c ... at present, chips and processors must be home-produced or else ...

d ... anyone displaying threatening behaviour will be liable to immediate arrest ...

72 Complaining and protesting

Expressions connected with complaining

It is important to use these expressions in appropriate situations. Some examples are given here. The expressions in each group go more or less from weaker to stronger, but much depends on who you are speaking to and what the situation is.

More common in informal situations

You've got to do something about that window of yours. It rattles in the wind and keeps me awake.

For goodness-sake! **I'm fed up with / sick of** all your moaning and grumbling. Cheer up!

Look here! **I've just about had enough of** your stupid comments.

Look, this is just not on! You promised to be here by two o'clock and it's almost three! [not acceptable]

Enough is enough! Please, no more arguments – be nice to each other!

More neutral in tone

I'm not at all satisfied about the service I've received.

Something will have to be done about that pile of rubbish. It can't be left in front of the house.

I wish you would turn your radio down. **I wish you wouldn't** play your music so loudly.

You never help around the house. **It just won't do!** You're going to have to change your ways.

More common in formal situations (typically in connection with bad service or behaviour)

I wish to complain about the delay in delivering my order.

The carpet in my room is stained and dirty. **This is most unsatisfactory.**

I take great exception to your unfair comments about our committee.

I really must object to being made to wait so long before seeing the manager.

The water pipe you have repaired three times in our kitchen is leaking again. **This is (simply) unacceptable.**

Your bus driver left the children by the roadside in pouring rain with no adult in attendance. **This is shameful.** [should make you feel embarrassed and guilty]

Verbs and nouns relating to complaining and protesting

verb	meaning	noun
complain (about)	express dissatisfaction or annoyance	**complaint**
protest (about) /prə'test/	strongly express complaint, disapproval or disagreement	**protest** /'prəʊtest/
object (to)	be against something or someone	**objection**
remonstrate with somebody / remonstrate about something	complain to someone / complain about something; *formal*	**remonstrance** (very formal and not common)
find fault (with)	criticise or complain about even small mistakes	**fault-finding**
grumble (about)	complain in a quiet but angry way	**grumble**
gripe (about)	to complain continuously; *informal*	**gripe**
grouse (about)	to complain, usually often; *informal*	**grouse**
whinge (about)	complain persistently; *informal*	**whinge, whingeing**

Common mistake

The verb *object to* is followed by a noun, a pronoun or an *-ing* form of a verb. Don't use the base form of a verb: *I object to being made to wait here for an hour before seeing the Principal* (NOT ~~object to be made~~).

Exercises

72.1 Where would you be more likely to hear these statements, in informal or more formal situations? Mark them I or F. How might the same idea be conveyed at the other end of the scale of formality?

1 Look here! I've just about had enough of your rudeness! ....
2 I am writing to remonstrate against some injustices in your regulations. ....
3 You've got to do something about the state of your desk. ....
4 I wish to complain about the poor facilities at the station. ....
5 You can't possibly come here not wearing a tie. ....
6 This behaviour is most unsatisfactory. ....
7 The lack of toilet facilities for disabled people is shameful. ....
8 The delay in completing my order is simply unacceptable. ....

72.2 Complete each of these sentences with one word.

1 What's Janet whingeing .... now?
2 We .... great exception to the proposed plans.
3 They objected loudly to .... forced to sit on the floor because there were no chairs.
4 He's always writing letters to the newspaper, finding fault .... something or other.
5 Something will have to be .... about traffic problems in the city.
6 I wish people .... smoke in restaurants.
7 This standard of work just won't .... !
8 You would be .... advised to start looking for another job.
9 I heard her remonstrating .... a police officer about the road being closed.
10 I'm tired of hearing you constantly moaning. Enough is .... !

72.3 How might you complain in the following situations?

1 You are complaining to your flatmate about your noisy neighbours; they've been having wild parties every weekend for several months now.
2 You're complaining in a fairly neutral way to your neighbours about a tree of theirs that has grown so high it blocks out the sun.
3 You're writing a formal email to the local newspaper about the problem of noise at night from a factory in your neighbourhood.
4 You're complaining to your boss, with whom you have a fairly informal relationship, about new and longer working hours.
5 You're complaining to a close friend about having to work longer hours.
6 You're writing an official, formal letter of complaint to the top level of management about a lack of safety procedures at work.

72.4 The people below are all complaining indirectly. What do they really mean in each case?

1 (*walking into a room*) 'It doesn't smell very nice in here!'
2 (*on a school report*) 'Jorge tends to complete his work rather too quickly.'
3 (*in a reference letter*) 'Punctuality is not Simone's highest priority.'
4 (*at a work appraisal*) 'You'd be well advised to reassess your long-term plans.'
5 (*commenting on a room*) 'It would benefit from a lick of paint.'
6 (*coming into a room*) 'The TV seems to be a bit loud.'

73 Apology, regret and reconciliation

A Apologies and excuses: collocations

adjective collocations	noun
sincere, heartfelt	apology
good, perfect, lame, flimsy, weak convincing, detailed, phoney	excuse explanation
cast-iron, convincing, perfect, phoney	alibi
flimsy, false	pretext [pretended reason for doing something rather than real reason]

He offered his most **heartfelt apology** for having offended everyone. [most sincere apology]
It was a rather **lame excuse,** and nobody really believed it. [weak excuse]
The police questioned her about the murder, but she had a **cast-iron alibi**: she had spent the whole day teaching at the local primary school. [firm reason why she was innocent]
The police were convinced the suspect's **explanation** was **phoney,** but could not prove it. [false]
He got an interview with her on the rather **flimsy pretext** of being interested in her research. [weak and not very believable excuse]

B Regretfulness in legal contexts

When he was pronounced guilty of fraud, Jack Mosley showed no **remorse**[1] whatsoever. He was sentenced to ten years in prison. All three of his companions who were on trial with him were **acquitted**[2] of the crime and walked out of the courtroom free. Mosley later **repented**[3] whilst in prison and his sentence was reduced by one year.

[1] feeling of guilt or regret   [2] declared not guilty (noun = acquittal)   [3] said he was sorry and asked for forgiveness (noun = repentance)

The President issued a **posthumous pardon** to the man who, it seems, had been wrongly accused of treason. [official forgiveness after someone's death for crimes they were unjustly convicted for]
The Committee of Inquiry **exonerated** the Minister from all responsibility for the disaster. [declared someone to be free of blame]
The condemned man received a last-minute **reprieve** the day before he was due to be executed. [official order stopping or delaying punishment]
It is hard for the victims of crime to **forgive and forget.** (these two verbs are always in this order)

C Peace and reconciliation

type of agreement	explanation and example
treaty	written agreement between two or more countries The two nations signed a **peace treaty** in 1996.
armistice	agreement to stop war while peace discussions take place The generals from the opposing armies **declared/signed an armistice.**
truce	agreement between two enemies to stop fighting for a period of time The two fighting politicians **called a truce** agreeing to put their differences behind them for the good of the country.
accord	official agreement, especially between countries There are fears that the current period of **accord** between the two sides in the civil war is at risk of collapsing.
ceasefire	agreement to stop fighting in order to allow discussions about peace Both sides have agreed to a **ceasefire** while talks are underway.

Exercises

73.1 Fill the gaps with suitable adjectives. There may be more than one possible answer.

1 She had a .... excuse for not mowing the lawn: she was allergic to grass.
2 I thought he gave rather a .... excuse and I'm not convinced at all.
3 He went around to her flat on the .... pretext of wanting to borrow a book.
4 The police had to let her go free, since she had a .... alibi.
5 I want to offer you all my most .... apology for the trouble I've caused.

73.2 Choose the correct adjective to complete each sentence.

1 I persuaded him to come on the rather *false* / *flimsy* pretext that I needed some help repairing my bike.
2 The police have struck George off their list of suspects as he has a *cast-iron* / *sincere* alibi.
3 Jilly's excuse for not coming to my party was pretty *convincing* / *lame* – you'd have thought she could have come up with something better than that.
4 Kate sends *heartfelt* / *perfect* apologies for not coming with me this evening – she's got a bad dose of flu.
5 The police officer asked us for a *detailed* / *phoney* explanation of the events leading up to the incident.
6 I hope you've got a *weak* / *good* excuse for forgetting it's my birthday today.

73.3 Complete the second sentence so that it means the same as the first, using the word in capitals. Do not change the form of the word in capitals.

1 'I'm sorry I broke your vase, Gina,' Matt said. (APOLOGISED)
  Matt .... her vase.
2 He had acted in a very inhumane way, but the criminal did not seem to repent. (REPENTANCE)
  The criminal did not .... the inhumane way in which he had acted.
3 At the end of the trial, the accused was acquitted. (ACQUITTAL)
  The trial ....
4 Sam did not offer any explanation for his strange behaviour. (EXPLAIN)
  Sam .... he had behaved so strangely.

73.4 Correct the errors in these sentences.

1 The President granted him a repentance just an hour before he was due to be executed.
2 He was exonerated of murder in 2004, but two years later was convicted of armed robbery in the same courtroom.
3 She showed a complete lack of reprieve for her evil deeds and just laughed when the judge sentenced her.
4 The Public Inquiry pardoned him from all blame for the accident at the factory.
5 Just before he died, the old man said he remorsed all the bad things he had done in his life.
6 Ten years after his death, Daniel Kehoe was given a humorous pardon by the government when another man confessed to the crime he had been hanged for.
7 He treated her badly and she says she simply cannot forget and forgive.
8 The ceasefiring is due to start at 9 pm.

73.5 Rewrite the underlined parts of the sentences using words from C on the opposite page and fill the gaps with a suitable verb. Use a dictionary if necessary.

1 The two armies .... a period without fighting during the religious holiday.
2 Both governments .... to the terms of the document ending the war permanently and it was signed on 15 August 1954.
3 The long-standing agreement to work together between the government and the unions is in danger of ....
4 The generals .... the agreement to end fighting while peace terms were worked out at midday on 25 February 1968.

74 A pat on the back: complimenting and praising

A Collocations with compliment and praise

The boss would get better results if she **paid** her staff **compliments** occasionally.
He asked us what we thought of his suit, but he was really only **fishing for compliments**.
Take it as a compliment that he feels relaxed enough to fall asleep at your dinner party!
A **back-handed compliment** and a **double-edged compliment** are ones that appear to be both positive and negative. Back-handed compliments tend to have a malicious intent whereas double-edged ones are usually made innocently.
I took it as a **back-handed compliment** when he said I was looking good for my age.
She **paid** me the **double-edged compliment** of saying my driving was pretty good for a beginner.
The phrase **give praise to** is usually used only (though not exclusively) for a god. An action or person that deserves praise is **praiseworthy** and people are **praised for** their actions.
Other common collocations are **widely/highly praised, praised to the skies, to sing someone's/ something's praises, to shower/heap praise on someone/something**. To **damn someone with faint praise** is to praise with such a lack of enthusiasm that you give the impression of actually having rather negative feelings.

> **Common mistake**
>
> The verb to compliment is followed by *on*:
> *He complimented me on my guitar playing*
> (NOT ~~He complimented me my guitar playing~~).

B Other expressions relating to praising

expression	meaning	example
pay tribute to	praise; *formal*	At the memorial service, I **paid tribute to** his kindness.
give someone a standing ovation	stand up and clap loudly for a long time	At the end of the concert, the audience **gave** the young pianist **a standing ovation**.
extol the virtues/ benefits of	praise highly; *formal*	At the conference, the Prime Minister **extolled the virtues** of the new trade treaty.
be the toast of	be admired for some recent achievement (often used about artists and celebrities)	A few months ago, hardly anyone had heard of her but now **she's the toast of** Hollywood.
pat someone on the back / give someone a pat on the back	praise, often children (used mostly metaphorically)	My teacher **patted me on the back / gave me a pat on the back** for my good marks in the maths test.
earn/win plaudits	get positive comments; *formal*	The exhibition **earned plaudits** from all the major reviewers.
laud (adj. = **laudable** (of behaviour), **laudatory** (of comments or remarks)	praise highly in official situations; *formal*	The Prime Minister has **lauded** the new peace initiative.

These mostly informal expressions imply praising someone for your own benefit: **to flatter, to make up to, to crawl, to suck up to, to lick someone's boots**. Someone who behaves like this can be called **smarmy, slimy** or **a crawler** (all informal), a **flatterer** (neutral) or **servile, obsequious** (more formal).
Flatter can also be used more positively. That dress **flatters** her figure. [makes her figure look better than it really is]
The noun **flattery** is often used in the phrase **Flattery will get you nowhere!** [insincere praise will not achieve anything]

Exercises

74.1 Look at A opposite and fill the gaps in these sentences with one word.

1 A: Do you like my new hairstyle? B: Don't .... for compliments.
2 At the meeting everyone was .... your praises.
3 He's not very good at .... people compliments.
4 Mrs Carrington is always praising her pupils .... the skies.
5 It may sound a bit double-edged, but I think you should .... what she says .... a compliment.
6 He never knows what to say when fans .... praise on him.
7 I didn't enjoy the film but it has been very .... praised by the critics.
8 Look at this reference. It's really .... the candidate with faint praise.

74.2 Look at the table in B opposite. Match the beginning of each sentence with its ending.

1 The performers were given   ☐   a tribute to her predecessor.
2 In the speech, the new manager paid   ☐   b a pat on the back for her drawings.
3 They're always extolling   ☐   c the toast of the tennis world.
4 Matt's design earned him   ☐   d a standing ovation.
5 The teacher gave Becky   ☐   e the virtues of living in the country.
6 The new young Czech player was   ☐   f the highest plaudits from the judges.

74.3 Look at the words below the table in B. Write each of the following sentences in four different ways. Indicate which of your sentences are particularly formal or informal.

1 He's always sucking up to the boss.
2 I wish she wasn't so smarmy.

74.4 Complete this word formation table. Do not fill the shaded boxes. Give two answers for some of the words. Use a dictionary if necessary.

verb	noun	adjective
compliment		
praise		
laud		
flatter		
crawl		
smarm		

74.5 Choose one of the words from the table in 74.4 to complete these sentences.

1 Although she didn't win a prize, the judges were very .... about her efforts.
2 Tim's a real .... , so I never take much notice of his compliments.
3 When he discovered the size of his mistake, he had to .... to the boss.
4 Her actions were foolish but her motives were ....
5 There's no point saying how good I am. .... will get you nowhere!
6 Whilst we cannot but .... the skill of their actions, we must express a certain disapproval of the risks they took.

75 Promises and bets

A Promises

If you **promise someone the earth/moon,** you promise them a great deal. It is usually implied that such a promise is unrealistic: The afternoon **promises** to be interesting! [the speaker expects it will be interesting = We **anticipate** that the afternoon will be interesting] **Anticipate** is to expect something before it happens.

Promise can also be used to indicate positive future development: The child already shows great **promise** as a violinist. She's a **promising** artist although her style is still rather immature.

An **oath / to swear** is a formal promise. In court, witnesses are **put on/under oath** when they have to swear to tell the truth.
Notice how **swear** is often used in informal spoken English in expressions:
I could have sworn I left my purse on the table. [was absolutely certain]
I think she lives on Rose Street but I **couldn't swear to** it. [am not totally sure]
My mother **swears by** these vitamin pills. [uses them and thinks they are wonderful]
Tom often uses **swear words / bad language.** [taboo expressions]

To **pledge (a pledge)** means to promise something, often friendship or money: Mayor Williams has **pledged** millions of dollars to improve the city centre.
To **vow (a vow)** is to make a determined decision or promise to do something: He **vowed** to discover who had killed his father. At a marriage ceremony, the couple exchange **vows.** Both **vow** and **pledge** are found more in written than spoken English.

New Year's resolutions are special promises **to turn over a new leaf** at the beginning of a new year. [to change one's behaviour for the better]
Resolutions and vows, like **promises** or **pledges,** can be **made, kept** or **broken.**
If you **go back on your word,** you break a promise.

> **Language help**
> Both *swear* and *oath* can mean either (make) a solemn promise or (use) taboo language.

B Bets

To **bet (a bet)** is to risk something, usually money, on the unknown result of something in the hope of winning more money. People spend (and lose) a lot of money **betting** on horse racing or football matches, for example. Putting money on the results of a game of some kind is called **gambling.** The amount of money that you risk is your **stake.** You can **stake** a sum of money on something happening. If something is **at stake,** then it is at risk. Many lives will be **put at stake** if the flood barrier is not built. A more formal word for **bet** is **wager:** She put a **wager** of £10 on a horse. Both words can be used in a non-literal sense: I'd **wager** that he will come to a bad end.

There are a number of colloquial expressions connected with betting.
Your best bet would be to look for a part-time job. [the best decision or choice]
You think Stuart'll win? **Don't bet on it!** [I think what you've just said is unlikely to happen]
My granny enjoys **having a flutter** on the horses. [having a small bet]
I'd **put (good) money / bet my life on** James getting the job. [I'm sure that James will get the job]
Do you feel like coming to the beach with us? **You bet!** [I certainly do!]
You can also **hedge your bets** by investing in several companies. [protect yourself from the results of making a single wrong choice]
The **odds** are the statistical or betting chances of something happening.
What are **the odds of** Olivia finishing her course, do you think? **The odds are against** her getting that promotion.

Exercises

75.1 **Which sentence in each pair sounds more formal?**

1 A: Ricky promised to love her always.
B: Ricky pledged to love her always.
2 A: Tom swore he would take revenge.
B: Tom vowed he would take revenge.
3 A: Lou wagered a lot of money on the result of the elections.
B: Lou bet a lot of money on the result of the elections.
4 A: Lina made a resolution at New Year to give up smoking.
B: Lina made a vow at New Year to give up smoking.

75.2 **Fill the gaps in these sentences with one word.**

1 He .... her the moon but they ended up in a tiny flat in the least attractive part of town.
2 At the trial, the witnesses were all under .... to tell the truth.
3 When you're revising, your .... bet would be to focus on Shakespeare. There are always lots of questions about him!
4 My mother's not a real gambler, but she does like to have the occasional .... on the horses.
5 Rob promised to give me his old car, but he's gone .... on his word and sold it to his neighbour.
6 Marina's bound to pass her driving test first time. I'd put my .... on it!

75.3 **Rewrite these sentences using the word in brackets, so meaning is the same.**

1 I think you should stay overnight in a hotel near the airport. (BET)
2 My father drinks these herbal teas and believes they are wonderful. (SWEARS)
3 John's been rather lazy with his homework, but he has promised to try harder next year. (LEAF)
4 I was sure I locked the door when I went out. (SWORN)
5 The writer's new play sounds as if it is likely to be as good as his last one. (PROMISES)
6 I'm sure that the Democratic Party will win the next election. (MONEY)
7 Do you ever buy national lottery tickets? (FLUTTER)
8 Her mother disliked the film because it contained so much bad language. (SWEAR)
9 The documentary promises to be controversial. (ANTICIPATE)
10 I minimised my risk by buying shares in both of the companies that had a serious chance of winning the contract. (HEDGE)

75.4

Over to you

Answer the questions.

1 'Promises and piecrusts are made to be broken, they say.' (*Jonathan Swift*, Irish writer, 1667–1745)
What point is Jonathan Swift making, in your opinion, and how is his use of language effective?

2 'To promise not to do a thing is the surest way in the world to make a body want to go and do that very thing.' (*Mark Twain*, American novelist, 1835–1910)
Do you agree with him?

3 Look at what some people promise one another during a wedding service:
'... to have and to hold from this day forward, for better for worse, for richer for poorer, in sickness and in health; to love and to cherish, till death us do part.' (*part of Church of England wedding vows*)
What wedding vows do people make in your country? Can you translate them?

4 In the UK and the US, witnesses in law courts swear that the evidence they give will be 'the truth, the whole truth and nothing but the truth.'
What oath do witnesses have to swear in your country?

76 Reminiscences and regrets

A Looking back: sharing memories

A: It's great to see you again. Gosh, it's ten years since we were at school together! Any idea what the school is like these days?

B: No, I've been a bit out of touch[1] with things ever since I moved away from London.

A: I wonder what became of[2] that maths teacher. I think his nickname, if I recall[3], was Goggles, because of those big glasses he used to wear. When I think back[4], I realise now how difficult things must have been for him, having to teach the likes of us! And do you ever hear anything of[5] James?

B: No, I haven't heard a thing.

A: And I often wonder what Sanjay ended up doing. I've lost touch with him too. Thinking back, we had some great times, didn't we?

B: Yeah. Seeing your phone there on the table reminds me of how we used to text under our desks right under the teacher's nose.

A: Yeah, that takes me back to[6] the day my phone rang when the government inspector was observing our class and I got into big trouble.

B: Yes, I have a vague memory[7] of that. Actually, it's all coming back to me now[8]. They confiscated your phone and you stormed out of the classroom!

A: Yeah. But I must say that what stands out in my mind[9] is the amazing freedom we used to have.

B: Me too. When I look back, I realise how much things have changed.

A: Yes, I often find myself reminiscing about[10] my teenage years and wonder if our children will have the same happy memories when they grow up.

B: Yes, we all tend to look at the past through rose-tinted spectacles[11], don't we? But I guess a bit of nostalgia[12] does nobody any harm!

[1] not knowing what has happened recently [2] where he is and what happened to him [3] if I remember correctly [4] think about the past [5] receive any news about [6] makes me remember [7] not a very clear memory [8] I'm beginning to remember it more clearly [9] what I remember more than other things (you can also say sticks out in my mind) [10] thinking about pleasant things that happened in the past [11] see only the pleasant things about a situation and not notice the things that are unpleasant (you can also say rose-coloured spectacles) [12] a feeling of pleasure and sometimes slight sadness at the same time as you think about things that happened in the past

B Expressing regret

I regret not spending more time with my aunt when she was ill.

He showed no sign of remorse for what he had done.

> **Common mistake**
>
> Don't confuse *remind* and *remember*. Seeing the class photo again reminded me of my unhappy schooldays (NOT remembered me).

She said she felt great shame for what had happened and apologised to us all. [embarrassment and guilt about something bad that happened]

I felt great pangs of guilt and remorse thinking of all the bad things that had happened and my part in them. [sudden sharp feelings, especially of painful emotion; collocates frequently with guilt, regret, conscience, remorse]

Some formal, rather literary ways of expressing regret:

I rue the day we ever met. [I regret very much that we ever met; collocates strongly with 'the day' and 'the fact that']

I lament the passing of time. [I feel sad that time passes]

I mourn my lost opportunities. [I feel sad about opportunities I had but did not take up]

Exercises

76.1 Fill each gap with one word.

1 .... back, I can't believe how I survived the first day in my old job. It was horrendous.
2 What .... in my mind when I think of my schooldays was our class trip to Edinburgh.
3 What .... of that friend of yours who wanted to be a pilot? Did he ever get to be one?
4 Do you ever hear .... your old college friend Martine these days?
5 When I .... , we had quite a hard life; my parents were poor.
6 When I get together with my old schoolmates, we often .... about the fun times we had.
7 I'm a bit .... of .... with what's happening with our old hockey team since I stopped playing, but someone said they're doing quite well these days.
8 I got a sudden feeling of .... as we drove past our old house. We'd had some happy times there.
9 When I saw the photo, it all .... back to me just what a wonderful holiday we had had.
10 You're always looking at the past through rose- .... spectacles. It wasn't all wonderful, you know.
11 I have only a very .... memory of my early childhood in Canada. It was all so long ago!
12 What happened to your sister? If I .... , she wanted to study chemistry, didn't she? Did she ever do that?

76.2 Look at C opposite. Match the beginning of each sentence with its ending.

1 I felt some pangs ☐   a my lost youth.
2 I rue the day ☐   b because I'd done nothing wrong.
3 I feel a certain remorse ☐   c not contacting her earlier.
4 I regret ☐   d I agreed to go into business with him.
5 I mourn ☐   e of guilt about what happened.
6 I felt no shame ☐   f about what happened. It was my fault.

76.3 Write these sentences in more formal language. Use the word in brackets.

1 I'm sorry that I didn't buy her a birthday present. (REGRET)
2 They didn't seem the least bit concerned about what they had done. (REMORSE)
3 I now greatly regret the fact that I discontinued my studies. (RUE)
4 I wish our relationship hadn't broken down. (LAMENT)
5 The whole village felt sad about the loss of the beautiful trees. (MOURN)

76.4 *Over to you*

Answer these questions for yourself.

- What stands out in your mind when you think about your own childhood?
- Do you ever think 'I wonder what became of ...?' When this happens, who or what do you think about?
- Is there any aspect or time of your life that you only have vague memories of?

77 Agreement, disagreement and compromise

Agreement: sharing views

verb + preposition	meaning
Her complaints **tally with** the comments we have received from other people.	match or agree with
His opinion **concurs with** the general opinion of the experts on this matter.	share/agree with an idea/opinion
The President **found** herself in full **accord with** the opposition.	be in complete agreement with
Your views **coincide with** mine on the question of crime and punishment.	be the same as
His behaviour doesn't **conform to** the school's expectations.	fit in with
My parents **approve of** my choice of profession and support me fully.	think something is right or good

The noun from **approve** is **approval**: an action can **meet with someone's approval**. [be liked by that person]
Note the expression **to agree to differ**, which is used when people continue to hold different opinions but see no point in continuing to argue about them.
We couldn't reach a consensus at the meeting, so we just **agreed to differ**.

Political and social disagreement

noun	meaning
There is **dissent** in the party on the issue.	opposition to the accepted way of thinking
The general **discord** between the committee members had a negative impact on the club.	lack of agreement or harmony (suggests arguments and rows)
The growing **rift** in the Democratic Party over defence policy is now public.	disagreement (with different groups/factions forming)
A major **split** in the Labour Party resulted in several ministers taking the decision to form a new party of their own.	when a larger group breaks up into two or more smaller groups because they disagree about something
There is (a) major **division** in the Socialist Party over economic policy.	similar to split but more abstract and formal (can be countable or uncountable)
Government plans to build a new airport in this area are bound to cause **controversy**.	a lot of disagreement about a subject usually because it affects a lot of people

Compromise

The two sides have **reached a compromise** over the plan to build the new road across a nature reserve.
The Minister was not prepared to **compromise on** the issue of raising university fees.
The government **made** several **concessions to** the protesters. [accepted some of the demands of]
The management and the union **reached a settlement** and the strike ended. [reached a decision/agreement]

Language help

A good way to agree with what someone has said is to say either **Absolutely!** or **Precisely!**
A: *It would be risky to leave your job without getting another one first.*
B: *Precisely!/Absolutely!*

In this particular case, we should **exercise** some **discretion** and not say anything that would cause more conflict. [be sensitive, use our judgement]

Exercises

77.1 Add the prepositions which normally accompany the verbs to the table. Then use these expressions to fill the gaps in the sentences below. Use each item once only.

verb	preposition	verb	preposition
approve		concur	
conform		compromise	
tally		(be in) accord	
coincide			

1 The list of principles .... to the normal idea of what a set of rules should be trying to achieve.
2 My views .... completely with yours. We think on exactly the same lines.
3 This plan is in .... with the proposal made by the committee in 2011.
4 Her latest statement simply does not .... with her earlier ones. She is contradicting herself.
5 I .... of all the changes suggested, and hope they can be made to work.
6 For once all the committee members .... with one another.
7 Even though I disagree, I'm willing to .... on your proposal to increase our expenditure.

77.2 Match these newspaper headlines with the most suitable extract below.

1 **RIFT OVER PENSIONS POLICY GROWS**

2 **DISSENT MUST BE KEPT WITHIN LIMITS, MINISTER SAYS**

3 **PARTY SPLIT OVER TAX CUTS NO LONGER A SECRET**

4 **DIVISION IN EUROPE OVER RESPONSE TO AFRICAN CRISIS**

5 **RELIGIOUS DISCORD THREATENS SOCIAL HARMONY**

a Approximately 50% of members now think it would have been better to leave things as they were.

b Intolerance towards others' beliefs seems to be increasing and there have been isolated outbreaks of violence.

c There is increasing pressure on the Minister to consider a change to his Party's approach to social welfare.

d Several different national approaches have emerged which could weaken unity.

e He made the point that to disagree is everyone's right, but a sense of responsibility is also important.

77.3 Rewrite the sentences using a noun from the same root as the underlined word. Make any other changes necessary.

1 The President conceded that the opposition party should be allowed a place on the committee.
2 I think one should always be as discreet as possible when it is a question of people's private lives.
3 The landowners settled their dispute with the authorities over the proposed factory site.
4 The negotiating team were able to compromise and put an end to the labour dispute.
5 The decision to close the railway line has proved very controversial.
6 There are a number of dissenting views among the Board members.
7 The forthcoming leadership election has divided the Green Party.
8 Javier's parents approved of his decision.

78 Academic writing: making sense

A Presenting arguments and commenting on others' work

If you **advocate** something, you argue in favour of it: He **advocated** capital punishment.
If you **deduce** something, you reach a conclusion by thinking carefully about the known facts:
Look at these sentences and see if you can **deduce** how the imperfect tense is used.
If you **infer** something, you reach a conclusion indirectly: From contemporary accounts of his
research, we can **infer** that results were slower to come than he had anticipated.
If someone's work **complements** someone else's, it combines well with it so that each piece of
work becomes more effective: Elswick's (2012) research **complements** that of Johnson (2007).
If someone's work **overlaps** with someone else's work, it partially covers the same material.
You might call someone's work: **empirical** [based on what is observed rather than theory],
ambiguous [open to different interpretations], **coherent** [logically structured], **comprehensive**
[covering all that is relevant], **authoritative** [thorough and expert].

B Talking about figures and processes

If figures are referred to as **arbitrary**, they are based on chance or personal choice rather than
a system or data that supports them.
Figures that **deviate from the norm** are different from what is typical.
If statistics **distort** the picture, they give a false impression.
If you refer to the **incidence** of something, e.g. a disease, you are talking about how often it
occurs.
If something, e.g. the incidence of brown eyes, is **predominant**, it is the largest in number.
If things, e.g. stages in a process, happen **in sequence**, they happen in a particular order.
If you want to say that something happens in many places or with many people, you can say
that it is **widespread**, e.g. widespread outbreaks of an illness, widespread alarm.

C Words typically used in academic contexts

academic verb	everyday verb
append	add (at the end)
conceive	think up
contradict	go against
demonstrate/indicate	show
denote	be a sign of, stand for
negate	make useless, wipe out
perceive	see
reflect upon	think about
reside	lie, live
trigger	cause
utilise	use
academic expression	**everyday expression**
an instance of something	an example of something
the converse	the opposite
crucial	very important
notwithstanding	despite this
somewhat	rather
thereby	in this way
whereby	by which (method)

Exercises

78.1 Which of the five verbs in A opposite best fits in each sentence?

1 The French and Swedish teams work in similar areas, but their research, fortunately, does not .... However, the French data .... the Swedish data very well.
2 Look at the complete set of graphs and see if you can .... the rules governing the data from them.
3 This article .... a different approach to the problem.
4 A great deal can be .... about the artist's state of mind from his later works.

78.2 Which of the five adjectives in A best describes each of these things?

1 a textbook written by the most highly regarded expert in the field
2 research based on a survey of the population
3 a poem which can be understood in two quite different ways
4 an argument which is well-expressed and easy to follow
5 a textbook which gives a broad overview of an entire discipline

78.3 Answer these questions which use vocabulary from B opposite.

1 If the incidence of asthma in children is increasing, what is actually going up: (a) the seriousness of asthma attacks or (b) the number of asthmatic children?
2 What are the next two numbers in this sequence: 1, 4, 9, 16, 25, 36?
3 If the average mark in a maths test was 68% and Ulla's mark deviated noticeably from that average, what do we know about Ulla's mark?
4 If facts are distorted, are they presented (a) accurately, (b) clearly or (c) in a misleading fashion?
5 If sociologists choose the subjects of their research in an arbitrary fashion, do they take care to get people from an appropriate balance of backgrounds?

78.4 Use items from C to rewrite the underlined parts of the sentences in a more formal academic style.

1 The information <u>lies</u> in archives that must not be opened until 2050.
2 He <u>thought up</u> his theory while still a young man.
3 Each of the symbols in the phonetic alphabet <u>stands for</u> a sound.
4 This study <u>went against</u> what was previously held to be true, and so <u>started</u> a great deal of discussion amongst specialists in the field.
5 Details of the experiment have been <u>added at the end of</u> the report.
6 Jelowski's book <u>thinks about</u> the rise and fall of great Empires over two millennia. She <u>sees</u> the Roman Empire as an <u>example</u> of a pattern that has repeated itself in other times and other parts of the world.

78.5 Rewrite this paragraph, using words from C, to make it sound more academic.

The present study was initially **thought up** in order to validate a new method of enquiry **by which** genetic information could be **used** to predict disease. The study **goes against** the findings of Hill (2009); indeed it would appear to **show** the **opposite** of what he claimed. It presents a **rather** different view of the genetic factors which **cause** disease. **Despite this**, the study does not **wipe out** Hill's, as his studies served the **very important** purpose of devising symbols to **stand for** certain tendencies, **in this way** facilitating further research.

79 Academic writing: text structure

Explaining, reinforcing, exemplifying

Look at these extracts and note the contexts in which the words in bold occur.

The Prime Minister **reiterated**[1] her concern that the debate should not be dominated by personal attacks. She **summarised**[2] the new policy as being progressive and radical ...

Peter Burnett's comments **epitomise**[3] the attitude of many parents nowadays in **asserting**[4] that schools are to blame for anti-social behaviour among children and that ...

It was a philosophy first **expounded**[5] by John Ruskin in the nineteenth century. If human ...

The recent events **underscore**[6] the need for a better understanding of the environmental impact of biotechnology. If this phase in the ...

Several scientists have **posited**[7] a link between climate change and bird migration patterns ...

In an attempt to **account for**[8] the lack of interest, political analysts have looked at past voting patterns. On the basis of ...

[1] repeated, restated [2] described briefly the main facts or ideas [3] are a perfect example of [4] saying that something is certainly true [5] developed, proposed [6] emphasise [7] suggested as a basic fact or principle [8] explain, find the cause of

B Categorising and including

Chinese visitors **comprised / made up** 70% of the hotel's guests last year. [consisted of]
The course **is comprised of** two elements: reading and writing. [is composed of]
These two approaches can be **subsumed** under one heading. [brought together, united]
The book **embraces** a number of issues, from economic to religious ones. [covers, includes]
Her philosophy is difficult to **categorise**. [label as belonging to a particular type or class]

> **Common mistake**
>
> Consist is followed by *of* when we refer to the elements which compose something: *The country consists of five major regions* (NOT ~~consists on/in~~ or ~~consists five~~).

C Structuring the text

Here are some words and expressions for ordering and arranging the parts of an essay.

function in the text	example
beginning	I should like to **preface** my argument with a true story. /ˈprefɪs/
mapping out the text	I shall **return** to this point later in my essay.
connecting points	This **brings me/us** to my next area of discussion, which is finance.
focusing	I should now like to **address** the question of the arms race.
ordering points	The arguments are presented **in ascending/descending order** of importance.
quoting/referring	The ideas of several writers will be **cited** in support of the argument. The text **alludes to** several themes that need closer examination.
including/excluding material	There will only be space to **touch upon*** the big question of political responsibility. It is impossible to **deal with** all the issues in this short essay. Discussion of the roots of the problem is **beyond the scope of** this essay.
drawing conclusions	We are **forced to conclude** that unemployment will always be with us.

*touch upon means to include something only briefly

Exercises

79.1 Look at these extracts from essays and use words from A opposite to improve their style, making the underlined words more formal.

1 The response from the public <u>really shows us</u> the importance of having a full investigation of the facts.
2 This view of the world was originally <u>laid out</u> by the Ancient Greek philosophers.
3 It is not easy to <u>find the reason</u> for the fall in population of these birds.
4 Economists have <u>said there might be</u> a link between exchange rates and a general lack of confidence in the European Union.
5 I should like to <u>say again</u> here that the issue is not one that can be easily resolved.
6 The recent events <u>are the best example of</u> the dilemma faced by politicians the world over.
7 In a 2005 article, Charles Plestow <u>said with great certainty</u> that the whole European Medieval era had been misinterpreted.
8 The lecturer <u>briefly repeated</u> the main arguments of her talk at the end.

79.2 Rewrite these sentences using the verb in brackets and making any other necessary changes.

1 70% of the landmass is mountain ranges. (COMPRISE)
2 A wide variety of subjects are dealt with in the book. (EMBRACE)
3 I think these three sections can all come under one heading. (SUBSUME)
4 The poems in this book have been divided up into different sections by topic. (CATEGORISE)
5 The course has five modules, from which students must choose three. (CONSIST)

79.3 Fill the gaps with words from C that express the meaning in brackets.

1 I shall .... to this line of argument later in the book. (come back to)
2 The question of monetary union .... us to our next topic: the idea of a federal Europe. (means we've arrived at)
3 Smithies just .... upon the subject of internet policing, but does not go into it in depth. (mentions only briefly)
4 I shall attempt to .... the problem of censorship later in this discussion. (attend to, consider)
5 Psychological factors in learning foreign languages are .... this article. (outside of the topic area)
6 I shall discuss the poets in .... order, that is to say I shall comment on the least important ones first. (going up)
7 In the final analysis, we are .... that there is little hope of stamping out illegal drugs altogether. (have no choice but to believe)
8 This unit has attempted to .... a range of useful vocabulary for formal writing. (give all the necessary information about)

79.4

Over to you

Choose six words or expressions from this unit which you could use in your special subject(s) of study. For each word or expression, write a sentence relevant to your subject(s). If possible, compare your writing with someone else.

80 Writing: style and format

Aspects of writing

If you're in a hurry, you can **scribble** a note to someone. [write quickly, without much care] A note is likely to be in a more **chatty** style than, say, a business letter. [when used about writing; *informal*]

I'll just **jot down** (informal) / **make a note of** (more formal) your phone number before I forget it. [write something down to remember it]

She got so bored at the meeting she spent the whole time **doodling**. [drawing and writing irrelevant things on the paper in front of her]

I'll **copy out** the information on hotels for you. [copy in writing]

I'm just **drafting** an application letter for that job I told you about. [making a first attempt at writing something] (noun = **draft**: the first **draft** of an essay)

Some students **write down** everything the lecturer says. [copy in writing what is spoken]

She's **writing up** her dissertation at the moment, so she's very tired and stressed. [making a proper final written text based on previous drafts]

She bought the **manuscript** of a famous poem at the sale. [original version produced by the author]

Type and print

Learning to **touch type** was one of the most useful things I've ever done. [type, using all your fingers without looking at the keyboard]

I've finished my book. I'll email the **typescript** to the publisher tomorrow. [an author's text that has not yet been published] I'll run you off a copy at the same time. [print out]

I've done the text, but I want to **format** it properly before printing it. [create the page as it will appear when printed]

I usually **cut and paste** or **copy and paste** bits of material from my notes when I'm writing an essay, then link them all together. [move text from one place to another electronically]

The letters and numbers on a keyboard can all be called **characters** – a password often needs to be at least eight **characters**, for example.

These words are in bold and *these words are italicised* / *in italics*.

These words are in a **shaded box**.

These words are in a different font size from the rest
and these words are in a different font or typeface.

"This sentence is in **double inverted commas / quotation marks**."
'This one is in **single quotation marks / quotes**.'

** This sentence has two **asterisks** in front of it.

• This sentence has a **bullet** (point) in front of it.

   This sentence **is indented**. [begins away from the normal margin]

Types of brackets: ( ) **round** brackets   < > **diamond/**
                        angle brackets
                    [ ] **square** brackets   { } **curly** brackets

CAPITALS or **UPPER CASE** (more technical) is the opposite of **small letters** or **lower case**. This person has written her name in **block capitals**: *MONICA KEEBLE*.

This is part of the first page of a typical academic book. Look at the structure and the names of the different elements. The numbers on the extract are in **superscript**. [written above the normal line]

Psychology **Today**[1]

Contents[2]

Chapter 1 What is psychology?[3]
  1.1 Some definitions[4]
  1.2 Psychology vs
       psychiatry

[1] title   [2] subtitle   [3] chapter heading
[4] sub-heading (within a chapter)

Exercises

80.1 Complete these sentences. The first letter of the missing word or phrase is given.

1 Let me just j.................................... your email address, or I'll forget it.
2 I'll just s.......................... a note for Preeti to tell her where we've gone.
3 I spent the whole lesson just d.......................... in the margin of my exercise book, I was so bored.
4 She's been w.......................... her PhD thesis for the last three months, that's why no one has seen her.
5 I'll email you a d.......................... of the letter, so you can suggest any changes before we send it.
6 In a bibliography, it is normal practice to put book titles in i.......................... rather than inverted commas, as some students do at first.
7 If you use even a sentence from someone else's work in your essay, then you must put it in q.......................... and acknowledge where it came from.
8 You computer password should consist of at least eight c.......................... , with at least one number.
9 Please r.......................... a copy of the agenda for everyone coming to the meeting.
10 Writers sometimes use an a.......................... to indicate that there is a footnote.

80.2 Circle the correct answer to describe these sentences.

1 **I love the summer.**	upper case	bold	italics
2 WILL YOU BE QUIET!	upper case	bold	italics
3 *This is crazy.*	upper case	bold	italics
4 Can you read this?	new typeface	new font size	
5 I've missed you.	new typeface	new font size	
6 so i wrote to mr smith.	upper case	lower case	block capitals
7 *ANNE TAYLOR*	small letters	lower case	block capitals
8 {See next page}	diamond	round	curly brackets	square brackets
9 [Not suitable for children]	diamond	round	curly brackets	square brackets
10 <johnjo@speedmail.com>	diamond	round	curly brackets	square brackets

80.3 Match up the words to make compound nouns.

1 bullet	☐	6 quotation	☐	a marks	f commas
2 type	☐	7 block	☐	b typing	g case
3 inverted	☐	8 lower	☐	c point	h brackets
4 square	☐	9 touch	☐	d heading	i face
5 font	☐	10 chapter	☐	e capitals	j size

80.4 Fill the gaps in these sentences with a word from the opposite page.

1 It's better to be more formal when you write an academic essay and not use such a .... style.
2 I think you should .... your CV differently if you want it to look good when it's printed out.
3 She works in the museum, conserving ancient ....
4 Dima got into trouble with the teacher because his essay was a cut and .... job straight from the internet.
5 You waste so much time typing with just two fingers – you really should learn to ....
6 I'll .... a letter of complaint to the restaurant, but I'd like you to check it before I finalise it.
7 Mrs Ward taught the children to .... the first line of each paragraph when they wrote stories.
8 My PhD thesis was called *Socialisation through children's literature* and its .... was *The Soviet example.*

81 Whatchamacallit: being indirect

A Vague and general words

In informal speech, we make frequent use of rather vague words and words with many different or rather general meanings like **thing** or **get**.

That's **one of the things** I want to talk to him about. [thing = subject]

Anne **has got a thing about** mice. [she either really likes or dislikes them]

Don't **make such a big thing of it**! [Don't make so much fuss about it!]

There **wasn't a thing** we could do about it. [a thing = anything]

For one thing, I haven't got time. **For another thing**, I can't afford it. [Firstly ..., secondly ...]

The thing is, I have to take my car for a service tomorrow morning. [used to introduce a topic or a problem, or to provide an explanation]

As things are at present, ... [as the situation is]

I don't **get** what you're saying. [understand]

We must **get** that parcel in the post today. [send]

She had big plans to travel the world but she just never **got it together**. [took positive action or organised herself]

Jill will **get things sorted (out)** today. [organise things so that the problem is solved]

I hope I can **get her to myself** this evening. [be alone with her]

B

When we can't remember a word or name, we often replace it with a vague word.

For objects: **thingy, thingummy** /ˈθɪŋəmi/, **thingumijig** /ˈθɪŋəmədʒɪɡ/, **thingamibob** /ˈθɪŋəməbɒb/, **whatsit, whatchamacallit** /ˈwɒtʃəməˌkɔːlɪt/, **whatnot**

Have you seen the **thingy** we use for keeping the door open?

For people: **whatsisname** /ˈwɒtsɪzneɪm/, **whatsisface** /ˈwɒtsɪzfeɪs/ (for a man); **whatsername** /ˈwɒtsəneɪm/, **whatserface** /ˈwɒtsəfeɪs/ (for a woman)

Did you see **whatsisname** today?

Note that these words can be written in different ways.

C

Some quantifiers are common in informal speaking but are rare in formal writing. For example, the following expressions mean a lot of:

bags of   a load of   loads of   a mass of   masses of   dozens of   tons of   umpteen

I can help you – I've got **bags of** time.

They can afford to go on expensive holidays as they've got **loads of** money.

I've tried phoning her **umpteen** times but she never seems to answer her mobile.

These expressions mean a little or some: **a bit of, a scrap of**.

I've got **a bit of** a headache.

You've been sitting there all day but you haven't done **a scrap of** work.

D Being indirect and less threatening

Here are some expressions which we can use in speech to make what we are saying sound less threatening and potentially offensive to the person we are talking to.

It's **not the most** practical/sensible/intelligent/appropriate thing you've ever done. [it's impractical / not very sensible / rather unintelligent / inappropriate]

It's not the most practical idea – and **I mean that in the nicest possible way**.

No offence intended, but I think you've misunderstood the basic problem.

If you don't mind my saying so, I think that you could have handled that better.

I gather you feel upset by the recent changes in the office. [I've heard it from someone]

Incidentally, have you paid your money for the club outing yet? [often used to introduce a new subject into the conversation in an indirect way]

What a load of idiots – **present company excepted**, of course. [not including you or me]

The staff here, **myself included**, have not been working quite as hard as we should.

Exercises

81.1 Look at A opposite. Explain what the underlined expressions with *thing* and *get* mean in the following sentences.

1 Don't <u>make such a big thing about</u> it. I'm only going for a few days.
2 Jess <u>has got a thing about</u> wanting straight hair, but her natural frizz suits her much better.
3 <u>The thing is</u>, I don't know when we'll be at home.
4 Unless <u>things</u> change, we won't be able to <u>get away for a holiday</u>.
5 We have a number of <u>things</u> to <u>get through</u> before lunchtime.
6 I don't <u>get on with</u> them very well. <u>For one thing</u>, we <u>like different things</u>. <u>For another</u>, I find them quite rude.
7 Did you <u>get</u> what the lecturer was saying? <u>I didn't get a thing</u>.
8 I hope we can <u>get everything sorted out</u> today. It's time we <u>got it together</u>!

81.2 What words do you think the speaker is looking for in each of these sentences? Choose from the words in the box.

> colander   hammer   rolling pin   protractor   sieve   Daniel Craig

1 Where's the thingummy for sifting the flour so there aren't any lumps in it?
2 Look, isn't that whatsisname? The actor who was in the latest *James Bond*?
3 I can't find the thingumibob for measuring angles.
4 Have you got a whatsit, you know, for bashing in nails?
5 Where's the thingy for draining potatoes?
6 I need a whatchamacallit – you know, one of those things for flattening pastry.

81.3 Look at the sentences in 81.2 again and find a different vague word from the one used in the exercise, e.g. *Where's the whatchamacallit for sifting the flour so there aren't any lumps in it?*

81.4 Look at C. Rewrite the underlined parts of these sentences in a more informal style.

1 The garden had <u>great numbers of</u> pink and yellow flowers.
2 I've asked her out <u>a great many</u> times, but she's always got some excuse.
3 He hasn't done <u>any</u> useful work here since he first got the job.
4 I've got <u>a large number of</u> papers I want to get rid of.
5 Alice invited <u>a great many</u> people to her party at the weekend.
6 Yasmin's got <u>a great deal of</u> energy – I don't know where she gets it all from!
7 <u>A great many</u> people were turned away because the lecture room was full.
8 She was told <u>many times</u> not to leave any valuables on her desk.

81.5 Look at D, and then fill the gaps in this text.

> This is a very boring party, present ¹............................ excepted, of course. No one, myself ²............................, seems to be making much of an effort to chat. I ³............................ a lot of people couldn't come. ⁴............................, no ⁵............................ intended, but don't you think you could have dressed a bit more smartly? If you don't ⁶............................ my saying so, I think you should have changed out of your gardening clothes. I mean that in the nicest ⁷............................ way, of course!

81.6 **Over to you**

Answer the questions for yourself.

- Have you got a thing about anything?
- Is there anything you need to get sorted out this week?

82 Give or take: more vague expressions

The words and phrases in this unit are mostly for informal conversation, except where indicated, and may sound inappropriate in more formal contexts.

A Vague expressions for numbers and quantities

He left a sum **in excess of** $1 million when he died. [more than; used in more formal contexts]
It'll cost you **somewhere in the region of** £800 a month to rent a flat. [less formal = around/ about £800]
It'll take five hours, **give or take** half an hour, to drive there. [could take 4.5 or 5.5 hours; *informal*]
The second meeting is **approximately** two and a half months after the first one. [could be a week before or after; *rather formal*]
It'll take a week **or so** to get the computer repaired. [more than a week, but unclear how much more; *informal*]
Quite a few students hadn't registered. [a surprisingly or undesirably *large* number]
There was only a **smattering** of women authors among the prize winners. [small proportion]
Would you like a **dash/smidgen** of chilli sauce with your kebab? [very small quantity]
I'd like a **dollop** of ice cream with my fruit salad. [usually a small amount; we can also say a large dollop]
Even though we put on **lashings** of suntan lotion, we still got sunburnt. [very large quantities]
I expect my business will never make **oodles** of money, but I enjoy running it. [very large quantities]
I used to have **stacks of** CDs with my files on, but now I have them all on one memory stick. [a large number or quantity of; *informal*]

B Making things less precise in informal conversation

More or less is often used with verbs and adverbs to make things more vague:
I think we've **more or less** solved the problem with the computer now.
My English is **more or less** the same level as the other students in the class.
A bit and **a bit of a** are used with adjectives and nouns to soften the meaning:
I'm **a bit** fed up with all the complaints I'm getting.
We were in **a bit of a** panic when we heard there was a strike at the airport.
Or whatever, or something, things like that and **that kind of thing** are useful expressions for referring vaguely to things and actions:
You could work on Saturday, then spend Sunday going to museums or galleries **or whatever**. [or similar activities]
If you don't want tea, have a lemonade **or something**. [any other kind of drink you want]
In the evenings we played board games **and things like that / and that kind of thing**. [different kinds of entertaining activities]
We need a big container made of plastic; a dustbin or **something along those lines** would do. [something fitting that description]
He said he was fed up with all the attacks and criticisms, **or words to that effect**. [or similar words expressing the same meaning]

Common mistake

We do not usually use *more or less* with people's ages:
He's about 35 (NOT He's ~~more or less~~ 35).

Exercises

82.1 Make the numbers in these sentences less precise, using expressions from A opposite. Follow the instructions in brackets.

1 The company will invest £10.3 million in new technology over the next five years. (formal, meaning 'more than')
2 It will cost you £10,000 to have the whole house redecorated. (less formal, approximately)
3 It could take six, seven or eight hours to drive to Aberdeen, depending on the traffic. (an informal *and* a more formal version)
4 Twenty-seven students failed the exam. I was rather surprised and disappointed. (a surprisingly large number)

82.2 These sentences contain some more vague language items used in conversation which are not presented on the opposite page. Underline the items that make the meaning less precise. Make a note of the grammar (i.e. is the item used with nouns, adjectives, etc?).

1 Her hair's a sort of reddish colour, and I'd say she's, well, forty, forty-fourish.
2 The garden was a bit on the big side, but it was very pretty.
3 There was a kind of elasticky thing that held the two parts together, and I've lost it.
4 They're good shoes. They're comfortable on long walks and that.
5 I've been to the doctor's and had treatments and suchlike, and I'm sure it helps in one way or another.

82.3 Fill the gaps in these sentences with a suitable word from A opposite.

1 I had a large slice of chocolate gateau with .... of cream.
2 Just a .... of milk in my coffee, please. I like it quite dark.
3 He put .... of hair gel on before going out to the disco.
4 Most of the people in the class were Spanish, with just a .... of other nationalities.
5 She put a .... of mayonnaise on her salad and mixed it all up.

82.4 Put an appropriate adjective or noun in the gap. There will usually be more than one possible answer. Then underline the vague expressions in each sentence.

1 It's a bit .... that she hasn't rung. I hope she's not ill.
2 The computer keeps crashing; it's a bit of a ....
3 It was a bit .... ; I couldn't remember his name. I'll apologise next time I see him.
4 If you don't want a big meal, you could have a .... or something.
5 Make yourself at home. There are some magazines there, or you can just .... or whatever.
6 It's a sort of craft shop; they sell .... and things like that.
7 When you go on business trips, do you have time to go .... and that?
8 There were six of us working, so we'd more or less .... by 5 pm.

82.5 **Over to you**

Which expressions from the opposite page could you use to talk about ...

- the amount of rent you pay for your accommodation or the amount you spend on food each week?
- how long it takes you to get from home to your workplace or place of study?
- any favourite items you like to add to your food, e.g. salt, cream, milk, ketchup?

83 The way you say it

A Verbs denoting volume: from quiet to loud

Mumble and **mutter** are both usually negative:
Stop **mumbling**! I can't hear what you're saying. He was **muttering** something under his breath, probably complaining, as usual.
Murmur can be more positive: They **murmured** their approval when he told them the plan.
The phrase **without a murmur** means without any protest, complaint or comment:
They accepted it all **without a murmur**. I was surprised; normally they argue about everything.
Raise one's voice can be used in positive or negative contexts:
You'll have to **raise your voice** a bit. She's a little hard of hearing. [speak louder]
'Don't you **raise your voice at** me!' [Do not speak in that loud, angry tone.]
Shout, yell, scream, roar and **shriek** are all followed by **at**: Don't **shout at** me!
Yell often conveys urgency, anger, frustration; it is also used when there is much surrounding noise: He **yelled** at the children to stop messing around with his computer.
'Stay where you are!' he **yelled** above the noise of the traffic.
Shriek means loud and very high-pitched. It can be used in positive and negative contexts:
'Oh, wow! That's fantastic!' she **shrieked**.
Roar suggests very loud volume, but deeper-pitched, like a lion. It is used in positive and negative contexts:
The crowd **roared** as he kicked the ball into the back of the net. 'How dare you come in here!' he **roared angrily**.

B Verbs describing speech and styles of conversation

Tom and Lily are always **nagging (at)** each other. [criticising faults or duties not done]
Stop **bickering over who sits by the window** you two! [arguing in an irritated way usually about something petty; synonym = **squabble**]
They spent all evening **slagging off** their colleagues. [criticising in an insulting way; *very informal*]
Jessie is always **whining** and **whingeing**. [complaining in an annoying way; *informal*, negative]
He's been **chatting away** on the phone all morning. [suggests light, non-serious talk; note how away is used to emphasise continuous/extended talk]
We always **gossip** about work when we go out together. [talk about people, rumours, etc.]
It took him a long time to realise they were **winding him up**. [/ˈwaɪndɪŋ/ teasing, fooling him; *informal*; noun = **wind-up**, often used in phrase, a **complete wind-up**]
I realised she was **buttering me up**. [saying nice things because she wanted something from me; negative]
Rick tends to **exaggerate** his problems, so don't take him too literally. [make something seem greater than it really is; noun = **exaggeration**]
Meg is inclined to **generalise** on the basis of her very limited experience. [make general statements about something; noun = **generalisation**]

C Speech and articulation problems

example	meaning
She speaks with a **lisp**. She **lisps**. She says 'thing' instead of 'sing'.	difficulty in making an 's' sound and making a 'th' sound instead
He hates speaking in front of people because he's got a really bad **stammer**.	speak with abnormal pauses and repetitions
'I want to t-t-t-tell you something,' she **stuttered** nervously.	repeat sounds at the beginning of words
He was **slurring** his words because he had drunk far too much alcohol.	his words had a slow, lazy sound; difficult to understand
I want to tell her I love her, but I **get tongue-tied**.	cannot say what I want to say because of nerves, i.e. emotional rather than physical problem affecting speech

Exercises

83.1 **Without looking at the opposite page, can you remember the following?**

1 a verb meaning 'to argue in an irritated manner' ....
2 a phrase meaning 'without complaining' ....
3 a verb meaning that someone often makes a 'th' sound instead of an 's' or 'z' sound

....
4 three verbs meaning 'speak very loudly' that are followed by *at* ....
5 how the verb *roar* is different from the verb *shriek* ....
6 a verb meaning talking about people, usually when they are not present, often about their private affairs ....
7 a verb meaning to tease someone or fool them to make them look silly ....
8 a noun meaning making something sound more important or worse than it really is

....

83.2 **Fill the gaps with one word.**

1 'I want to c-c-c-c-come with you,' she .... nervously.
2 Lara got .... , perhaps because of the famous people present, and didn't say a word all evening.
3 I wish you'd speak up and stop .... I can't hear a word you're saying.
4 I had to .... at him to be heard, the noise of the plane was so loud.
5 'I love you,' he .... softly.
6 I hate people who .... about their workmates. I never talk about other people.
7 The drugs had made her speech very incoherent. She was .... all her words.
8 She speaks with a .... – she says whithper, instead of whisper.
9 I know Ben is a little strange but you can't .... about all Canadians just because of him.

83.3 **Choose the correct word to complete these sentences.**

1 They're always *wining* / *whining* and whingeing about everything. Take no notice of them.
2 I don't believe you. I think you're winding me *up* / *down*.
3 Do you think Peggy was trying to *bicker* / *butter* me up for some reason? I wonder why she was saying all those nice things about me?
4 You're always *nagging* / *slagging* me! Just leave me alone and let me watch TV!

83.4 **Complete the crossword.**

Across

3 people often do this on the phone for hours
4 speak in a soft voice

Down

1 speak loudly
2 another word for stutter
5 make a loud, deep sound like a lion

84 Abbreviations and acronyms

A Abbreviations pronounced as individual letters

e.g.	for example, from *exempli gratia* (Latin)
i.e.	that is, from *id est* (Latin)
AD	the year of our Lord, from *Anno Domini* (Latin), used in the Christian calendar to count years since the birth of Christ; many people prefer CE as an alternative [Common Era]
BC	before Christ, used to count the years before the birth of Christ; many people prefer BCE [before the Common Era]
EU	European Union
ID	identity document
NB	note well, from *nota bene* (Latin), used as a warning or to point out something important
IQ	intelligence quotient: a way of measuring people's intelligence using a system of numbers
PTO	please turn over
USB	Universal Serial Bus: a type of connection between a computer and an electronic device
FAQ	frequently asked questions
ASAP	as soon as possible
VIP	very important person
RSVP	please reply (used on invitations, from French, *répondez s'il vous plaît*)
UFO	/juːef'əu/ unidentified flying object

B Shortened and blended words

bedsit	one room which is a **bed**room and a **sit**ting room
sitcom	short for **sit**uational **com**edy: a kind of humorous TV programme
sci-fi	/'saɪfaɪ/ science fiction
info	information
biodata	/'baɪəʊ deɪtə/ biographical data: details about someone's life, job and achievements
biopic	/'baɪəʊpɪk/ biographical picture: a film about the life of a real person
wi-fi	/'waɪfaɪ/ wireless fidelity: wireless connection for computers and electronic communications

C Acronyms

Some abbreviations are **acronyms**, i.e. they are formed from the first letters (or occasionally syllables) of a word or series of words and are pronounced as a word.

AIDS	/eɪdz/ acquired immune deficiency syndrome
NATO	/'neɪtəu/ North Atlantic Treaty Organisation
PIN	personal identification number (used on credit cards, bank cards, etc.)
VAT	value-added tax (a kind of tax on goods), pronounced /væt/ or /ˌviːeɪ'tiː/

D Abbreviations used in academic writing and bibliographies

fig.	figure (a picture or drawing, often with a number, in a book or other document). Example: See **fig.** 2.
ed. (plural eds)	editor/editors (often used in bibliographical references)
p. (plural pp.)	page/pages. Examples: see **p.** 26, see **pp.** 58–61 (from page 58 to page 61).
cf.	compare. Example: Carter (1997) investigated core vocabulary (**cf.** Lee 1987).
et al.	and others (used in bibliographical references to refer to a book or article with several authors, usually three or more). Example: O'Keeffe **et al.** (2010) discuss this problem.

Exercises

84.1 Insert the correct Latin abbreviations from A opposite into the gaps.

1 This helmet dates from 500 .... It's over 1,500 years old.
2 The file extension, ... the letters that follow its name, such as .docx, .jpg, .mp3, tells you what type of file it is.
3 Type your message here. .... , press 'save' before pressing 'send', or you may lose your message.
4 Fruits, ... lemons, pears and grapes, are sometimes added when cooking poultry.

84.2 How are the abbreviations and shortened expressions in these sentences pronounced? What do they stand for?

1 NATO is an alliance of North American and European countries.
2 Their FAQ page is completely useless. You can never find what you're looking for.
3 She's very fond of sci-fi films. I prefer biopics.
4 I forgot my PIN and couldn't get into my bank account online.
5 Do you believe in UFOs?
6 Write back asap.
7 Most of the cafés in town have free wi-fi.
8 The VAT rate is different in different countries of the EU.
9 A lot of people now prefer to use BCE instead of BC.
10 AIDS spread rapidly in the 1980s.
11 He manages to get into the VIP lounge at most airports. I don't know how he does it.
12 Where's the USB connection on this camcorder? I can't find it.

84.3 Answer the questions.

1 If someone asks you to send them your biodata, what will you send them?
2 Which is likely to be cheaper to rent in the same street in a city, a two-bedroom flat or a bedsit?
3 If someone asks you for ID, what do they want?
4 If you're watching a sitcom on TV, are you more likely to want to cry or to laugh?
5 If a party invitation says RSVP, what should you do?
6 If someone asks you to take an IQ test, what do they want to find out?
7 If you see PTO on a document, what should you do next?
8 What would you expect to find if you clicked on 'live traffic info' on a website?

84.4 Correct these false statements about academic abbreviations.

1 *Smedley and Jones (eds)* means Smedley and Jones wrote the book or article referred to.
2 *See fig.* 7 means look at number 7 in a list.
3 *Markov et al.* means Markov wrote a book or article with another person.
4 *See pp. 33–37* means see the information on page 33 and on page 37.
5 *Cf. Oswald (1987)* means 'read Oswald (1987)'.

85 Prefixes: creating new meanings

Common prefixes

In- (and its variations im-, il-, ir-) can make a word negative as in **inappropriate**, **incapable**, **inaccuracy**, **inability** and **imperfect**.

Mis- means wrongly or badly, e.g. **misbehave** and **misuse**. [use in the wrong way or for the wrong purpose]

Out- suggests being greater or better than something, e.g. **outnumber** [to be larger in number than another group] and **outweigh**. [be greater or more important than something else]

Re- has the meaning of 'do again' as in **reconsider** [think again about a decision or opinion], **redevelop** and **rethink**. [change what you think about something or what you plan to do]

Preposition-based prefixes

Over- may indicate (a) an excess of something, (b) being above something, or (c) going across something.

(a) EXCESS That film was **overrated** in my view. [people said it was better than it really was] It was a bad restaurant, with an **overpriced** menu. [too high prices]

(b) ABOVE Several of our neighbour's large trees **overhang** our garden. [their branches go over our garden]
Our garden is **overshadowed by** the block of flats next door. [the flats cast a shadow over our garden]
She always felt **overshadowed by** her older, more successful, sister. [metaphorical use, felt less important than]

(c) ACROSS He **overstepped the mark** when he said that. [crossed a barrier into offensive/ unacceptable behaviour] Will you be staying **overnight**? [cross from one day to the next]

Under- may indicate (a) less than the desired amount, (b) something below another thing, or (c) some kind of negative behaviour.

(a) LESS Don't **underestimate** the time it will take. [think it will be less than it really is]
The company is seriously **understaffed**. [lacking staff]

(b) BELOW It's quite wet **underfoot**. Did it rain last night? [on the ground, beneath your feet]
The **underlying** question is a very difficult one. [the deeper question]

(c) NEGATIVE I wish you would not **undermine** everything I do. [attack, weaken] He did it in a very **underhand** way. [secretly and possibly dishonestly]

Up- can suggest a change of some kind, often positive.

The airline **upgraded** me to business class. [changed my ticket to a better class]
There has been an **upturn** in the economy. [change for the better]

Less frequent prefixes

Con-/com- often suggests mixing things together (often in verbs of communication).
converse commiserate condolences congeal contaminate

Pro- can often suggest pushing something forward or increasing it.
promote proliferate procrastinate procreate

E- can give the idea of something coming out of something.
They were **ejected** from the restaurant for bad behaviour. [thrown out; *formal*]
The machine **emitted** a loud noise and then stopped working. [gave out; *formal*]

Exercises

85.1 Choose a word from A opposite to complete each sentence.

1 They are planning to .... the area around the old bus station.
2 It is .... to use colloquial language in a formal essay.
3 The yes votes .... the no votes by two to one.
4 Ivan's English is excellent but he still tends to .... idioms occasionally.
5 We all hope you will .... your decision to turn down our offer of a job.
6 I'm afraid I only have an .... understanding of the situation myself.
7 These pupils do not usually .... in class.
8 An .... to drive is a serious problem for anyone in this line of business.
9 Lance seems to be .... of understanding even the simplest instructions.
10 Paula lost marks in her science test because of the .... of her measurements.

85.2 Decide which of the meanings of *over-* and *under-* are most obvious in the words in bold. Use the labels (a), (b) or (c), as in B opposite. Circle the correct letter. Use a dictionary if necessary.

1 I really think she **overstated** her case, and lost a lot of sympathy.   a   b   c
2 The plane's **undercarriage** failed to open and it crashed.   a   b   c
3 A detailed list of awards is given **overleaf**.   a   b   c
4 He has a very **overbearing** personality.   a   b   c
5 The project was **underfunded** from the outset.   a   b   c
6 During the cruise, a child fell **overboard** and drowned.   a   b   c
7 Priya's contribution to the project has sometimes been **underrated**.   a   b   c
8 Phil always gets an **underling** to do the tasks he doesn't enjoy.   a   b   c

85.3 Rewrite these sentences using words from the opposite page.

1 There are more women than men on my course. *Women outnumber men on my course.*
2 The hotel gave me a luxury room instead of the ordinary one I'd booked.
3 Would you like to spend the night there or come back the same day?
4 The problem that lies under the surface is a very serious one.
5 For me, the advantages of air travel are more significant than the disadvantages.
6 I think this hotel charges too much.
7 It's slippery walking just here. Be careful.
8 The company experienced a rise in popularity after it changed its name.
9 I felt that what she said was critical of my position and weakened it somewhat.
10 It would be a mistake to think Frances was less intelligent than she really is.

85.4 Match these definitions to a word in C opposite. Use a dictionary if necessary.

1 to keep delaying something that must be done ....
2 to make something poisonous or less pure ....
3 to throw out with force ....
4 suddenly to increase a lot in number ....
5 to sympathise with someone's unhappiness ....
6 to change from a liquid or soft state to a solid or hard state ....
7 to produce young (formal) ....
8 to chat (formal) ....
9 to send out (a beam, noise, smell or gas) ....
10 to encourage people to buy or use something ....

86 Suffixes: forming new words

A Productive suffixes

Many suffixes (and prefixes too) are **productive**. [still used to create new words] You might feel adventurous enough to try **coining** some words of your own! [creating] The meaning of the example words below is clear from the meanings of the root and the suffix.

-able can be used productively, whereas *-ible* never is. It combines with verbs to form adjectives. Note that **-able** means 'can be': a **washable** jacket [one that can be washed] **disposable** nappies   **predictable** results   **avoidable** problems   a **manageable** situation

-conscious combines with nouns to form adjectives that describe people who consider one aspect of their lives especially important: **health-conscious** person   **class-conscious** society **safety-conscious** company   **time-conscious** workforce

-free combines with nouns describing something undesirable to form adjectives to describe nouns without that undesirable aspect: **stress-free** life   **tax-free** shop   **additive-free** food

-rich combines with nouns (often chemical or organic substances) to form adjectives to describe nouns with a lot of that substance: **fibre-rich** diet   **calcium-rich** foods

-led combines with nouns and nationality adjectives to form adjectives describing things that are controlled or influenced by the original noun or nationality: **community-led** initiative **student-led** protest   **worker-led** uprising

-minded combines with adjectives or nouns to form new adjectives describing people with particular characters, opinions or attitudes: **like-minded** friends [with similar interests] **career-minded** young women   **money-minded** managers   **high-minded** [having high moral standards]

-proof combines with nouns to form adjectives describing things that can resist the damage or difficulty caused by that noun: **ovenproof** dish   **waterproof** jacket   **soundproof** room **idiot-proof** instructions

-related combines with nouns to form adjectives to describe one thing as connected with another: **stress-related** absence from work   **age-related** illness

-ridden combines with nouns to form adjectives describing people or things with a lot of that noun: **guilt-ridden** person   **crime-ridden** city   **bedridden** [a person has to stay in bed because they are ill]

-worthy combines with nouns to form adjectives that describe people or things that merit whatever the original noun refers to: **newsworthy** incident [worth reporting in the news] **praiseworthy** action/pupil [deserving praise]

> ### Language help
> The first part of words with –ed, –related, –conscious, etc. is usually a singular rather than a plural noun: *university-led, crime-related, age-conscious* (NOT ~~universities-led, crimes-related, ages-conscious~~).

B Suffixes in different word classes

-ly is not only an adverb ending, it also forms quite a few adjectives: **lively** children [full of energy]   **costly** holiday [expensive]   **leisurely** walk [relaxed]   **miserly** man [mean with money]

-ant is most familiar as an adjective ending (**relevant** information, **distant** hills) but it can also make nouns from verbs to describe a person: an **applicant** for a job   an insurance **claimant** a police **informant**   a quiz **contestant**   an **occupant** of a house

-en makes adjectives from nouns (**woollen** jumper, **golden** hair) but it also makes verbs from adjectives: **to moisten** your lips   **to sweeten** tea   a situation **worsens**   a face **reddens**

Exercises

86.1 Complete the table below with the correct phrases.

suffix	new example in phrase	meaning
-able	*a debatable issue*	an issue that can be debated
-conscious		employers who are very aware of money
-free		a city centre without any cars
-rich		a drink which provides a lot of energy
-led		fashion that is dictated by the French
-minded		friends who are very focused on sports
-proof		a car with protection against bullets
-related		crime that is connected in some way with drugs
-ridden		a society where there is a lot of poverty
-worthy		a person who deserves others' trust

86.2 Match each adjective with the two nouns it best collocates with in the box.

EXAMPLE
student-led: *rebellion, demonstration*

1 additive-free
2 avoidable
3 disposable
4 guilt-ridden
5 high-minded
6 newsworthy
7 oil-rich
8 ovenproof
9 soundproof
10 stress-related

knives and forks   income   drinks
mistake   ~~rebellion~~   delay   foods   room
criminal   expression   glove   story
booth   illness   speech   personality
dish   country   ~~demonstration~~   principles
problems   economy

86.3 Which of the suffixes in A opposite could combine with the words in the box below to make new words? Note that there is more than one possibility for each word.

child   dust   calorie   work

86.4 Rewrite the sentences using the suffix given in brackets.

1 The weather can't be predicted. (-able) *The weather is unpredictable.*
2 Poisonous mushrooms can be easily identified. (-able)
3 He thinks so much about his career that he has no time for his family. (-minded)
4 The new speed cameras are supposed to be indestructible by vandals. (-proof)
5 During the Civil War, the country was totally overcome by terror. (-ridden)
6 The soil on that farm contains a lot of nutrients. (-rich)
7 The bank decided that he did not have enough income to allow him credit. (-worthy)

86.5 Using a suffix from A, make up words with the following meanings.

1 food for vegetarians must be this
2 connected with class
3 containing a lot of vitamins
4 can be dry-cleaned
5 very aware of people's clothes
6 initiated by the government

86.6 Are the following words adverbs, adjectives or verbs? Use a dictionary if necessary.

1 dampen
2 friendly
3 dearly
4 silken
5 roughen
6 masterly
7 kindly
8 darken

87 Word-building and word-blending

A Common well-established word parts

Many literary or academic words in English are formed using Latin and ancient Greek prefixes and roots. Many English speakers are not aware of the meanings of the word parts listed here, but knowing them can help you to understand and remember new words.

word part	meaning	example
auto-	self	an **autonomous** region [self-ruling]
bio-	life, living things	**biodegradable** packaging [able to decay naturally]
cyber-	relating to computers and robots	a **cybercafé** [café where customers can use computers and the internet]
de-	opposite action	**demotivate** [make someone feel less interested and enthusiastic about something]
mono-	single, one	**monocycle** [cycle with just one wheel]
-graph-	writing	a **monograph** [long article or short book on a single subject that the writer has studied for a long time]
-gress-	step, walk, go	a **congress** [a conference, i.e. a meeting where people come together]
-ics	an area of study or knowledge	**obstetrics** [the study of childbirth]
-phon-	sound	**phonetics** [the study of human speech sounds]
-ology	study	**criminology** [the study of crime and criminals]
pre- (*opp.* = post-)	before	**prepaid** tickets [tickets paid for in advance]
retro-	back, backwards	**retroactive** law [taking effect from a date in the past]
techno-	relating to advanced machines	**technophobia** [fear of using technology such as computers]
tele-	over a distance	**telepathic** experience [feeling something from a distance]

Language help

Although the word parts above will help you to understand words, you cannot use them as freely to form new words as the prefixes and suffixes in Units 85 and 86.

B Blends

An interesting, if much less common, way of forming words is by combining two well-established words, e.g. **brunch** = a meal that is a combination of breakfast and lunch.
heliport: a place where helicopters can land and take off (helicopter + airport)
smog: polluted fog (smoke + fog)
motel: a roadside hotel for people travelling by car (motor + hotel)
webinar: a seminar delivered over the internet via a designated website (web + seminar)
guesstimate: an approximate calculation (guess + estimate; verb = to guesstimate)
docudrama: TV programme that dramatises real historical events (documentary + drama)
breathalyser: a device to find out how much alcohol a person has drunk (breath + analyse)

Exercises

87.1 Using information from the table in A, explain the basic meanings of these words.

1 biography = *writing about a life*
2 monologue
3 telephone
4 autobiography
5 phonology
6 to retrogress
7 graphology
8 to destabilise
9 autograph

87.2 Look at the following word parts. Use a dictionary to find two new words beginning with these and write them in your vocabulary notebook. Choose only words that use the meanings studied in this unit. *Postman*, for example, clearly has not been formed using the prefix *post-* meaning 'after'.

1 mono
2 techno
3 retro
4 tele
5 auto
6 pre
7 post
8 bio

87.3 Rewrite these sentences, replacing the underlined words with a word that includes the word part given. Use a dictionary if necessary.

1 I had to put off my trip to Japan. (POST)
   I had to postpone my trip to Japan.
2 She asked the singer for his signature on the back of her table napkin. (GRAPH)
3 She took a degree in the science of crime at Stockholm University. (OLOGY)
4 The novel is largely based on the writer's own life. (BIO)
5 It's an exhibition looking back at the painter's life and work. (RETRO)
6 He believes in the idea that you can cure yourself by suggesting to yourself that you are cured. (AUTO)
7 Working at home and keeping in contact with the office by phone, text-messaging and email is now quite common. (TELE)
8 Some English philosophers in the 19th century believed in the abolition of industry. (DE)
9 Crime committed through the internet is a huge cause for concern. (CYBER)

87.4 Rewrite these sentences, replacing the underlined word with an explanatory phrase.

1 Most of the time, planes fly on autopilot.
   Most of the time planes fly automatically, controlled by a computer rather than the pilot.
2 The firm makes job applicants do a graphology test.
3 The school always takes very seriously any case of cyberbullying.
4 Matt's a bit of a technophobe.
5 He's giving a paper at a pre-conference event in Spain.
6 She did a course in informatics.

87.5 What words have been combined to make these blends? What do you think they mean?

1 infomercial
2 podcast
3 camcorder
4 veggieburger
5 swimathon
6 freeware

88 English: a global language

A The origins of English vocabulary

Some languages do not easily accept words from other languages into their **lexicon**[1], but English has always welcomed them. It is estimated that English vocabulary has its **sources**[2] in at least 120 languages. Some languages have, of course, provided English with more words than others. English started out with a basic **Anglo-Saxon**[3] **word stock**[4]. **Viking**[5] and **Norman**[6] invaders from the 9th century onwards **enriched**[7] the language enormously with large numbers of words brought from their own languages. The Vikings brought new words of Germanic origin while the Normans spoke a form of French. Both sets of invaders **had** an enormous **impact on**[8] English vocabulary, explaining why English may sometimes seem to have several words for the same basic **concept**[9]. During the Renaissance of the 15th to the 17th centuries, scholars introduced many words of **classical origin**[10]. And throughout history, English speakers' contact with the world as explorers, scientists, traders, pirates and holiday-makers has had **linguistic consequences**[11] in a wealth of new words from every part of the world that they reached. These words taken from other languages are sometimes referred to as **loan words** or **borrowings**.

[1] vocabulary (specialist term)   [2] where something comes from   [3] Old English   [4] set of words
[5] Norse, from the north of Europe, e.g. Denmark or Norway   [6] from Normandy, a region in the north of France   [7] made richer   [8] influenced, had an effect on   [9] idea   [10] from Latin or Ancient Greek
[11] results affecting language

B English words from other languages

language	word	meaning	phrase
Arabic	amber	yellowy-orange substance originating from tree resin and used in jewellery	an **amber** necklace
Dutch	roster	list of people's turns for jobs	the cooking **roster**
Farsi	tabby	grey and brown stripy cat	our old tabby
German	gimmick	an amusing or unusual way of attracting attention	advertising **gimmicks**
Greek	tonic	medicine to make you feel stronger and better	take a **tonic**
Hindi	cot	child's bed with high vertical sides	sleep in a **cot**
Icelandic	mumps	a childhood illness	have **mumps**
Japanese	karaoke	type of entertainment where ordinary people sing to popular music	a **karaoke** machine
Portuguese	palaver	unnecessary trouble	What a **palaver**!
Russian	intelligentsia	social class of intellectuals	19th century **intelligentsia**
Spanish	hammock	net hung and used as a bed	sleep in a **hammock**
Turkish	turban	type of men's headwear, made from a long piece of cloth	wear a **turban**

C False friends

Some English words may look like words in your language but have a different meaning. Such words are known as **false friends**, e.g. the German word *Gift* looks like the English word **gift** [present] but actually means *poison* in German. The English word **sympathetic** resembles a word meaning, simply, *nice* in many other European languages, but in English **sympathetic** has a much narrower meaning [understanding and caring about someone else's suffering]. Note also that the pronunciation of a word borrowed into English may be quite different from its pronunciation in its language of origin.

Exercises

88.1 Complete the sentences with a word from A opposite.

1 A linguist may talk about a language's vocabulary as its ....
2 Old English is also known as ....
3 Ancient Greek and Latin are referred to as .... languages.
4 A loan word can also be termed a ....
5 Where something originates from can be called its ....
6 A word for something that happens as a result of something else is ....
7 A synonym for effect or influence is ....
8 The opposite of impoverish or make poorer is ....

88.2 Which of the words in B opposite do these pictures illustrate?

1 .... 2 .... 3 .... 4 ....

88.3 Fill the gaps with one of the words from B.

1 We're having a .... evening at school tonight – it should be great fun.
2 Most babies these days have an injection to protect them from getting ....
3 I have some lovely .... earrings. They match my orange scarf perfectly.
4 Have a refreshing drink of lemon and honey every morning – it'll be just the .... you need to make you feel better again.
5 Who's on the .... for the cleaning this week?
6 The clowns went out into the street as a .... to advertise their circus.

88.4 Think of words that have come from your own language into English. Try to find words from these topic areas, which are particularly rich in loan words in English.

- food and drink
- animals, flowers and landscape features
- industrial products and inventions
- clothing and the home
- politics and society
- the arts, sports and leisure activities

88.5 Make a list of false friends for English and your own first language. Here is a list begun by a Spanish speaker.

English word	similar word in my language + meaning	meaning in English
complexion	complexión = person's physical build	appearance of skin on a person's face (a clear complexion)
destitute	destituido = removed from job	without money, food, home or possessions

88.6 These words are said to have moved from English into a number of other languages. Which of them exist in your language?

thematic fields	English source words
food and drink	beefsteak, jam, pudding, sandwich
animals	bulldog, dog, skunk
clothing	blazer, cardigan, pullover, sweater
political and social life	parliament, Tory, boycott, budget, inflation, strike
industry and inventions	car ferry, container, freight, computer chip, cable TV
arts, sports and leisure	ace [1 in playing cards], boxer, football, break-dance

89 False friends: words easily confused

A Words similar in form and close in meaning

The United Nations should **intervene** to stop the civil war. [step in; neutral in meaning]
She shouldn't **interfere** in things that don't concern her. [involve herself; negative and critical]
The phone's been ringing **continually**. It's driving me crazy. [very frequently; often negative]
Stir the mixture **continuously** until it boils. [without stopping; from a recipe]
There's a new **series** on TV about space exploration. [set of related programmes]
I don't want to miss this week's episode of *Oliver Twist*. It's a **serial** – if I miss one I'll lose track of the story. [set of programmes where the story continues over different episodes]
We sat **in the shade of** a big oak tree. [out of the sun; pleasant connotation]
The evening sun cast long **shadows**. [dark areas or shapes]
They lived **in the shadow of** a chemical factory. [in a place dominated by; negative connotation]
She **complimented** me on my performance at the concert. [praised, expressed admiration for]
I took a course in programming to **complement** my other IT skills. [make them seem better, more complete or more attractive in combination]

B Words of different form but from the same area of meaning

The cake mixture should be **moist** but not sticky. [slightly wet; from a recipe]
The climate in the north is **damp** and rather cold. [slightly wet in an unpleasant way]
The **theme** of the festival was '1,000 years of culture'. [the main idea that everything followed]
The **topic** of conversation soon changed to the news. [what the people talked about]
The **security** officer noticed a broken window. [concerned with protection of property, etc.]
The **safety** officer told him that he must wear a helmet. [concerned with prevention of accidents, etc.]
We took a smaller road in order to **avoid** the roadworks on the motorway. [stay away from]
The escaped prisoner **evaded** capture for three months. [escaped from; more formal]

C Phrasal combinations

Phrasal verbs may have noun forms with different meanings.

verb	noun
Six men **broke out** of the prison.	There was a **breakout** at the prison.
The disease has **broken out** in several villages in the north of the country.	There has been an **outbreak** of the disease in several villages in the north of the country.
Economists are **looking out** for signs of an end to the recession.	The **outlook** is not good. The economy seems to be stagnant.
He stood at the corner **looking out** for police cars.	He was the **lookout** while the others robbed the bank.
The Swimming Club decided to **set up** a committee to look into the club rules.	The company **setup** is quite complex, with branches in 30 different countries.

In some cases, two verb forms have the same words in a different order and different meanings.

verb 1: particle first	verb 2: particle second
upend [move into a vertical position]	**end up** [finish]
uphold [confirm, support]	**hold up** [delay]
outdo [do better than]	**do out** [decorate]
outrun [run faster than]	**run out** [use something so there is none left]
upset [make someone worried, unhappy or angry]	**set up** [organise or arrange something]

Language help

Common prepositions often occur as prefixes, (e.g. *up* and *out* in the table above). Other examples include *over* (*overcook*, *overcome*), *in* (*input*, *income*). Make a note of new examples as you meet them.

See also Unit 85.

Exercises

89.1 Choose the correct word in these sentences.

1 I have always tried not to *intervene / interfere* in things that are not my business.
2 *Security / Safety* at the factory is not good. There have been several accidents involving machinery recently.
3 There are some *themes / topics* I don't like to talk about with my friends, such as politics and religion.
4 He was dozing happily in the *shade / shadows* of an old beech tree.
5 The *theme / topic* of her latest novel is growing up as an only child in the 1970s.
6 The teacher *intervened / interfered* to stop the argument between the two students.
7 The receptionist called the *safety / security* officer once it became clear that there had been a burglary.
8 He was *continually / continuously* complaining about something or other.
9 The moon sometimes casts wonderful *shadows / shade* on the sea.
10 You have to press the button *continually / continuously* until the green light comes on. Don't take your finger off it, or it won't work.

89.2 Decide whether the particle should go *before* or *after* the verb in these sentences.

1 The cheetah is so fast it can .... run .... a fast-moving vehicle. (OUT)
2 The police .... held .... the traffic while the President's car passed. (UP)
3 Sean made an insensitive comment and didn't realise how much he'd .... set .... Wendy. (UP)
4 The committee .... held .... her complaint, and she was awarded compensation. (UP)
5 We decided to .... do .... the living room and went online to choose paint colours. (OUT)
6 We .... ended .... eating in a dingy café on the edge of town. (UP)
7 The radio's not working. The batteries have .... run .... (OUT)
8 We .... ended .... the sofa and used it to block the doorway. (UP)

89.3 Choose a noun from the box that can be associated with the following sentences.

> lookout   outbreak   breakout   upset   outlook   setup

1 There has been violence in the capital city.
2 My stomach was bad so I couldn't go to work.
3 The prospects for the economy are good over the coming years.
4 I wanted to learn more about how the business was organised.
5 She made sure nobody was looking, and her husband did the shoplifting.
6 Four prisoners have escaped from a maximum security prison.

90 One word, many meanings

A Polysemy

A great many words in English have more than one meaning. Linguists call this aspect of vocabulary polysemy.

Look at these sentences and think about how you would translate the words in italics into your own language.

fair   It's only *fair* that we should share the housework.
        The Frankfurt Book *Fair* is a very important event for most publishers.
        The forecast is for the weather to stay *fair* for the next week.
        I've got *fair* skin and burn easily in the sun.
        His marks in his final exams ranged from excellent to *fair*.

flat   The firefighters managed to save the children from the burning third-floor *flat*.
        The countryside round here is terribly *flat* and boring.
        To join the Fitness Club you pay a *flat* fee of £500.
        The sonata is in B *flat* minor.
        She finished the exercise in five minutes *flat*.

capital Fill in the form in *capital* letters.
         Wellington is the *capital* of New Zealand.
         You need plenty of *capital* to open a restaurant.
         Capital punishment has been abolished in many countries.

mean   What does 'coagulate' *mean*?
        I didn't *mean* to hurt you.
        He's far too *mean* to buy her flowers.
        The *mean* temperature for July is 25°C.
        You shouldn't be so *mean* to your little sister.

You probably need a different word to translate *fair*, *flat*, *capital* and *mean* in each sentence. Sometimes the meanings are clearly related – *flat* as in *countryside* has a connection with *flat* as in *apartment* in that they both include an idea of being on one level. Sometimes, however, there is no connection at all. For example, the meaning of *fair* as in Book *Fair* has no obvious connection with any of the other meanings of *fair*. Words like this can be called **homographs** (words with the same spellings but different meanings).

B Being aware of polysemy

It is useful to be aware of polysemy in English for several reasons.

- You need to remember that the meaning you first learnt for a word may not be the one that it has in a new context.
- You need to be aware that in English, words can sometimes be used as different parts of speech. *Flat* with its *apartment* meaning, for instance, can become an adjective, e.g. a set of *flat keys*.
- Learning about the range of meanings that a word can have can help you to learn several meanings for the price of one.
- It will also help you to understand jokes in English as these are often based on polysemous words.

Language help

The context of a word with multiple meanings will usually make it absolutely clear which of the word's possible meanings is intended. So you can understand what, for example, the noun **drill** probably means in (a) a dental context, (b) an army context, (c) a road-building context, (d) a language-learning context.

Exercises

90.1 Find the example sentence in A opposite in which *fair, flat, capital* or *mean* has the following meaning.

1 intend
2 exactly
3 proper, just
4 city with the seat of government
5 light in colour

6 unkind
7 fixed
8 neither very good nor very bad
9 money
10 unwilling to spend money

90.2 What part of speech is the italicised word in each of the example sentences in A? Write a synonym or explanation for each of the examples not used in 90.1.

90.3 Here are some more examples of polysemous words in English. Which word can fill all the gaps in each group of sentences?

1 He struck a .... and we slowly began to look around the dark cave.
   The teenage cooks in the competition were a .... for any of the adults.
   Their marriage has been called a .... made in heaven.
2 That bird has an unusually long ....
   Don't forget to keep the receipt when you pay your hotel ....
   Parliament is currently discussing a .... proposing changes to copyright legislation.
3 Hannah gave us a lovely .... of glasses as a wedding present.
   Let's now try and .... a date for our meeting next week.
   My father has very .... opinions about how people should behave.
4 I've applied for a .... in our company's Paris office.
   The end of the race is indicated by a .... with a flag on it.
   Why not .... your query on an online forum? You're bound to get a quick response.
5 I didn't get my assignment back because the teacher hadn't had time to .... it.
   Sales have already passed the million ....
   You've got a red .... on your cheek. It looks like lipstick.
6 You need to be a special kind of person to .... a successful business.
   Do you fancy going for a .... this evening?
   Thanks to the hot weather, our shop has had a .... on ice cream.

90.4 Look at the Language help box. What does *drill* mean in each of the four contexts suggested?

90.5 What would the given word be most likely to mean in each of the contexts suggested? Use a dictionary if necessary.

1 register: a a primary school   b a post office
2 interest: a people planning a festival b a bank
3 dice: a a kitchen   b people playing a board game
4 service: a people playing tennis   b in a restaurant
5 case: a in a lawyer's office   b at an airport
6 cue: a people playing snooker   b in the theatre

90.6 Explain these one-line jokes. They are all based on polysemy.

1 I wondered why the tennis ball was getting bigger. Then it hit me!
2 Smaller babies may be delivered by stork but the heavier ones need a crane.
3 Time flies like an arrow. Fruit flies like a banana.
4 You know prices are rising when you buy a winter jacket and even down is up.

91 Collocation: which words go together

A Adjective + noun collocations

Nouns often have typical adjectives which go with them. Here are some examples. Compare **thing** and **article**:

we say	we don't usually say
the **real thing**	the genuine thing
the **genuine article**	the real article

I don't like five-a-side football, I prefer the **real thing**. [i.e. real, live football]
These trainers are the **genuine article**. Those others are just cheap imported copies.

You can give a **broad summary** of something. (NOT a wide summary)
You can describe something **in great detail**. (NOT in big detail)

Some adjectives go with a restricted range of nouns. For example:
a **formidable opponent / reputation / task / challenge**

B Verb + adverb collocations

Often, verbs have typical adverbs that collocate with them. The lines here show which collocations are normal:

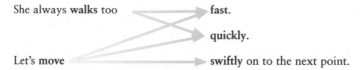

She always **walks** too   **fast.**

    quickly.

Let's **move**   **swiftly** on to the next point.

It's something I **feel strongly** about. (NOT I feel powerfully about)
If I **remember rightly**, it happened at about 6.30. (NOT If I remember perfectly)

C Adverb + adjective collocations

It is useful to learn which adverbs most typically modify particular types of adjectives. For example, the adverb **utterly**, which means totally or completely, very frequently occurs before adjectives with negative connotations, although it can also be used with neutral or positive words. Typical examples are: **appalling, dismal, depressed, disgusting, distasteful, exhausted, false, fatuous, impossible, lost, ludicrous, naive, pointless, wrong, ridiculous, unacceptable, useless.** Try to notice this kind of regularity when learning words.

D Verb + object collocations

Verbs and their objects often form collocations.
You **raise your hand** to ask a question. (NOT lift your hand)
You can **raise a family.** [bring up children] (NOT lift a family)
You can **visit / go to / click on / check out a website.**

> **Language help**
> Collocation is concerned with the way words regularly occur together, often in unpredictable ways. It is a very good idea when learning new words to learn any typical collocations that go with them.

Exercises

91.1 Is the correct word *real* or *genuine* in these sentences? Choose the more normal collocation. If both are acceptable, choose them both.

1 The photos of the pyramids are wonderful. One day I'd love to see the *real / genuine* thing.
2 He just doesn't live in the *real / genuine* world. He lives in a fantasy world all the time.
3 This handbag is made of *real / genuine* leather.
4 She is a very *real / genuine* person. If she promises something, she'll do it.
5 This home-made champagne is nice, but it's not as good as the *real / genuine* article.

91.2 Choose one of the words below each sentence to fill the gaps. In each case only one of them is the normal collocation for the underlined word. Use a dictionary if necessary.

1 After his death, she went to the hospital to collect his <u>personal</u> ....
  A affairs   B objects   C effects   D extras
2 He made a rather .... <u>attempt</u> at an apology, but it didn't convince anyone.
  A faint   B frail   C fragile   D feeble
3 George was a .... <u>opponent</u>, and I respected him for that.
  A formidable   B dreadful   C forbidding   D threatening
4 I began to feel .... <u>anxious</u> when she didn't arrive.
  A totally   B pretty   C utterly   D blatantly
5 She seemed to be .... <u>bewildered</u> by the answer they gave her.
  A vividly   B strongly   C utterly   D heavily

91.3 Choose the most suitable collocation in these sentences. The word you choose should have the approximate meaning given in brackets. Use a dictionary if necessary.

1 A *brisk / brusque / brash* walk before breakfast helps to *enforce / sharpen / grow* the appetite. (quick and energetic; increase, make stronger)
2 The death *tally / tale / toll* in the earthquake has now risen to 20,000. (number or total)
3 Let's take a *sluggish / plodding / leisurely* stroll along the beach, shall we? (slow and not energetic)
4 If you want to stay at home tonight, that's *utterly / perfectly / blatantly* OK with me. (completely, 100%)
5 My aunt *bequeathed / bequested / bereaved* £20,000 in her will to cancer research. (gave after her death)
6 If I remember *rightly / keenly / fairly*, she had two brothers, both older than her. (correctly)
7 If you want information about the publisher of this book, you can *accede / call / visit* their website at www.cambridge.org. (consult, look at)
8 Eating all those peanuts has *spoilt / attacked / lowered* my appetite. I don't feel like dinner now. (destroyed, decreased)

91.4 Which collocation is more likely? Choose the correct answer.

1 a strong car / a powerful car
2 strong tea / powerful tea
3 auburn hair / auburn carpet
4 a doleful party / a doleful expression
5 a lengthy room / a lengthy meeting

91.5

Over to you

During the next week, try to find one new collocation that you were not aware of before for each of these categories:

ADJECTIVE + NOUN   VERB + OBJECT   VERB + ADVERB

92 Metaphor: seeing the light

A What are metaphors?

Metaphor is concerned with using words in abstract rather than literal ways. It is a way of expressing something by comparing it indirectly with something else that has similar characteristics.

If we call a city a **jungle**, for example, we are using a metaphor. We are suggesting that a city is like a jungle in that it is wild and full of dangers.

If we say that someone **lights up our life**, we are using a metaphor. We are suggesting that person is like a light in our life in that they bring us great happiness.

B Idioms and metaphors

Many idioms are metaphorical expressions which are in common use.

be on the ball [be very aware of things and ready to act – like a good footballer]

to **keep someone/something on a tight rein** [have a lot of control over someone/ something – like a rider having control over a horse]

Some of the most common idiom-metaphors are based on parts of the body. So we might say that a building is in the **heart** of the city. [centre] We can call the place where a river joins the sea its **mouth** and the person in charge of an organisation its **head**. If you say that someone **has an eye for** a bargain, you mean they are good at finding a bargain. If you **keep a (close) eye on** someone/something, you watch them carefully. If you say that something is **in safe hands**, you mean that the person in charge is capable. If you say that something **goes hand in hand with** something else, you mean that they exist together and are interconnected. Rights **go hand in hand with** responsibilities. If you talk about doing something using a **rule of thumb**, you mean you are calculating something in a way that is not exact but will allow you to be accurate enough.

C Common metaphorical concepts in English

Many words in English are so frequently used in a metaphorical way that English speakers may no longer notice that they are metaphors. Here are some examples.

- Intelligence and understanding are equated with light; for example, a clever person is called **bright** and a less intelligent person **dim**. If you **see the light**, you understand something. To **cast light on** something means making it easier to understand. The discovery of the poet's letters **has cast light on** his troubled relationship with his brother.
- Intensity of feeling or passion is equated with temperature; someone who is enthusiastic at one time and not at another is said to **blow hot and cold**. If someone is **hotheaded**, then they react quickly on the basis of their feelings without thinking first. If you call someone **cold-hearted**, then you think they are without feeling.
- The movement of people or traffic is equated with the movement of water; we can, for example, talk of people **flooding** or **trickling** out of a hall. There was a constant **stream** of traffic past the window.
- Time is likened to money; both are seen as commodities that can be **spent** or **wasted** or **used profitably**. You can also talk about **investing** time, using it in a way that you think will **pay dividends** in future. [bring you advantages]
- Business is likened to a military operation; **strategies**, **tactics** and **campaigns** are used in both contexts. So a company might **launch an advertising campaign**, for example, or work on its **marketing strategy**.

Exercises

92.1 Choose a word from the box that can be used metaphorically to complete the sentence.

> ball   eye   hands   head   heart   jungle   mouth   light   rein   thumb

1 Helen asked me to keep a close .... on her little boy while the children were playing in the garden.
2 You don't need to worry about your grandfather – he's in safe .... in the hospital.
3 Our hotel offers excellent facilities in the .... of the old city centre.
4 When the writer refers to the urban .... , he is suggesting that the city is a dangerous and unpleasant place.
5 As a rule of .... , you can expect to deal with about 20 orders a day.
6 Joe is always on the .... ; he always knows what's going on.
7 Can you see that small boat at the .... of the river?
8 It is up to the .... of the school how the budget is spent.
9 I'm afraid we need to keep a tight .... on our spending this year.
10 I never used to understand opera, but an excellent TV series helped me to see the ....

92.2 Here are some more idioms which are based on metaphors. What is the idiom in each sentence and what does it mean? What aspect of life does it draw its image from?

1 Oscar's going to be holding the reins while the boss is on holiday.
2 It's hard to know what to do when management keeps moving the goalposts.
3 Starting his own dry-cleaning business was just another of his half-baked ideas.
4 We've had to tighten our belts since Sam lost his job.
5 The company needs to take its customers' criticisms on board.
6 Are you still on track to finish your essay by this evening?
7 Jana worked around the clock to finish decorating the room before her parents came home.
8 I'm sure you can take him at face value – he seems perfectly honest to me.

92.3 Here are some more examples of the five metaphorical concepts in C opposite. Underline the metaphor and say which concept it exemplifies and what it suggests.

1 This book throws a great deal of fresh light on the history of the period.
2 We could save half an hour at least if we went through the wood.
3 Try to keep cool even if he argues with you.
4 We spent months trying to achieve our sales targets.
5 Police tried to control the flow of the fans as they left the concert.

92.4 More unusual and original metaphors are used a great deal in literature. Here are some famous metaphors from Shakespeare. Underline the metaphors in each case and explain what they suggest.

1 All the world's a stage and all the men and women merely players.
2 We are such stuff as dreams are made on; and our little life is rounded with a sleep.
3 There is a tide in the affairs of men, which, taken at the flood, leads on to fortune.

93 Idioms for everyday situations and feelings

A When things go right

If something ...	this means ...
worked like a dream	a plan succeeded absolutely perfectly
went/ran like clockwork	it went smoothly, with no difficulties
is up and running	it has begun to work as planned
is falling into place	it is on the point of starting to work well
is looking up	it is looking very positive

B When things go wrong: reacting in conversation

Oh no! That's all we need/needed! [in response to news that makes current problems even worse]
That's the last thing I wanted to hear! [in response to news that fulfils your worst fears]
This is like a bad dream! [when one bad thing after another happens in quick succession]
It's a real nightmare / my worst nightmare. [used very generally, e.g. about traffic jams, computers going wrong]
What a pain! [used very generally, in response to any situation that causes you difficulty]

C Confusing situations or situations you don't understand

Her sudden question **threw me completely.** [I didn't know how to respond]
The meeting was **a complete shambles.** [a totally disorganised and chaotic event]
It's a mystery to me how people know about my private life. [it's something I cannot understand]
I'm sorry, we must have **got our wires crossed.** I thought the meeting was at 11, not 10.30.
[there must have been a miscommunication/misunderstanding]
I'm not with you. / You've lost me there. [what you have said has confused me]

D Happiness and sadness

expression	meaning
to be on top of the world / on cloud nine / over the moon	to be extremely happy
to be in (your) element / to be made for	to be ideally suited for
to be fed up to the back teeth	to be extremely unhappy, disappointed
to be down in the dumps / down in the mouth	to be depressed

Exercises

93.1 Rewrite the underlined words using an idiom based on the word in brackets.

1 The system is now working as planned, so we should be able to get some useful data soon. (RUN)
2 Things are becoming very positive now that we've increased our online sales. (LOOK)
3 The whole project was 100% successful. (DREAM)
4 After a problematic start, things are beginning to work well now. (FALL)
5 The school open day ran very smoothly without difficulties or problems. (CLOCK)

93.2 Fill in B's missing words in these conversations.

1 A: 'I'm afraid your insurance policy expired a month ago, so you can't claim for the
      fire damage.'
   B: 'Oh no! This is like a bad .... !'
2 A: 'I'm afraid the boss is away this week so we'll have to wait to sort this out till next week.'
   B: 'Oh, what a .... ! Ah well, I suppose there's nothing we can do.'
3 A: 'Tarek is ill and can't come. Now Sheena's phoned in to say she's sick too!'
   B: 'Oh no! Two people sick! That's all we .... !'
4 A: 'Wow! Look at this traffic jam. We'll be stuck here for hours!'
   B: 'I know. It's a real .... !'
5 A: 'The lawyers have said we can't hold the festival because we haven't done a proper risk
      assessment.'
   B: 'Oh no! That's the last thing we wanted to .... !'

93.3 Read the comments and then answer the questions.

1 ALEX: 'It's a mystery to me how those papers just disappeared.'
2 SABINA: 'Sorry. I'm not with you. You've lost me there.'
3 RICARDO: 'That shop is a complete shambles these days.'
4 MONICA: 'The news threw me completely.'
5 MICHELLE: 'Sorry. I think we got our wires crossed yesterday.'

	name
1 Who is talking about something disorganised and chaotic?	
2 Who thinks there's been a misunderstanding?	
3 Who can't follow what someone has said?	
4 Who can't find an explanation for something?	
5 Who didn't know how to respond to something?	

93.4 Correct the mistakes in the idioms in these sentences.

1 Jessica's on cloud seven now she's at university.
2 She's on her element now she's got a job in an architect's office.
3 You look a bit down in the damp. What's the matter?
4 Just look at him! He looks fed up to the front teeth!
5 I was above the moon when they told me I'd got the job.

93.5 Look up these idioms in a dictionary. Do they fit best into A, B, C or D opposite?
Circle the correct letter.

1 Oh no! That's the last straw!   A B C D
2 I can't get my head round it.   A B C D
3 You look as miserable as sin.   A B C D
4 It worked like a charm.   A B C D
5 I was walking on air.   A B C D

94 Brushing up on phrasal verbs

A Learning phrasal verbs

There are a great many phrasal verbs in English and many learners find them particularly difficult to master. The best way to learn them is in context. When you **come across** [meet] one, write it down in an example sentence.

There are a couple of important points to remember about phrasal verbs. Firstly, a verb + preposition/particle combination may have more than one meaning. **Come across**, for example, can also mean *give an impression of being*, as in He can **come across** as unfriendly when you first meet him. **Come over** can also be used with the same meaning, as in He can **come over** as unfriendly.

Secondly, it is sensible to concentrate first on understanding phrasal verbs rather than using them. There is usually an alternative way in which you can say the same thing using a single verb. So, for example, instead of **put forward** a plan you can *propose a plan*, and instead of **rush into** a decision you can *make a hasty decision*.

B The verb

A very large number of phrasal verbs are formed using common verbs such as *come, do, get* or *go*, for instance. Here are some more examples with **come**.

I hope our plans to visit Russia **come off**. [happen successfully]

Sandro's family **came over** from Italy for the wedding. [travel to one place from another]

I wouldn't usually say something like that. I don't know what **came over** me. [influence someone to behave in a particular way]

The proposal has **come under** a lot of criticism. [experience something (usually unpleasant)]

If the opportunity to work in the US **comes up**, you must take it. [occur unexpectedly]

Our plan has **come up against** some obstacles. [have to deal with a problem or difficulty]

C The preposition/particle

The second part of a phrasal verb is a preposition or particle. This can sometimes help you understand the meaning of the phrasal verb. For example, **on** can often convey an idea of continuing over a period of time.

Selina decided to **stay on** at university and do a Master's degree. [remain]

Try not to **dwell on** the past. [keep thinking about, usually something unpleasant]

I didn't expect platform shoes to **catch on**. [become popular]

I wish she'd stop **going on** about her new car. [talking at length]

The crowd was **urging** the runners **on**. [encouraging]

The weather was terrible but the climbers **pressed on** regardless. [continued in a determined way]

D Phrasal verbs in topics

It can be useful to learn phrasal verbs in sets connected with a topic. Here, for example, are some from the context of work.

I need to **brush up on** my computer skills for my new job. [improve knowledge of something already learnt but partly forgotten]

The company **laid off** half its staff during the recession. [stopped employing]

Tomorrow's meeting has been **called off** because Jack is ill. [cancelled]

Sasha has **thrown himself into** his new job. [start doing something with great energy]

It took me a few weeks to **settle in** at my new office. [feel relaxed and happy]

It took me ages to **put together** the report. [prepare by collecting information from several sources]

Language help

When you learn a phrasal verb, note down the positions of the preposition/particle and the object, if there is one. For example, you can say **put a report together** or **put together a report**, but you can only say **rush into a decision**.

Exercises

94.1 Reword these sentences using a phrasal verb with *come*.

1 Meena can seem a little arrogant at times, but she's just shy.
2 Charlie was quick to take advantage of a chance for promotion that arose at his workplace.
3 The project was going well until we encountered some legal problems.
4 I found some lovely old photos when I was sorting some boxes yesterday.
5 I'm afraid it looks as if our plans to move to a new flat may not happen.
6 Something strange happened to me and I shouted at him angrily.

94.2 Complete the sentences with a verb, using the appropriate form.

1 Ian is always .... on about how rich he is.
2 You can't change what happened, so don't .... on it.
3 We'd better .... on if we're going to get to the hostel before dark.
4 I'm going to .... on after work to finish the report.
5 Taekwondo has really .... on – all my friends are learning it.
6 Hugo's family tried their best to .... him on to complete his novel.

94.3 Do these sentences have the correct preposition or particle? If not, correct them.

1 Do you think the company will have to lay any staff out?
2 I learnt Spanish at school but need to brush it on before I go to Spain.
3 I'm putting a presentation together for the board to consider.
4 If you rush for a decision, you may regret it later.
5 We'll have to call out tomorrow's picnic if the weather is bad.
6 The family soon settled on to their new flat in the city.
7 I love the way Suzie always throws herself onto everything she does.
8 Nita put forward some very interesting ideas at the meeting.

94.4 Which of the phrasal verbs on the opposite page can have the preposition or particle either before or after the object? Write the verbs in phrases both ways using one of these objects.

> team   skill   report   staff   meeting   plan

EXAMPLE: *urge a team on – urge on a team*

94.5 These sentences use some other phrasal verbs. Can you work out what the verbs mean from the context? Match the phrasal verbs in the sentences with the definitions in the box.

> delay   explode   abolish   waste time
> not tell   criticise   occur   start to work

1 Most of the students say they would like to **do away with** school uniform.
2 The new arrangements won't **kick in** till next month.
3 Stop **messing around** – go and tidy your room.
4 Problems always seem to **crop up** at the most inconvenient times.
5 These complications will **set** the building work **back** by several weeks.
6 However hard he tries, his teacher always seems to **run** him **down**.
7 I heard the bomb **go off** at midday.
8 It's foolish to **hold** something so important **back** from your partner.

95 Connotation: making associations

Different kinds of associations

We often **associate** words [make connections] with something that is not obvious from the literal meaning of the word. The dove, for example, is a white bird that has associations with peace. So if a journalist calls a politician a **dove**, they are suggesting that he or she is a peacemaker. Similarly, they might call a more aggressive, hard-line politician a **hawk**, a bird which hunts its prey. Some associations like those of dove and hawk will be shared by most speakers of English and they may even be included in a good dictionary for learners.

Sometimes associations are not the same for all native speakers of the same language but may vary from one geographical area to another. **Black cats**, for example, have associations with *good luck* in Britain but with *bad luck* in the USA. Many associations are purely personal. Someone who had a bad experience of dogs in childhood may think of a dog as being fierce and frightening, whereas for others dogs may represent loyalty and friendship. The most commonly shared association of the word dog in English is 'faithfulness'. However, the phrase **a dog's life** is used to refer to a very unhappy and unpleasant life.

Understanding associations

Journalists, advertisers and other writers or speakers who want to interest and entertain their audience often make use of word associations. A fashion advert might ask, for example, 'Would you like to have that **Paris** look?', which draws on the associations of Paris with glamour and style. Or someone might refer to **cowboy builders** meaning builders who are not careful or trustworthy.

It might seem difficult at first to understand this kind of language, but your knowledge both of the world and of the primary meanings of words will help you. Paris, for example, is known throughout the world as a centre of high fashion and it is quite possible that the name Paris is associated with glamour in your own language too. If you have seen a Western, you will have seen how cowboys behave in a careless and dishonest way.

Think, for example, about the words **shark**, **scar** and **diamond**. You probably know their literal meanings – a large sea creature with sharp teeth, a mark left on the skin after a cut has healed, and a precious stone, respectively – but what associations do you think they have for English speakers in general? What might someone mean if they said the following?

'They're all **sharks** in that garage.'
'I think that new office block is a **scar** on the landscape.'
'Emma's a real **diamond**.'

The idea of sharks as sharp-toothed creatures with an aggressive reputation should help you to understand that the speaker does not like the garage. The fact that a scar is a mark of a wound on something that was once unspoilt should help you to appreciate that the speaker does not like the new office block. The beauty and high value of a diamond as a precious stone should help you to see that the speaker has a high opinion of Emma.

Language help

Research into language learning shows that words are better remembered if you have personal associations in mind as you learn them. Remember to think about what your associations with a word are as you learn it.

Exercises

95.1 Answer these questions about the associations discussed on the opposite page.

1 Would you recommend a cowboy plumber to a friend?
2 Would a politician be more likely to be called a dove if they were a peacemaker or if they argued for military action?
3 What is more likely to be a scar on the landscape – a waterfall or a factory chimney?
4 Would you be pleased to be called a diamond?
5 Would you be pleased to be called a hawk?
6 In Britain would you be likely to see a black cat on a good luck card or not?
7 What characteristic is a dog most typically said to have in English?
8 Would you be likely to call a business Supersharks?

95.2 Match the colours with their associations in English. Are any of these the same in your language? (See Unit 64 for more about the associations of colour in English.)

1 purple ☐   4 red ☐   a purity   d inexperienced
2 green ☐   5 white ☐   b evil   e danger
3 yellow ☐   6 black ☐   c royalty   f a coward

95.3 Are these statements about the associations of animals in English correct? When a statement is wrong, correct it.

1 If you say someone has a dog's life, you think they have an easy life.
2 If you call a businessman a snake, you trust him.
3 If you say someone's hair is mousy, you mean it is dark brown and strikingly attractive.
4 If you say someone is being ratty, you mean they are irritable.
5 If you say someone can be catty, you mean they tend to be lazy.
6 If you say something is fishy, you mean it is suspicious.
7 If you call someone a sheep, you mean they are very independent-minded.
8 If you say that someone is hawk-eyed, you mean that they have very big eyes.

95.4 Can you make any associations between the colours in 95.2 and the animals and their associations in 95.3 that will help you to understand why these associations have been made?

95.5 Some of these have associations of good luck in English and some have associations of bad luck. Decide whether each picture represents good luck or bad luck.

Friday 13th   a horseshoe   walking under a ladder   a four-leaved clover

1 ....   2 ....   3 ....   4 ....

95.6 Over to you

Write down five colours and five animals. What are your own associations for these words?

96 Register: degrees of formality

A Formal and informal words

Some words are formal or informal, and others are quite neutral.
Is your **partner** (neutral) / **other half** (informal) not with you today? [husband/wife]
Rick's a really nice **bloke/guy**. [man; *informal*]
She is able to **converse** with everyone, which is a great gift. [have a conversation; *formal*]
Sometimes it is possible to arrange words into sets of neutral, formal and informal words.

neutral	formal	informal
TV/television		**the box / (the) telly**
glasses	**spectacles**	**specs**
clothes	**clothing/garments**	**gear**
use	**employ/utilise**	
try	**endeavour/attempt**	**have a go/stab/bash/crack/shot at**

Language help

Register is concerned with the overall tone of a text or conversation, and the relationship that is built between the speaker and listener, or reader and writer. It is important to speak and write in the appropriate register for the situation.

B Speech and writing

Some words are more associated with *either* spoken *or* written language. It is worth noting if a word has a particularly strong association with speech (S) or writing (W).

word/phrase	S/W	comment and example
subsequently	W	Linking adverb: in speech more likely to be 'later' or 'afterwards', e.g. The police found some important clues. **Subsequently**, three people were arrested.
in sum	W	Linking expression: means 'to sum up', e.g. **In sum**, we may say that most, but not all, English adverbs end in -ly.
whatsisname/whatsername	S	vague word: used when we cannot remember the name of a person, e.g. I met **whatsername** at the party, you know, the woman who works at the university.
thingy	S	vague word: used as a noun, of people and things whose name one cannot remember, e.g. Give me that **thingy** there, yes, that bottle opener.
mind you	S	discourse marker: used to bring attention to an important point, e.g. He's a good actor. **Mind you**, he should be – he went to the best drama college.
now then	S	discourse marker: used to get people's attention when you want to ask or tell them something, e.g. **Now then**, is everybody's luggage here?

C Outdated words

Some words and expressions may be correct, but may sound archaic (outdated) or old-fashioned, e.g. **asylum** [hospital for the mentally ill], **frock** [dress], **wireless** [radio], **consumption** [tuberculosis/TB], **eyeglasses** [glasses].

English Vocabulary in Use Advanced

Exercises

96.1 Make the underlined words in these sentences formal or informal, as instructed.

1 She works in a shop that sells women's <u>clothes</u>. (formal)
2 I've got some new <u>spectacles</u>. Do you like them? (informal)
3 Did you see that documentary about Wales on <u>TV</u> last night? (informal)
4 Gerry's a decent <u>man</u>. I wouldn't want to upset him. (informal)
5 I spent the morning <u>talking</u> with the Director. (formal)
6 Molly was there with her <u>other half</u>. He's a nice <u>guy</u>. (neutral; informal)

96.2 Complete the table using the words from the box. Do not fill the shaded boxes.

> shades   kids   endeavour   cop   really useful
> ensure   umbrella   employ   children

neutral	formal	informal
	offspring	
sunglasses		
policeman/woman	police officer	
		brolly
	invaluable	
make sure		
try		
use		

96.3 Decide whether these words are more likely to be associated with everyday spoken or everyday written English. Write S or W next to the word.

1 frequently   2 start   3 begin   4 maybe   5 moreover

96.4 What do you think are the present-day equivalents of these now outdated English words? Use a dictionary if necessary.

1 apothecary   2 damsel   3 poesy   4 whither

96.5 Look at these text extracts and decide which register types you would classify them in. Underline key words which help you decide the register. For example, if you think the text is 'written, formal, poetic and archaic', which word(s) make you think that?

Some register types: literary / poetic / non-literary   academic / non-academic
archaic / modern   technical / non-technical   spoken / written   formal / informal

1 When you have created a file that is to be stored in a shared folder, or one that is located on a server, you can use the tools in the client software to restrict access to the file.

2 Views are certainly divided on the answers to the questions listed above; even whether it matters that pluralism and different paradigms reign in SLA is a matter of heated debate.

3 Sweetest love, I do not go,
For weariness of thee,
Nor in hope the world can show
A fitter love for me;
But since that I
Must die at last, 'tis best,
To use myself in jest
Thus by feigned deaths to die.

4 And so, my fellow Americans: ask not what your country can do for you – ask what you can do for your country. My fellow citizens of the world: ask not what America will do for you, but what together we can do for the freedom of man.

5 Mind you there was a lot of rain in Germany over Christmas wasn't there, cos I saw the river in Bonn on the news on telly, the Rhine. Yeah, the river in Bonn.

97 Divided by a common language

Very few words and expressions are used exclusively in either British or American English, and you are likely to hear and read words from both varieties in use in English-speaking countries and on the internet.

A Streets and roads

Street has a wider range of meaning in American English.

American speaker: Let's cross the **street** here. There's more traffic further down.

However, a British speaker would normally say cross the **road**, especially in a busy city.

Here are some more examples of American English words and expressions not used in British English. The British English expressions are given in square brackets.

Go two blocks down and the car rental office is **kitty-corner** to the **gas station**. [diagonally opposite; *informal*] [petrol station]

You should always use the **crosswalk** to cross the street. [pedestrian crossing / zebra crossing]

There's a **trail** that leads down to the **creek**. [path] [stream, small river]

Take a left here and you'll come to the **Interstate** after about three miles. [turn left] [major motorway in the US connecting different states]

After the **intersection**, look for a sign saying 'International Airport'. [junction]

I hit a shopping **cart** in the **parking lot** when I was **backing up**. [trolley] [car park] [reversing]

Look for the **overpass** and then take the next exit for downtown Chicago. [flyover, i.e. bridge that carries one road over another]

> **Language help**
>
> In British English road numbers use *the*; in American English no article is used.
> British English: *Take the M4 as far as Newbury, then turn off on to the A34 for Oxford.*
> American English: *Take I-45 north for about 20 miles, then take 25 west.*

B Educational terminology

American	British
My older brother never went to **college**.	My older brother never went to **university**. (college in Britain usually means a place for specialised education for people over 16)
What **courses** are you taking next semester?	What **modules** are you taking next semester/term?
Are you a **freshman**? No, I'm a **sophomore**.	Are you a **fresher** / **first year** (student)? No, I'm (a) **second year**.
Most of my friends are **juniors**.	Most of my friends are **third years** / **third year students**.
She's **majoring** in French.	She's **doing honours** in French. / She's doing a French **honours** degree.
My **professors** are all very friendly. (used as a general term for university teachers)	My **lecturers** are all very friendly. (used as a general term for university teachers – a **professor** is a person with the highest academic rank)
I want to be an **elementary** school teacher.	I want to be a **primary** school teacher.
My years in **high school** were not very happy.	My years in **secondary school** were not very happy.

C Around the home

This cable is the **ground** (US) / **earth** (UK). [cable that takes electricity safely into the ground]

We need a **dumpster** (US) / **skip** (UK) to put all this old stuff in. [large metal container for rubbish]

The **faucet** (US) / **tap** (UK) in the kitchen never stops dripping!

I have to cook for five people, so we need a big **stove** (US) / **cooker** (UK). [piece of kitchen equipment to cook food]   I fried the fish in a **skillet** (US) / **frying pan** (UK).

Exercises

97.1 Who do you think is most likely to be speaking, an American or a British person? What would someone who speaks the *other* variety probably have said instead?

1 I lost my way at the big intersection just south of the city.
2 Why are there always so many shopping trolleys left in the car park?
3 Cross the road at the pedestrian crossing, then turn left.
4 You can't drive any further; you'll have to back up, the street is very narrow.
5 You'll see the petrol station just after the flyover on the A34.
6 Once you get on to the Interstate, it will only take you two hours to get there.
7 The office is kitty-corner to the Chinese restaurant.
8 There's a creek at the end of the trail. It's about three miles from here.

97.2 Match the words on the left with their equivalent on the right, and write US for American English and UK for British English in the boxes.

1 dumpster   a skillet
2 ground   b tap
3 frying pan   c stove
4 cooker   d earth
5 faucet   e skip

97.3 Answer the questions.

1 Who do you think is more likely to get homesick, a fresher or a junior?
2 Does a primary school teacher teach at more or less the same level as an elementary school teacher or at a different level?
3 How might calling someone 'Professor' in the US mean something different from calling someone 'Professor' in Britain?
4 Where are you more likely to register for a module, the US or Britain?
5 What year of study are you in if you are a sophomore?
6 If someone says they are majoring in psychology, what do they mean?
7 If an American says they're going to college next year, does that necessarily mean the same as if a British person said it?
8 If someone says they're a secondary school teacher, are they more likely to be British or American?

98 Language and gender

A Gender awareness and vocabulary

A number of vocabulary changes have occurred thanks to heightened awareness of the sexist nature of some traditional English vocabulary. David Crystal in *The Cambridge Encyclopedia of the English Language* writes:

Attention has been focused on the replacement of 'male' words with a generic meaning by neutral items – *chairman*, for example, becoming *chair* or *chairperson* (though not without controversy) or *salesman* becoming *sales assistant*. In certain cases, such as job descriptions, the use of sexually neutral language has become a legal requirement. There is continuing debate between extremists and moderates as to how far such revisions should go – whether they should affect traditional idioms such as *man in the street*[1] and *Neanderthal Man*[2], or apply to parts of words where the male meaning of man is no longer dominant such as *manhandle*[3] and *woman*. The vocabulary of marital status has also been affected, notably in the introduction of *Ms* as a neutral alternative to *Miss* or *Mrs*.

[1] a typical person (could be replaced by *person in the street*)   [2] a now extinct species that were the ancestors of present-day humans   [3] handle roughly, using force

Here are some examples of non-sexist variations of vocabulary.

older usage	current usage
spokesman	**spokesperson**
fireman, policeman	**firefighter, police officer**
male nurse	**nurse**
man-hours	**working hours**
air hostess	**flight attendant**
cleaning lady	**cleaner**
foreman	**supervisor**
man-made	**artificial**
mankind	**the human race / human beings**
to man	**to staff**

B Words relating to gender

words	meaning/comment	example
male, female	used for gender classification in biology	**male** and **female** bees
masculine, feminine	having qualities traditionally felt to be typically male or female	**masculine** pride, **feminine** charm
manly, womanly	having positive qualities traditionally felt to be typically male or female	**manly** strength, **womanly** grace
effeminate	resembling a woman (used of men, negative)	his **effeminate** walk
a tomboy	a young girl who behaves and dresses like a boy	She's a real **tomboy**.
a sissy	a boy who behaves like a girl, or a weak and cowardly person (informal, negative, often used by children)	He's such a **sissy**!
butch	used of men and women, aggressively masculine in looks and behaviour (informal)	**butch** stars of cowboy films

Exercises

98.1 **Answer these questions about the text opposite.**

1 Why do you think there have been attempts to introduce non-sexist language of the kind described by David Crystal?
2 How would you explain this expression: 'male' words with a generic meaning?
3 Why do you think there might have been controversy about attempts to change the word *chairman*?
4 What do more extreme advocates of making English gender-neutral want to do that is unacceptable to the moderates?
5 Why was *Ms* introduced and why is it useful?

98.2 **Change these sentences so they reflect modern usage.**

1 Three firemen helped put out a fire at a disused warehouse last night.
2 A spokesman for the Department of Education provided us with a statement.
3 Cleaning lady wanted for house in Priory Street.
4 The helpline is continuously manned even during holiday periods.
5 All our air hostesses are fluent in at least three languages.
6 The fibres in this garment are man-made.
7 Policemen today spend more time in cars than on the beat.
8 Brenda's husband is a male nurse.
9 It took a great many man-hours to clean up the stadium after the concert.
10 This was a great step for mankind.
11 The man in the street has little time for such issues.
12 Salesmen are often well trained and can be very persuasive.

98.3 **Choose the correct word to complete each sentence.**

1 She looks rather *butch / male* in that suit.
2 Go on, jump. Don't be such a *tomboy / sissy*!
3 You'd never know now that Serena was a real *female / tomboy* as a child.
4 She always dresses in a very *feminine / womanly* way.
5 The *masculine / male* cat is less aggressive than his sister.

98.4 **Answer these questions.**

1 Do you think that using gender-specific language affects people's attitudes to men and women's roles in society?
2 Does your language ever use male words generically? If so, give examples of words you use to avoid sexual stereotyping?
3 How do you feel about imposing language changes of the different kinds that David Crystal describes?
4 Do terms of address (i.e. Mr, Mrs, etc.) in your language indicate whether people are married?
5 Do you think it is better if terms of address indicate marital status or not? Why?
6 A grammatical problem in this area is the use of *he/his* to refer to a person of either gender. In the sentence 'A government minister may have to neglect his family', the minister could be a man or a woman. However, the use of 'his' assumes, perhaps wrongly, that it is a man. How could you rewrite this sentence to avoid this problem?

99 In the headlines

A Features of headline language

If a story **hits the headlines** it suddenly receives a lot of attention in the news.
Here are some typical examples of headlines from **tabloid newspapers** with comments on
their use of language. [popular papers with small pages and short simple reports]

EXPERT REVEALS NEW CLOUD DANGERS

- Articles, prepositions and auxiliary verbs are often omitted from headlines.
- This use of the present simple instead of the past tense makes the story sound more
  immediate.
- The use of language is often ambiguous. It is not entirely clear, for example, what **cloud** refers
  to here. It is actually about the dangers of storing electronic information on a 'cloud' [hosted
  services on the internet for storing personal data], but it could have referred to dangers relating to
  the weather. Readers have to look at the story in order to find out.
- Words with dramatic associations such as **danger** are often used.

TV STAR TRAGIC TARGET FOR CRAZED GUNMAN

This story is about how a well-known television actor was shot by a mentally unstable killer.
- In order to attract readers' attention, tabloid newspapers often feature celebrities, e.g. film/pop
  stars and sports personalities.
- Alliteration such as **TV Star Tragic Target** is often used to attract the eye in headlines and to
  make them sound more memorable.
- Newspapers tend to use strong, simple words such as 'gunman' in order to express an idea or
  image as briefly and as vividly as possible.
- Strongly emotional words like **crazed** are often used to attract attention. [behaving in a wild or
  strange way, especially because of strong emotion]

B Violent words

Violent and militaristic words are often used in headlines, especially in tabloid newspapers,
in order to make stories seem more dramatic. For example, people who cause trouble may be
referred to as **thugs**, **yobs** or **louts**.

EU acts to **crush**[1] **terror** of **thugs**   **Crackdown**[2] on soccer **louts**

Palace **besieged**[3] by journalists

Typhoon **rips**[4] through town

[1] destroy [2] taking serious measures to deal with a problem
[3] surrounded, as if by army   [4] moves in a destructive way

> **Language help**
> The kind of language that is common in
> headlines may sound strange in other
> contexts. So the vocabulary in this unit
> is more likely to be useful to you when
> you are reading rather than when you
> are speaking or writing.

C Playing with words

Many newspaper headlines attract readers' attention by playing on words in an entertaining
way. For example, a story about a very heavy rainstorm which caused a landslide on a
narrow mountain road was headlined **Rain of terror**. This headline was a play on words
based on the expression **reign of terror**, an expression used about a period in which a
country's ruler controls people in a particularly cruel way.
Another example is the use of the headline **Moon becomes shooting star** to describe a
football match where a player called John Moon shot [scored] the winning goal. **Shooting star**
is an informal expression for a meteor. Here it is used to play on the expression **shoot a goal**,
and also to link to the player's name, Moon (another astronomical body). The headline is
particularly effective because of the association between star and moon in the sky.

Exercises

99.1 Read these headlines. What do you think the stories might be about?

1 **BLAST TERROR IN CAPITAL**
2 PM TO REVEAL SOCCER LOUT PLANS
3 TOP PLAYERS DEFEND COACH
4 CRACKDOWN ON DISSENT
5 **THUGS BESIEGE TEEN STAR**
6 COPS TARGET YOBS

99.2 Look at these headlines from a fictitious tabloid newspaper about Ancient Greece. Match them with the subjects of their stories and comment on the features of headline language they contain.

1 **NUDE SCIENTIST IN BATHTUB SCANDAL**

2 **KING PHIL'S MACEDONIAN MASSACRE**

3 **MARATHON MAN IN DROP-DEAD DASH**

4 **QUADRUPLE ROYAL MURDER SENSATION**

5 **IT'S CURTAINS FOR CORINTH**

a Four members of the royal family die in mysterious circumstances.
b Philip of Macedonia wins a battle against the city states of Athens and Thebes.
c Archimedes discovers the law governing the displacement of water.
d The city of Corinth is burnt to the ground by the Romans.
e A long-distance runner brings news of a battle victory to Athens and then dies.

99.3 Match the headline to its story and explain the play on words in each case.

1 Bad blood
2 Happy days?
3 *Shell-shocked*
4 False impressions
5 Happy haunting
6 *Hopping mad*
7 Flushed with success
8 Highly embarrassed
9 Round-up

a A grandfather's breathing problems were solved when doctors found four false teeth at the entrance to his lungs. They had been forced down his windpipe in a car crash eight years before.
b A 25-year-old terrapin is being treated for a fractured shell after surviving a 200-foot drop.
c A Shetland teacher has suggested sheepdogs could be used to control pupils in playgrounds.
d A ghost society has been told not to scare off a friendly female apparition at a hotel.
e An unusual travel company is offering adults the chance to experience going back to school again – they will spend a week wearing school uniform, sitting through lessons and eating school dinners..
f An ex-public loo in Hackney, East London, is to be sold for £76,000.
g A Whitby vicar has attacked the resort's attempts to profit on its connections with Dracula: 'a pale-faced man with a bad sense of fashion, severe dental problems and an eating disorder'.
h A toad triggered a police alert when it set off a new hi-tech alarm system.
i Firefighters had to scale a 30-foot tree to rescue a man who was trying to capture his pet iguana.

100 Red tape

Characteristics of bureaucratic language

A student shall not be eligible for a loan in relation to an academic year if he/she:

(a) has **attained**[1] the age of 50 years before the first day of the course;

(b) has received another loan in relation to the same academic year;

(c) has received another loan in relation to another academic year which began during the same period 1st August to the following 31st July during which the academic year began;

(d) is eligible in respect of that year to receive:

(i) any payment under a bursary or award of similar description **bestowed on**[2] him/her under section 63 of the Health Services and Public Health Act 1968(2) the amount of which is not calculated by reference to his/her income ...

[1] reached   [2] given to

Your request to **demolish**[1] the garage **adjoining**[2] your property is hereby rejected. Any and all appeals regarding this decision must be submitted to the **undersigned**[3] by Jan 31 2013. No exceptions to the **aforementioned**[4] procedure will be considered.

[1] knock down   [2] next to   [3] the person who wrote this letter   [4] above

Some publications produced by companies or government departments are difficult to understand because they use language that is very different from everyday English.

- They frequently use words that are longer and 'grander' than their ordinary equivalents.
- They often use a passive form instead of an active one, e.g. 'Normal service will be resumed as soon as possible' instead of 'We will resume normal service as soon as possible.'
- They use nouns as the subject of the sentence when they are not necessary, e.g. 'Achievement of this module is dependent upon candidates meeting the assessment outcomes' instead of 'To achieve this module, candidates must meet the assessment outcomes.'
- They use a noun instead of You, e.g. Customers will be informed of ...' instead of 'You will be informed of ...' or even 'We will tell you about ...'

These words are more frequent in a bureaucratic context.

Work will **commence** in May. [start] (noun = **commencement**)

The company **ceased operations** last year. [stopped functioning] (noun = **cessation**)

Property belonging to the **deceased** will be returned to the **next of kin**. [dead person] [closest relative]

In the event of an emergency, call 121. [if there is]

In the event of fire, the building **must be evacuated** immediately. [people must leave]

Tenants must **endeavour** to keep communal areas tidy at all times. [try]

The developments will **facilitate** movement of traffic in the area. [make possible, easier]

Residents **will be instructed** what to do in the event of an emergency. [will be told]

The project will **proceed** to the next phase in June. [move]

We are currently attempting to **rectify** the situation. [put right]

Normal service **will be resumed** as soon as possible. [start again]

Bureaucratic correspondence

There is some specific vocabulary that characterises bureaucratic letters.

Please **acknowledge receipt of** payment. [inform us that you have received]

With the compliments of Smith and Co. [written on a slip of paper sent with an item from a company]

Please **notify** us immediately of any change of address. [inform]

I would be grateful for a reply **at your earliest convenience**. [as soon as possible]

Contact us if **further clarification is required**. [you need more of an explanation]

I enclose payment **in respect of** your invoice. [relating to, for]

I am writing **with regard to** your advertisement. [about]

Exercises

100.1 Look at the two texts in A opposite. Find an example in the texts of each of the four characteristics of bureaucratic language listed in the bullets in A.

100.2 Read each sentence. Choose the word in the second sentence which gives the same meaning in simpler language.

1 Roadworks will commence on 1 June.
Roadworks will *begin / end* on 1 June.
2 (*on a form*) Contact details for next of kin.
Write the name and address of your *neighbour / nearest* relative.
3 With the compliments of Jane Bramwell.
With *best wishes / love* from Jane Bramwell.
4 Call me at your earliest convenience.
Call me early *in the morning / as soon as you can.*
5 In the event of fire, lifts should not be used.
If there is a fire / At the start of a fire, don't use the lifts.
6 Passengers should await instruction from the captain before proceeding to the car deck.
Passengers should not *go to / leave* the car deck until the captain tells them to.
7 I am writing with regard to the editorial in today's paper.
I am writing *for / about* the editorial in today's paper.
8 I am writing in respect of your letter of 6th June.
I am writing *in connection with / in favour of* your letter of 6th June.

100.3 Match the words with their synonyms. Which word or phrase in each pair exemplifies bureaucratic language?

deceased	acknowledge	end	make easier	rectify	let us know
start	clarification	put right	start again	commencement	dead
endeavour	try	facilitate	cessation	explanation	resume

100.4 Complete the word formation table below. Note that not all the words are on the opposite page. Use a dictionary if necessary.

verb	noun	adjective
	clarification	
facilitate		
instruct		
		notifiable
rectify		

100.5 Rewrite the sentences using everyday, non-bureaucratic English to replace the underlined words and phrases. Use a dictionary if necessary.

1 Clients must comply with the following regulations.
2 Insert coins into the slot below.
3 Your complaints have been investigated and are considered to be without foundation.
4 Passengers are requested to refrain from smoking.
5 Tick your country of residence.

Answer key

Unit 1

1.1
1 His PhD **thesis** ...
2 Little Martha did her first **composition** ...
3 We have to hand in a **portfolio** ...
4 The teacher gave us the title of this week's **essay** ...
5 At the end of this course you have to do a 5,000-word **assignment** ...
6 I think I'll do a study of people's personal banking habits for my MSc **dissertation** ...
7 I've chosen to do the **project** ...

1.2
When I'm studying **intensively** because I'm **cramming** for an exam, I don't see any point in looking up **past papers,** nor is there any point in just learning things **(off) by heart.** I know some people develop very clever **mnemonics** to help them remember the material, but there's no real substitute for **revising** the term's work. It's a good idea to have some sort of **mind map** to organise your ideas, and **rote-learning / memorising** is useful, but in a limited way. At the end of the day, you just have to **bury yourself in your books** until you feel you know the subject **inside out.**

1.3
1 a first draft
2 a deadline
3 plagiarism
4 submit; assess
5 drop out
6 a paper; in (academic) journals
7 inter-library loan
8 feedback
9 a genius
10 carry out research

1.4
1 acknowledge
2 resources
3 revision
4 plagiarism
5 well-qualified
6 paper
7 access
8 inside

Unit 2

2.1
1 league tables
2 selective education
3 equality of opportunity
4 perpetuate inequalities
5 tertiary education

2.2
1 Inequality is **inherent in** the education system.
2 **Elitism** is bad for the country in the long term.
3 **Comprehensive education** is a basic political ideal in many countries.
4 A **two-tier system** of schools **depresses** the opportunities for children from **less well-off** families and favours those from **better-off** families.
5 Some private schools **are well-endowed / have endowments,** and this means they can have better resources.
6 All parents want their children to **excel** at school.
7 Emphasis on the three Rs is **perceived** by parents to be the key to success.
8 The government is increasing its provision for **tertiary** education.

2.3
2 Literacy refers to the ability to read.
Numeracy refers to the ability to count and do maths.
3 A student who is doing a doctorate is a postgraduate.
A student who is doing a first degree is an undergraduate.
4 Bullying is when a pupil uses frightening or threatening behaviour towards another child who is smaller or less powerful in some way.
Excelling is when a student does exceptionally well.
5 Secondary education is the stage that follows primary education.
Tertiary education is the stage that follows secondary education.
6 Selective schools choose the best students to study there.
Comprehensive schools take all students regardless of their academic ability.
7 League tables list schools from good to bad according to their exam results.
Guidelines offer advice on how to do something.

2.4
1 scholarship
2 distraction
3 guidelines
4 mature
5 fees
6 loan
7 three
8 one-to-one

Unit 3

3.1
I'm a **technician** in a factory. I think I have a good **working** relationship with my colleagues. I tried to establish a good **rapport** with them from the very beginning. The person I like most is my opposite **number** in our office in Paris. My boss likes me to **take** the initiative. Generally, when I socialise with my **workmates** outside of work, we try not to talk ~~about~~ shop, but it's not easy and sometimes we have a good gossip about colleagues and events at work.

3.2 1 d 2 a 3 e 4 b 5 f 6 c

3.3
1 went in with, start-up
2 workload
3 behind a desk
4 a rut
5 freelance
6 self-employed
7 (dead-) end job
8 off
9 antisocial / irregular

3.4 *Possible answers:*
1 repetitive, mechanical, challenging
2 mundane, monotonous, mind-numbing
3 varied, challenging, glamorous
4 glamorous, stressful, varied
5 stressful, challenging, rewarding
6 stressful, monotonous, glamorous
7 varied, repetitive, monotonous
8 stressful, stimulating, challenging
9 repetitive, monotonous, mundane
10 monotonous, challenging, stressful

Unit 4

4.1
1 Do you often look at the job **advertisements**?
2 I have no **sales experience**.
3 Developing good apps for phones and tablets is a **lucrative** activity.
4 I thought I would apply for the job since **I fitted the description.**

4.2
1 a **close-knit** team
2 a (very) **rewarding** job
3 a person with **drive**
4 a **dynamic** profession
5 a salary **increment**
6 **voluntary** redundancy
7 a **skeleton** staff of workers
8 someone who **is overworked and underpaid**

4.3
1 seeking   2 run-of-the-mill   3 rewarding   4 team player   5 drive
6 job satisfaction   7 holiday entitlement
A person who is 'going places' is a person who is likely to succeed in his/her career in the future, and if you are working in tourism, you will probably go to many places in the literal sense.

4.4
1 She was on **maternity** leave for three months after the birth of her baby. Then her husband took **paternity** leave for three months. (You can also combine the two terms and refer to **parental leave.**)
2 Sarah has been on **adoption** leave since she and Brian welcomed their new two-year old child into their family. Brian took **voluntary** redundancy from his job, which means he is at home too.
3 My holiday **entitlement** is four weeks a year. The atmosphere in my **workplace** is very pleasant, so I'm happy.
4 When I applied for the job, I was looking **to** join a dynamic team. However, the interview **panel** gave an impression of complete boredom and lack of drive.
5 The factory had to operate with a **skeleton** staff during the economic crisis. There had been a large number of **compulsory** redundancies.
6 I get some good **perks** in my new job. I get a company car and free health **insurance**.

Unit 5

5.1   1 c   2 g   3 e   4 b   5 h   6 a   7 f   8 i   9 d

5.2 1 under 2 around 3 back 4 cold 5 part 6 bid 7 telesales
8 niche 9 stock

5.3 1 hammer out a deal / hammer out an agreement 2 red tape 3 a takeover
4 lucrative 5 start-up 6 swallowed up 7 proposition 8 administration

5.4 1 reach
2 priced
3 merchandise
4 down
5 back
6 red tape

Unit 6

6.1 1 Do you have many **outstanding accounts**?
2 When does your **contract expire**?
3 Is there a **penalty clause** in the contract?
4 It is very important that you **meet the deadline**.
5 We would like to invite companies to **submit / put in tenders** for the job.
6 It is company policy to take legal action against customers who **default on payment**.
7 Our factories **distribute** their products by rail.
8 We received a large **shipment** from the States this morning.

6.2 1 stock market
2 morale
3 liquidation
4 funding
5 sector
6 bonus

6.3 1 how to encourage effective teamwork
2 how to secure enough funding
3 how to avoid bankruptcy
4 how to improve staff morale
5 whether to offer staff bonuses or not

6.4 1 affinity
2 reward, tuned
3 entrepreneurs
4 assessment
5 propulsion
6 intuition

6.5 1 c 2 h 3 b 4 a 5 g 6 d 7 e 8 f

Unit 7

7.1 1 Sophie 2 Rowan 3 Tatyana 4 Andrey 5 Alice 6 Graham

7.2 Positive: Eliza and Marco
Negative: David and Julie

7.3
1 opportunistic
2 intuitive
3 morose
4 naive
5 magnetic
6 methodical
7 brusque
8 superficial
9 insecure
10 good company
11 courageous
12 perfectionist

7.4
1 altruistic
2 parsimonious
3 diligent
4 placid
5 industrious
6 rebellious
7 distrustful
8 terse
9 naive
10 unscrupulous

7.5
Possible answers:
1 altruistic: unselfish
2 parsimonious: thrifty
3 diligent: hard-working
4 placid: calm, easy-going
5 industrious: hard-working, energetic
6 rebellious: disobedient, defiant, unruly
7 distrustful: suspicious, wary
8 terse: abrupt, short
9 naive: green, trusting
10 unscrupulous: dishonest, dodgy

Unit 8

8.1
1 She looks as if she needs a good meal; her body is so **scrawny**.
2 Marian and David are very suitable for each other; they're both rather **lanky** individuals.
3 Being **obese** is very unhealthy.
4 A **gangly/gangling** boy carried our bags for us.
5 They were taking photos of a beautiful, **slender** model.
6 A **stocky** man offered to lift the stone so we could look underneath.
7 That **stout** woman on the left of the photo is Charlie's wife.

8.2
Possible answers:
1 He looks very unkempt.
2 She never has a hair out of place. / She looks immaculate.
3 She's got a double chin.
4 He looks rather haggard.

8.3
2 He's folding his arms.
3 She's clenching her fists.
4 She's pouting.

5 He's biting his nails.
6 She's shrugging her shoulders.
7 She's scowling.
8 He's grinning.

8.4
1 The two meanings: positioning one's lips in a sexually attractive way; positioning one's lips in a look of annoyance.
2 They are probably angry or annoyed.
3 A swarthy complexion is dark, a sallow one is rather yellowish and unhealthy-looking.
4 When you feel really angry or frustrated.
5 When they want to show that they don't understand or know something, or that they don't care about something.
6 You might tap or drum them.
7 People often fold their arms when they are listening to a lecture or to the teacher in class, or when sitting for a photograph. Folding your arms can also express a refusal to respond, confrontation or hearing something you don't like. People often cross their legs when sitting and waiting for something.
8 A 'lean and wiry' person is thin, healthy and strong.

Unit 9

9.1
1 An approachable teacher or boss is one that you can easily talk to.
2 pig-headed
3 little
4 an effusive greeting
5 difficult
6 impetuous
7 conscientious
8 extrovert

9.2
1 Don't be so **conceited**! You're not the only one to get an A-grade!
2 People **with / who have low self-esteem** can find it difficult to achieve their goals.
3 He's generally **an outgoing** sort of person.
4 She is a **well-balanced** person overall.
5 You always seem **restless**. What's the problem?
6 He's so **excitable**. He should try to calm down more.
7 She is **rather naive** when it comes to politics.
8 He's **pushy** and cares little what happens to others.
9 Frances was very **aloof** at the party.
10 At times, Joel is quite **haughty**.

9.3

adjective	noun	adjective	noun
excitable	excitability	reserved	reserve
gullible	gullibility	diffident	diffidence
disdainful	disdain	pig-headed	pig-headedness
impetuous	impetuosity (or, much less commonly, impetuousness)	respectful	respect
obstinate	obstinacy	self-important	self-importance
approachable	approachability	modest	modesty

9.4 1 One of her main character traits is **impetuosity/impetuousness**.
2 It's difficult to get him to change his ways. He **is very obstinate**.
3 Luke **is very reserved**, but his wife is **more approachable**.
4 One of her nicest characteristics is **(her) modesty**.
5 She **is very respectful towards/to** her elders. It's important in her culture.
6 **Pig-headedness** seems to be a family trait among my relatives.
7 She is so **self-important**; it irritates everyone.
8 Online identity thieves prey on **people's gullibility**.

Unit 10

10.1 1 e 2 f 3 a 4 b 5 d 6 c
1 ... love at first sight.
2 ... kindred spirits.
3 ... bosom pals.
4 ... mutual acquaintances.
5 ... head over heels in love.
6 ... hit it off.

10.2 1 eyes
2 well-matched
3 on, on fire
4 infatuated / besotted
5 regard
6 heart
7 thick
8 family

10.3

noun	adjective	noun	adjective
loyalty	loyal	respect	respectful
consideration	considerate	affection	affectionate
passion	passionate	romance	romantic
devotion	devoted	support	supportive
fondness	fond	amiability	amiable
faithfulness/faith*	faithful	trust	trusting/trustworthy†
adoration	adoring	infatuation	infatuated

*_Faithfulness_ is when you are completely loyal to someone; _faith_ is the complete trust or confidence that you have in someone or something.
† If someone is very _trusting_, they trust you (or other people); if they are _trustworthy_, you (or other people) can trust them.

10.4 1 to
2 for
3 to
4 of
5 of
6 in
7 towards
8 about

Unit 11

11.1
1 disloyal
2 untruthful
3 dishonest
4 unsupportive
5 friendly
6 disrespectful

11.2
1 We both own the company: we're business **partners.**
2 I've made several casual **acquaintances** since moving to London, but no close friends yet.
3 Were Britain and the USA **allies** in the First World War?
4 The two companies hate each other: they're **(bitter/arch) rivals.**

11.3
1 close / staunch
2 scrupulous
3 deeply
4 complete, unswerving
5 bitter / arch
6 true / loyal

11.4
1 with
2 of
3 to
4 behind
5 on, with
6 towards

11.5
1 Sandra and her sister **didn't see eye to eye** on a lot of things.
2 Carla's affection for Andrew has **turned sour** lately. I expect they'll **split up.**
3 Our relationship **broke down** because we were **untruthful** to each other.
4 Henry's brothers are **sworn enemies.**

11.6
1 It was a **genuine misunderstanding.**
2 They come from a **broken home.**
3 It has **had its ups and downs.**
4 A serious **rift** has **developed** between the two union leaders.
5 I think it's a **family feud.**

Unit 12

12.1 1 B crave   2 C defusing   3 B thrilled   4 B appease   5 C coveted   6 B blissfully

12.2 1 Katie   2 Ashley   3 Rowan   4 William   5 Laura

12.3 1 d   2 f   3 b   4 e   5 a   6 c

12.4
1 No. Appease(ment) is usually associated with disapproval.
2 Jubilant.
3 They would probably be trying to find a compromise or a solution that would be acceptable to both neighbours.
4 Angry.
5 They are probably not ready to forget the conflict because they very much want revenge.

Unit 13

13.1
1 I have a strong **aversion** to people who always want to be the centre of attention.
2 He always **scorns** our amateur theatrical productions.
3 She **abhors** injustice, wherever it occurs.
4 I am **not averse to** a vegetarian diet. I've just never tried it.
5 His attitude was very **irritating**. / I was very **irritated** by his attitude.
6 We were all **alarmed** when we heard the news.

13.2
1 b upset
2 very strong dislike / intense hatred
3 c actively and strongly dislike them
4 b annoyance

13.3
1 d   2 e   3 a   4 b   5 c

13.4
1 ostentatious
2 fickle
3 pretentious
4 nit-picking
5 sloppy
6 obnoxious
7 offhand
8 pompous
9 puerile
10 officious
11 forlorn
12 distraught

Unit 14

14.1
1 conceive
2 labour, birth
3 delivery, caesarean
4 placenta, uterus/womb
5 tube
6 midwife
7 expecting
8 pregnancy, foetus

14.2
1 The whole country is in **mourning** after the President's death.
2 I'd like my **ashes** scattered in my favourite forest.
3 My **late** grandfather was a shepherd all his life.
4 I'm afraid her elderly step-mother has just passed **away**.
5 My car is on its last **legs**.
6 My father **bequeathed** me his gold watch in his will.
7 Mrs Wilson seems to have been at death's **door** for years.
8 Over 2,000 people **perished** in the earthquake.
9 It was amazing there **were** no **fatalities** when the bridge collapsed.
10 My aunt left me a **bequest** of £500 in her will.

14.3 1 Both my sisters **are expecting** at the moment.
2 Amanda Harrison **gave birth** to twins last Monday.
3 She has been taking **fertility drugs** (to help her conceive).
4 All my grandparents lived to **a ripe old age.**
5 My neighbour is 90 but she still **has all her wits about her.**
6 Unfortunately, the deceased died **without leaving a will.**
7 **John's three nephews each inherited £1,000 from him.**
8 **Please accept my condolences.**

14.4 1 perished
2 slaughtered
3 fatalities
4 deceased
5 passed away
6 pensioner
7 bequeathed
8 inherited
9 bequest

Unit 15

15.1 1 therapeutic
2 lucrative
3 relaxing / calming / therapeutic
4 fruitful
5 rewarding
6 time-consuming

15.2 1 a couch potato
2 a shopaholic
3 a culture vulture
4 a dabbler

15.3 *Possible answers:*
1 It's a matter of personal choice but, for me, tidying is more of a chore than washing my clothes.
2 It depends, of course, but once a week in the grass-growing season is normal in England.
3 No, he/she doesn't.
4 No, they do a bit of photography but are not seriously into it.
5 Again, it's a matter of personal choice but, for me, being a participant is more appealing than being a spectator.

15.4 1 My daughter's **into** folk music. She downloads a lot of traditional folk songs.
2 He **locks** himself **away** in the attic and plays with his model railway for hours on end.
3 She's **(totally) hooked on** football these days. She watches every match on TV.
4 I have a **full diary** for the rest of the month.
5 What do you **get up to** when you aren't working, Nigel?
6 Martine **was a keen participant** in the end-of-term concert.

15.5 1 therapeutic
2 couch potato
3 gone off
4 time-consuming
5 full diary
6 lucrative

Unit 16

16.1 *Possible answers:*
1 You mean that they tend to dress in an untidy, careless way.
2 Smart but fairly casual clothes.
3 Scanty, skimpy, clingy, baggy, revealing or frumpy clothes would not be appropriate for a job interview.
4 It would be appropriate for both men and women to wear a smart suit to a job interview.
5 Jeans and a baggy shirt.
6 A nice belt, with boots and simple jewellery.
7 Trousers and a T-shirt.
8 Nurses, police officers, firemen, airline staff, the military.
9 Jobs involving risk, e.g. construction workers, miners.
10 She means it's extremely useful.

16.2 1 the nines
2 smart-casual
3 skimpy / scanty
4 designer (label), High Street
5 height, chic
6 baggy
7 on
8 must

16.3 1 I'm no good at speaking **off the cuff**.
2 Simon is bound to have **something up his sleeve** for tomorrow's meeting.
3 I think we should **draw a veil** over what happened on Monday, don't you?
4 Be careful what you say to Helen – she's **hand in glove** with the boss.
5 The new legislation **has put us in a straitjacket**.
6 We'll still have a great party even if we have to do it **on a shoestring**.

16.4 1 The literal meaning of *belt* is a piece of cloth or leather that you wear round your waist. You need to tighten it if you lose weight. The metaphorical meaning of *tighten one's belt* is to start living in a more economical way.
2 The literal meaning of the verb *hem* is to sew up the bottom edge of, e.g. a dress so that it does not develop loose threads. *Hemmed in* means completely surrounded.
3 A *seam* is a line of sewing joining two pieces of material so that if, say, a bag is *bursting at the seams*, it is almost splitting open. The metaphorical meaning of *bursting at the seams* is very, very full.
4 Literally, *to cloak* is to cover with a cloak. The metaphorical meaning of *cloaked* is kept secret.
5 Literally *a feather in someone's cap* is simply a feather decorating one's cap or hat. The metaphorical meaning of the expression is an achievement to be proud of.

16.5 *Possible answers:*
1 Very high heels and dresses with uneven hemlines.
2 Silk and velvet.
3 That they may be rather superficial to need to follow fashion so closely.
4 Not very interested at all.
5 Film stars, pop stars, business people who wish to make money from selling new fashions – they are all possible trend-setters.
6 Shoes, because they would fit perfectly.

Unit 17

17.1 *Possible answers:*

accommodation	What kind of person lives there?	Would you like to live there? Why/Why not?
furnished flat	someone who does not have their own furniture, perhaps a young person or someone living in a place for a short period of time	I wouldn't want to live in this kind of accommodation now because I have too many pieces of furniture of my own now.
social housing	people who do not have enough money to buy a house of their own	It would depend on the area – some social housing is very nice and there is a friendly atmosphere. But in other areas, the social housing is rather run-down and depressing.
granny flat	an elderly relative of the people who live in the main house	When I'm old, I would like to live close to my family but with at least a degree of independence.
high-rise	any type of person might live in one of these, though it would probably be someone in a large city	I wouldn't like to live very high up, as it would mean using a lift or lots of stairs to get down to the bottom and go outside.
hovel	someone who is not good at or interested in looking after themselves	I should hate to live somewhere dirty and in a bad condition.
penthouse	someone with a lot of money	I'd like to live in a spacious modern penthouse with the very latest in design and technology, and a fantastic view over a city.

17.2
1 on fire
2 home truths
3 write home about
4 life and death
5 fast lane
6 led
7 breathe
8 make

17.3
1 We **had the time of our life/lives** on holiday this year.
2 As soon as spring comes, I feel as if I'm **getting a new lease of life**.
3 The problems caused by the floods are only **hitting home** now.
4 I imagine that being a servant in the past must have been **a dog's life**.
5 All over the world, McDonald's **is a household name**.
6 He's **taking his life in his hands** if he gets in a car with Paul at the wheel!
7 Because we were such frequent customers, the restaurant gave us a meal **on the house**.
8 Our holiday apartment was quite adequate but **nothing to write home about**.

17.4
1 committing suicide
2 was extremely popular with the audience
3 occupations
4 very unstable
5 eat an enormous amount
6 be energetic and funny at a social occasion

Unit 18

18.1 1 male: a stag party or stag night; female: a hen party or hen night
2 the wedding reception and/or an evening party
3 a housewarming (party)
4 a launch party / a book launch
5 a reception / an official reception
6 a fancy-dress party

18.2 1 It's always good to see Hugh, but somehow he always manages to **outstay his welcome.**
2 I'm going to a dinner at the Royal Plaza Hotel tonight. It's a **black tie** event.
3 Don't forget your old friends when your film becomes a hit and you're **rubbing shoulders / hobnobbing / hanging out** with the rich and famous.
4 We're going to have **a girls' night out** on Friday.
5 We must invite Jasmine to our do. She's a real **party animal!**
6 Don't always wait for people to do things for you. You should be more **proactive.**
7 It's good to see you! We must **do lunch** sometime and discuss business.
8 It irritates me the way he's always **hobnobbing** with the managers.

18.3 1 He usually hangs **out** with his college friends at the weekend and they go to football matches and things.
2 Nella and her friends are very **cliquey.** They don't mix with anyone else.
3 I'd better go home now. You've been very kind, but I don't want to **outstay** my welcome.
4 She said she wanted to go out with me, then she stood me **up!**
5 Rita and Nick are an **item.** They've been together for months. Didn't you know?
6 Laurie's **crowd** are really fun people. I often meet up with them in town.

Unit 19

19.1 1 far-fetched
2 hackneyed
3 overrated
4 understated
5 disjointed
6 tedious

19.2 *Suggested answers:*
1 The musical **was (rather/a bit) risqué** and was attacked by several politicians and religious figures. (*Risqué* is often used with a modifier such as *rather, very, a bit,* etc.)
2 Her dance performance was **memorable/unforgettable,** simply marvellous.
3 I can't remember the last time I saw such a **gripping film.**
4 It was a **very/deeply moving** play.
5 It's a **harrowing** film.
6 His first stand-up routine **was hilarious.**

19.3 1 flop   2 booed   3 panned   4 interpretation   5 glowing   6 ovation

19.4 1 portrayal
2 miscast
3 cliffhanger
4 keep you on the edge of your seat
5 budding (like the buds of a flower, which will open up and grow)
6 blockbuster (film/movie)
7 cops-and-robbers
8 masterpiece

19.5 *Possible answers:*
1 No, because then it's difficult for them to get a variety of different parts.
2 False. An *ovation* means applause, and if people stand up to applaud, it means they have enjoyed the performance a great deal.
3 He/she is likely to feel nervous.
4 Not much. I prefer to read reviews after seeing something myself rather than before.

Unit 20

20.1
1 Surrealism
2 Op-art
3 Cubism
4 Impressionism
5 subject matter
6 visually literate

20.2
1 Low – as is made clear by the use of the word *dauber*, which suggests speed and lack of care.
2 Formal – because *deem* is typical of more formal speech or writing.
3 Not affected at all – the use of the word *inured* suggests that the sculptor has developed a hard skin when it comes to criticism.
4 An art school is a place where students study art, while a school of art is an artistic movement.

20.3 *usually positive associations*: dazzling, evocative, exquisite, intriguing, original, peerless, priceless, skilful, thought-provoking
usually negative associations: predictable, highbrow, lowbrow, impenetrable, undemanding, pedestrian, uninspiring, unstimulating, clumsy, dreary, run-of-the-mill, worthless, poorly done
negative or positive associations: transparent, challenging, tongue-in-cheek, earnest, sophisticated, primitive

20.4 *Possible answers:*
I think Picasso's painting called *Guernica* is very original because he treated his subject matter in such an unusual and powerful way.
I think the pictures on chocolate boxes could be called rather lowbrow as they are intended to appeal to a mass audience.
I find some modern sculpture rather impenetrable as I don't know what it is meant to represent and I don't find it beautiful in any way.
I think you could call some classical paintings sophisticated in that you appreciate them more if you have had some artistic education.
I find paintings by the surrealist artist Salvador Dali rather challenging as they contain so many curious and unexpected images.
I went to an exhibition of a new art school graduate which I thought was rather pedestrian because it contained nothing original.
I find paintings by Toulouse-Lautrec very evocative because they make me feel as if I am there myself.
I find the sculptures by Anish Kapoor very thought-provoking in that you want to look at them for a long time to work out what he intended to convey.
In my opinion, the designs on ancient Chinese porcelain are often exquisite as they are so delicate and so carefully executed.
I found a recent work that won a prestigious art prize – an unmade, rather grubby bed – extraordinarily dreary as it made me feel miserable rather than uplifted, as I believe art should.

I believe that Turner's paintings of the sea are peerless as no other painter seems to capture the colour and light of the sea so effectively.

Most political cartoons in newspapers are tongue-in-cheek as they do not take anything too seriously.

The beautiful paintings of Leonardo da Vinci are, of course, priceless.

I can see that the works of the modern British painter Tracey Emin are skilful, but personally I don't like them very much.

20.5
1 lowbrow
2 tongue-in-cheek
3 primitive
4 dreary
5 exquisite
6 challenging

20.6

verb	noun	adjective
paint	painting, painter	painted
sketch	sketch	sketchy
depict	depiction	depicted
portray	portrayal, portrait ·	portrayed
colour	colour	colourful, colourless
shape	shape	shapely
illustrate	illustration, illustrator	illustrative
illuminate	illumination	illuminating

Unit 21

21.1
1 memoir/memoirs
2 manual
3 anthology
4 journal

21.2 *Suggested answers:*
1 I just could not **get into** the story, so I stopped reading it.
2 It's **lightweight.**
3 It's **heavy going.**
4 It's **good bedtime reading;** it's just right when you're settling down at night. All the time I was reading it, I just couldn't **put it down.**
5 It's **compulsive reading,** it's so fascinating. / It's a **gripping story.**
6 The book is **very informative.**
7 Her second novel did not attract a large **readership.**
8 This book contains some great moments of **insight.**
9 It is an **engaging tale** about a boy who nurses an injured bird.
10 Mena Harrap's self-help book was a **product of its time,** but what was true in the 1980s doesn't necessarily apply nowadays.

21.3
1 The story takes place against a rather **lugubrious** background in 18th century London.
2 It's full of **wry** comedy and satire.
3 The book is a **chilling** documentation of abuse in a prison.
4 The novel is full of **evocative** passages depicting life in Australia at the turn of the 19th century.
5 It's a very **enigmatic** novel; you never really know what is happening until right at the end.
6 The novel is a **poignant** portrayal of life in a coal-mining community during the last economic recession.

7 John Farr's latest novel is a **breathtaking** masterpiece.

8 *House of the Dead* is a **macabre** story of torture and death in a medieval castle.

9 The novel's **eponymous** heroine, Maria Selune, leaves home at the age of 18 and travels through Asia.

10 Laisha and Asoka are the **protagonists** in this unusual tale of rural family life.

21.4 1 c   2 a   3 d   4 b

Unit 22

22.1 1 Rowan
2 Thomas
3 Atsuko
4 Hannah
5 Beth
6 Carlos

22.2 1 nutrition (or you could use the adjective *nutritional*)
2 traffic-light
3 wholesome
4 unprocessed
5 gluten-free
6 battery farming
7 vegan
8 wholefoods

22.3 1 My mother **grilled** me about where I had been last night.
2 I feel I need a complete change of career, something more exciting to **spice up** my life.
3 What's been happening while I was on holiday? You must fill me in on all the **juicy** gossip.
4 Don't tell her that her phone has been found. Let her **stew (in her own juice)** – perhaps she'll be more careful with it in future.
5 He wanted me to go to the match with him, but rugby just isn't **my cup of tea.**
6 They lived together happily for many years, but things **turned sour** when his mother came to live with them.
7 Patience combined with interest in your pupils is **a recipe for** success for a teacher.
8 Lance's ideas are always **half-baked.**
9 There were some **unsavoury** characters at that party.
10 He has **cooked up** a crazy scheme for making money on the internet. It has all the **ingredients** of a complete disaster.

Unit 23

23.1 *Suggested answers:*
1 When we eat out as a group, **we usually split the bill.**
2 Let me **get this (one).** You can pay next time.
3 Visitors to the company's head office in London are always **wined and dined in/at** the best restaurants.
4 **Would you like to join us** for lunch tomorrow?
5 No, please. Put your credit card away. **Dinner's on me.**
6 **I'd like you to be my guest** at the theatre tomorrow night.

23.2
1 I'm **teetotal.**
2 I **haven't got a sweet tooth.**
3 **Do you have any special/particular dietary requirements?**
4 Just a small **portion** for me, please. I don't want to overdo it.
5 She's become **very calorie-conscious.** / She's **counting the calories.**
6 Sasha is such a **fussy eater.** It's difficult to find things she likes.

23.3
1 a savoury dish
2 a sullen/overbearing waiter
3 an informal get-together
4 courteous staff
5 sluggish service
6 impeccable service

23.4
1 take pot luck
2 say when
3 grab a bite to eat
4 nibbles
5 seconds (note plural)
6 an informal get-together

Unit 24

24.1
1 tow-away
2 tailback
3 pile-ups
4 give way
5 right of way
6 hit-and-run
7 (exhaust) emissions
8 breathalyser, drink-driving, penalty points
9 sound/beep, horns
10 disruption

24.2 *Suggested answers:*
2 B: Oh, so you **skidded.**
3 B: Oh, I guess it was a case of **road rage.**
4 B: Oh, so your tyres were **bald,** were they?
5 B: Oh, so it was a **head-on collision.**
6 B: Oh, really? I didn't know they could give **on-the-spot fines.**
7 B: Oh, so it's not **roadworthy.**
8 B: Oh, really? Do you have to pay a **toll?** I didn't know that.

24.3 *Suggested answers:*
1 All the traffic in all directions was unable to move.
2 The police car made me stop at the side of the road.
3 I had a small accident where I hit something or another car, but without serious damage. (*Bump* is an informal alternative to *collision.*)
4 My car broke down. (*Conk out* is very informal.)
5 He's an irritating person who sits in the passenger seat and thinks he can tell the driver how to drive.

Unit 25

25.1 *Suggested answers:*
2 I hate **charter flights.**
3 The ticket allowed us a three-night **stopover** in Singapore on the journey from London to Sydney.
4 You can get a **shared cabin** on the ferry. / You can get a **four-berth cabin** on the ferry.
5 Our seats were in the **front/first carriage.**

6 When you arrive, the **transfers** are included in the cost of the holiday. / The cost of the holiday is inclusive of **transfers**.

7 It was a cheap fare, but there were (some) **restrictions**.

8 The ticket is relatively cheap, but it's **non-refundable**.

25.2 1 e 2 f 3 a 4 c 5 j 6 b 7 d 8 g 9 h 10 i

25.3 *Suggested answers:*
1 self-catering holiday: to be your own boss
2 camping at a beach resort: to rough it (i.e. to live in very basic conditions, without any extra comforts), to sleep under the stars (i.e. out in the open, without a roof over your head)
3 staying in an inn or a guest house: a cosy atmosphere
4 skiing holiday staying in a chalet: an exhilarating experience, perhaps also a real learning experience
5 trekking holiday camping in the mountains: to keep on the move, to be out in the wilds (i.e. away from civilisation), to sleep under the stars, an exhilarating experience
6 cruise: to lounge around (i.e. to sit or lie and relax for long periods), to just drift along (to go along with the pace and rhythm of the ship)
7 sightseeing holiday staying in a hotel in a historic city: to spend a fortune on entrance fees, a real learning experience
8 touring holiday in hire car: to come and go as you please, to just drift along (i.e. not drive fast, no particular plan), to keep on the move

25.4 *Suggested answers:*
1 lounged around / drifted along
2 be my own boss
3 roughing it / sleeping under the stars / being out in the wilds
4 an exhilarating experience
5 to spend a fortune on entrance fees
6 a real learning experience
7 a cosy atmosphere
8 to keep on the move

Unit 26

26.1 1 boasts
2 sector
3 fauna
4 get, beaten
5 hordes
6 get, nature
7 seeking, ordinary
8 escape
9 tracts, virgin, wealth
10 parks, reserves

26.2 1 unrivalled
2 scenic
3 stunning
4 unbeatable
5 awe-inspiring
6 waterfront
7 unwind
8 recharge

26.3 1 trek, hike, ramble
2 savour
3 discerning
4 outside of the cities in wild areas, covered with grass, bushes and trees, especially in Africa and Australia
5 four by four: the vehicle has driving power on all four wheels (often used to cross rough terrain or snow and ice)
6 positive

Unit 27

27.1 1 c   2 e   3 d   4 b   5 a
Note that some other matches could be made although they do not appear in the text. Less strong but also possible is *coniferous plantation*. Note, however, that *paddy* cannot collocate with anything else and it is not possible to talk about 'crop fields'.

27.2 *Suggested answers:*
plantation: tea, coffee, rubber
industry: manufacturing, pharmaceutical, textile
forest: deciduous, rain, dense
field: oil, wheat, magnetic
nation: civilised, independent, sovereign
Note that *oil, cotton* and *rubber* could also collocate with 'industry'.

27.3 1 ancestors
2 emigrants
3 immigrants/migrants
4 migrants/immigrants
5 descendants

27.4 1 Recently, the country's economy has suffered a decline in **manufacturing industry**.
2 The university has long been **at the forefront of** agricultural science.
3 The river delta **is prone to** catastrophic flooding on a regular basis.
4 One can often see local shepherds **tending** large flocks of sheep on the hillsides.
5 In the late 18th century, migrants **settled** in the uncultivated lands towards the north of the country.
6 In the **arid** southern provinces, **vegetation** is sparse.
7 In the cold northern regions, the landscape consists mostly of **tundra**.
8 The **indigenous tribes** in the eastern jungles are now facing threats to their way of life.
9 The farmlands are dotted with **deciduous woods**, while the large **evergreen forests** provide the country with much-needed timber.
10 The **prairies** of the northern USA experienced a severe **drought** last year.

Unit 28

28.1 *Possible answers:*
1 Yes, extremely chilly / cold.
2 Mm. Isn't it hot!
3 Yes, terribly humid.
4 Very windy!

28.2 *Suggested answers:*
2 unfriendly, unwelcoming
3 to confuse
4 having too much of something
5 rapid, moving quickly
6 lots of hard, unpleasant things that one can't stop or escape from
7 general atmosphere or situation
8 unclear
9 to move, making a loud, deep noise

28.3 *Possible answers:*
1 moral, social, economic, current, mild, harsh **climate**
2 **prevailing** winds, view, climate, opinion, mood
3 **to cloud** the issue, the horizon, someone's judgement, someone's thinking, someone's vision
4 **the winds of** change, democracy, discontent
5 **a frosty** reception, look, glance, response
6 **a hail of** bullets, gunfire, abuse, missiles, insults

28.4

1 mean	6 solar radiation
2 arid	7 moderates
3 elevation	8 continental
4 latitude	9 seasonality
5 precipitation	

Unit 29

29.1
1 c glass ceiling = invisible barrier
2 d ivory tower = life away from unpleasant realities
3 e brick wall = barrier
4 f back door = unofficial way in
5 b window of opportunity = time when there is the chance to do something
6 a tower of strength = very supportive person

29.2
1 gone
2 hold / provide
3 opens
4 come
5 hit
6 towers
7 shut / closed
8 fell

29.3
1 My brother is always **a tower of strength** whenever I have a problem.
2 We'll never know what the US and Russian Presidents said to each other **behind closed doors.**
3 The fee for this work will depend on the time it takes but **there is / it has a ceiling** of $20,000 / **the ceiling is** $20,000.
4 The cost of petrol **has gone through the roof** in the last six months.
5 Having children often **cements a marriage.**
6 Winning an Olympic medal can be **the gateway to** a career in the media.
7 The **key** decision we have to take now is where to locate our business.
8 The professor has spent all his life **in an ivory tower** and really finds it very difficult to cope in the real world.
9 Lena **has built Max up** so much – I hope I won't be disappointed when I meet him.

29.4 *Suggested answers:*
1 He earns very little, barely enough to **survive on**.
2 The speaker's request for questions was met with **total silence**.
3 Working on this project together should help to **provide the starting point** for a good relationship in the future.
4 Jack's prolonged illness **led to the collapse of his business**.
5 This government should **put things right in its own immediate sphere of influence / close to home / here** before criticising other countries.

Unit 30

30.1 1 f   2 c   3 e   4 a   5 g   6 b   7 d

30.2 1 roots
2 rooted
3 take
4 seeds
5 branches
6 put
7 stemmed
8 budding

30.3 *Verbs associated with growth and health:* flourish, germinate, sprout, thrive
Verbs associated with decline and death: fade, shrivel, wilt, wither

30.4 *Possible answers:*
1 budding: pop star, novelist, politician
2 flourishing: business, campaign, enterprise
3 withering: glance, expression, remark
4 fading: optimism, ambitions, dream
5 deeply rooted: prejudice, hatred, tradition
6 thriving: industry, business, agriculture

30.5 1 My hopes of getting a job are **fading**. Unemployment is at an all-time record.
2 The firm is **pruning back** the labour force in order to become more competitive.
3 She **shed** her inhibitions at the party and danced with everyone!
4 He and his wife are now **reaping the rewards** of many years of hard work building up their business.
5 The party is trying hard to **weed out** the extremists and create for itself a more moderate political image. They want to reflect the views of **the grass roots** supporters.
6 Some people seem to **thrive** on difficult challenges.
7 A blogger **dug up** some alarming facts about government spending.
8 Well, if you won't study for your exams, don't be surprised if you **reap what you sow**.

Unit 31

31.1 1 There are a lot of different types of **rodent** living in the woods.
2 A whale isn't a fish, as it doesn't lay eggs. It's actually **a mammal**.
3 There are some interesting **reptiles** near the river.
4 Everyone thinks these animals **are carnivores**, but in fact they **are herbivores**.
5 The mother bird protects her eggs from **predators**.
6 May different species **have become extinct** because their habitat has been destroyed.

31.2 1 docile
2 fierce/savage
3 domesticated
4 tame
5 wild

31.3 1 habitat
2 sanctuary
3 reserve
4 scavenger
5 stray
6 marsupial
7 migration
8 dodo

31.4 1 blood sports
2 the ivory trade
3 poachers
4 They would say that it is cruel to kill animals just to provide people with luxury clothes.
5 its horn
6 animal (rescue) shelter
7 game park / game reserve
8 warm-blooded
9 cold-blooded

31.5 Stressed syllables are in bold for comparison.

noun	verb	adjective
carnivore		car**ni**vorous
herbivore		her**bi**vorous
predator	prey (on)	**pred**atory
poacher	poach	
mi**gra**tion	mi**grate**	**mi**gratory
domesti**ca**tion	do**mes**ticate	do**mes**ticated

Unit 32

32.1 *Suggested answers:*
1 **Carbon (dioxide) emissions from** cars and factories **are** a major problem.
2 These flowers here are **an endangered species,** so it's illegal to pick them.
3 A lot of wild animals have to survive in **shrinking habitats.**
4 A lot of Patagonia is a **pristine environment.**
5 We have to look after **the finite resources of the planet.**
6 If **deforestation** continues, there will be no forest left ten years from now.
7 Burning **fossil fuels** causes a lot of pollution.
8 **Sea levels will rise / There will be rising sea levels** if **global warming** continues.
9 Increasing population **exerts severe pressure on** economic resources.
10 The **ecological balance** is very delicate.

32.2

noun	verb	adjective	adverb
climate		climatic	
demography		demographic	demographically
projection	project	projected	
sustainability	sustain	sustainable	sustainably
contamination	contaminate	contaminated	
toxin		toxic	toxically
depletion	deplete	depleted, depleting	

32.3 Prophets of doom and gloom are always saying that we are heading for an environmental catastrophe, and that unless we adopt a policy of sustainable development, we will cause irreparable damage to the planet. The worst-case scenario is of a world choked by overpopulation, the greenhouse effect and traffic gridlock. Much of what is claimed is exaggerated, but politicians are influenced by such voices and are always trying to improve their green credentials in the eyes of the voters.

32.4 1 d   2 e   3 g   4 h   5 f   6 c   7 a   8 b

Unit 33

33.1
1 on hold, back to
2 dispatch
3 responsive
4 prompt
5 backlog
6 substandard / shoddy
7 accommodating / obliging
8 helpline
9 in-store
10 set up

33.2 1 i   2 h   3 b   4 f   5 a   6 g   7 d   8 e   9 c

33.3
1 The plumber we got **was incompetent** and he caused a flood in our kitchen.
2 If you have any **queries** about the service, there's a helpline you can ring.
3 The new TV came with a two-year **guarantee / warranty**.
4 The service **is (very) impersonal**; they just treat you as a number.
5 Do they offer a **nationwide** service?
6 The woman at the tax office **was impeccable.**
7 It's a **secure site.**
8 It didn't feel like a **secure transaction,** so I cancelled it and logged off.

Unit 34

34.1
1 You'll have to show a **vaccination certificate** for tropical diseases when you enter the country.
2 People entering from war-torn countries often **claim asylum.**
3 You have to **clear customs** if you arrive on an international flight at San Francisco airport, even if you are flying on within the USA.
4 You may have to fill in a **customs declaration (form)** before going through customs control.
5 At the airport now, they use **facial recognition technology.**
6 *Passenger to airline cabin attendant:* Could you give me **a landing card** before we arrive, please?
7 At the airport, the security guards had **sniffer/detector dogs.**
8 You'll need a visa; the **entry regulations** are very strict.
9 You have to fill in the **port of entry** in this box here.

34.2 1 g   2 j   3 h   4 e   5 i   6 d   7 b   8 a   9 f   10 c

34.3 1 a plain-clothes (police) officer
2 a traffic warden
3 the anti-corruption squad
4 a parking ticket
5 an undercover police officer
6 the security forces

34.4 1 detected
2 refugees
3 persecution
4 exceeding
5 enforce
6 allowance
7 search
8 suspicions / a suspicion

Unit 35

35.1

noun – person	noun –abstract	verb	adjective
adherent	adherence	adhere	
convert*	conversion	convert*	converted
radical	radicalism	radicalise	radical
reactionary	reaction		reactionary
fanatic	fanaticism		fanatical

* Note the change in stress.

35.2 1 seeks
2 derives from
3 are anxious to
4 eradicate
5 exploitation
6 campaigned
7 leave
8 commitments

35.3 1 implausible
2 credible
3 benefit
4 prejudiced
5 presumed
6 salt
7 point of view
8 attributed

35.4
1 eradicate
2 converts
3 prejudiced
4 subjective
5 adherents
6 attribute
7 objective
8 commitments
9 pinch

Unit 36

36.1
1 For Christians, Christmas **celebrates** the birth of Jesus Christ.
2 The **festivities** included parades, sports and musical gatherings.
3 There was a **celebratory feeling** about the whole weekend.
4 For people who live in the country, the spring festival **is a renewal of** the fertility of the land.
5 There was a **ceremonial atmosphere** as the military bands **paraded** around the main square.
6 People were **in a festive mood** when the harvest was successfully completed and a huge **feast** was held in the village.
7 You should go and see the lantern festival. It's always **a spectacle**.
8 The festival **always falls** on the first Monday in July. It **commemorates** a famous battle.
9 It was the **centenary** of the founding of the university and the **bi-centenary** of the city itself.
10 The gymnastic display involving 300 children was **really spectacular**.

36.2 Well, it was called the Festival of Flowers, and it was **associated** with the coming of spring, after the **sombre** winter months. It was a time of **renewal**. Its origin can **be traced back to** the religious tradition of taking flowers to offer them to the gods. Spring flowers were the main **focus of** the festival, and there was always a big **parade** through the streets. It was all very lively and **flamboyant** and probably rather **raucous**, and it **was very atmospheric**. The flowers **symbolised** new life, and people thought they would be guaranteed a good harvest later in the year if they were offered to the gods. Nowadays most people **are not (so) superstitious**, but there are still some **pagan festivals** celebrated every year.

Unit 37

37.1
1 Slavic
2 Sino-Tibetan
3 Semitic
4 Germanic
5 Austronesian
6 Romance
7 Indo-Iranian
8 Altaic

37.2 *Suggested answers:*
1 The **orthography** of Burmese / Burmese **orthography** is quite difficult for a foreign learner.
2 Japanese uses several different writing systems with hundreds of **characters**.
3 The **lexicon** of a language like English is constantly changing. A lot of new technical words are **derived from Graeco-Latin** roots, rather than the **Anglo-Saxon lexicon**.
4 Unlike English, some world languages have very few vowel **phonemes** and no **diphthongs**.
5 This ancient and beautiful alphabet uses **pictograms** to express meaning.
6 **Modality is** expressed in different forms in different languages.

37.3 *Stressed syllables are shown in bold:*

noun	adjective	change in stress?
ortho**gra**phy	ortho**gra**phic	yes
lexicon	**le**xical	no
mo**da**lity	**mo**dal	yes
metaphor	meta**pho**rical	yes
polysemy	poly**se**mous	no

37.4 1 metaphor
2 obsolete language
3 polysemy
4 computer jargon

Unit 38

38.1 1 reign
2 dynasty
3 heir (the heir has a legal right to take over, for example, by birth; the successor is any person who actually takes over, for example, by being elected)
4 manuscript
5 coronation
6 empire
7 dawn
8 shred
9 the Bronze Age
10 the pre-colonial era

38.2

person	noun	verb
king	kingdom	
emperor	empire	
successor	succession	succeed
	coronation	crown
conqueror	conquest	conquer
archaeologist	archaeology	
	reign	reign
labourer	labour	labour
migrant	migration	migrate
ruler	rule	rule
monarch	monarchy	

38.3 1 d 2 g 3 a 4 f 5 h 6 b 7 e 8 c

38.4 1 b 2 a 3 a 4 b 5 b

Unit 39

39.1
1 deprivation
2 illiterate
3 affluent
4 Denial
5 destitution
6 violation

39.2
1 relative
2 threshold
3 shelter
4 fundamental
5 absolute
6 impoverished

39.3
1 line
2 bracket
3 context
4 ends
5 belts
6 stricken

39.4
1 destitute
2 mouth
3 tight
4 deprived
5 poverty line
6 bracket
7 classed
8 affluence
9 malnourishment
10 sanitation

Unit 40

40.1
1 False. It is down to the MP to make up his or her own mind.
2 False. They only make a statement about some of them. Others are simply placed in the Petitions Bag.
3 True.
4 False. Only on the substantive ones.
5 False. It is an example of a Select Committee that crosses departmental barriers.
6 False. They do investigate the conduct of individual MPs.
7 True. (Presumably because they do not have the same constituency work to do.)
8 False. They don't. They focus on five key areas (Europe, etc.) whereas Commons Select Committees focus on shadowing government departments (as well as some other things).

40.2 1 d 2 h 3 e 4 b 5 g 6 a 7 f 8 c

40.3
1 debating chamber
2 briefing material
3 wide-ranging expertise
4 select committee
5 party policy
6 committee stage
7 Speaker's chair
8 government department

40.4 1 conduct
2 allegations
3 down / up
4 shadow
5 set
6 crosses
7 expertise
8 scrutinises

Unit 41

41.1 1 conquer
2 injustice
3 minorities
4 establish
5 negotiations
6 humanity
7 justify
8 pursue

41.2

verb	noun
constitute	constitution
found	foundation, founder
undertake	undertaking
negotiate	negotiation, negotiator
justify	justification
conquer	conquest, conqueror
liberate	liberation, liberator
unite	unity
delegate	delegate, delegation
recognise	recognition

41.3 1 B march
2 C delicate
3 D infrastructure
4 B undertook
5 A foundation
6 D delegate

41.4 1 undeniably
2 customary
3 injustice
4 solidarity
5 movements
6 integrated

Unit 42

42.1   1 impeached
       2 lodge
       3 overturned
       4 sets
       5 award/grant
       6 bend
       7 are infringing / infringed
       8 perverting
       9 annulled
      10 quashed

42.2   1 trespass / trespassing
       2 embezzlement
       3 discrimination
       4 perjury
       5 harassment
       6 insider trading / dealing

42.3   1 amendments
       2 harassment
       3 infringement
       4 contravention
       5 perversion
       6 allegation
       7 annulment
       8 impeachment

42.4   1 You should let the police deal with the situation – it's far too risky to **take the law into your own hands.**
       2 Sam started getting into trouble when he got in with a gang of habitual **law-breakers.**
       3 You shouldn't start **laying down the law** on your first day in a new job.
       4 Masha will never be able to get Vadim to conform – he's **a law unto himself.**
       5 Jack is far too **law-abiding** to agree to bring extra cigarettes into the country.

Unit 43

43.1   1 diplomacy, sanctions
       2 escalated, out
       3 cleansing
       4 massacre
       5 regime, overthrown
       6 resolution
       7 resort
       8 casualties
       9 clashes
      10 weaponry

43.2   1 **Irrational hatred** of people of other ethnic groups is one of the root causes of conflict.
       2 The **intervention** of the United Nations in the situation has helped to reduce the violence.
       3 The **rival** political groups finally negotiated a peace agreement.
       4 The general was a **brutal** dictator who ruled for 18 years.
       5 There had been a longstanding **mistrust** between the two tribes.
       6 The **rebellion** began in 2010.

43.3   1 suicide
2 peacekeeping
3 ambushed
4 observers
5 waged
6 siege
7 truce / ceasefire
8 campaign

43.4   1 d   2 e   3 f   4 a   5 b   6 c

Unit 44

44.1   1 sustainable
2 following / pursuing, eradicate
3 encouraging, taking
4 deep / abject
5 recovered
6 achieve
7 allocate
8 access

44.2   1 Over a period of five years, the country **incurred** huge debts which it could not **repay**.
2 **Debtor countries** are completely at the mercy of wealthier nations.
3 **The debt burden** is so great in some countries that their economies are collapsing.
4 Wealthier countries could do a lot to **ease / alleviate** the debt of poor countries, and indeed, in some cases, could **cancel** the debt altogether.
5 Over a period of three years, the country suffered a **double-dip** recession.
6 The following year, there was a **slump** in the price of crude oil.
7 While some countries **devalued** their currencies, one country alone **revalued** its currency due to its strong economy.
8 Urgent measures were needed to **boost** the economy.

44.3   1 a trade war
2 impose sanctions, lift embargoes
3 restrictive practices
4 monetary union
5 development grants
6 a war-torn economy
7 ailing
8 debt relief

44.4   1 **Monetary union** was agreed between the five countries in 2003.
2 The government introduced a package of measures to rescue the **ailing** economy.
3 The two Trade Ministers got together to try to abolish **restrictive practices**.
4 A **trade war** broke out between the two countries in 1999.
5 The **war-torn** economy is slowly recovering now that peace has come.
6 The United Nations **imposed** sanctions on the country in 1995 and did not lift them until 2008.
7 The region received a **development grant** from the World Bank.
8 **Debt relief** has been crucial for some developing nations.

Unit 45

45.1
1 debit card
2 credit card fraud (you can also say *identity theft*)
3 put it / stick it
4 direct debit
5 electronic transfer
6 broke / skint
7 strapped
8 tight

45.2
1 She got a huge golden **handshake** when she left the company.
2 My old aunt Jessie is **rolling** in it. Every time I go to see her, she gives me £100.
3 My father got a **lump** sum when he retired, so he bought a weekend cottage.
4 She put her **life** savings into an online company and lost everything when it collapsed.
5 The bank tried to persuade me to put my money into a share **portfolio**, with stocks and shares in different companies.
6 If you need a very large sum of money, it's not a good idea to **borrow** from friends or neighbours.

45.3
1 d 2 f 3 e 4 b 5 a 6 c

Unit 46

46.1
1 classified ads (or adverts/advertisements) / classifieds
2 an agony aunt
3 the obituaries (or obituary column)
4 an editorial / a leader (or leading article)
5 a supplement
6 a feature
7 circulation
8 coverage

46.2
1 manual
2 flyers / leaflets
3 brochures
4 pamphlets
5 journal
6 press release
7 prospectus
8 newsletter

46.3
edition is used about both books and magazines (a book, magazine, etc. that is one of a large number that are the same and were produced at the same time)
<u>Books</u>
spine (the vertical edge of the book which usually has the title on it)
blurb (short description usually on back cover, written to encourage people to read the book)
foreword (a piece of text before the main text of the book begins)
index (alphabetical list of subjects or names at the end of a book, showing on what page they are found in the text)
edition – see above

<u>Magazines</u>
subscription (a payment that buys you a certain number of issues in advance, e.g. for one year)
issue (publication printed for a particular day/week/month)
edition – see above
quarterly (a magazine issued every three months)

46.4 1 B 2 C 3 A

46.5 1 c
2 d
3 a
4 e If something **tells you all you need to know about something** (informal), it gives all the most important information.
5 f
6 b **Small print** refers to the details, rules and restrictions that often accompany legal documents such as guarantees, contracts, insurance policies, etc., which are often written in very small letters.

Unit 47

47.1 1 chat room
2 webinar
3 ISP
4 cookie
5 attachment
6 spam

47.2

word	opposite	exists	doesn't exist
delete	undelete	✓	
download	upload	✓	
update	downdate		✓
inbox	outbox	✓	
online	offline	✓	
install	uninstall	✓	

47.3 1 upload, online
2 inbox
3 install
4 undelete
5 offline
6 update

47.4 *Suggested answers:*
1 E-signatures are a way of identifying yourself on the internet with a unique code or name, which you can use, for example, to agree to pay for goods.
2 E-learning means taking courses over the internet instead of going to a school or college to do your studies.
3 E-enabled here means that all the study materials can be accessed and worked with through the internet.
4 E-books are books which you buy from the internet, and which you then read on your computer, tablet, e-reader or smartphone.

5 The dotcom economy refers to internet companies, whose web addresses typically end in '.com', e.g. a company that sells bicycles over the internet might call itself *newbikes.com*, which would be read aloud as 'new bikes dot com'.
6 A tablet is a very thin (and often quite small) portable computer used mostly for email and online activities.
7 Parental controls are controls on the computer which allow parents to decide which websites their children can visit and to restrict certain activities.
8 I can't stop doing this activity; I want to do it all the time and can't stop myself.

Unit 48

48.1
1 lap
2 crowd
3 rock
4 the art
5 pamper
6 sumptuous
7 leave/put
8 galore
9 indulge
10 slashing

48.2 1 d   2 h   3 g   4 f   5 a   6 b   7 c   8 e

48.3
1 B
2 A / C
3 E
4 C
5 D
6 A / C / E
7 E
8 B

48.4
1 a logo (on clothing)
2 a billboard
3 a sandwich board
4 a pop-up ad (on a website)
5 a flyer
6 sky-writing

Unit 49

49.1 1 h   2 g   3 e   4 b   5 a   6 d   7 c   8 f

49.2
1 rag
2 copy
3 inches
4 deadline
5 went
6 archive

49.3
1 No, because rag is too informal a word for this context and also it implies that you think the newspaper is not of good quality.
2 You have a low opinion of them.
3 Deadlines.
4 'Exclusive' and 'scoop'.
5 The story breaks and the story hits the headlines.
6 Libel and defamation of character: these both involve saying things that lower a person's reputation. (Defamation is broader than libel in that it covers slander as well as libel. Slander is spoken defamation of character and libel is written defamation of character.)

49.4
1 Every news report inevitably **puts its own spin** on events.
2 I have to find some articles from some **back copies** of *The Times*.
3 The TV news yesterday **ran a story** about my favourite singer.
4 The floods took up more **column inches** in the papers than any other story this week.

5 Politicians are always ready and willing to **air their views to/in** the press.
6 The story about the scandal surrounding her uncle **hit the headlines** on her wedding day.
7 Any newspaper does all it can to prevent being sued for **defamation of character**.
8 Muck-raking is a characteristic activity of **the gutter press**.

49.5
1 conference
2 broke
3 publicity
4 media
5 airtime
6 Social
7 hero
8 occurrence

Unit 50

50.1
1 anaesthetist
2 cardiologist
3 paediatrician
4 opthalmologist
5 dermatologist
6 acupuncturist
7 aromatherapist
8 psychiatrist

50.2
1 surgery
2 chronic
3 prescription
4 refer
5 condition
6 locum
7 organ
8 acute

50.3
1 What is the name of your **family doctor**?
2 Is there a **prescription charge** in your country?
3 In your country is there a similar structure of primary care and **secondary care**?
4 Do doctors often do **home visits** in your country?
5 Are there **insurance schemes** for private healthcare in your country?
6 When it comes to healthcare, do many people in your country **go private**?
7 How popular is **complementary medicine** in your country?
8 Have you ever been to a specialist who practises some kind of **alternative medicine**?

Unit 51

51.1
1 She was feeling **under** the weather and a bit **feverish**, so she took the day off.
2 I felt really **off-colour** yesterday and my head was **throbbing**, so I took a painkiller.
3 I felt a bit **out of sorts** and seemed to have more **aches and pains** than usual.
4 Mo has **backache** after carrying that heavy suitcase of yours.
5 Gary has been **fighting off a cold** for the last few days.
6 I'm sorry I won't make it to your party because I've **come** down with flu.
7 Do you suffer **from** any allergies?
8 How did you get all those **cuts and bruises**?

51.2　1 I was feeling quite **feverish.**
　　　2 The smell of paint always made her feel **nauseous.**
　　　3 I felt **dizzy** so I went and lay down for an hour.
　　　4 My nose was **bunged up**, so I got a spray from the chemist.
　　　5 I got **a stiff neck** from driving for a long time in an awkward position.
　　　6 Joanna was **shivery** and looked unwell, so I told her to go to bed.
　　　7 My knee hurts today because I **twisted it** getting out of Andrei's sports car yesterday.
　　　8 I **had a sleepless night** last night.

51.3　*Positive meanings:* be over the worst, fight off*, be on the mend, be back on one's feet again, get over
　　　Negative meanings: suffer from, fight off*, come down with, under the weather
　　　*Whether you consider *fight off* to be positive or negative depends on whether you feel that 'fighting something off' is always used in a negative situation, or whether you are succeeding in 'fighting off' your cold/flu/headache, etc., in which case you might see it as positive.

51.4　1 Hello, Dan, good to see you **back on your feet again.**
　　　2 Nadja, I won't be in today, I've **come down with** a cold.
　　　3 Oh, I'm OK. I'm **over the worst** now. I still feel bad, but I should be out within a week or so. (*over the worst* suggests getting better, but that you are still quite ill; *on the mend* (see 6 below) suggests the person is getting back to normal health)
　　　4 Don't worry, darling. Everyone has a cold now and then. You'll **get over** it.
　　　5 I'm trying to **fight off** the flu, but nothing seems to help. I don't think I'll be at work tomorrow.
　　　6 Hilary was quite ill last week, but she's **on the mend / back on her feet again** now and should be back at work on Monday.
　　　7 I feel a bit **under the weather** today, but I'm sure I'll be fine tomorrow.
　　　8 I used to **suffer from** a dust allergy, but I don't think I do any more.

Unit 52

52.1　1 disorder
　　　2 history
　　　3 allergic
　　　4 exceed
　　　5 adverse
　　　6 stroke
　　　7 poo
　　　8 are
　　　9 Disorientation
　　10 duration

52.2　1 Excitement **reached fever pitch** as the day of the final match dawned.
　　　2 Although industry is doing well in the north of the country, in the south it is **ailing.**
　　　3 The manager said that there had been a **rash of** complaints about the hotel.
　　　4 Unfortunately, she **still carries the scars of / is still scarred by** her divorce.
　　　5 The problems we have experienced in our neighbourhood are **symptomatic of** wider problems in society.
　　　6 What do you think the **prognosis** is for the peace talks?
　　　7 I voted for the Green Party because they seem to **have their finger on the pulse.**
　　　8 The business has been **ailing** for some time now.
　　　9 I'm afraid I have rather a **jaundiced** view of the banking industry.

52.3
1 paralysed
2 ailing
3 fatal
4 rash
5 contagious
6 fever
7 disease
8 prognosis

Unit 53

53.1
1 Eggs and shellfish are **nutritious**.
2 **Cholesterol-rich foods** are fine if eaten in moderation.
3 These foods do not necessarily **pose** a danger to health.
4 The most important thing is not to **impede** the flow of blood.
5 Fatty plaque can **clog** the arteries.
6 Scientists recommend a **high-fibre diet**.
7 Running is a good form of **cardiovascular exercise**.
8 **Brisk** walking is also good for you.
9 Jogging is a great way to **burn** calories.
10 To do enough of this kind of exercise, you don't have to be **sporty**.

53.2
1 heart attack and stroke
2 high
3 rich
4 they contain a lot of fibre / they are fibre-rich
5 He is intent on doing more exercise.
6 diabetics

53.3
football: score an own goal, move the goalposts, level playing field
horse racing: in the running, neck and neck
skating: skate around
sailing: sail through

53.4
1 Elsa **sailed through** her exams.
2 I wish he'd **stop skating around** the point.
3 I've been told that **I'm in the running** for the job of supervisor.
4 Although he meant it as a compliment, Rick **scored an own goal when he told** Helen she looked as if she had put on some weight.
5 **It's hardly a level playing field** when 18-year-olds take the same exam as 15-year-olds.
6 It's hard to know what to do when the **goalposts are constantly being moved**.
7 The two candidates are **neck and neck** in the race to become President.

Unit 54

54.1 *Suggested answers:*
1 The economy cannot depend only on **service industries**. We need to encourage **manufacturing industries**.
2 In this area, there are a lot of **high-technology / high-tech industries**, while in the north, they depend more on **low-technology / low-tech industries**.
3 **Cutting-edge** technology is very expensive, so the company has to rely on **conventional** technology.
4 **State ownership / Nationalisation** is less popular than it was, but the trend towards **privatisation** has slowed down.
5 **Heavy industry** has declined, and now we're more dependent on **light industry**.

54.2 1 a public-private partnership
2 subsidy
3 inward investment
4 piecework
5 a sweatshop economy
6 to switch production, to relocate
7 retraining, reskilling
8 a multinational (company)
9 a cost-cutting exercise
10 child labour

54.3 1 Industrial piracy (illegal production of goods using another company's brand name)
2 industrial espionage (stealing or destroying a rival company's plans or secrets)
3 Copyright infringement (publishing or copying a book or work of art without the author's permission)
4 Money laundering (passing money illegally earned through the normal banking system without being caught)
5 black market (secret, illegal trade)

Unit 55

55.1 1 satellite communications
2 ergonomics
3 biotechnology
4 digital technology
5 artificial intelligence

55.2 1 tablet / iPad
2 interactive TV
3 laptop
4 desktop computer
5 e-reader / Kindle
6 router

55.3 1 thumbnail (small pictures you can make bigger before downloading them)
2 computer nerd (a rather negative term for a person obsessed with computers and who devotes most of their time to them at the expense of a normal social life)
3 techie (this has none of the negative associations that nerd has)
4 app (short for application = special software)
5 screensaver (image that appears on your computer screen if you do not use the computer for a certain period of time)
6 footprint
7 icon (small symbol representing the program)
8 trackpad

55.4 1 technician
2 technically
3 technology
4 technique
5 technologically

Unit 56

56.1
1 c gridlocked traffic
2 e genetic modification
3 d human genome
4 a population explosion
5 b global village

56.2
1 population explosion
2 genetic modification
3 a global village
4 Gridlocked traffic
5 the human genome

56.3
1 a mega-city
2 keyhole surgery
3 nanotechnology
4 cloning
5 extraterrestrial beings
6 genetic engineering / modification
7 (our) destiny
8 a designer baby

56.4
1 The **doomsday scenario** is that we will destroy the world with nuclear weapons.
2 **Interplanetary travel** for scientific exploration will become normal in the coming centuries.
3 He belongs to a team of scientists who are trying to improve our understanding of the **human genome**.
4 Governments need to take **drastic measures** to save the planet.
5 Many people **envisage / foresee** a world in which the poor simply get poorer.

56.5
1 genetically modified (GM) food
2 the nuclear family
3 cloning
4 gene therapy
5 the global village / globalisation
6 space tourism

Unit 57

57.1   1 pipeline   2 offshore drilling platform   3 solar panels   4 coal mine   5 wind farm

57.2
1 A new 100-kilometre **pipeline** has been built to bring oil from **wells** in the north of the country to a refinery on the coast.
2 The power station is **coal-fired,** but it will soon be replaced by a **nuclear plant.**
3 Fire has broken out on **an offshore** drilling platform.
4 **Tidal power and wave power** could solve the energy problems of countries with extensive coastlines. Other parts of the world may be able to use **geothermal** energy.
5 '**Renewables** are important,' the Prime Minister said. 'We intend to give grants for people to install **solar panels,** as well as developing **wind farms.**'
6 The country is developing two main energy sources: **biomass** and **hydroelectric** power stations. At the same time, inefficient **coal mines** will gradually be closed.

57.3 1 food miles
2 appliances, energy-efficient
3 carbon footprint
4 gas-guzzler, consumption
5 monitoring, consume
6 finite, deposits

Unit 58

58.1 1 poky (suitable in this informal context)
2 roomy (often used for cars)
3 compact (in fact, a whole class of small cameras is referred to as 'compact cameras' by manufacturers and advertisers)
4 cramped (suitable in this slightly more formal context – compare with 1)
5 spacious
6 extensive

58.2 The property is **spacious,** with a **compact** garden, and is situated only ten minutes away from the **bustling** town centre. There are **extensive** leisure facilities nearby.
Notes on the incorrect choices:
Rambling usually suggests a rather chaotic collection of rooms. A *labyrinth* suggests they are confusingly laid out.
Cramped and *poky* suggest that somewhere is too small to be comfortable.
Congested and *crowded* are negative. *Bustling* suggests that somewhere is busy, interesting and full of life.
Excessive means too many. No one wants *expensive* facilities.

58.3 1 The kitchen is so small you **can't/couldn't swing a cat / there isn't enough room to swing a cat** in it.
2 There's **ample space / room** for your clothes in this wardrobe.
3 I **got / was hemmed in** in the office car park the other day.
4 Holidays in Australia are great if you love **wide open spaces.**
5 I hate the London underground during rush hour. Everyone is **packed in like sardines** in the trains.
6 I dropped a glass and tiny pieces **(were) scattered** all over the floor.
7 The buildings in the holiday complex are **(quite / rather) spread out.**
8 The train was very full but I just managed to **squeeze in** before the doors closed.

58.4 1 **It might be a bit of a squash** on the bus at this time of day – I hope you don't mind.
2 I quickly **stuffed** a few clothes and a couple of books in a rucksack and set off at once.
3 The Ural Mountains **mark the boundary** between Europe and Asia.
4 We'll all have to try and **squeeze into** my little car; Larry hasn't got his with him today.
5 Your room is at the **rear** of the hotel, so you won't hear any traffic.
6 I don't think we should try and **cram / squeeze / stuff** everything into one suitcase. Let's take two.

Unit 59

59.1 1 They've been living in the same house since the year dot.
2 I'll be with you in a sec.
3 John gave it to Magda for keeps. / Magda gave it to John for keeps.
4 Together we can get it done in less than no time. / We can get it done together in less than no time.
5 He's never been further than the nearest town in all his born days.
6 We got to the hospital in the nick of time.

59.2 1 a lingering scent
2 a transient (feeling of) joy
3 persistent criticism
4 an incipient headache
5 a lengthy process / a protracted process
6 the inexorable ageing process
7 a fleeting grin
8 a protracted investigation / a lengthy investigation

59.3 1 d 2 c 3 g 4 h 5 f 6 a 7 e 8 b

59.4 1 We'll be ready to leave **in less than no time.**
2 Most of the members of the band may be in their sixties, but they're certainly not **over the hill.**
3 You can argue with him **till the cows come home,** but he'll never see sense.
4 Kit promised he'd get here **in a flash** and he kept his word.
5 I've told her **repeatedly** not to phone me at work.
6 The two events happened **simultaneously.** / The two events were **simultaneous.**
7 The hotel staff were very good; they let me cancel the reservation **at short notice.**
8 I didn't want to **prolong** the meeting.
9 He had his moment of fame. Now he's (just) **a has-been.**
10 The press were excluded **for the duration** of the delicate negotiations.

Unit 60

60.1 1 trudged (If you strut, you can't have your shoulders hunched. You are also unlikely to be weary.)
2 tiptoed (If you trudge, you are tired and weary and your steps are heavy, so you might well wake someone who is sleeping lightly. A bedroom is also a very small place for someone to trudge across.)
3 hopping (Rabbits move quickly with feet all off the ground at the same time, so, as with birds, their movement is described as hopping. Stamping is too heavy a movement for a small animal.)
4 limped (Stamping is something which you usually do when you are angry and there is no obvious connection between having an accident and stamping.)
5 staggered / lurched (Striding cannot be unsteady.)
6 trample (Daisies are too small to be stumbled on.)
7 chased (Tramped suggests moving slowly and so the dog would then be unlikely to catch the postman. Tramped also suggests too heavy a movement to be appropriate for a small dog as opposed to a big, heavy dog.)
8 lurching / staggering (It would be extremely difficult to tiptoe if the sea is rough and the ship is moving violently.)

60.2 *Possible answers:*
1 It was not at all successful or enjoyable – the verb limped makes that clear.
2 No, it was clearly in difficulties for a few years before it failed totally.
3 People didn't expect her to do as well as she did.
4 No, the government gives the impression of being out of control.
5 She is probably calm, easy-going and relaxed.
6 They destroy or spoil them, for example, by laughing at them.
7 He or she might send them emails or letters reminding them to pay, or they might phone them.
8 Not at all confident. They were hesitant and uneven in quality.

60.3 flowed: moved smoothly, without ceasing

spilled: fell out, in an uncontrolled fashion, starting suddenly and moving in all directions

streamed: a lot of people moving at a fairly constant pace from one direction

pouring: coming all the time, in large numbers, possibly from all directions

trickle: a few people, here and there

meandered: not going in a straight line, no definite purpose

flooding: coming in large numbers, spreading in all directions

60.4 1 flow
2 spilling
3 meander
4 trickle
5 pouring / streaming (flooding is less likely to be used about people moving into a relatively restricted area like a football stadium)

60.5

verb	type of movement	reason for type of movement
file	lots of people moving in a straight line, one after the other	to control large numbers of people
saunter	relaxed, confident	pleasure
sidle	approaching someone in a slightly sneaky way	intending to do something dishonest or unpleasant in some way
glide	smooth, as if not moving one's feet	to make effortless movement or to make movement seem effortless
mill around/ about	lots of people all moving in different directions	to meet or to talk to different people

60.6 1 Graceful dancers glide.
2 Guests at a cocktail party mill around / about.
3 Schoolchildren file into a classroom.
4 Someone who is irritatingly anxious to make you like them might sidle up to you.
5 Tourists exploring in a relaxed way might saunter round a city.

Unit 61

61.1 1 done
2 netiquette
3 offhand
4 manners
5 ceremony
6 insolent
7 straitlaced
8 courteous, discourteous

61.2 *Suggested answers:*
1 No, he was probably feeling nervous.
2 She didn't like them.
3 He probably flinched because his arm hurt.
4 It must have been rather surprising or shocking in some way; maybe they were being very rowdy or swearing a lot.
5 Tanya, because a smirk is not a pleasant smile.
6 No, he was probably not pleased. A titter is rather a weak laugh and more from embarrassment than amusement.

7 She probably felt embarrassed or nervous.

8 Badly. Perhaps they leant across the table and grabbed food, didn't say 'thank you' or didn't use the cutlery properly.

61.3
1 snorted	4 tittered
2 twitch	5 flinch
3 squirming	6 beamed

61.4 eyes: raise your eyebrows
mouth: titter, smirk, beam
nose: snort, sniff
no specific part of the body: twitch, squirm, flinch

Unit 62

62.1 *Suggested answers:*
1 noiseless
2 quiet
3 silent
4 soundlessly (we might normally expect some sound from its wings)
5 silent

62.2 *Possible answers:*
2 Suddenly, a shot **rang out**. Somebody was firing at the birds on the lake.
3 The door **creaked**. It was very old, made of oak and difficult to open.
4 The music **was pounding** through the walls. It was as if the musicians were playing in our bedroom.
5 The chicken **sizzled** in the frying pan. The sound and the smell made me even more hungry.
6 The rusty door hinges **are squeaking**. I think they need some oil.
7 She **tooted** her horn. I looked out of the window and saw her car parked outside.
8 I could hear the waves **crashing**. It was wonderful to be so near the sea.
9 We heard police sirens **wailing**. There must have been an accident, or perhaps a robbery.

62.3
1 deafening
2 eerie
3 piercing
4 grating
5 high-pitched
6 inaudible

62.4
1 It was so quiet you could have **heard a pin drop**.
2 I've had some noisy, hectic days with all those kids, now I'm looking forward to some **peace and quiet**.
3 Turn that music down! I can't **hear myself think!**
4 I don't even notice that Jack is in the flat sometimes. He's **as quiet as a mouse.**

Unit 63

63.1
1 cumbersome / unwieldy
2 ponderous
3 weighty
4 lumbering
5 burdensome
6 cumbersome / unwieldy

63.2
1 lumbering
2 cumbersome
3 weighty
4 ponderous

63.3
1 I weighed **out** a kilo of flour and then added water to it.
2 He's very irritating. When you're trying to have a rational discussion, he always has to weigh **in** with his own selfish point of view.
3 I owe Gina £250; it's been weighing **on** my mind for weeks. I must pay her back.
4 We were weighed **down** with huge suitcases and bags, and the airport was terribly crowded; it was a nightmare.
5 I have to weigh **up** the various options before I decide which job to accept.

63.4 *Suggested answers:*
1 To thin out the customer's hair.
2 thicken, e.g. The fog has thickened.
3 It will probably congeal and be difficult to wash out.
4 It means you must add water. You have to dilute it / water it down before using it.
5 You might sift flour (in a sieve) when you are cooking, so there are no lumps.
6 No, because insults do not worry them.
7 It is likely to be large and difficult to handle
8 The story or argument is so dense, you cannot begin to understand it.
9 It lacks complexity and seriousness.
10 thin out, e.g. The traffic is thinning out.

Unit 64

64.1
1 ginger
2 pitch black
3 chestnut
4 scarlet
5 navy
6 turquoise

64.2
red: ruby, coral, scarlet, crimson
blue: sapphire, navy, turquoise
green: emerald, lime, jade

64.3 1 C 2 A 3 C 4 B 5 B

64.4 1 d 2 g 3 f 4 b 5 h 6 a 7 c 8 e

64.5 *Possible answers:*
There are some great **black and white** films on TV on Sunday afternoons (NOT ~~white and black~~).
He gave me such **a black look** that I stopped talking immediately.
At last I have received the cheque I was waiting for and our account is **in the black** again.
It was only **a white lie** when I told her I loved her new hairdo.
I'd love to go **white-water rafting**, though I know it's quite dangerous.
That shop sells mainly **white goods** – fridges, cookers and the like.
I wouldn't pay any attention to what they're suggesting – it's only **a red herring**.
I hate it when my bank account is **in the red** – they charge so much interest.
Don't talk to him about the present government – it's like **a red rag to a bull**.
Come and sit next to the fire – you look quite **blue with cold**.

We were driving along when, **out of the blue**, another car turned out of a side street and stopped just in front of us.
I'm not very keen on **blue cheese**.
He likes to imply that he's **blue-blooded**, but really most of his ancestors were farm labourers.
You can't park there – there are **double yellow lines**.
If you want to find a plumber, look in the **Yellow Pages**.
Her garden is wonderful – she has **green fingers**.
It's almost impossible to get permission to build houses in the **green belt**.
The government has recently published a **green paper** on the Health Service.

Unit 65

65.1
1 in a hurry
2 speed up
3 dawdling
4 a traffic jam
5 rocket
6 totter
7 career
8 person who races
9 to be creeping up
10 fast

65.2
1 not pleased   4 pleased
2 not pleased   5 not pleased
3 not pleased   6 not pleased

65.3
1 C
2 B
3 D
4 C (accelerate is not normally used for people)
5 B
6 D
7 D
8 B

Unit 66

66.1
1 generated (*produced* is also quite acceptable here, with little difference in meaning, except perhaps that it focuses more on the result, while *generated* focuses more on the process of getting the result)
2 produce (*produce* is the most frequent collocation for *list*, but in more formal, technical contexts, *generate* can also be used)
3 caused (*brought about* is also possible here)
4 sparked off / precipitated (*caused*, *produced* and *provoked* would all also be possible here, but *spark off* and *precipitate* are ideal for things which explode suddenly and violently)
5 resulted (no other possibilities: *result* collocates with *in*)
6 given (*brought* or *provided me with* could also be used with the same meaning here)
7 provoked (*caused*, *produced* and *generated* are also possible, but *provoke* is ideal for negative responses and emotions)
8 precipitate (*cause* or *bring about* are also possible here, but would be less dramatic)

66.2 1 I have good grounds **for** believing that he is lying.
2 My suspicions are based **on** what I saw with my own eyes.
3 The government's decision has serious implications **for** the economy.
4 His fear of flying stems **from** a film he once saw.
5 I'm glad to say that all her hard work has resulted **in** success.
6 The riots will probably bring **about** a change of government.
7 A considerable amount of damage was caused **by** the tornado.
8 The President's visit to the university sparked **off** a number of demonstrations.

66.3 *Suggested answers:*
1 The crash on the motorway has caused all traffic to be severely delayed.
2 Your advice resulted in our getting there on time.
3 The minister's comments about tax law have generated a lot of interest.
4 Her many problems stem from her previous poor decisions.
5 The bad weather brought about many flight cancellations.

66.4 *Possible answers:*
2 The higher taxes **have sparked off** riots in three cities.
3 Icy roads **have caused** a number of serious accidents this week.
4 My old car **has caused me / given me** endless problems and involved me in a lot of expense.
5 This software **can generate** stunning images and graphics.
6 Jealousy **caused** the breakup of his marriage.

Unit 67

67.1 Distinct is followed by **from**. All the others are followed by **to**.
1 dissimilar to
2 tantamount to
3 corresponds to
4 akin to
5 distinct from

67.2 1 between, and
2 with
3 from
4 with
5 to
6 with

67.3 1 distinct
2 dissimilar
3 discrete
4 divergent
5 disparate
6 diverse
7 comparable
8 diverged
9 comparative
10 diversified

Unit 68

68.1
1 dilemma
2 glitches
3 chore
4 ordeal
5 snag
6 impediment
7 pitfalls
8 stumbling block

68.2
1 obstructive
2 traumatic
3 abstruse
4 wayward
5 insufferable
6 convoluted / abstruse
7 gruelling / arduous / tough
8 tough

68.3
1 into
2 guts
3 death
4 hassle
5 drag / pain
6 fix / spot / hole
7 with
8 sticky / tricky
9 problematic
10 difficulty
11 downside
12 torture
13 hook
14 woods

Unit 69

69.1 1 g 2 e 3 a 4 f 5 h 6 b 7 d 8 c

69.2
2 It is **obligatory** to put on a life jacket.
3 The **odds are** (that) Karl will take over his father's job.
4 You **have no option but to** do what the police officer says.
5 They're **bound to** settle down eventually.
6 **The chances are** we'll meet someone we know at the party.
7 **It was apparent** that there was going to be trouble.
8 You **might well / may well** end up with no job at all if you don't try.
9 **This is unquestionably** the most serious problem we've encountered.
10 With all this snow, the train will be late, **for sure / I'm sure**.
11 I was in the park today, and **who should I see** but Marilyn.
12 She is really **eager** to get into university next year.

69.3 *Possible answers:*
1 It is **essential** to arrive at school on time every day.
2 Attendance at all lessons is **compulsory**.
3 Wearing uniform is **optional**.

69.4 1 determination
2 yearning
3 resolutions
4 desirous
5 eagerness
6 longing
7 ambitious
8 aspirations

69.5 1 It was a hard day. I was just **longing** to get home and go to bed early.
2 c – he's almost certain to work in the oil industry
3 synonyms: resolved – determined, eager – keen, desire – wish, likelihood – probability
odd one out: obligation

Unit 70

70.1 1 fourfold
2 expenditure
3 factor
4 drastic
5 revise
6 correlation
7 GDP / Gross Domestic Product
8 quadrupled

70.2 *Suggested answers:*
1 **There seems to be a discrepancy between** the two reports of the accident.
2 Oil prices **seesawed** last year.
3 Monthly average temperatures **have deviated from the norm** this year.
4 The water levels didn't **fluctuate** as much as we'd expected last year.
5 I don't need to know all the individual figures – just give me the **aggregate**.
6 His moods **are erratic** – one minute he's happy, the next he's depressed.

70.3 1 b
2 a
3 a
4 at least $1,000
5 55
6 the weather forecast, competing companies' advertising campaigns
7 girls
8 b

70.4

verb	noun	adjective
deviate	deviation	deviant
	discrepancy	discrepant
flaw	flaw	flawed
	inconsistency	inconsistent
err	error	erratic
multiply	multiplication	multiple

Unit 71

71.1
1 vetoed
2 condone / countenance
3 acquiesced
4 outlaw / ban
5 authorised / endorsed
6 barred / banned
7 accede
8 clamp down

71.2
1 Alex parked his car outside the shop regardless of the No Parking sign.
2 The Minister said he would never accede to the union's demands.
3 It's time the police clamped down on cyclists going through red lights.
4 The President has assented to the latest world environment plan.
5 The Minister is likely to acquiesce in / to the proposal.
6 The college principal has given the green light to the students' proposal for an end-of-term festival.
7 The company been given the go-ahead for a new factory in the city.
8 The inspector had carte blanche to investigate every aspect of the business.

71.3
1 c An **embargo** means an official prohibition on something. If the prohibition is cancelled, the embargo is **lifted**.
2 a A **franchise** is permission to operate some sort of service or commercial activity, usually for a set period of time.
3 d **Zero-tolerance** means that not even the smallest crime or misbehaviour will be allowed.
4 b **Sanctions** are restrictions on some activity.

Unit 72

72.1 *Possible answers:*
1 Informal
A more formal version: I take great exception to your rudeness!
2 Formal
A more informal version: You've got to do something about your unfair rules.
3 Informal
A more formal version: The state of your desk is most unsatisfactory!
4 Formal
A more informal version: I've just about had enough of the awful station facilities!
5 Informal
A more formal version: I really must object to your coming here not wearing a tie.
6 Formal
A more informal version: I'm fed up with this behaviour!
7 Formal
A more informal version: The lack of toilet facilities for disabled people is disgusting / pretty awful.
8 Formal
A more informal version: The delay with my order is just/simply not on.

72.2
1 about
2 take / took
3 being
4 with
5 done
6 wouldn't
7 do
8 well
9 with
10 enough

72.3 *Possible answers:*
1 Honestly! I'm fed up with / sick of their noisy parties week after week!
2 I wish you/we could do something about that big tree that blocks out the sun. (we is more indirect)
3 Most people take considerable exception to being awoken by loud noise from the factory when they are trying to sleep.
4 I'm not at all satisfied about the changes to our working hours.
5 I've just about had enough of working longer hours.
6 I wish to complain about the lack of safety procedures on the company's premises.

72.4 *Possible answers:*
1 We must open the window / clean the room / spray some air-freshener.
2 Jorge's work is very careless.
3 Simone is often late for work.
4 You're not suited to this job.
5 This room really needs decorating.
6 The TV must be turned down.

Unit 73

73.1
1 perfect
2 lame / flimsy / weak
3 flimsy
4 cast-iron / perfect
5 sincere / heartfelt

73.2
1 flimsy
2 cast-iron
3 lame
4 heartfelt
5 detailed
6 good

73.3
1 Matt **apologised to Gina for** breaking her vase.
2 The criminal did not **show any (sign of) repentance for** the inhumane way in which he had acted.
3 The trial **ended in acquittal.**
4 Sam **did not explain why** he had behaved so strangely.

73.4
1 The President granted him a **reprieve** just an hour before he was due to be executed.
2 He was **acquitted** of murder in 2004, but two years later was convicted of armed robbery in the same courtroom.
3 She showed a complete lack of **remorse / repentance** for her evil deeds and just laughed when the judge sentenced her.
4 The Public Inquiry **exonerated** him from all blame for the accident at the factory.
5 Just before he died, the old man said he **repented of** all the bad things he had done in his life.
6 Ten years after his death, Daniel Kehoe was given a **posthumous** pardon by the government when another man confessed to the crime he had been hanged for.
7 He treated her badly and she says she simply cannot **forgive and forget.**
8 The **ceasefire** is due to start at 9 pm.

73.5 *Suggested answers:*
1 The two armies **declared / announced / agreed a truce / ceasefire** during the religious holiday.
2 Both governments **agreed / assented** to the terms of **the peace treaty** and it was signed on 15 August 1954.
3 The long-standing **accord** between the government and the unions is in danger of **collapsing / collapse.**
4 The generals **signed the armistice** at midday on 25 February 1968.

Unit 74

74.1 1 fish
2 singing
3 paying
4 to
5 take, as
6 shower / heap
7 widely / highly
8 damning

74.2 1 d   2 a   3 e   4 f   5 b   6 c

74.3 *Suggested answers:*
1 He's always **flattering** the boss. (neutral)
He's always **licking the boss's boots.** (informal)
He's always **making up to** the boss. (informal)
He's always **crawling to** the boss. (informal)
2 I wish she wasn't so **slimy.** (informal)
I wish she wasn't **such a crawler.** (informal)
I wish she wasn't so **servile.** (formal)
I wish she wasn't so **obsequious.** (formal)

74.4

verb	noun	adjective
compliment	compliment	complimentary
praise	praise	praiseworthy
laud		laudable, laudatory
flatter	flattery, flatterer	flattering
crawl	crawler	crawling
smarm		smarmy

74.5 1 complimentary
2 flatterer
3 crawl
4 laudable / praiseworthy (laudable is a little more formal)
5 Flattery
6 laud / praise (laud is a little more formal)

Unit 75

75.1 1 B
2 B (*swore*, possibly because of its close associations with taboo language, sounds much less formal than *vowed*)
3 A
4 B (because *New Year's resolutions* is the standard phrase and such resolutions are perhaps best known for being quickly broken, *vow* sounds much more formal)

75.2 1 promised
2 oath
3 best
4 flutter
5 back
6 life

75.3 *Suggested answers:*
1 **Your best bet** would be to stay overnight in a hotel near the airport.
2 My father **swears by** these herbal teas.
3 John's been rather lazy with his homework, but he has promised to **turn over a new leaf** next year.
4 **I could have sworn** I locked the door when I went out.
5 The writer's new play **promises** to be as good as his last one.
6 **I'd put money on** the Democratic Party winning the next election.
7 Do you ever **have a flutter** on the national lottery?
8 Her mother disliked the film because it contained **so many swear words / so much swearing.**
9 **I/We anticipate** that the documentary will be controversial.
10 I **hedged my bets** by buying shares in both of the companies that had a serious chance of winning the contract.

75.4 *Suggested answers:*
1 Swift is making the point that many people don't take promises seriously. His point is effective because of the comparison of a solemn thing like a promise with such an everyday thing as a piecrust, which is of course intended to be broken; it has to be broken for the pie to be eaten.
2 Most people probably do agree that making someone promise not to do something may often serve to put the idea of doing it actually into their head!

Unit 76

76.1 1 Looking / Thinking   7 out, touch
2 stands / sticks, out   8 nostalgia
3 became   9 came
4 anything of   10 tinted / coloured
5 look / think, back   11 vague
6 reminisce   12 recall

76.2 1 e   2 d   3 f   4 c   5 a   6 b

76.3 *Suggested answers:*
1 **I regret not buying** her a birthday present.
2 They **showed no remorse** for what they had done.
3 I now **rue the fact** that I discontinued my studies.
4 **I lament the fact** that our relationship has broken down.
5 The whole village **mourned the loss** of the beautiful trees.

Unit 77

77.1

verb	preposition
approve	of
conform	to
tally	with
coincide	with
concur	with
compromise	on
be in accord	with

1 conforms
2 tally / coincide
3 accord
4 tally / concur
5 approve
6 concur / concurred
7 compromise

77.2 1 c   2 e   3 a   4 d   5 b

77.3 *Suggested answers:*
1 The President **made a/the concession** that the opposition party should be allowed a place on the committee.
2 I think one should always **exercise/use** as much **discretion** as possible when it is a question of people's private lives.
3 The landowners **reached a settlement in** their dispute with the authorities over the proposed factory site.
4 The negotiating team were able to **reach a compromise** and put an end to the labour dispute.
5 The decision to close the railway line has **caused a lot of controversy.**
6 There is **some dissent** among the Board members.
7 The forthcoming leadership election has **caused division(s) in/within** the Green Party.
8 Javier's decision **met with his parents' approval.**

Unit 78

78.1 1 overlap, complement(s)
2 deduce
3 advocates
4 inferred

78.2 1 authoritative
2 empirical
3 ambiguous
4 coherent
5 comprehensive

78.3 1 b
2 49, 64 (they are square numbers: 7 squared and 8 squared)
3 Ulla's mark was either much higher or lower than 68%.
4 c
5 No, they select their subjects in a random fashion.

78.4 1 The information **resides** in archives that must not be opened until 2050.
2 He **conceived** his theory while still a young man.
3 Each of the symbols in the phonetic alphabet **denotes** a sound.
4 This study **contradicted** what was previously held to be true and so **triggered** a great deal of discussion amongst specialists in the field.
5 Details of the experiment have been **appended to** the report.
6 Jelowski's book **reflects upon** the rise and fall of great Empires over two millennia. She **perceives** the Roman Empire as an **instance** of a pattern that has repeated itself in other times and other parts of the world.

78.5 The present study was initially **conceived** in order to validate a new method of enquiry **whereby** genetic information could be **utilised** to predict disease. The study **contradicts** the findings of Hill (2009); indeed it would appear to **demonstrate/indicate** the **converse** of what he claimed. It presents a **somewhat** different view of the genetic factors which **trigger** disease. **Notwithstanding**, the study does not **negate** Hill's, as his studies served the **crucial** purpose of devising symbols to **denote** certain tendencies, **thereby** facilitating further research.

Unit 79

79.1 1 The response from the public **underscores** the importance of having a full investigation of the facts.
2 This view of the world was originally **expounded** by the Ancient Greek philosophers.
3 It is not easy to **account for** the fall in population of these birds.
4 Economists have **posited** a link between exchange rates and a general lack of confidence in the European Union.
5 I should like to **reiterate** here that the issue is not one that can be easily resolved.
6 The recent events **epitomise** the dilemma faced by politicians the world over.
7 In a 2005 article, Charles Plestow **asserted** that the whole European Medieval era had been misinterpreted.
8 The lecturer **summarised** the main arguments of her talk at the end.

79.2 *Suggested answers:*
1 70% of the landmass is **comprised of** mountain ranges. / Mountain ranges **comprise** 70% of the landmass.
2 The book **embraces** a wide variety of subjects. (*embrace* is usually used in the active voice)
3 I think these three sections can all **be subsumed** under one heading.
4 The poems in this book have been **categorised** by topic.
5 The course **consists of** five modules, from which students must choose three.

79.3 1 return
2 brings
3 touches
4 address
5 beyond the scope of
6 ascending
7 forced to conclude
8 deal with

Unit 80

80.1 1 jot down   6 italics
2 scribble   7 quotes
3 doodling   8 characters
4 writing up   9 run off
5 draft   10 asterisk

80.2 1 bold
2 upper case
3 italics
4 new font size
5 new typeface
6 lower case
7 block capitals
8 curly brackets
9 square brackets
10 diamond brackets

80.3 1 c 2 i 3 f 4 h 5 j 6 a 7 e 8 g 9 b 10 d

80.4 1 chatty
2 format
3 manuscripts
4 paste
5 touch type
6 draft
7 indent
8 subtitle

Unit 81

81.1 1 make such a big thing = make such a fuss
2 has got a thing about = is obsessed with
3 The thing is = the problem is
4 things = the situation; get away for a holiday = go on holiday
5 things = subjects, items; get through = deal with
6 get on with = have a good relationship with; For one thing = firstly; like different things = have different tastes; For another (thing) = in addition, secondly
7 get = understand; I didn't get a thing = I didn't understand anything
8 get everything sorted out = solve all our problems; got it together = organised things

81.2 1 sieve 2 Daniel Craig 3 protractor 4 hammer 5 colander 6 rolling pin

81.3 *Possible answers:*
2 Look, isn't that **whatsisface**? The actor who was in the latest *James Bond*?
3 I can't find the **thingumijig** for measuring angles.
4 Have you got a **whatchamacallit**, you know, for bashing in nails?
5 Where's the **thingummy** for draining potatoes?
6 I need a **whatsit** – you know, one of those things for flattening pastry.

81.4 *Possible answers:*
1 The garden had **masses of / a mass of / loads of / a load of / dozens of** pink and yellow flowers.
2 I've asked her out **umpteen / loads of / masses of** times, but she's always got some excuse.
3 He hasn't done **a scrap of** useful work here since he first got the job.
4 I've got **loads of / masses of / dozens of** papers I want to get rid of.
5 Alice invited **masses of / dozens of / tons of** people to her party at the weekend.
6 Yasmin's got **bags of / loads of / tons of** energy – I don't know where she gets it all from!
7 **Loads of / Dozens of / Masses of** people were turned away because the lecture room was full.
8 She was told **dozens of / masses of / umpteen** times not to leave any valuables on her desk.

81.5 1 company
2 included
3 gather
4 Incidentally
5 offence
6 mind
7 possible

Unit 82

82.1 *Suggested answers:*
1 The company will invest **in excess of** £10.3 million in new technology over the next five years.
2 It will cost you **in the region of / around / about** £7,000 to have the whole house redecorated.
3 Informal: It could take **seven hours, give or take an hour / or so,** to drive to Aberdeen, depending on the traffic.
Formal: It could take **approximately seven hours** to drive to Aberdeen, depending on the traffic.
4 **Quite a few** students failed the exam. I was rather surprised and disappointed.

82.2 1 Her hair's a sort of reddish colour, and I'd say she's, well, forty, forty-fourish.
Sort of is used here with an adjective, but it can be used with almost any type of word. The *-ish* suffix is used here with a descriptive adjective and a number denoting age, but it is also often used with clock times, e.g. We arrived around half-past sevenish. *Well* is often used to make things less direct.
2 The garden was a bit on the big side, but it was very pretty.
The expression *a bit on the ... side* is used with adjectives to denote a quality that is not what we want or hope for, e.g. The living room was a bit on the dark side, but we bought some new lamps and then it was OK.
3 There was a kind of elasticky thing that held the two parts together, and I've lost it.
Kind of and *sort of* can both be used with adjectives and with almost any other word class. Putting the -y suffix on a noun or adjective to make it indirect or less precise occurs in informal conversation, e.g. It was a browny colour with a kind of acidy taste.
4 They're good shoes. They're comfortable on long walks and that.
And that just means 'and similar things'. It is very informal. Here it is used with a noun, but people often use it with verbs too, e.g. They were singing and that at the party last night.
5 I've been to the doctor's and had treatments and suchlike and I'm sure it helps in one way or another.
And suchlike normally follows a plural noun, but it could also be used with an uncountable one, e.g. It'll be useful for your work and suchlike.

82.3 1 lashings / oodles / stacks (could also be dollops)
2 dash / smidgen
3 stacks / lashings
4 smattering
5 dollop

82.4 *Possible answers:*
1 worrying / strange / odd
2 nuisance / pain / problem
3 embarrassing
4 sandwich / snack
5 relax / watch TV / have a sleep

6 souvenirs / pots / jewellery / pictures

7 sightseeing

8 finished / done everything / completed the job

Expressions to underline:

1 a bit

2 (it's) a bit of a

3 a bit

4 or something

5 or whatever

6 a sort of, and things like that

7 and that

8 more or less

Unit 83

83.1
1 to bicker

2 without a murmur

3 to lisp / to speak with a lisp / to have a lisp

4 shout, yell, scream (also roar, shriek)

5 roar is a deeper sound, like a lion; shriek is a very high-pitched sound

6 to gossip / to slag (someone) off

7 to wind (someone) up

8 exaggeration

83.2
1 stuttered / stammered

2 tongue-tied

3 mumbling / muttering

4 yell / shout

5 murmured

6 gossip

7 slurring

8 lisp

9 generalise

83.3
1 whining

2 up

3 butter

4 nagging

83.4

Unit 84

84.1 1 AD / CE 3 NB
2 i.e. 4 e.g.

84.2 1 /ˈneɪt əʊ/ North Atlantic Treaty Organisation
2 F – A – Q frequently asked questions
3 /ˈsaɪfaɪ/ science fiction, /ˈbaɪəʊpɪk/ biographical picture (a film about the life of a real person)
4 /pɪn/ personal identification number
5 U – F – Os unidentified flying objects
6 A – S – A – P as soon as possible
7 /ˈwaɪfaɪ/ wireless connection for computers or smartphones (wireless fidelity)
8 V – A – T / /væt/ value added tax
9 B – C – E before the Common Era , B – C before Christ
10 aids acquired immune deficiency syndrome
11 V – I – P very important person
12 U – S – B universal serial bus

84.3 1 a short account of your life and achievements
2 a bedsit
3 proof of identity, e.g. a passport or driving licence
4 laugh
5 you should reply
6 your level of intelligence according to the Intelligence Quotient system
7 turn the page
8 information on the state of the traffic in a particular area that is continuously updated as the situation changes

84.4 1 Smedley and Jones **edited** the book or article (they oversaw the contents and structure of the book but did not write it).
2 This means see the figure (picture or illustration) which is marked as number 7.
3 Et al. normally refers to three or more co-authors. If there are just two, both names are normally given.
4 This means all the information from page 33 to (and including) page 37.
5 This means **compare** a work already being discussed or referred to with Oswald's 1987 work.

Unit 85

85.1 1 redevelop
2 inappropriate
3 outnumber / outnumbered
4 misuse
5 reconsider
6 imperfect
7 misbehave
8 inability
9 incapable
10 inaccuracy

85.2 *Suggested answers:*
1 a 2 b 3 c 4 b 5 a 6 c 7 a 8 b

85.3 *Suggested answers:*
2 The hotel **upgraded** me to a luxury room instead of the ordinary one I'd booked.
3 Would you like to stay there **overnight** or come back the same day?

4 The **underlying** problem is a very serious one.
5 For me, the advantages of air travel **outweigh** the disadvantages.
6 I think this hotel is **overpriced.**
7 It's slippery **underfoot** just here. Be careful.
8 The company experienced an **upturn** in popularity after it changed its name.
9 I felt that what she said **undermined** my position and weakened it somewhat.
10 It would be a mistake to **underestimate** how intelligent Frances is / to **underestimate** Frances's intelligence.

85.4
1 procrastinate
2 contaminate
3 eject
4 proliferate
5 commiserate
6 congeal
7 procreate
8 converse
9 emit
10 promote

Unit 86

86.1

-conscious	money-conscious employers
-free	car-free city centre
-rich	energy-rich drink
-led	French-led fashion
-minded	sport(s)-minded friends
-proof	bullet-proof car
-related	drug(s)-related crime
-ridden	poverty-ridden society
-worthy	trustworthy person

86.2 Here are the most likely adjective + noun combinations. You may find others that also work.
1 additive-free drinks, foods
2 avoidable mistake, delay, problems
3 disposable knives and forks, income, glove
4 guilt-ridden expression, speech, personality
5 high-minded speech, principles
6 newsworthy story, speech, mistake
7 oil-rich country, economy
8 ovenproof glove, dish
9 soundproof room, booth
10 stress-related illness, problems

86.3 *Suggested answers:*
child-led, child-minded, childproof, child-related
dust-free, dustproof, dust-related
calorie-conscious, calorie-rich, calorie-related
workable, work-conscious, work-free, work-rich, work-led, work-minded, work-related

86.4
2 Poisonous mushrooms are easily **identifiable.**
3 He is so **career-minded** that he has no time for his family.
4 The new speed cameras are supposed to be **vandal-proof.**
5 During the Civil War, the country was **terror-ridden.**
6 The soil on that farm is **nutrient-rich.**
7 The bank decided that he was not **creditworthy.**

86.5
1 meat-free
2 class-related
3 vitamin-rich
4 dry-cleanable
5 clothes-conscious
6 government-led

86.6
1 verb
2 adjective
3 adverb
4 adjective
5 verb
6 adjective
7 adverb and adjective
8 verb

Unit 87

87.1
2 a long speech by one person (e.g. in a film or play)
3 sound carried from a distance
4 something written by yourself about your own life
5 study of sound
6 to go back to an earlier, worse state
7 study of writing
8 to make something unstable
9 something written to represent yourself

87.2 *Possible answers:*
1 monotonous, mono-culture
2 technocrat, technology
3 retrograde, retroactive
4 telescope, telecommunications
5 automatic, automobile
6 pre-war, pre-flight
7 postnatal, postpone
8 biological, biodiversity

87.3 *Suggested answers:*
2 She asked the singer for his **autograph** on the back of her table napkin.
3 She took a degree in **criminology** at Stockholm University.
4 The novel is largely **autobiographical**.
5 It's **a retrospective** exhibition of the painter's life and work.
6 He believes in **auto-suggestion** to cure yourself.
7 **Teleworking** is now quite common.
8 Some English philosophers in the 19th century believed in **de-industrialisation**.
9 **Cybercrime** is a huge cause for concern.

87.4 *Suggested answers:*
2 The firm makes job applicants do a test that analyses their handwriting for what it reveals about their personality.
3 The school always takes very seriously any case of bullying carried out over the internet or by phone.
4 Matt has a fear of anything technical.
5 He's giving a paper at a special event taking place just before a conference in Spain.
6 She did a course in information science.

87.5 1 information + commercial, i.e. a television advert that gives information instead of selling something (e.g. explaining new social welfare regulations)
2 iPod + broadcast, i.e. radio programmes that you can download after they are broadcast and listen to on a personal audio player such as an iPod or smartphone.
3 camera + recorder, usually a small, portable video camera
4 vegetable + hamburger, i.e. a vegetarian hamburger
5 swimming + marathon, i.e. an event in which people attempt to swim a very long distance (probably done in order to raise money for charity)
6 free + software, i.e. software you can download without charge from the internet

Unit 88

88.1 1 lexicon
2 Anglo-Saxon
3 classical
4 borrowing
5 source
6 consequence
7 impact
8 enrich

88.2 1 hammock
2 turban
3 tabby
4 cot

88.3 1 karaoke
2 mumps
3 amber
4 tonic
5 roster
6 gimmick

88.4 *Here are some possible answers for speakers of Spanish:*
• food and drink – paella, tapas, rioja
• animals, flowers and landscape features – mosquito, cork, banana
• industrial products and inventions – fumidor, lasso
• clothing and the home – sombrero, mantilla, hammock
• politics and society – junta, guerilla, embargo, mañana, macho
• the arts, sports and leisure activities – flamenco, guitar, toreador

88.5 If possible, compare your answers with those of other speakers of your language.

88.6 Notice that these words may not all have originated in English. *Pudding* originates from an old French word, for instance, but it seems to have moved into some other languages from English rather than going directly from French.

Unit 89

89.1 1 interfere
2 Safety
3 topics
4 shade
5 theme
6 intervened

7 security
8 continually
9 shadows
10 continuously

89.2
1 outrun
2 held up
3 upset
4 upheld
5 do out
6 ended up
7 run out
8 upended

89.3
1 outbreak, e.g. There has been an **outbreak** of violence.
2 upset, e.g. I had a stomach **upset** and couldn't go to work.
3 outlook, e.g. The **outlook** for small businesses is bleak because of the economic crisis.
4 setup, e.g. After the merger, the **setup** of the company was radically changed.
5 a lookout, e.g. Thieves or robbers often have one person as a **lookout**, watching for police, etc.
6 a breakout, e.g. There were three **breakouts** from this prison last year.

Unit 90

90.1
1 intend: I didn't **mean** to hurt you.
2 exactly: She finished the exercise in five minutes **flat**.
3 proper, just: It's only **fair** that we should share the housework.
4 city with the seat of government: Wellington is the **capital** of New Zealand.
5 light in colour: I've got **fair** hair and burn easily in the sun.
6 unkind: You shouldn't be so **mean** to your little sister.
7 fixed: To join the Fitness Club you pay a **flat** fee of £500.
8 neither very good nor very bad: His marks in his final exams ranged from excellent to **fair**.
9 money: You need plenty of **capital** to open a restaurant.
10 unwilling to spend money: He's far too **mean** to buy her flowers.

90.2
It's only *fair*: adjective (right)
The Frankfurt Book *Fair*: noun (large show)
the weather to stay *fair*: adjective (pleasant)
I've got *fair* skin: adjective (light)
ranged from excellent to *fair*: adjective (satisfactory)
the burning third-floor *flat*: noun (apartment)
terribly *flat* and boring: adjective (level)
a *flat* fee of £500: adjective (fixed)
B *flat* minor: noun (♭ = a note that is a semitone lower than B itself)
in five minutes *flat*: adverb (only; emphasises how quick a time is)
in *capital* letters: adjective (upper case)
the *capital* of New Zealand: noun (city where the country's government sits)
capital to open a restaurant: noun (money)
Capital punishment: adjective (punishable by death)
'coagulate' *mean*: verb (convey a meaning, express an idea)
mean to hurt you: verb (intend)
too *mean* to buy her flowers: adjective (opposite of generous)
be so *mean*: adjective (unkind)

90.3
1 match
2 bill
3 set
4 post
5 mark
6 run

90.4
a an instrument a dentist uses to make holes in your teeth
b training for marching
c a powerful tool used for making holes in a road
d an exercise practising grammar in a fairly mechanical way

90.5
1 a the list on which students are marked present or absent every day
  b to send a letter or parcel in a special way so it has protection against being lost
2 a how much performers might appeal to the public
  b money earned on an investment or paid for a loan
3 a to cut up into small cubes (usually vegetables)
  b a cube with a number from one to six on each side
4 a throwing the ball into the air and hitting it at the start of a turn
  b the attention given to customers by staff
5 a specific problem being dealt with by lawyers
  b a piece of luggage
6 a the long stick that players use in snooker or billiards
  b the words or actions that tell an actor that it is his or her turn to speak

90.6
1 Then it hit me! This means 'then I suddenly understood and then the ball suddenly struck my body.'
2 This is based on the traditional saying that babies are delivered to a home by a big bird called a stork. A crane is another kind of large bird rather like a stork. But a crane can also be a piece of heavy machinery used to lift heavy objects.
3 In the first sentence, *flies* is a verb and *like* is a preposition – the sentence is comparing the flight of time with that of an arrow. In the second sentence, *flies* is a noun and *like* is a verb and the sentence says that fruit flies [very small insects] enjoy bananas.
4 As well as being a preposition, *down* is the word for very soft feathers used to stuff, for example, pillows or winter jackets. If prices are *up*, they have risen and if they are *down* they have fallen.

Unit 91

91.1
1 real
2 real
3 real / genuine
4 genuine
5 genuine

91.2 1 C   2 D   3 A   4 B   5 C

91.3
1 brisk, sharpen
2 toll
3 leisurely
4 perfectly
5 bequeathed
6 rightly
7 visit
8 spoilt

91.4
1 a powerful car
2 strong tea
3 auburn hair
4 a doleful expression
5 a lengthy meeting

Unit 92

92.1
1 eye
2 hands
3 heart
4 jungle
5 thumb
6 ball
7 mouth
8 head
9 rein
10 light

92.2
1 holding the reins = in charge; idiom taken from horse riding
2 moving the goalposts = changing the rules; idiom from football
3 a half-baked idea = an idea that is not fully thought through or developed; idiom from cookery
4 to tighten our belts = to reduce our spending; idiom from dressing
5 to take (something) on board = to understand and accept; idiom from loading a ship
6 on track = likely to complete a planned course of action; idiom from travel (e.g. along railway tracks)
7 around the clock = day and night; idiom based on the movement of the hands of a clock
8 take something/someone at face value = to accept something/someone as how they appear at first, without thinking they could be something else; idiom based on the image of a coin or stamp where the value is stated on its 'face'

92.3
1 This book throws a great deal of fresh light on the history of the period. = This books tells us a great deal that is new about the history ...; from the concept of intelligence as light
2 We could save half an hour at least if we went through the wood. = We could gain half an hour ...; from the concept of time as money
3 Try to keep cool even if he argues with you. = Try to keep calm ...; from the concept of intense feeling as temperature
4 We spent months trying to achieve our sales targets. = (two metaphors) We devoted a long time to trying hard to sell as many of our products as we were aiming for; from the concepts of time as money and business as a military operation
5 Police tried to control the flow of the fans as they left the concert. = Police tried to control the movement of the fans ...; from the concept of movement of people as water

92.4
1 All the world's a stage and all the men and women merely players.
The line suggests that life is like a theatre and that possibly the roles are written in advance, with people being like actors in that they all have different parts to play. (from *As You Like It*)
2 We are such stuff as dreams are made on; and our little life is rounded with a sleep.
The line suggests that people's lives have as little substance as a dream. Death is likened to sleep at the end of the short day that is all that life is. (from *The Tempest*)
3 There is a tide in the affairs of men, which, taken at the flood, leads on to fortune.
The line suggests that our lives have tides like the sea and we must take advantage of lucky opportunities, metaphorical flood tides, in order to be transported to good times. (from *Julius Caesar*)

Unit 93

93.1
1 The system is now **up and running** so we should be able to get some useful data soon.
2 Things are **looking up** now that we've increased our online sales.
3 The whole project **worked like a dream**.
4 After a problematic start, things are **falling into place** now.
5 The school open day **went / ran like clockwork**.

93.2
1 dream
2 pain
3 need / needed
4 nightmare
5 hear

93.3
1 Ricardo
2 Michelle
3 Sabina
4 Alex
5 Monica

93.4
1 Jessica's on cloud **nine** now she's at university.
2 She's **in** her element now she's got a job in an architect's office.
3 You look a bit down in the **dumps / mouth**. What's the matter?
4 Just look at him! He looks fed up to the **back** teeth!
5 I was **over** the moon when they told me I'd got the job.

93.5
1 B (the last straw means a final, very damaging event in a series of bad events)
2 C (I can't understand it because it is too complex/complicated)
3 D (you look very unhappy indeed)
4 A (it worked perfectly, as if by magic)
5 D (I was feeling very happy/elated)

Unit 94

94.1
1 Meena can **come across/over** as a little arrogant, but she's just shy.
2 Charlie was quick to take advantage of a chance for promotion that **came up** at his workplace.
3 The project was going well until we **came up against** some legal problems.
4 I **came across** some lovely old photos when I was sorting some boxes yesterday.
5 I'm afraid it looks as if our plans to move to a new flat may not **come off**.
6 Something strange **came over** me and I shouted at him angrily.

94.2
1 going
2 dwell
3 press
4 stay
5 caught
6 urge

94.3
1 Do you think the company will have to lay any staff **off**?
2 I learnt Spanish at school but need to brush it **up** before I go to Spain.
3 Correct
4 If you rush **into** a decision, you may regret it later.
5 We'll have to call **off** tomorrow's picnic if the weather is bad.
6 The family soon settled **in** to their new flat in the city.
7 I love the way Suzie always throws herself **into** everything she does.
8 Correct

94.4 These verbs can have the particle before or after the object:
to brush up a skill – brush a skill up
to put together a report – put a report together
to lay off staff – lay staff off
to call off a meeting – call a meeting off
to put a plan forward – put forward a plan

94.5 1 abolish
2 start to work
3 waste time
4 occur
5 delay
6 criticise
7 explode
8 not tell

Unit 95

95.1 1 No, you wouldn't.
2 a peacemaker
3 a factory chimney
4 Yes, it's a compliment.
5 No, you wouldn't.
6 Yes, as it's a symbol of good luck.
7 faithfulness
8 No, you wouldn't. Although super suggests something extra good, shark has a negative meaning in a business context.

95.2 1 c
2 d (also associated with growth, fertility)
3 f (also associated with cheerfulness)
4 e (also associated with fierceness)
5 a (also associated with birth)
6 b (also associated with death, nothingness)
Note that these are not the only associations which these colours have. Blue, green and red, for instance, can also be used to refer to different political parties.

95.3 1 No. If you say someone has a dog's life, you think they have a difficult life.
2 No. If you call a businessman a snake, you don't trust him.
3 No. If you say someone's hair is mousy, you mean it is light brown and not especially striking or attractive.
4 Correct.
5 No. If you say someone can be catty, you mean they tend to say unkind things about people.
6 Correct.
7 No. If you call someone a sheep, you mean they just follow others and are not independent at all.
8 No. If you say that someone is hawk-eyed, you mean that they have very sharp eyes.

95.4 *Possible answers:* (but you may have some better ones!)
<u>Colours</u>
Purple is often the colour of royal robes (and was the colour of the most important Romans' togas, because it was made from an expensive dye).
Green is the colour of new growth and this may suggest inexperience.
Yellow might be seen as the colour white people's skin goes when they are afraid.
Red is the colour of fire, so may suggest danger.
White is the absence of colour, which suggests purity, a blank sheet.
Black is dark, and seems to suggest things that are hidden and frightening, hence evil.
<u>Animals</u>
'A dog's life' may come from the idea that a dog is totally under the thumb of its master.
A snake is a creature that many people are afraid of. They know that snakes can be dangerous.
A mouse is usually light brown or grey in colour and it is not generally a popular animal, so it is not surprising that 'mousy' has negative and dull associations as a hair colour.
Rats generally have very unpleasant associations for most English speakers, so it is not surprising that rattiness is a negative quality.
Cats have sharp claws which can scratch and hurt people.
Fish can have a rather unpleasant smell, one that can hang around for a long time, so this may suggest something suspicious, i.e. what is causing that unpleasant smell?
Sheep tend to follow one another rather than all acting in an independent way.
As a bird of prey, the hawk needs very sharp eyes.

95.5　1 bad luck
2 good luck
3 bad luck
4 good luck

Unit 96

96.1　1 She works in a shop that sells women's **clothing**. (Ladies' **garments** might be an even more formal equivalent.)
2 I've got some new **specs**. Do you like them?
3 Did you see that documentary about Wales **on the telly / on the box** last night?
4 Gerry's a decent **bloke / guy**. I wouldn't want to upset him.
5 I spent the morning **conversing** with the Director.
6 Molly was there with her **husband / partner**. He's a nice **man**.

96.2

neutral	formal	informal
children	offspring	kids
sunglasses		shades
policeman/woman	police officer	cop (*bobby* can also be used, but it is becoming increasingly rare nowadays)
umbrella		brolly
	invaluable	really useful
make sure	ensure (or guarantee)	
try	endeavour	
use	employ	

96.3 In a database from the Cambridge International Corpus totalling ten million words of everyday spoken and written English texts, the words in the list occurred approximately in the ratios given in the second column (for example, *frequently* is 11 times more frequent in written English than in spoken).

word	ratio spoken : written
1 frequently W	1 : 11
2 start S	2 : 1
3 begin W	1 : 5
4 maybe S	5 : 1
5 moreover W	1 : 60

96.4
1 pharmacist / chemist
2 girl (or young unmarried woman)
3 poetry / poem
4 to where / where to

96.5
1 This computer text could be called written, modern, technical. Terms such as *shared folder* and *server* are technical. The style is typically written, especially with the use of passive voice verbs and the word *located*; in non-technical spoken language, we would probably just say 'one that is on a server'.
2 This is typical modern, written academic text; *above* indicates it is written. Typical academic words are *paradigm* (which means a dominant set of beliefs or methods in an academic field) and the initials *SLA* (which mean Second Language Acquisition).
3 This is rather archaic poetry (by the English poet John Donne, 1572–1631). *Thee* is an archaic form of singular *you*; *'tis* is an archaic form of *it is*; *in jest* is rather formal and/ or literary and means 'as a joke / not serious'. Other rather formal or literary words are *weariness* and *feigned* (pretended).
4 This is formal spoken language. It is from a speech by US President John F. Kennedy (1917–1963). Key items are the formal *ask not* instead of 'don't ask', *my fellow*, and *the freedom of man* instead of human freedom or freedom for everyone. Formal speeches and lectures are often very close to formal written texts, and this text could possibly also have been a written text (e.g. a political pamphlet or electioneering literature).
5 This is informal, modern conversation. Key items are *mind you* (rare in written language), *telly* instead of television, *cos* instead of *because*, and *yeah* instead of yes. The text is quite fragmented too (*the Rhine. Yeah, the river in Bonn*). Written registers tend to be more integrated (e.g. *the River Rhine in Bonn*).

Unit 97

97.1
1 American. British version: I lost my way at the big **junction** just south of the city.
2 British. American version: Why are there always so many shopping **carts** left in the **parking lot**?
3 British. American version: Cross the **street** at the **crosswalk**, then **take a left**.
4 American. British version: You can't drive any further; you'll have to **reverse**, the **road** is very narrow.
5 British. American version: You'll see the **gas station** just after the **overpass** on I-34.
6 American. British version: Once you get on to the **motorway**, it will only take you two hours to get there.
7 American. British version: The office is **diagonally opposite** the Chinese restaurant.
8 American. British version: There's a **stream** at the end of the **(foot)path**. It's about three miles from here.

97.2
1 e dumpster US = skip UK
2 d ground US = earth UK
3 a frying pan UK = skillet US
4 c cooker UK = stove US
5 b faucet US = tap UK

97.3
1 A fresher, as they are younger.
2 At more or less the same level.
3 'Professor' is an appropriate form of address for any university teacher in the US. In Britain it is a title given only to those of the highest academic rank.
4 Britain
5 The second year.
6 They mean psychology is their main subject of study
7 No. In Britain it is likely to mean going to an institution for 16+ students to learn some special knowledge or skill (e.g. a teacher-training college). In the USA, it usually means going to university.
8 British

Unit 98

98.1
1 To try to make the language less stereotyped with regard to gender and also perhaps to try to alter sexist attitudes in this way.
2 The expression means words that have male connotations but are referring to people in general.
3 There might have been controversy perhaps because some people felt it was an unnecessary change or that it was impossible to try to impose language change artificially.
4 They want to get rid of 'male' words in traditional idioms like *man in the street* by using such phrases as the *person in the street* or the *average person* instead. They even want to get rid of *man* in words like *manhandle* and *woman* where the male idea has really been lost.
5 It was introduced as a title which does not focus on whether a woman is married or not. It is useful if you do not know what a woman's marital status is or if a woman does not want people to know her marital status.

98.2
1 Three **firefighters** helped put out a fire at a disused warehouse last night.
2 A **spokesperson** for the Department of Education provided us with a statement.
3 **Cleaner** wanted for house in Priory Street.
4 The helpline is continuously **staffed** even during holiday periods.
5 All our **flight attendants** are fluent in at least three languages.
6 The fibres in this garment are **artificial**.
7 **Police officers** today spend more time in cars than on the beat.
8 Brenda's husband is **a nurse**.
9 It took a great many **working** hours to clean up the stadium after the concert.
10 This was a great step for the **human race**.
11 The **average person** has little time for such issues.
12 **Sales assistants** are often well trained and can be very persuasive.

98.3
1 butch
2 sissy
3 tomboy
4 feminine
5 male

98.4 1–5 *Personal answers*
6 The sentence can be altered by either using *his* or *her*: A government minister may have to neglect **his or her** family.
Or by making it plural: **Government ministers** may have to neglect **their families**.
It is also becoming increasingly common and acceptable for *their* to be used as a generic pronoun to refer to one person, e.g. A government minister may have to neglect **their family**. Note that some people consider this to be incorrect. Note also that some writers use the pronoun *s/he* instead of *he* or *she*.

Unit 99

99.1 *Suggested answers:*
1 A bomb explosion in a capital city terrorises the population there.
2 The Prime Minister is going to announce plans for dealing with football hooligans.
3 Some highly successful footballers are speaking up for their coach after he has been criticised.
4 A strong campaign against people who disagree with a government has been launched.
5 Violent men surround a teenage star.
6 The police decide to focus on dealing with badly behaved and offensive young men.

99.2 1 c It uses nudity and the dramatic word 'scandal' to attract attention.
2 b It uses a familiar name for the King, which shows either lack of respect or friendly familiarity, and the dramatic word 'massacre' for battle, with alliteration on 'Macedonian' and 'massacre'.
3 e It uses alliteration in 'Marathon man' and 'drop-dead dash', with a dramatic image and words.
4 a It is about royalty and scandal, which are favourite topics for tabloids.
5 d It uses the colloquial expression 'It's curtains for …' [It's the end for …], and alliteration in 'curtains' and 'Corinth'.

99.3 1 g Dracula was a vampire known for drinking blood. 'Bad blood' is also an expression used to mean bad feelings between people. There will probably be bad blood between the vicar of Whitby and the people who are making a profit from the Dracula connections of the town.
2 e School days are often referred to as the 'happiest days of one's life'.
3 b 'Shell-shocked' means traumatised or in a state of great shock. It describes how soldiers in the trenches in World War I felt after they had been subjected to shells or bombs for a long time. Terrapins and tortoises have shells and they would certainly be shocked (in the medical sense) by falling from such a height.
4 a Dentists make impressions of teeth and 'false impressions' is a common collocation used to mean incorrect impressions created by a person.
5 d This is meant to recall the phrase 'happy hunting'. 'Haunting', however, is what a ghost does. An 'apparition' is a kind of ghost.
6 h 'Hopping mad' is a collocation meaning extremely cross. It is appropriate here as toads and frogs hop along the ground. Hopping mad is also no doubt how the police felt when they discovered they had been called out by a toad.
7 f Toilets 'flush' [water passes through them]. 'Flushed' also means to be red in the face. It collocates strongly with the phrase 'with success'; the people who have sold the toilet for such a large sum of money are likely to feel successful.
8 i 'Highly embarrassed' means extremely embarrassed. It is doubly appropriate here as the man is so high up the tree that he has to be rescued by the fire brigade – certainly an embarrassing situation.
9 c Sheepdogs 'round up' sheep. They are a kind of dog and it is suggested that they should round up the children.

Unit 100

100.1 *Possible answers:*
Use of 'longer' and 'grand' vocabulary: *attained* instead of reached; *bestowed on* instead of given to; *adjoining* instead of next to; *property* instead of home
Use of passive when active would do: *Your request ... is hereby rejected* instead of We hereby reject your request to ... ; *No exceptions ... will be considered* instead of *We will not consider any exceptions*
Use of noun as the subject of the sentence: *No exceptions to the aforementioned procedure will be considered* instead of We will not consider any exceptions ...
Avoidance of 'you': *Any and all appeals regarding this decision must be submitted* instead of You must submit any appeal

100.2
1 Roadworks will **begin** on 1 June.
2 Write the name and address of your **nearest** relative.
3 With **best wishes** from Jane Bramwell.
4 Call me **as soon as you can.**
5 **If there is a fire,** don't use the lifts.
6 Passengers should not **go to** the car deck until the captain tells them to.
7 I am writing **about** the editorial in today's paper.
8 I am writing **in connection with** your letter of 6th June.

100.3

bureaucratic word	more everyday equivalent
acknowledge	let us know
cessation	end
clarification	explanation
commencement	start
deceased	dead
endeavour	try
facilitate	make easier
rectify	put right
resume	start again

100.4

verb	noun	adjective
clarify	clarification	clarifiable
facilitate	facilitation	facilitating
instruct	instruction	instructive
notify	notification	notifiable
rectify	rectification	rectifiable

100.5
1 Clients must **obey** the following **rules.**
2 **Put** coins into the slot below.
3 Your complaints have been investigated and are considered to be **unjustified.**
4 Passengers are **asked not to smoke.**
5 Tick **the country where you live.**

Phonemic symbols

Vowel sounds		Consonant sounds	
Symbol	*Examples*	*Symbol*	*Examples*
/iː/	sleep me	/p/	put
/i/	happy recipe	/b/	book
/ɪ/	pin dinner	/t/	take
/ʊ/	foot could pull	/d/	dog
/uː/	do shoe through	/k/	car kick
/e/	red head said	/g/	go guarantee
/ə/	arrive father colour	/tʃ/	catch church
/ɜː/	turn bird work	/dʒ/	age lounge
/ɔː/	sort thought walk	/f/	for cough photograph
/æ/	cat black	/v/	love vehicle
/ʌ/	sun enough wonder	/θ/	thick path
/ɒ/	got watch sock	/ð/	this mother
/ɑː/	part heart laugh	/s/	since rice
		/z/	zoo surprise
		/ʃ/	shop sugar machine
/eɪ/	name late aim	/ʒ/	pleasure usual vision
/aɪ/	my idea time	/h/	hear hotel
/ɔɪ/	boy noise	/m/	make
/eə/	pair where bear	/n/	name now know
/ɪə/	hear cheers	/ŋ/	bring
/əʊ/	go home show	/l/	look while
/aʊ/	out cow	/r/	road
/ʊə/	pure fewer	/j/	young
		/w/	wear

ˈ This shows that the next syllable is the one with the stress.

ˌ This is used when some longer words have a second stress, less strong than on the main stressed syllable.

Index

The numbers in the Index are Unit numbers not page numbers.

New Year's resolution
/ˌnju: jɪəz ˌrezəl'u:ʃən/ 75
newsgroup /'nju:zgru:p/ 47
newsletter /'nju:z,letə/ 46
newsworthy /'nju:z,wɜ:ði/ 86
next of kin /ˌnekst ɒv ,kɪn/ 100
nibbles /'nɪbəlz/ 23
niche market /ˌni:ʃ 'mɑ:kɪt/ 5
night shift /'naɪt ˌʃɪft/ 3
nip /nɪp/ 65
nip in the bud 30
nippy /'nɪpi/ 28
nit-picking /'nɪtpɪkɪŋ/ 13
no offence intended 81
nobility /nəʊ'bɪləti/ 38
no-frills /ˌnəʊ'frɪlz/ 16
noiseless /'nɔɪzləs/ 62
noiselessly /'nɔɪzləsli/ 62
non-refundable /ˌnɒnrɪ'fʌndəbəl/ 25
Norman /'nɔ:mən/ 88
nostalgia /nɒs'tældʒə/ 76
not enough room to swing a cat 58
not the most 81
notebook /'nəʊtbʊk/ 55
nothing to write home about 17
notifiable /'nəʊtɪfaɪəbəl/ 100
notification /ˌnəʊtɪfɪ'keɪʃən/ 100
notify /'nəʊtɪfaɪ/ 100
notwithstanding /ˌnɒtwɪθ'stændɪŋ/
78
now then 96
nuclear /'nju:klɪə/ 57
nuclear family /ˌnju:klɪə 'fæməli/ 56
numeracy /'nju:mərəsi/ 2
nurse /nɜ:s/ 98
nutrition /nju:'trɪʃən/ 39, 53
nutrition label 22
nutritious /nju:'trɪʃəs/ 53
oath /əʊθ/ 75
oatmeal /'əʊtmi:l/ 53
obese /əʊ'bi:s/ 8
obituary /əʊ'bɪtʃʊəri/ 46
object /əb'dʒekt/ 72
objection /əb'dʒekʃən/ 72
objective /əb'dʒektɪv/ 35
obligation /ˌɒblɪ'geɪʃən/ 69
obligatory /ə'blɪgətəri/ 69
obliging /ə'blaɪdʒɪŋ/ 7, 33
obnoxious /əb'nɒkʃəs/ 13
obsequious /əb'si:kwɪəs/ 74
observation /ˌɒbzə'veɪʃən/ 40
obsolete /'ɒbsəli:t/ 37
obstacle /'ɒbstəkl/ 68
obstinate /'ɒbstɪnət/ 7, 9
obstructive /əb'strʌktɪv/ 68

occupant /'ɒkjəpənt/ 86
occurrence /ə'kʌrəns/ 49
odds /ɒdz/ 75
the odds are 69
off the cuff /ˌɒf ðə 'kʌf/ 16
off the hook 68
off the peg /ˌɒf ðə 'peg/ 16
off the rack /ˌɒf ðə 'ræk/ 16
off-colour /ˌɒf'kʌlə/ 51
offensive material 47
offhand /ˌɒf'hænd/ 13, 61
officious /ə'fɪʃəs/ 13
off-putting /ˌɒf'pʊtɪŋ/ 23
offshore /ˌɒf'ʃɔ:/ 57
oil well /'ɔɪl ˌwel/ 57
-ology /'ɒlədʒi/ 87
on a shoestring 16
on me 23
on the High Street 16
on the house 17
on the mend 51
on trend 16
once in a blue moon 59
one-to-one /ˌwʌntə'wʌn/ 2
online /ˌɒn'laɪn/ 1
online journalism 49
only have eyes for 10
onshore /ˌɒn'ʃɔ:/ 57
on-the-spot 24
oodles /'u:dəlz/ 82
Op-art /'ɒp,ɑ:t/ 20
open doors 29
open educational resources 1
open-minded /ˌəʊpən'maɪndɪd/ 7
ophthalmologist /ˌɒfθæl'mɒlədʒɪst/
50
opponent /ə'pəʊnənt/ 91
opportunistic /ˌɒpətʃu:'nɪstɪk/ 7
opposite number /ˌɒpəzɪt 'nʌmbə/ 3
oppressive /ə'presɪv/ 28
option /'ɒpʃən/ 69
optional /'ɒpʃənəl/ 69
opulent /'ɒpjələnt/ 48
or so 82
or something 82
or whatever 82
or words to that effect 82
ordeal /ɔ:'di:l/ 68
organ /'ɔ:gən/ 50
original /ə'rɪdʒənəl/ 20
orthography /ɔ:'θɒgrəfi/ 37
ostentatious /ˌɒsten'teɪʃəs/ 13
out- /aʊt/ 85
out of sorts 51
out of the wood(s) 68

out of touch 76
outbreak /'aʊtbreɪk/ 89
outdo /ˌaʊt'du:/ 89
outfit /'aʊtfɪt/ 16
outgoing /ˌaʊt'gəʊɪŋ/ 9
outlaw /'aʊtlɔ:/ 71
outlook /'aʊtlʊk/ 89
outnumber /ˌaʊt'nʌmbə/ 85
outrun /ˌaʊt'rʌn/ 89
outstanding /ˌaʊt'stændɪŋ/ 6
outstanding account 6
outstay your welcome 18
outweigh /ˌaʊt'weɪ/ 85
ovenproof /'ʌvənpru:f/ 86
over- /'əʊvə/ 85, 89
over the hill 59
over the moon 12
over the worst 51
overalls /'əʊvərɔ:lz/ 16
overbearing /ˌəʊvə'beərɪŋ/ 23
overdo it 23
overhang /ˌəʊvə'hæŋ/ 85
overjoyed /ˌəʊvə'dʒɔɪd/ 69
overlap /ˌəʊvə'læp/ 78
overnight /ˌəʊvə'naɪt/ 85
overpass /'əʊvəpɑ:s/ 97
overpriced /ˌəʊvə'praɪst/ 85
overrated /ˌəʊvə'reɪtɪd/ 19, 85
overshadow /ˌəʊvə'ʃædəʊ/ 85
overstep the mark 85
overthrow /ˌəʊvə'θrəʊ/ 43
overturn /ˌəʊvə'tɜ:n/ 42
overworked and underpaid 4
p. 84
package /'pækɪdʒ/ 25
packed in like sardines 58
paddy field /'pædi ˌfi:ld/ 27
paediatrician /ˌpi:dɪə'trɪʃən/ 50
pagan times 36
page-turner /'peɪdʒ,tɜ:nə/ 21
pain /peɪn/ 51
paint /peɪnt/ 20
palaver /pə'lɑ:və/ 88
pamper (yourself) /'pæmpə/ 48
pamphlet /'pæmflɪt/ 46
pan (v.) /pæn/ 19
pang /pæŋ/ 76
paper /'peɪpə/ 1
parade (n. and v.) /pə'reɪd/ 36
paradise /'pærədaɪs/ 26
pardon /'pɑ:dən/ 73
parental control 47
Paris /'pærɪs/ 95
parking lot /'pɑ:kɪŋ ,lɒt/ 97
parking ticket /'pɑ:kɪŋ ,tɪkɪt/ 34

English Vocabulary in Use Advanced   **291**

How to use the *English Vocabulary in Use Advanced* CD-ROM to learn vocabulary

Your copy of *English Vocabulary in Use Advanced* comes with a CD-ROM. You can use the CD-ROM to improve your English vocabulary. These two pages answer some common questions about the CD-ROM.

What is on the CD–ROM?

The CD-ROM contains

- two practice activities for each unit of the book (200 in total)
- a test maker
- a record and play-back function
- a dictionary function
- a reference section.

When should I use the CD–ROM?

You can use the CD-ROM before or after you do a unit in the book. This section will give you some suggestions.

Using the CD–ROM before you look at a unit in the book

The CD-ROM can help you discover how much vocabulary you already know about a topic. Try this:

- Choose a topic from the *Exercises* menu, for example *The visual arts* in the *Leisure and lifestyle* section.
- Complete the two exercises. After each exercise, click *Check your answers* to see how many questions you got right. Make a note of any words you found difficult.
- Now go to the relevant unit of the book. Study the notes on the left-hand page. Try to find the words you didn't know from the CD-ROM. Complete the exercises on the right-hand page.
- Finally, return to the CD-ROM. Look at the *My progress* section. Can you improve your score this time? Complete the two exercises again for the same unit.

Using the CD–ROM after you look at a unit in the book

The CD-ROM can help you to remember words you learnt from the book. This kind of revision is very important if you want to remember vocabulary. Try this:

- When you complete a unit from the book, write the date at the top of the page.
- One week later, go to the CD-ROM and do the two exercises from that unit. How much vocabulary can you remember? Make a note of any words you found difficult or couldn't remember.
- Go back the unit in the book and look for the words you didn't know. Study the words again.
- Finally, return to the CD-ROM and complete the two exercises again. Did you remember those difficult words?

The CD-ROM can also help you test yourself. You can even personalise the tests to cover the topics that *you* want to practise. Try this:

- When you finish a group of units in the book (for example, the four units in the *Health* section), go to the CD-ROM and make a test on the vocabulary from those units. The CD-ROM will create five test questions from each of those units. For an extra challenge, use the time limit function. If your score is low, look at the units again. Then create a new test and try to improve your score.
- Alternatively, create a test when you have completed the whole book. Choose units at random or concentrate on units that you found difficult.

Can the CD-ROM help me with my pronunciation?

Yes, it can. The CD-ROM has a record and play-back function which you can use to practise your pronunciation. Try this:

- When you have completed an exercise on the CD-ROM, click the green arrow to hear a model pronunciation of the words or sentences.
- Then click the red *Record your voice* button at the bottom of the screen. Practise saying the word or sentence.
- Now click the green *Play your voice* arrow at the bottom of the screen. Does your pronunciation sound correct? Listen to the model pronunciation again to check.
- Record your voice again if necessary.

What's in the reference section?

Here you will find a really useful wordlist, with all the key words from the book. You can hear the American English and British English pronunciation of every word and phrase. You can also make notes on this page. All the left-hand book pages are available to help you with the exercises.

What else can the CD-ROM do?

The CD-ROM also has a dictionary function. You can use it to look up any words that you don't know. You will need an internet connection for this. Also, you can click on any word in the CD-ROM and it will look up the word in the online dictionary.

You can also check your progress at any time using the *Progress* section. This will help you to see which exercises you have completed. It can also show you areas where you need more practice. In those cases, study the left-hand pages again.

Remember you can print out tests, exercises and the answers.

We hope you enjoy using the *English Vocabulary in Use Advanced* CD-ROM.

English Vocabulary in Use Advanced 2nd Edition

English Vocabulary in Use Advanced (EVU) can be run directly from the CD-ROM and does not require installation. However, you can also install EVU and run it directly from your hard disk. This will make EVU run more quickly. See the section below called *Installation Instructions*.

To use EVU on your computer, you must have:

- a PC running Windows® XP, Windows Vista®, Windows 7 or Windows 8
- a Mac® running OSX 10.6, 10.7 or 10.8

For both PC and Mac, you also need:

- 1 GB RAM
- 250 MB free hard disk space if installing to your hard drive
- Internet access (only required for dictionary)
- Flash Player 10 (free download from Adobe.com/products/flashplayer)
- PDF reading software such as Adobe® Reader (required for book PDFs)
- a microphone if you wish to record yourself speaking
- a mouse or other pointing device

To run EVU directly from the disc on a PC

1. Insert the EVU CD-ROM into your CD-ROM drive.
2. If Autorun is enabled (Windows XP, Vista and 7), the CD-ROM will start automatically. For Windows 8, go to My Computer, right click on the CD/DVD-ROM drive and choose Open.
3. If Autorun is not enabled: For Windows 7/Vista, click on Start > Computer. For Windows XP, double-click on My Computer. Then double-click on the EVU icon.

To run EVU directly from the disc on a Mac

1. Insert the EVU CD-ROM into your CD-ROM drive.
2. Double-click on the CD icon on the desktop to open it.
3. Double-click on the EVU Mac OS X icon.

Installation instructions

To install EVU on a PC

(You must be allowed to install software on your computer, i.e. have Administrator privileges.)

1. Close EVU if you are already running it from the CD.
2. For Windows 7/Vista: Click on Start > Computer. For Windows XP: double-click on My Computer. Windows 8: Go to Computer, and double-click on the CD-ROM to display all the files and folders.
3. For Windows 7/XP, right-click on D: and choose Open to display all the files and folders. For Windows Vista, right-click D: and choose Explore to display all the files and folders.
4. Double-click on *install* to begin installation.
5. Follow the installation instructions on your screen.

To install EVU on a Mac

1. Insert the CD into your CD-ROM drive.
2. Double-click on the CD icon on the desktop to open it.
3. Create a folder on your desktop.
4. Copy the contents of the CD-ROM into this folder.
5. Double-click on the EVU Mac OS X icon to run EVU.

Uninstallation instructions

To uninstall EVU from a PC

1. Close EVU.
2. Open the Control Panel.
3. For Windows 7/Vista, click on Uninstall a Program. For Windows XP, click on Add/Remove Programs. For Windows 8, click Uninstall a program. A dialogue box is displayed, listing all the software on your computer.
4. Click on *English Vocabulary in Use Advanced*.
5. For Windows 7/Vista, click Uninstall/Change. For Windows XP, click on Change/Remove. For Windows 8, follow the instructions on your screen.

To uninstall EVU from a Mac

1. Close EVU.
2. Delete the folder you created and copied the EVU files to.

Support

If you experience difficulties with this CD-ROM, please visit: www.cambridge.org/elt/support

Terms and conditions of use

This is a legal agreement between 'You' (which means the individual customer) and Cambridge University Press ('the Licensor') for **English Vocabulary in Use Advanced 2nd Edition**. By placing this CD-ROM in the CD/DVD-ROM drive of your computer You agree to the terms of this licence.

1. Licence

(a) You are purchasing only the right to use the CD-ROM and are acquiring no rights, express or implied to it or the software other than those rights granted in this limited licence for not-for-profit educational use only.

(b) Cambridge University Press grants the customer the licence to use one copy of this CD-ROM (i) on a single computer for use by one or more people at different times, or (ii) by a single person on one or more computers (provided the CD-ROM is only used on one computer at one time and is only used by the customer), but not both.

(c) The customer shall not: (i) copy or authorise copying of the CD-ROM, (ii) translate the CD-ROM, (iii) reverse-engineer, disassemble or decompile the CD-ROM, (iv) transfer, sell, assign or otherwise convey any portion of the CD-ROM, or (v) operate the CD-ROM from a network or mainframe system.

2. Copyright

(a) All original content is provided as part of the CD-ROM (including text, images and ancillary material) ('Original Material') and is the copyright of the Licensor, protected by copyright and all other applicable intellectual property laws and international treaties.

(b) You may not copy the CD-ROM except for making one copy of the CD-ROM solely for backup or archival purposes. You may not alter, remove or destroy any copyright notice or other material placed on or with this CD-ROM.

3. Liability

(a) The CD-ROM is supplied 'as-is' with no express guarantee as to its suitability. To the extent permitted by applicable law, the Licensor is not liable for costs of procurement of substitute products, damages or losses of any kind whatsoever resulting from the use of this product, or errors or faults in the CD-ROM, and in every case the Licensor's liability shall be limited to the suggested list price or the amount actually paid by You for the product, whichever is lower.

(b) You accept that the Licensor is not responsible for the persistency, accuracy or availability of any URLs of external or third party internet websites referred to on the CD-ROM and does not guarantee that any content on such websites is, or will remain, accurate, appropriate or available. The Licensor shall not be liable for any content made available from any websites and urls outside the Software.

(c) Where, through use of the Original Material you infringe the copyright of the Licensor you undertake to indemnify and keep indemnified the Licensor from and against any loss, cost, damage or expense (including without limitation damages paid to a third party and any reasonable legal costs) incurred by the Licensor as a result of such infringement.

4. Termination

Without prejudice to any other rights, the Licensor may terminate this licence if You fail to comply with the terms and conditions of the licence. In such event, You must destroy all copies of the CD-ROM.

5. Governing law

This agreement is governed by the laws of England, without regard to its conflict of laws provision, and each party irrevocably submits to the exclusive jurisdiction of the English courts. The parties disclaim the application of the United Nations Convention on the International Sale of Goods.